A Reader's Guide to
Fifty British Novels 1600–1900

A Reader's Guide to
Fifty British Novels
1600–1900

by Gilbert Phelps

823. 09
P

Heinemann – London
Barnes & Noble – New York

Heinemann Educational Books Ltd
LONDON EDINBURGH MELBOURNE AUCKLAND HONG KONG
SINGAPORE KUALA LUMPUR NEW DELHI IBADAN NAIROBI
JOHANNESBURG KINGSTON PORT OF SPAIN

First published 1979 by Pan Books as
An Introduction to Fifty British Novels 1600–1900
in the Pan Literature Guides Series
First published in this casebound edition 1979

ISBN (UK) 0 435 18751 1
ISBN (USA) 0-06-495533-8

Library of Congress Number 79-53436

Published in Great Britain by
Heinemann Educational Books Ltd
22 Bedford Square, London WC1B 3HH
Published in the U.S.A. 1979 by
Harper & Row Publishers, Inc.
Barnes & Noble Import Division

Printed and bound in Great Britain by
Richard Clay (The Chaucer Press) Ltd,
Bungay, Suffolk

For my wife, but for whose editorial help this
book would not exist

Contents

Introduction

The main purpose of this book is to present fifty representative British novels from the beginnings of the genre to the end of the nineteenth century, when the main outlines of our fictional tradition had been established. The fifty titles have not been chosen for exclusively historical reasons. Every one of them is worth reading for its own sake, as a genuine work of the creative imagination. At the same time the fifty titles do, by and large, represent the peaks in a continuous chain of development. It is certainly not claimed that the book will provide a comprehensive survey of the British novel; but it will indicate the general features of the landscape and the chief areas where further exploration is necessary.

In attempting even the sketchiest of surveys, though, problems of definition inevitably arise. Story-telling itself, of course, is as old as mankind. But what exactly *is* a novel? Today most of us would probably agree that at least six conditions are essential to it. First and most obvious, it is fictitious: even if it is based on historical, biographical or autobiographical fact, it is shaped by the imagination: it does not pretend to tell the truth, though imaginatively it may indeed be 'true'.

The second condition, almost as obvious, is that of length. A novel is not a short story, or even that hybrid known as a 'long short story'. Allowing for a small number of exceptions, we would generally expect a novel to be not less than seventy thousand words.

But length must not be merely a matter of stringing together a series of miscellaneous items. A novel may not necessarily tell a continuous story, and it can stray all over the place in both time and space – but the third requirement is that of unity. This unity may be one of plot, theme, tone, atmosphere, or vision: but any novel worthy of the name is an organic whole.

Fourth, although a novel is fictitious, it must create the illusion of reality. The majority of English novels are indeed 'realistic' in the sense that they approximate to the day to day actualities of 'real life'. This kind of realism, though, is not essential. A novel may be allegorical, fantastic, or even *sur-realistic*: But to convince, it must accomplish what the great Romantic poet and critic Coleridge called the 'willing suspension of disbelief for the moment, which constitutes poetic faith'.

Fifth, we expect a novel to be very closely concerned with character. Usually this means the analysis of clearly differentiated types of individuals. There may be cases of the poetic or impressionist novel where these differentiations are deliberately dispensed with in order to communicate a sense of the primitive, molten flux of human experience – but the preoccupation with human nature and behaviour is just as intense as in the more normal kind of novel.

And finally, we generally assume that a novel must be written in prose.

This is not to say that these conditions constitute a watertight formula (a living art is always full of surprises) but they are applicable to the vast majority of English novels.

The works of fiction that most obviously appear to stray outside these definitions, at least in part, are those which belong to the category of the Moral Fable. Books, that is, which adopt the methods of the novel not for their own sake, not because the basic definitions seem inevitable to the writer (so that his book really grows out of them) – but merely because they seem 'useful' for conveying a preconceived ideological position. A work composed in this way cannot really be called a novel in the fullest meaning of the term. At its weakest it can be crude propaganda, with utterly lifeless characters and situations. But at its best it can be a literary masterpiece. The outstanding instances in this selection are John Bunyan's *The Pilgrim's Progress*, Jonathan Swift's *Gulliver's Travels*, and Samuel Johnson's *Rasselas*. Genius will out, and in all these cases inherent intelligence, aesthetic instinct, and creative vitality have transmuted the primary moral or satiric intentions and prevented the novelistic devices from becoming flat and mechanical. Much the same might be said, at a lower level of attainment, of such novels as Benjamin Disraeli's *Sybil* and Charles Kingsley's *Alton Locke*, which are discussed in this selection, or of such twentieth-century examples as Aldous Huxley's *Brave New World* and George Orwell's *Animal Farm*. Although in reading such works we are seldom unaware of the fact that in a sense a deception is being practised upon us, and that the dominant motive is the canvassing of a specific set of ideas, nevertheless they generate sufficient interest in story-line, character and situation to compel us to respond to them, with at least part of our minds, *as if* they were novels as we normally understand the word. Certainly no account of the British novel would be really satisfactory that excluded these fringe instances.

At the same time it is also evident that the complete 'packet' of conditions only begins to be applicable in the eighteenth century. There are many reasons for this, some of which are discussed in the essays that follow. Outstanding among them are: the perfection of a supple and lucid prose style; the advent of the scientific spirit, evinced in particular in the work of the physicist Isaac Newton and of the empirical philosopher John Locke; the resultant emphasis on the rational, the factual, the observable, the demonstrable and the measurable, in the physical universe and human affairs alike; the accompanying – or, some would say, motivating – changes in economic and social organization, among them the rapidly increasing importance of the city as the focus of culture and the pre-eminence of London; the rise, closely associated with these factors, of a thrusting, confident middle class, with a desire for self-improvement and entertainment, and greater means and leisure to achieve them; and – most important from the purely literary point of view – the fact that the heyday of the drama as the great popular medium of story-telling and presentation of character had passed.

Although, however, the origins of the novel as a specific genre lie in the eighteenth century, there is a considerable pre-history. It could be argued, indeed, that the germs of the novel are discernible in the very earliest forms of storytelling. These primitive forms, it is true, were usually cast in verse, because, before the advent of literacy such devices as rhythm, rhyme and alliteration were essential aids to memory if any kind of continuity and transmission was to be achieved. But there were two types of verse story-telling: a short one, designed to be sung or recited (and often danced as well) in a single session; and a long one that would demand a whole series of sessions. From the first evolved the folk-ballad, the fairy tale, and ultimately the short story; from the second evolved the saga, the epic – and ultimately perhaps the novel.

For many centuries, in fact, narrative poetry was the basic form of literary art – and from this point of view a particularly plausible starting-point for the English novel might be Geoffrey Chaucer's long narrative poem *Troilus and Criseyde*, probably written between 1372 and 1386. Not only does it tell a story with all the variety, all the alternations of light and shade, and all the amplitude of a great novel, but its analysis of character, behaviour and motive is as sophisticated, subtle and complex as anything in the mature novel, while it also possesses a genuine organic unity. It might be said to contain practically every requisite for a novel, as we understand the term, except one – that it is not written in prose. That exception,

though, is a vital one. There have been reasonably successful examples of the 'verse novel' in more modern times,
such as Elizabeth Barrett Browning's *Aurora Leigh* (1856),
but fundamentally they are bound to be hybrids. Verse
inevitably involves different approaches on the part of
the author, and expectations on the part of the reader. In
spite of everything, *Troilus and Criseyde* remains a
mediaeval poem. It is only in prose that the novel can
breathe in the way that is natural to it.

It is sometimes argued that one of the preliminary
conditions for the development of prose fiction was the
advent of the printed book. From this point of view, it
could be claimed therefore, that the proper starting-point
of the English novel is Sir Thomas Malory's *Morte
D'Arthur*, which was issued by William Caxton, the first
English printer, in 1485. There is plenty of personal invention in both the incidents and the characterization of
Malory's book, not to mention the frequently beautiful,
though archaic, prose in which they are conveyed; but it
was largely a reconstruction, derived from foreign sources,
of the traditional Arthurian legends and it does not add
up to a novel in any meaningful sense of the word.

The last two decades of the sixteenth century, on the
other hand, undoubtedly witnessed a whole series of
prophetic developments. One of the most potent influences on these was the Italian *novella*. This term had
been applied to the prose story as early as the thirteenth
century, and from it derives our own word 'novel'. But
the word is also the equivalent of the English 'news' – and
many of the Italian *novelle* were roughly similar to the
sensational items in a modern popular newspaper. They
were shaped, however, with great skill, while a good deal
of creative planning went into the grouping and linking
of the stories into collections. The most famous of these
collections is *The Decameron* of Giovanni Boccaccio (written between 1348 and 1358) which provided Chaucer,
Shakespeare and many others with some of their plots.
The sixteenth-century collections of Matteo Bandello and

Giraldi Cinthio also provided a rich storehouse of source material. The vivid detail, the illusion of matter-of fact *rapportage*, and the brilliant narrative of the *novelle* certainly helped to establish the principle of realism in English fiction, and to inculcate the idea that prose fiction might be as much an art as poetry or drama. Thus the various collections of translations from, or imitations of, the Italian *novelle*, such as William Painter's *Palace of Pleasure* (1566–1567), also played a part in the evolution of the English novel.

Another training-ground in fictional realism was provided by the numerous pamphlets on the various rogues of the Elizabethan underworld, like Robert Greene's *A Notable Discovery of Coosnage* (or cozenage – that is deception) which was published in 1591. Many of these pamphlets contained anecdotes which were in effect short stories. The vogue which had its origins in the Middle Ages was eventually absorbed into the novel proper – for example in Daniel Defoe's *Moll Flanders* (1722), where the exploits of the heroine recall those of the Elizabethan confidence tricksters. These Elizabethan developments belong more properly to the short story than to the novel. Short story and novel may nourish each other, but at a more sophisticated level they are, because of their different spatial and chronological scales (and hence of their rhythms of being), quite distinct forms. At this formative stage, however, we are dealing with the raw materials of both forms and it is too early to differentiate between them.

Another possible stepping-stone towards the novel was the popular jest-books, beginning with *A Hundred Merry Tales* in 1525, especially when a crude continuity was introduced by assigning the anecdotes to a single character, as in *Scogan's Jests* (1566), *Tarleton's Jests* (*c.* 1592), and *Long Meg of Westminster* (1594). Long Meg in particular (a brawny Lancashire lass who came to London, met Will Sommers, jester to King Henry VIII, assumed man's clothing and went to the wars, married a soldier and set up a public house in Islington) emerges as a considerable character, almost to the extent of providing a cohesive element.

The vogue for the portrayal of low life was further strengthened by the appearance in 1576 of a translation of the anonymous *Lazarillo de Tormes* (published in Spain in 1554). Although little more than a series of episodes, this work achieved a degree of unity from the personality of the central (and fictional) character, the ne'er-do-well son of a miller on the banks of the river Tormes (near Salamanca), who sets out on an itinerant career of witty stratagems, cunning, and fraud. *Lazarillo de Tormes* is regarded as the origin of the 'picaresque novel' (after *picaro*, the Spanish word for 'rogue'), although it came to denote not only a narrative about amusing scoundrels, but any type of loosely constructed, episodic novel centred on the adventures of a wandering hero.

Close to the spirit of the jest-books and the homely world of shop, tavern and market place for which they catered, were the narratives of Thomas Deloney, the Norwich silk weaver. It has been suggested that Deloney may have been subsidized by the cloth manufacturers, at a time when trade was bad, in order to enlist popular sympathy. For two of the narratives which he wrote between 1596 and 1600 were devoted to the exploits and legends surrounding real-life heroes of the textile industry. These were *The Pleasant History of John Winchcomb, in his Younger Years Called Jack of Newbury* and *Thomas of Reading*. The first of them in particular demands attention. Although it is episodic and anecdotal, it has something approaching a central plot – the primitive but perennially popular one of a hard-working youth's rise from poverty (Jack of Newbury began his career as an apprentice and rose to wealth and influence, eventually becoming a powerful magnate who enjoyed the confidence of King Henry VIII himself). The character of the hero is also clearly and convincingly drawn.

During the same period, Deloney also published *The Gentle Craft*, a series of anecdotes, some comic, some serious or romantic, about the shoemakers from the days of their patron saints down to Deloney's own time – but in spite of its great charm it has less cohesion than his other books. At the same time, all of them come somewhere near the length of a short novel and all of them are written in a style which, though artless and homespun, is lively and energetic. They contain passages of dialogue which display something of the humour and naturalness of Shakespeare's lower-class characters. What is more, they grew out of, and catered for, the very class whose rise to economic power was eventually to provide some of the basic conditions for the emergence of the novel as the predominant literary form. At the same time, it must be remembered that the incidents and characters in Deloney's books are drawn from history, legend or hearsay and not *invented*. If it were not for that, *Jack of Newbury* might well have been chosen as the first embryonic English novel.

However, in the pastoral romances the Elizabethan period does furnish instances of longer prose narratives which are entirely fictional. These grew up under two main influences. The first of them was that of the Greek pastoral story writers of the second century AD and their Roman imitators: *The Golden Ass* of Apuleius, for example, was translated into English in 1556, and the *Daphnis and Chloe* of Longus in 1587. The second source was a group of highly conventionalized elaborations of the mediaeval romances of chivalry by various Italian, Spanish and Portuguese authors of the sixteenth century which were also extremely popular in England, especially among the cultivated classes, either in the originals or in translation.

The most important English practitioners of the pastoral romance were John Lyly and Sir Philip Sidney. Lyly's *Euphues: The Anatomy of Wit* was published in 1578, and was followed by a second part in 1580 entitled *Euphues and his England*. Their outstanding characteristic is the very elaborate and mannered style (hence the adjective 'euphuistic'). Obviously such a style, though it gave full scope to the Elizabethan delight in language for its own sake, was too complicated and slow-moving for anything approaching narrative pace or naturalness of dialogue. In any case, Lyly's purpose (apart from the sheer joy of revelling in language) was to advance his ideas about the follies of youth, the illusions of love and the inconstancy of women (in the first part of *Euphues*) and to extol the glories of England and the Virgin Queen (in the second part). The characters are merely mouthpieces for these ideas, which are expressed in debates of interminable length. There is little attempt at consistency of story-line or appropriateness of action to character. Nevertheless there is *some* attention to plot, especially in the second part, and it has been pointed out that Lyly was one of the first writers to appreciate that fiction can exert a social influence because he demonstrates precepts in action instead of merely stating them in general terms. Some critics have also suggested that the fact that some of the lengthy discussions on love in *Euphues* are conducted by means of an exchange of letters points forward to the employment of the epistolary technique in the eighteenth century, notably by Samuel Richardson, 'the father of the English novel'.

Sir Philip Sidney's *Arcadia* was originally written to entertain his sister the Countess of Pembroke and her friends, and was not published until 1590, four years after his death. Here, there is certainly no lack of either plot or action. There is a veritable tangle of battles, disguises, mistaken identities, disappearances, cross-purposes, coincidental meetings, oracles, love-potions and intrigues, and many other ingredients. Although it is difficult to find one's way through the enchanted mazes, Sidney's *Arcadia* is not merely a random collection of episodes, and there is a story-line to be disentangled. There are, too, no less than eighty-eight characters, and although they are not easily differentiated they do represent varied types of human personality, exhibit some genuine psychological insight, and in some cases come sporadically to life as individuals. Sidney's pastoral romance cannot be regarded as a novel, but it may well have had some influence on later developments. It is possible, for example, that his elaborate disquisitions on the behaviour and emotions of his lovers paved the way to some extent for the sentimental refinements of Samuel Richardson (oddly enough, one of the characters in the *Arcadia* is named Pamela). In fact the twentieth-century novelist and critic Virginia Woolf had considerable justification when she declared: 'In the *Arcadia*, as in some luminous globe, all the seeds of English fiction lie latent.'

Among the other pastoral romances which might also be taken as precursors of the novel are Thomas Lodge's *Rosalynde: Euphues' Golden Legacie* (1590), strongly influenced, as the title indicates, by Lyly, and combining Lyly's style and Sidney's pastoralism in an attractive plot, on which Shakespeare drew for his play *As You Like It*.

One important point that must be made about the various types of Elizabethan fiction is that the two major modes into which (with numerous overlaps and subdivisions) the novel of the future was to fall – a continuation of opposed basic aesthetic and philosophical attitudes established far earlier – are already clearly illustrated. On the one hand there was the realistic, tough-minded, pragmatic, comic-satiric mode, which was to issue in the so-called 'masculine' novel, as practised by writers like Defoe, Fielding, Smollett and their successors. And on the other hand, there was the romantic, idealistic mode, more sensitive and poetic in approach and often with a strong moral purpose (as with both Lyly and Sidney, especially the latter with his blend of Platonism and Puritanism) which was to lead to the so-called 'feminine' novel of writers like Richardson and his successors.

Nevertheless, in spite of the claims of the narratives considered above and of others like them, it is Thomas Nashe's *The Unfortunate Traveller*, the subject of the first of the essays in this book, that comes closest to being the genuine starting-point for a history of the English novel. It is perhaps surprising though, in view of so much activity in the field of fiction during this period, that the fully-fledged novel took so long to appear, and that, with the exception of Bunyan's isolated masterpiece *The Pilgrim's Progress*, there was no real advance from *The Unfortunate Traveller* until the publication of Defoe's *Robinson Crusoe* in 1719.

In the intervening period there was, it is true, the vogue of the prose heroic romances. These engaged the same sort of interests and used very much the same methods as Lyly's *Euphues* and Sidney's *Arcadia*, but they were mostly composed in France. They were set in Ancient Greece or Rome, or in Asiatic countries of the same period, though there was no attempt at historical or topographical accuracy. The characters, who were usually clearly recognizable portraits of living personages, were invariably noble, and invariably indulged in interminable discussions and disquisitions on high-flown sentimental and moral problems, which were in effect separate essays embedded in the main narrative. The debates were often conducted by means of long letters. The exotic backgrounds were described in passages full of florid, baroque decoration. There was plenty of violent action (battles, shipwrecks, capture by pirates, recognitions of disguised princes, and so on), but much of it was contained in separate 'histories' in which one of the characters related his past adventures or those of a friend. Above all, the heroic romances were of vast length; *Artamène, ou le Grand Cyrus* by Madeleine de Scudéry (1649–1659), which was one of the most popular, ran to ten large volumes.

The heroic romances were avidly read in cultivated circles, either in the originals or in translations, and there were also a number of English imitations. Their greatest merit was their polished dialogue, which approximated to the real conversation of the aristocracy of the day. But obviously such vast and heterogeneous compilations could not achieve the sort of narrative pace and organic unity needed to establish the novel as a mature art form, and on the whole the heroic romances represent a regressive tendency.

The truth of the matter is that no real advance could take place in the novel until the drama had lost its pre-eminence. A forward spurt might have been expected after the closing of the theatres by the Puritans in 1642. But to the Puritan mind story-telling and playwriting were equally frivolous and morally harmful. After the Restoration of 1660, drama once again claimed most of the best energies and talents – Bunyan's *Pilgrim's Progress* was at this stage looked down upon by the intelligentsia as a primitive product catering for the lowest tastes. The case of the young William Congreve is symptomatic. In 1692 he published, under a pseudonym, a short novel entitled *Incognita, or Love and Duty Reconciled*. In his preface Congreve proclaimed that he had set out to 'imitate dramatic writing ... in the design, contexture, and result of the plot', and the novel does display some of the naturalness of characterization and dialogue and the discipline of structure that were necessary for further progress in the form. But on the whole it is a mechanical work, and Congreve's heart was not in it. He makes it clear in his preface that he regarded it as no more than an unimportant by-product of his interest in the drama, and before long he was directing his genius exclusively into his comedies of manners.

There is, however, one other novel of this intervening period which might well have featured in this selection – Mrs Aphra Behn's *Oroonoko, or The Royal Slave* (1678). This is the story of a young African prince whose sweetheart, Imoinda, is sold into slavery by a jealous king, and who is himself captured by an English slave-trader and sold, like Imoinda, in Surinam (at that time part of British Guiana). *Oroonoko* is distinguished by the authenticity of its Surinam backgrounds – Aphra Behn (the first professional female author) had herself lived there for a number of years; by the sympathetic portrayal of the hero – who exercised a considerable influence on the later Romantic cult of the noble savage – and by the frequently moving account of his sufferings and the tragic outcome of his love for his fellow slave Imoinda. On the whole, however, *Oroonoko* (like Aphra Behn's other novels) was too close to the tone of the heroic romances, and, minor classic though it undoubtedly is, it did not possess the kind of positive strengths needed to initiate a tradition.

The pre-eminence of the heroic romances did not mean that the realistic tradition had been superseded. The most powerful corrective to them (though it is very much more as well) was the great Spanish classic *Don Quixote de la Mancha* by Miguel de Cervantes Saavedra, which had been published in 1605 (with a second part ten years later) and which (though not itself a fully-formed specimen) was to have a great influence on the development of the novel throughout Europe. But there were developments in England, too, that had an important bearing on realism in fiction. The various seventeenth-century collections of 'characters', such as John Earle's *Microcosmographie* (1625), and their successors in the early eighteenth century – all of them indebted to the character sketches of the Ancient Greek philosopher Theophrastus – provided a valuable training ground in realistic observation and analysis of various character-types in contemporary society. So, too, did the increasing output of memoirs, autobiographies and biographies, and the growing fashion of letter-writing. Then again, the periodicals of the late seventeenth and early eighteenth centuries contained ingredients which would eventually be taken over by the novel, and which helped to prepare a public for it. Many of the periodicals used the devices of fiction to add variety and heighten interest. Whole numbers were sometimes entirely fictional, and some of them come close to being not only short stories but embryo novels. Johnson's 'Lingering Expectations of an Heir' in *The Rambler* is an outstanding example. There were strong fictional elements too in *The Tatler* of Richard Steele and Joseph Addison, and these were expanded in *The Spectator*, which succeeded it in 1710. The fictional characters, headed by Sir Roger de Coverley, who appeared in it from time to time are handled with such skill and panache that it is evident that Steele and Addison too, if they had addressed themselves to the task, might well have produced the first authentic English novel.

In a survey of this kind it is more satisfactory to concentrate on the more obvious landmarks. However, for a period of over four hundred years, fifty titles cannot possibly do full justice to the subject. Personal preferences are bound to enter into any selection, and individual readers will inevitably have reason to complain either of choices that seem to them eccentric or of glaring omissions. To take one obvious example: it may seem strange that Mary Shelley's *Frankenstein, or the Modern Prometheus* (1818) is not included as a potent symbol of many aspects of Romanticism and the precursor of so many later horror novels and movies. This is not the result of any lack of respect for the novel itself, but because on the whole it seemed that the relevant points were more easily covered by attention to other novels of the Romantic period.

It might be objected that it would have been better to make way for such omissions by assigning only one title to each author. But as the genre advanced, individual geniuses contributed so much to it that often the history of the novel resolves itself into a tracing of the various stages of their personal progress. Even so, no-one would pretend that the allocation of only two titles, for instance, to Sir Walter Scott and Jane Austen, or even three to Charles Dickens, comes anywhere near to paying adequate tribute either to them or to the parts they played in moulding the English novel.

One principle of selection at any rate can be reiterated without apology. The fifty titles have been chosen because, in their very varied ways, they are valuable in themselves – and it must be stressed that the essays on them are designed not as substitutes for reading the novels firsthand, but to stimulate interest in doing so.

The Unfortunate Traveller,
or The Life of Jacke Wilton

Thomas Nashe

Thomas Nashe was born at Lowestoft, on the Suffolk coast, in 1567, the son of a clergyman. He was educated at St John's College, Cambridge, and in 1588 he settled in London and became a member of the circle known as the 'University Wits' – writers, that is, who had been educated at one of the ancient universities – which included such well-known men of letters as Robert Greene, John Lyly, and Christopher Marlowe. He came into prominence with his polemical pamphlets, many of them directed against the Puritans, whose influence in religious affairs was rapidly growing in the last years of the sixteenth century. These prose works were marked by the vigour and pungency of their style, their vivid and realistic comedy, and their savage satire. Troubled with religious doubts, in 1593 he published his repentant reflections under the title *Christes Teares over Jerusalem*. He engaged in a battle of words with Gabriel Harvey (who had attacked his friend Greene) which became so ferocious that the government itself ordered the two combatants to desist. Just as ferociously he attacked various current abuses in the State in his lost play *The Isle of Dogs* (1597), and was sent to prison for several months for his pains. In 1599 he published *Lenten Stuffe*, a burlesque panegyric of the red herring, written to repay hospitality enjoyed at Yarmouth (a centre of the herring fisheries), and in the following year a comedy, still extant, called *Summer's Last Will and Testament*. This contained a particularly fine lyric, and he wrote other delightful poems. He died in 1601.

Summary

The hero of *The Unfortunate Traveller* (which was published in 1594) introduces himself as 'a certaine kind of appendix or page' at the court of King Henry VIII at the time of the siege of Tournai in 1513. He practises his wits on various gullible members of the camp, among them a fat and niggardly cider merchant, conning him into providing the army – and of course himself – with free cider ('syder in bowles, in scuppets, in helmets ... if a man would have fil'd his boots full, ther he might have it'), by leading him to believe that the king suspects him of dealings with the enemy.

The four anecdotes in this part of the book are similar to those of the popular contemporary jest-books which were also mostly concerned with practical jokes or dupings, and the cunning and audacity of those who perpetrate them. But whereas the approach of the jest-books was simple and crude, that of Nashe is skilful and sophisticated.

In order to gull the cider merchant, Jack first softens him up with a long complimentary speech (which parodies the typical official address of the day) and then plays on his nerves by means of various rhetorical tricks. In this way Nashe builds up suspense and brings out the character of the cider merchant in a vignette of sparkling comedy.

After these escapades, Jack is sent back to England where he lords it over the other pages at court with his Frenchified dress and behaviour. An epidemic of the 'sweating sickness' then breaks out, and here Nashe draws on one of the 'chronicles' (also very popular among the Elizabethans) containing an account of an actual visitation of this type of plague in 1517. Nashe's description, however, is marked by a grotesque and horrific kind of humour which is entirely his own:

I haue seene an old woman at that season, hauing three
chins, wipe them all away one after another, as they melted
to water, and left hir selfe nothing of a mouth but an
upper chap . . .

To escape the sickness Jack travels to Italy and witnesses
the battle of Marignano (actually fought two years
earlier), and Nashe again draws on the chronicles, largely
to demonstrate how much better he can handle the bloody
details of war.

By another chronological manipulation Jack goes
straight from Italy to Münster in Germany, where he
witnesses the defeat and slaughter, in 1535, of the Ana-
baptists, an extreme Protestant sect which sought to overthrow established forms of religion and to set up a kind
of theocratic primitive Christian communism.

Jack now travels to the Low Countries, where he enters
the service of Henry Howard, Earl of Surrey, a celebrated
courtier and poet of the reign of Henry VIII and pioneer
in England of the Petrarchan sonnet form. It was the
convention of the day to address love poems to some unattainable lady fair, in terms of extravagant worship
largely derived from the mediaeval Courts of Love. The
'goddess' of Surrey's poems was 'Fair Geraldine' and Nashe
takes the opportunity for guying the fashion and for
parodying Surrey's own poems.

After various other adventures, they proceed to Venice,
Jack and Surrey changing places, in order to allow the
latter more liberty of movement. They are caught in the
snares of a courtesan named Tabitha, who plots with
the supposed Jack to kill and rob his 'master'. They expose
her villainy, but she manages to turn the tables on them
by having them thrown into prison, accused of possessing
counterfeit currency (planted on them with the help of
an alchemist).

In prison they meet Diamante, arrested on an unjust
charge of adultery. The love-sick Surrey imagines that
Diamante is Geraldine, woos her in the strained language
of courtly love, and of course writes a sonnet to her. Jack's

reaction is more earthy: 'My master beate the bush and kept a coyle and a pratling, but I caught the bird.' In other words, he makes Diamante his mistress.

Surrey and Jack are eventually released from prison. Diamante's husband conveniently dies, and she too is set free. As she proves to be with child by Jack, the lovers leave Venice, financing themselves with Diamante's inherited money. On their journey, Jack keeps up the pretence that he is the Earl of Surrey, and when Surrey himself catches up with them in Florence he takes the deception in good part. He also visits the house in Florence where Geraldine was born, covers the windows with Latin tags expressing his lovelorn condition, writes another and even more extravagant sonnet, and issues a challenge to all-comers in defence of his fair Geraldine's beauty. That, of course, gives Nashe plenty of scope for mocking at the whole mediaeval code of chivalry which was still being observed (together with tournaments) in the royal courts.

After this, Surrey is summoned home by the king, but Jack and Diamante go to Rome, where Jack sees the tourist sights, among them the beautiful gardens of the wealthier citizens – thus providing Nashe with an excuse for a highly successful exercise in the manner of the Elizabethan pastoral.

From a vision of the 'Golden Age' which these gardens suggest, the story plunges into horror and villainy. The plague of 1522 has arrived in Rome, and two villainous Spaniards named Esdras and Bartol are taking advantage of it to break into the stricken houses. They come to the house where Jack and Diamante are lodging. Locking Jack in his room, Bartol seizes Diamante while Esdras rapes Heraclide, virtuous wife of the owner of the house, who is ill with the plague. After the rape Heraclide delivers a long lament (similar to that of Lucrece after she has been ravished by Tarquin in Shakespeare's narrative poem *The Rape of Lucrece*) and then commits suicide.

Heraclide's husband unexpectedly recovers, and accuses

Jack of murdering his wife. Jack is saved from the gallows in the nick of time by the arrival of an English nobleman, who has overheard the deathbed confession of Bartol, mortally wounded in a quarrel with Esdras.

But Jack is soon in trouble again. He falls into the clutches of Zadoch the Jew. Diamante has also landed up in Zadoch's house, but the reunion between the lovers is short-lived, for Zadoch sells Jack to another Jew, Dr Zacharie, the Pope's physician, who wants to dissect him alive for an anatomy lecture. He is rescued from this predicament by Juliana, the Pope's mistress, who has caught sight of Jack and taken a fancy to him. Dr Zacharie tries to avenge himself on Juliana by borrowing Diamante from Zadoch, and sending her to Juliana with a phial of poison. But Diamante reveals the plot to Juliana, who out of gratitude takes her on as her maid – and so she and Jack meet again.

Juliana persuades the Pope that Dr Zacharie has been plotting to poison him, and so the Pope expels the Jews from Rome, while Dr Zacharie is executed by a series of fiendish tortures, which Nashe, true to the Elizabethan demand for horrors, describes in detail.

Eventually Jack and Diamante manage to escape, helping themselves to as much of Juliana's treasure as they can carry. Juliana accidentally drinks the phial of poison which Diamante has brought from Zadoch.

The lovers reach Bologna, and there they listen to the public confession and witness the execution (by tortures even more horrific than those inflicted on Dr Zacharie) of a cobbler named Cutwolfe, who turns out to be Bartol's brother, and who has been condemned for the murder of Esdras.

Jack is deeply affected by Cutwolfe's horrible end, regarding it as a final act of divine retribution for the rape of Heraclide. He marries Diamante and resolves to lead a better life in future. With his wife he returns to the English camp in France, arriving in time to witness 'the great triumphs' attending King Henry VIII's meeting with the King of France and the German Emperor at the Field of the Cloth of Gold in 1520.

Critical commentary

The Unfortunate Traveller is clearly a rather disorganized composition, consisting of a series of episodes very loosely strung together. Sometimes, indeed, there are no connecting links at all: the first section for example, dealing with Jack's escapades in the English camp in France, is in effect self-contained, with no real relationship to the rest of the book. In addition, there are a number of loose ends and all manner of stops and starts, dictated by Nashe's whim of the moment.

To a large extent, in fact, the book is a rag-bag, into which two main kinds of material are crammed. First, there are the varied subjects on which Nashe was itching to employ his brilliant satirical gifts; and second, there were the topics in which Nashe, as a professional writer, knew his public had an avid interest, including (as the Elizabethan dramatists also knew) violence, rape, torture and bloodshed.

Although some critics feel that *The Unfortunate Traveller* cannot really be treated as a novel in any meaningful sense of the term, there can be no doubt at least that Nashe's book was quite different from anything that had gone before, if for no other reason than that it recounts a series of adventures at something approaching normal novel length through the mouth of a single hero. It is true that the personality of this hero tends at times to change according to the nature of the incident in which he is involved, but on the whole he does create the impression of a real, and intensely vivid, character.

There is no doubt that Nashe possesses the power of rapid character delineation in his separate scenes, for example in the presentation of the cider merchant at Tournai; in the very skilful depiction of Juliana, the Pope's mistress, and in the very telling self-portrait of

Cutwulfe, strapped to the torture-wheel. In all these cases the characterization is conveyed both in action and through a masterly handling of dialogue or soliloquy.

Nashe also shows a marked gift for developing the more grotesque aspects of a character's appearance and personality, in a way that sometimes reminds one of Dickens. The two writers, so widely separated in time, seem to have shared the ability to put the streak of sadism in their temperaments to effective artistic use. In both, the scenes of horror and bloodshed are often attended by a kind of grotesque humour, and both Nashe and Dickens endow their human monsters with a certain ferocious joviality.

An outstanding aspect of Nashe's characterization is the mixing of fictional creations, like Jack Wilton, with real historical persons, like the Earl of Surrey. He also uses real historical events alongside fictional ones, and in each of these cases the blending is controlled by his imaginative purposes and not by historical or chronological exactitude. Even G. R. Hibbard, who in other respects is sceptical about claims that *The Unfortunate Traveller* is a genuine novel, has to admit: 'It looks as though Nashe stumbled on the historical novel before anyone else.'

There is also no denying at least one element essential to fiction in the book, and that is Nashe's sheer narrative skill. Moreover, it can be argued that it does not entirely lack signs of the organizing principle necessary for the creation of a genuine novel. Nashe reveals considerable expertise in his use of contrast: for instance, when Surrey's artificial fantasies about Geraldine are immediately followed by the evocation of a flesh-and-blood Diamante and Jack's possession of her; or when the descriptions of the Roman gardens as miniature Edens of peace and innocence are succeeded by a whole series of Italianate villainies.

After Jack's departure from Tournai there are also several attempts to provide proper narrative links. Surrey and his Platonic infatuation for Geraldine furnish a certain *raison d'être* for the itinerary: Surrey is travelling both to escape the pangs of unattainable love, and to visit the house in Florence where Geraldine was born – and, of course, as Jack is his attendant he has to go where his master goes. Then there is Diamante. While far from being a fully realized heroine, she does play an integral part in the plot and from the moment she first appears in the prison she is seldom entirely lost sight of. Her relationship with Jack is, in fact, a real cohesive factor.

After Surrey's departure, too, the threads of the story are more firmly held, and Jack's decision to marry Diamante and return with her to the English camp in France – so that he finishes up where he began – shows some intention of conscious shaping.

Finally, it could be argued that the incoherence and discontinuity of the story are right for the nature of the material. As H. F. Brett has suggested, the 'inconsequence' is that of life itself, 'which never proceeds according to plan.' Looked at from this point of view *The Unfortunate Traveller*, whatever its defects, may be seen as the first in a long line of English novels in which the inner dynamic is provided by the continuing presence or personality of a wandering hero.

What is certain, too, is that *The Unfortunate Traveller* reveals an impressive unity of tone, whether this comes from the fictional creation, Jack Wilton, or from Nashe himself. However much the material may change, however varied the objects and methods of the satire, however disjointed the episodes, there is, throughout the book, a single forceful and vigorous voice.

This is perhaps another way of saying that Nashe is a brilliant prose writer. What is more, he is one who transcends limitations of time and place – and in this he has influenced many modern English writers who have sought to make their style vigorous, muscular and supple enough to convey the sensations and actualities of experience, not only its semblance.

To sum up, then, *The Unfortunate Traveller* may not be a novel in any modern sense of the term. At the same time it displays, if in rudimentary fashion, some of the basic elements that go to the making of a novel of a certain type, as well as being a superb piece of prose literature. As such it deserves a place in any comprehensive survey of the history of the English novel.

The Pilgrim's Progress
from This World to That Which is to Come

John Bunyan

John Bunyan was born in Bedfordshire, the son of a tinker, in 1628. He learned to read and write at the village school, but his formal education stopped there, and while still a boy he was apprenticed to his father's trade.

During Bunyan's boyhood and youth, the Puritan spirit in England was rapidly approaching its zenith, and was particularly strong in Bedfordshire. Bunyan's imaginative and highly-strung temperament was strongly affected, and he was subject to all kinds of religious terrors and guilts, and to nightmares populated by fiends from Hell.

The Civil War between King and Parliament broke out in 1642, and Bunyan was old enough to enlist in the Parliamentarian army and to take part in the decisive campaign against the Royalists of 1645. On his return home, Bunyan's religious fervour and fears intensified. He heard voices, saw visions, was seized by urges to utter terrible blasphemies. He gave up such innocent pastimes as dancing on the village green, bell-ringing, and even reading his favourite chap-book romance of *Sir Bevis of Southampton*, seeing them all as heinous sins.

In 1646 he married a poor but devout girl, who brought him as her only dowry a few pious books, which he studied avidly. He joined a Baptist society in Bedford and began to preach. The death of his wife in 1656, leaving him with four children to care for, deepened his religious convictions, and from now on, he tells us, he was 'never out of the Bible either by reading or meditation'. But the demoniacal torments continued. 'None', he wrote in his spiritual autobiography *Grace Abounding to the Chief of Sinners* 'knows the terrors of those days but myself.'

It seems to have been outside persecution that eventually relieved his inner sufferings and led him to emotional stability. In 1660 (a year after he had remarried) Bunyan was thrown into Bedford gaol for his preaching, under the law enacted against those who dissented from the established Church of England. Bunyan refused to compromise, and apart from a few brief intervals he remained in prison for the next twelve years. There he tried to support his wife and family by making and selling laces to the hawkers. He preached to his fellow inmates and assiduously studied the Bible and other religious books. He also wrote *Grace Abounding* (published in 1666) and other works.

He was released in 1672, under Charles II's Declaration of Indulgence, and the Baptist group to which he belonged appointed him their pastor. In 1675, however, he was again sentenced for public preaching, and it was during this six-month imprisonment that he wrote *The Pilgrim's Progress*, which was published in 1678. He continued to preach in secret and became so famous among the dissenters that he was nicknamed 'Bishop Bunyan'.

In 1680 he published *The Life and Death of Mr Badman*, which some critics consider as powerful as *The Pilgrim's Progress* itself; and, in 1682, *The Holy War*, an allegory which relates the attempts of the powers of evil to gain possession of the city of Man's soul. He published many other works, among them the second part of *The Pilgrim's Progress* which appeared in 1684. He died four years later and was buried in Bunhill Fields, London.

Summary

Bunyan subtitles the first part of *The Pilgrim's Progress* 'In the Similitude of a Dream' – and it is in a dream that he sees 'a man clothed with rags, standing in a certain place, with his face from his own house, a book in his hand' (the Bible) 'and a great burden on his back' (his sins). He is distraught because his reading in the Bible has convinced him that the wrath of God is about to descend on the City of Destruction in which he lives. The name of the man is Christian.

Christian, after unsuccessfully trying to persuade his family to escape with him, meets a preacher named Evangelist who indicates the route to the far-distant Celestial City. Their conversation, like all the others in the book, is set out in dramatic form, with the names of the characters in the left-hand margin.

So, crying 'Life! Life! Eternal Life!' Christian runs away, putting his fingers in his ears when his wife and children call after him. Two of the watching neighbours, Obstinate and Pliable, go after him in the hope of persuading him to return. Obstinate soon turns back in disgust, and when Pliable and Christian fall into a deep quagmire, the 'Slough of Despond', Pliable scrambles out and thankfully scampers back home, leaving Christian (weighed down by his burden) to be rescued later by a passer-by named Help.

Christian continues on his way, meeting Mr Worldly Wiseman, who tries to convince him that his journey is quite unnecessary, and that his friends Mr Legality and Mr Civility can easily show him how to get rid of his crippling burden (a reflection perhaps of the well-meaning attempts by the kinder-hearted magistrates of Bedfordshire to persuade Bunyan himself to conform and save himself from prison. However, Evangelist arrives and exposes the tempters.

Christian continues on his way, reaching a wicket-gate on which is written 'Knock, and it shall be opened to you'. Here the Christian mysteries are explained and he is shown a vision of the Day of Judgment, which fills him with fears of Hell, and hopes of Heaven.

After further travelling, Christian comes upon the Cross of Christ and the Holy Sepulchre, the sight of which causes his burden of sins to fall from his back, and he rejoices in the heavenly bliss to come. This passage is a reminder that Bunyan's Baptist faith contained the Calvinist idea of the pre-ordained division of human souls into the Damned and Elect. Christian is now convinced that he belongs to the latter, and after encounters with Sloth, Presumption, Formalism and Hypocrisy, he reaches the House Beautiful, where the virtuous young maidens Charity, Discretion, Prudence and Piety give him the sword, shield and other armour of the Christian Faith. They also show him a distant prospect of the Delectable Mountains, from which he will be able to see the Celestial City itself.

His conviction of salvation however, still has to undergo many trials. In the Valley of Humiliation, he is attacked by Apollyon, 'clothed with scales like a fish', who reveals himself as the Prince of the City of Destruction, and when Christian refuses to offer him allegiance a terrible fight ensues. Christian finally wins, though badly wounded by the monster's flaming darts.

Now, however, comes an even greater ordeal as Christian enters the Valley of the Shadow of Death. Surrounded by terrible dangers, he passes the mouth of Hell from which devils taunt him, and, as day breaks, comes upon the 'blood, bones, ashes and mangled bodies' of previous pilgrims, and nearby the caves of the giants Pagan and Pope who had put them to death.

As he struggles out of the dreadful valley, Christian catches up with another pilgrim, a neighbour of his from the City of Destruction named Faithful.

Before long they come to the town of Vanity, in which a Fair, set up by Beelzebub, is perpetually in progress. When the pilgrims refuse to be enticed by any of the false worldly wares of Vanity Fair they are arrested on a false charge.

The trial follows the formal procedure which Bunyan personally knew so well. Envy, Superstition, and Pick-thank bear false witness against the prisoners. The judge, Lord Hate-good, gives a biased summing up. The equally biased jury pronounce them both guilty. Faithful, who has dared to defend himself, is condemned to be burned and his body is devoured by the flames. A chariot of the Lord descends and carries his soul straight to the Celestial City.

Christian, however, manages to escape from prison, and is joined by Hopeful, who has been inspired by Faithful's example. Another traveller, By-ends, also attaches himself to them. But when they overhear him explaining that whereas Christian and Hopeful are 'for Religion when in rags and contempt' he, By-ends, favours Religion only 'when she is in golden slippers, in the sunshine, and with applause', they shake him off and continue alone.

After various other adventures, they come to the River of Life, where they refresh themselves, before falling into the clutches of Giant Despair of Doubting Castle, who throws them into one of his dungeons, starving and beating them and advising them to commit suicide. They pray fervently for the spiritual strength to resist this temptation (as Bunyan himself must often have done in the midst of his own sufferings in prison). With a key called Promise they eventually escape from the castle, and soon they reach the Delectable Mountains, from which they catch a distant glimpse of the Celestial City itself.

They now meet various other travellers, including a country lad named Ignorance, whom they unsuccessfully try to enlighten; a gaudily dressed young man named Flatterer; and Atheist, who is travelling in the opposite direction.

At long last they are within sight of the Celestial City, gleaming with pearls and precious stones, its streets paved with gold. To reach it, however, they have to cross the wide and deep River of Death. They plunge in boldly, but as Christian finds himself sinking, 'a great horror and darkness' falls upon him. Hopeful supports and comforts him, and at last both pilgrims reach the further bank. Two of the Shining Ones meet and escort them up the steep hill to the Celestial City.

This isn't quite the end, though. A final paragraph

describes how Ignorance also reaches the gates of the Celestial City – but when he fails to satisfy the questioning of the guards he is bound and thrust through an opening in the hillside – in other words there is a way to Hell 'even from the gates of Heaven, as well as from the City of Destruction!' The book ends with the words: 'So I awoke, and behold it was a dream.'

In the second part of *The Pilgrim's Progress*, Christian's wife Christiana, her children, and her friend and neighbour, Mercy, set out after Christian, and their pilgrimage follows much the same route. Inevitably, there is less sense of desperate urgency about it, and not so much direct personal conflict, because the women have a guide and protector in Mr Great-heart – who fights and overcomes Giant Despair and other monsters for them. In this part of the book Bunyan was dealing with the aspirations of the ordinary believer, and with the religious community as a whole (including the place of women within it) rather than with the spiritual temptations of the struggling individual soul. The more relaxed atmosphere is also probably a reflection of Bunyan's own greater equanimity.

But this certainly does not lead to any creative relaxation. The action is as vivid and exciting as ever; Christian warriors like Mr Great-heart and Mr Valiant-for-truth have a simple heroism about them, as well as a pious, almost zestful, joy in doing battle for the Lord that suggests that Bunyan had met their counterparts in the Parliamentary army.

There is more homely humour, too, in the second part, and passages of great beauty, many of which reveal an intense feeling for Nature. The final section where the various pilgrims cross the River of Death – 'pages without a false or faltering note', F. R. Leavis has said – is one of the greatest in the whole of English literature.

Critical commentary

It is obvious that *The Pilgrim's Progress* was not intended to be a novel in any sense in which the term is used today. Indeed, Bunyan would not even have known the word, for it did not come into general use until towards the end of the eighteenth century. His overriding aim was, like that of Milton when he wrote his great religious epic *Paradise Lost*, 'to justify the ways of God to men'. Bunyan regarded the narrative framework of his book as entirely subordinate to his religious intention of showing the right path to salvation.

It is also obvious that *The Pilgrim's Progress* is an allegory of this quest, a figurative narrative used to convey the spiritual content – and the characters bear names that label the moral or religious qualities they embody. In this, as in his use of the framework of a dream, Bunyan was drawing on a tradition that went back to the Middle Ages and beyond. There were also allegorical precedents closer to Bunyan's own time – in particular *The Plain Man's Pathway to Heaven*, a religious dialogue written in 1601 by an Essex minister named Arthur Dent, with which Bunyan was familiar.

But of all the influences entering directly or indirectly into *The Pilgrim's Progress* by far the most important was that of the Bible. Bunyan's mind and imagination were soaked through and through with it. From its simple, forceful language and majestic rhythms came much of the strength and beauty of his prose style – while the superb story-telling in many of the familiar tales of the Old Testament and, even more so perhaps, in the parables of the New Testament, profoundly affected his narrative methods.

In addition, Bunyan knew from experience that the best way of reaching an uneducated audience was by means of a story, and he had behind him a long line of preachers who drew their illustrations, full of practical experience and folk wisdom, from everyday life. To a large extent, in fact, *The Pilgrim's Progress* can be seen as a blending of the twin traditions of the Bible and of popular culture. As well as biblical expressions, Bunyan uses a large number of the pithy, everyday terms in common rural use such as 'slithy rob-shop' and 'all on a dung sweat'; and farming metaphors like 'make hay while the sun shines'.

The consequence of all this is that the allegory in *The Pilgrim's Progress* is never purely abstract. In spite of their names, the characters are flesh-and-blood, three-dimensional creations. They talk, despite the frequently abstract nature of their religious arguments, like real men and women, and the passages of dialogue have the force and variety of Elizabethan drama.

Far and away the strongest element of realism in *The Pilgrim's Progress* is, of course, the presence of Bunyan himself. Throughout the book there is the urgent and passionate pressure of his own personal experiences, both spiritual and actual, a pressure which holds the whole book together and gives it an impressive unity. Also, Bunyan was a born story-teller, with an instinctive command of those variations of pace and mood, light and shade, that capture and sustain the reader's interest. The book seldom remains on the same note for long, and incorporates such diverse elements as folk humour, lyricism, pungent conversation, dramatic debate, religious exaltation, and sheer narrative excitement.

Perhaps this was one of the reasons why, for a long time, *The Pilgrim's Progress* was looked down on by the serious critics, who regarded it as too primitive for civilized tastes. Among ordinary people, on the other hand, it was from the beginning a tremendous success. By 1692 one hundred thousand copies had been sold. By 1792 it had gone into no less than one hundred and sixty editions, and there were many translations into foreign languages as well. Until quite recent times, in fact, it was one of the two books (the other being the Bible) to be found in practically every British household.

Continuing popularity of this kind belongs only to a work of supreme genius, and it would be difficult today to find a critic who would disagree with **F. R.** Leavis's estimation of *The Pilgrim's Progress* as 'one of the great classics', outstanding because of 'its rich, poised and mature humanity'. As Professor Ifor Evans has said, it has 'entered into that part of our literature which transcends its age and is permanent.'

Although Bunyan was not consciously writing a novel, it is evident that *The Pilgrim's Progress* possesses many of the characteristics of great fiction, influencing many later novelists, and, in particular, initiating a whole line of novels to which the label 'moral fable' can be attached (though, with its wandering hero it also belongs in part to the picaresque tradition). An obvious example in the following century is Jonathan Swift's *Gulliver's Travels*, which despite its very different tone – bitter, worldly and misanthropic – is also fundamentally an allegory with a moral purpose. Other notable examples of the same genre are William Makepeace Thackeray's *Vanity Fair* (1848) – the title of which is of course derived directly from Bunyan's book; Samuel Butler's *Erewhon* (1872); Aldous Huxley's *Brave New World* (1932), and George Orwell's *Animal Farm* (1945).

The moral fable type of novel is a notoriously difficult one to write with success. It can only too easily exhibit the dullness and deadness of a moral or political tract – unless it is informed with some of the realism, passion and imagination which are such pre-eminent features of John Bunyan's great Christian novel.

Robinson Crusoe

Daniel Defoe

Daniel Defoe, like John Bunyan, was a Dissenter, and like him he came from a humble background and passed through many vicissitudes. He was born in London, the son of a butcher, probably in 1660. After some schooling in a Dissenting Academy, he became a hosiery merchant, and as such travelled in many European countries. In 1685 he took part in the Protestant rebellion led by the Duke of Monmouth against the Roman Catholic King James II, and also joined the army of the Protestant William of Orange, returning after the 'Glorious Revolution' of 1688 (which put William and his English wife, Mary, on the throne) to his commercial activities. In 1703 and again in 1713 he was pilloried and imprisoned for writing pamphlets against the established church. In spite of his interrupted early education he became a man of wide learning – he spoke six languages and read seven. He wrote numerous pamphlets, political as well as religious, and was also on various occasions a government secret agent in Scotland. He edited a number of newspapers, one of them a trade journal. Although he published over 250 works, he was nearly sixty when *Robinson Crusoe* and its sequel, *The Farther Adventures of Robinson Crusoe* appeared in 1719. These were followed by a string of other brilliant fictional or semi-fictional works. He died in 1731, and, like Bunyan, was buried in Bunhill Fields.

Although there are some obvious similarities between Defoe and Bunyan it is the differences that are most significant. For Bunyan his religion was all in all, and his whole life was a spiritual pilgrimage: for Defoe, in spite of his ardent Dissenting faith, religion had a powerful rival – what he himself called 'the grand affair of business'.

In many respects for Defoe, as for several of his contemporaries, religion and business had run into each other. Individualism in religious matters (the stress on salvation as a personal matter between each man and his God) inculcated by Protestantism – and especially Puritanism – had in part become merged with the kind of individualism necessary for successful commercial activity in the atmosphere of eighteenth-century free enterprise.

Whereas, too, Bunyan lived during a period when religious zeal was at its height, Defoe was born in the year when the Puritan Commonwealth had collapsed with the restoration of King Charles II. In *The Serious Reflections of Robinson Crusoe* which Defoe published in 1720 (thus completing a Robinson Crusoe trilogy, though this third part is now little read) he has his hero reflecting on a general ebbing of the Christian religion in the face of advancing secularization.

Defoe was very much a product of the eighteenth century, the Age of Reason, which eschewed religious and political extremes and anything approaching emotionalism or mysticism and, supported by the empirical science of Isaac Newton and the empirical philosophy of John Locke, emphasized the concrete, the actual and the practical at a time when Britain was rapidly expanding her economic power both at home and abroad.

Summary

Robinson Crusoe begins with the nineteen-year-old hero going to sea to make his fortune. On an expedition to Africa to buy more slaves for his successful Brazilian plantations, his ship is wrecked near an unknown island, somewhere off the north-east coast of South America, and Crusoe is the only survivor to reach shore.

To begin with he has nothing but his knife, pipe and tobacco. But by constructing a crude raft he is able to ferry back all kinds of stores, including firearms and powder, from the foundered ship. He keeps a careful diary of his activities and reflections – and daily reads his Bible and gives thanks to God for his deliverance.

While recovering from a fever, Crusoe gradually teaches himself all kinds of crafts, builds himself a permanent shelter protected by a stockade, makes rough utensils, hunts for food and skins for clothing, and succeeds in cultivating crops. He tries to build a boat, only to find it is too heavy for him to get it to the beach. Slowly he makes his living conditions more tolerable, especially after he has domesticated some of the wild goats – and tamed a parrot as a pet.

After twelve years of solitude comes one of the most memorable scenes in fiction, when Crusoe finds a human footprint in the sand. But, although he keeps constant watch, nearly ten more years pass before he finds human bones and flesh on the shores, left by cannibals who return shortly afterwards with several captives. Crusoe attacks them with his musket and sword. They escape in their canoes, leaving behind one of their captives – and so Crusoe meets Man Friday, named after the day of his rescue.

Crusoe converts the savage to Christianity and teaches him enough English for them to communicate with each other. Friday tells Crusoe that there are seventeen white prisoners on his own island. Crusoe determines to rescue them, and with Friday's help builds a seaworthy boat. But before they can launch it, another band of cannibals land with three prisoners. Crusoe and Friday attack them, kill many of the savages and rescue two of the captives. One of them is Friday's father and there is a joyful reunion between them. The other is a white man, an old Spaniard.

Crusoe sends him and Friday's father in the newly-built boat to try and rescue the other white prisoners.

Then an English ship appears. Mutineers put the captain and two of the loyal crew ashore, and Crusoe and Friday help them to recapture the ship. The mutineers decide to stay on the island, and the others set sail.

During the homeward voyage, Crusoe learns that the old Spaniard and Friday's father have succeeded in freeing the other white men, and vows one day to visit them. First, though, he returns with Friday to England, finds that both his parents are dead, but learns too that he is now a rich man, his plantations in Brazil still intact. He marries and has a family. When his wife dies, however, he sets sail again with Friday, and their adventures (in the course of which Friday is killed) are recounted in the sequel.

Critical commentary

Robinson Crusoe is very much a product of his age, the practical-minded eighteenth century. There is nothing about him of the romantic adventurer who goes to sea in search of excitement. On the contrary, as David Daiches has pointed out, he is 'a sober and prudent merchant engaged in a business enterprise. Prudence rather than heroism is the key to his actions; he is, in fact, the first significant example in English literature of the prudential hero.'

This is pinpointed by the very lively interest Crusoe takes in money, even on his desert island. When he finds some coins on the wreck he cannot resist the temptation of taking them, even though he knows they will be of no use to him. Then, when he finally returns to England and his faithful agent reveals the extent of his riches, Crusoe records: 'I turned pale and grew sick; and had not the old man run and fetched me a cordial, I believe the sudden surprise of joy had overset nature, and I had died on the spot.' It is probably the most emotional utterance in the whole book.

Much of the fascination of the story, indeed, lies in the loving catalogue of all the varied goods he brings from the wreck. 'I had everything so ready at my hand that it was a great pleasure to me to see all my goods in such order, and especially to find my stock of all necessaries so great,' he reports with true merchant glee.

There is also much genuine piety in the book, but Crusoe's attitude towards God often seems to be one of business partnership, and his religious faith serves to confirm and strengthen his robust and materialistic individualism.

A number of economic theorists have cited Robinson Crusoe as the perfect example of 'economic man', pointing out, for example, that he regards his island primarily as a property to be developed for his own use. Another major source of the book's fascination is in the detailed accounts he gives of his taming of Nature and his harnessing of her resources. He has no wish to adapt himself to his wild environment and little feeling for its natural beauties: his aim, rather, is to adapt it to his own ideas and make it as far as possible a replica of the social and economic organization he has left behind.

Crusoe is, of course, desperately lonely on his desert island: but it is noticeable that his craving for human society is largely satisfied by the advent of Friday, even though their communication is necessarily limited. Their relationship, moreover, is very much that of master and servant. Basically, Crusoe treats Friday as a native to be tamed (like the wild creatures of the island) and set to profitable use. In fact Crusoe represents exactly the kind of attitudes which were eventually to make Britain the richest country in the world and lead her to establish a vast overseas empire.

It is important to realize that Defoe's emphasis on the actual, the concrete and the observable, which Crusoe exemplified, was essential in the development of the novel, at any rate in its early stages. Indeed, many contemporary readers thought that Defoe's novel was a true account based on the experiences of Alexander Selkirk, a sailor who, from 1704 to 1710, *did* live alone on the uninhabited island of Juan Fernandez in the Pacific Ocean. But although Defoe may have met Selkirk, and read his manuscript narrative of his experiences, he drew on many other travel books as well, and the novel is pure fiction.

Robinson Crusoe may bear a superficial resemblance to these travel books but its spell goes far deeper. It holds an appeal to the pioneering instinct deep in human nature that seeks to pit itself, alone, against the unknown. 'Defoe's excellence', Coleridge wrote, 'is to make me forget my specific class, character, and circumstance and to raise me, while I read him, into universal man.'

As far as *Robinson Crusoe*'s contribution to the development of the English novel is concerned, it was Defoe's thoroughgoing realism which was of prime importance. It was the first time that a continuous prose narrative had been written with no other specific object than to create the illusion of day-to-day living. Crusoe's preoccupation with time is symptomatic of this. In previous works of fiction there had been little attempt to establish a natural chronological sequence: events had usually succeeded each other with the abruptness and inconsequentiality of a dream. Much the same thing is true of place. In many earlier works of fiction it is often impossible to tell the exact location, and real and imaginary places often exist side by side without any clear distinction between them. Whereas earlier authors had mixed obvious fantasy with their fact, Defoe was the first to take it for granted that the storyteller's task was to achieve as far as possible the verisimilitude of real life. Also, in his innovatory use of the form of an autobiographical memoir, he was the first to achieve something approaching real pattern and unity.

Obviously the novel needed to contain all these elements if it was to become a coherent art form. Why is it, then, that Defoe is not generally considered to be the true progenitor of the English novel?

The main answer to that question is related to the fact that Crusoe, like Defoe himself, was so thoroughly the embodiment of the social and economic drives of the early eighteenth century. Inevitably this meant the absence of some of the qualities most needed to give the novel warmth and depth. The concentration on the practical and the rational left little room for any real exploration of character. Crusoe does not change morally or psychologically in spite of his long and frightening experiences. Neither is there any exploration of personal relationships – so essential an element in the mature novel. True, Crusoe gets married after his return to England, but only after he has characteristically made sure of his financial position. His attitude towards marriage is the reverse of romantic: in his typically practical view it was 'neither to my disadvantage or dissatisfaction', but nothing more. The birth of his three children and the death of his wife are dismissed in a few words. As for his other relationships, they are almost entirely dominated by economic motives – including even that with Friday. Consequently there is none of that carefully spun web of interrelating characters which was to be the distinguishing mark of later English fiction. Nevertheless, none of this alters the fact that *Robinson Crusoe* is one of the classics of world literature, and so inevitably occupies an important place in the history of the English novel.

Moll Flanders

Daniel Defoe

Among Daniel Defoe's other fictional or semi-fictional
works one in particular stands out as a major contribution
to the development of the English novel. Its full title is
*The Fortunes and Misfortunes of the famous Moll Flan-
ders* and it was published in 1722. Like *Robinson Crusoe*
it is a first-person narrative, and has been described as 'a
spoof autobiography', because, as with Defoe's other
fiction, it has that air of matter-of-fact reporting which
makes it appear absolutely authentic.

Summary

Moll Flanders is born in Newgate Gaol, the daughter of a
woman about to be transported to Virginia for theft. The
abandoned child is brought up, in ignorance of her
origins, in the household of the compassionate mayor of
Colchester. She is seduced in her teens, but then retrieves
her fortunes by making a respectable marriage. On the
death of her first husband, however, she goes from marriage to marriage – five in all, and some of them bigamous
– and into all sorts of other liaisons, some of them solely
for money. She visits Virginia, and discovers that her current husband is her half-brother. Leaving him behind,
she returns to England. There, for a time, she is reduced
to destitution. But then she becomes a highly successful
pickpocket and thief. Eventually, though, she is caught

and, like her mother, lands up in Newgate Gaol. There she meets her favourite among her many husbands, a convicted highwayman named James. Both of them are transported to Virginia. Somehow they manage to take their ill-gotten gains with them, and, in addition, Moll finds that she has inherited a plantation from her mother. She and James pass the remainder of their lives in an atmosphere of prosperity and penitence.

Critical commentary

In his preface to the book, Defoe stresses his moral intention, pointing out that 'there is not a wicked action in any part but is first and last rendered unhappy and unfortunate.' He cannot, however, prevent himself entering into Moll's career of crime with his customary gusto. The strength of the book lies in its vivid objectivity, in the absence of any ingrained moral revulsion which would have weakened the impact. Moll's intermittent bouts of repentance and moralizing, in consequence, do not ring true in themselves, though they can be seen as part of her character. But what we do have is an unforgettable evocation of the seamy side of eighteenth-century London life.

Clearly Defoe has, to a considerable extent, identified himself with his heroine, revealing more than a sneaking sympathy for her. In part this is a purely human sympathy occasioned by Moll's unfortunate beginnings. In part, too, it is the kind of sympathy shared by many in the eighteenth century for the victims of a vicious penal code which could hang a man, woman, or child, or transport them for life, for stealing (like Moll and her mother) some quite paltry article. In addition, it was a period when crime was on the increase: it has been described as the golden age of the highwayman – and a certain glamour grew up round many criminal activities. The highwayman Dick Turpin, for example, became a kind of folk hero, and John Gay's *The Beggar's Opera* (1728), with its highwayman 'hero' Macheath, was a tremendous popular success.

Some social historians have suggested that this growth

of crime, and the increasingly harsh laws to combat it, were a distorted reflection of the new economic forces with their stress on individualism, free enterprise, and success in financial matters as criteria of human value.

It is noticeable that Moll frequently insists that she is not basically different from anybody else, that her over-riding aim is merely to be prosperous and respectable – except that unfortunate circumstances have denied her a respectable outlet for her economic drives. 'With money in the pocket one is at home anywhere,' she says. These sentiments form her basic 'morality', and fundamentally they were the product of the same instinct that prompts Robinson Crusoe to take gold coins from the shipwreck merely for the comfort of having them in his pocket.

Moll Flanders may have some basic similarities in atti-tude to *Robinson Crusoe*, but how does it compare with it purely as a novel? Some critics believe that *Moll Flanders* is inferior in form and structure, too close to the picaresque novel in its diffuse and episodic nature to be really effec-tive. Certainly there are all kinds of loose ends, gaps, and discontinuities, and, as in all Defoe's novels, the ending is frustratingly abrupt. As Ifor Evans puts it: 'Form, in its subtler sense, does not affect Defoe: his novels run on until, like an alarm clock, they run down.'

It could, of course, be argued that the inconsequentiality of the plot in *Moll Flanders* is further evidence of Defoe's special brand of realism in that it expresses the random nature of life itself. However, there is at least some evi-dence of shaping and structure in the reappearances at crucial points in the narrative of Moll's mother, her half-brother, her favourite husband and her favourite child – and, above all, in the continuing presence of Moll herself.

The characterization of Moll has been much discussed. Adverse critics have considered her devoid of any real depth – the Victorian critic Sir Leslie Stephen, for ex-ample, complained of a lack 'of all that goes by the name of psychological analysis in modern fiction'. On the other hand his daughter, the novelist Virginia Woolf, declared

Moll Flanders to be an 'indisputably great' novel, largely on account of the obsession to impart character that it displays in the depiction of Moll, which Virginia Woolf regarded as the distinguishing mark of the true novelist. Another novelist of our time, E. M. Forster, picked on *Moll Flanders* as the prime example of a novel 'in which character is everything'. Moll, he says, 'fills the book which bears her name, or rather stands alone in it, like a tree in a park, so that we can see her from every aspect.' Whereas, too, the adverse critics see Defoe's heroine as essentially amoral and in any case existing only on the surface, Forster sees her as brave, impulsive and fundamentally warm-hearted and sincere – and, above all, a concrete human presence: 'Moll is a character physically, with hard plump limbs that get into bed and pick pockets.'

What is certain is that *Moll Flanders*, whatever its defects, was another notable step forward in the progress of the still infant novel – and perhaps the controversy among modern critics is the most telling evidence of its inherent vitality.

Gulliver's Travels

Jonathan Swift

Jonathan Swift was born in Dublin of English parents in 1667, and was educated at Trinity College, Dublin. In 1689 he came to England to work as secretary to Sir William Temple, a notable Whig statesman, scholar, and patron of learning and letters. Chafing at his position of dependence, Swift returned to Ireland and in 1694 he was ordained. Two years later he returned to the service of Sir William Temple and, encouraged by him, wrote his first two major works of satire, *The Battle of the Books* and *A Tale of a Tub* (published together in 1704), both of which contained fictional characters.

When Sir William Temple died in 1699 Swift hoped to obtain some substantial ecclesiastical position. These hopes were not fulfilled, but he was given some minor preferments in Ireland. He continued to spend much of his time in London, and to write pamphlets on Church matters. The most famous of these is the ironically titled 'An Argument to Prove the Inconvenience of Abolishing Christianity' (1708), which pretends to defend the retention of Christianity on grounds of pure expediency.

In 1710, disgusted with the Whigs for their failure to reward his efforts and with their alliance with the Dissenters, he went over to the Tories, and wrote for them some of his most famous political pamphlets. Despite Swift's intimacy with the Tory leaders, the only ecclesiastical prize they bestowed on him was the deanery of St

Patrick's Cathedral in Dublin. On the death of Queen Anne in 1714 his Tory friends went out of power, his hopes of advancement were at an end, and the misanthropic element already apparent in his satirical writings was deepened by a profound sense of failure and frustration.

It would be wrong, however, to assume that the misanthropy was of a petty and personally vindictive nature. He was, for example, deeply moved by the plight of the Irish, and wrote pamphlets on their behalf, the most famous of which is 'A Modest Proposal for Preventing the Children of Poor People from Being a Burthen to Their Parents or Country' (1729). In this, instead of directly attacking the English government's attitude towards the miseries of the Irish poor, he solemnly, and in a tone of sweet reasonableness, advances his 'modest proposal' for the solution of the problem, which turns out to be even more monstrous – no less than the breeding of children for butchers' meat – so that the real cruelty and inhumanity are, of course, mercilessly and horrifically exposed.

In addition, Swift spent a third of his income on charities, and saved up another third to found a charitable institution after his death. He was tremendously popular in Ireland, and as an individual, too, he was certainly capable of inspiring love. Two women followed him to Ireland. One of these, Hester Vanhomrigh, he addressed as Vanessa in various poems. The other was Esther Johnson (or Stella, as Swift called her), an illegitimate daughter of Sir William Temple. Some of Swift's biographers think they may have been secretly married; they were certainly very close, as is shown in the *Journal to Stella*, which consists of letters Swift wrote daily from London between 1710 and 1713 to Stella in Ireland. Swift never really recovered from her death in 1728, and from that date the morbid elements in his nature became more pronounced. After a period of great wretchedness when he probably suffered from a form of insanity, he died in 1745 and was buried beside Stella in St Patrick's Cathedral.

Summary

The full title of Swift's best-known work, published in 1726, is *Travels into Several Remote Nations of the World, by Lemuel Gulliver, first a Surgeon, and then a Captain of Several Ships*, though it is usually known simply as *Gulliver's Travels*. The Preface, ostensibly written by Richard Sympson, explains that his 'ancient and intimate friend' and distant relative, Lemuel Gulliver, had handed his papers to him to edit for the public.

Gulliver begins his account with a quiet, factual, unemphatic record of his origins, education, studies in medicine and navigation, and of his first uneventful voyages as a ship's surgeon. In exactly the same disarming manner he introduces the first of his extraordinary adventures, recounting how, after the ship had been driven on to a rock 'to the north-west of Van Dieman's land' (the exact latitude is given), some of the crew had embarked in a boat which overturned, and how he himself had managed to struggle ashore, the sole survivor.

Up to this point, therefore, there was nothing to suggest that the book was going to be anything more than another of the many narratives of exploration and travel which were enjoying a great vogue at the time. It reads, in fact, very much as if it were written by the author of *Robinson Crusoe*. Indeed, Swift had been Daniel Defoe's main competitor in the field of journalism for twenty years, and it is obvious from *Gulliver's Travels* that he had been influenced by Defoe, both in the adoption of fiction as a vehicle for his purposes, and in the use of a plausible, matter-of-fact realism.

The result is that the reader of *Gulliver's Travels* is lulled in the course of the first few pages into a mood of complete confidence, security, and credulity. The tale, however, suddenly takes a very different turn in the famous scene of Gulliver's awakening, after a long sleep of exhaustion, to find himself the prisoner of tiny human beings who have fastened him securely to the ground.

By now, of course, the majority of Swift's contemporary readers would have realized that this was not a travel book but a work of fantasy – but the fascination of the detail in his description of how Gulliver coped with the Lilliputians might well have carried the more unsuspecting among them right through 'A Voyage to Lilliput' without regarding Swift's satire as much more than an additional spice to the story.

That, after all, is how generations of children have been able to read *Gulliver's Travels* in the shortened (and suitably expurgated) editions prepared for them, and there are thousands of readers in consequence who regard the book as a juvenile classic (in much the same way as they do *Robinson Crusoe*), unaware that it is one of the most devastating and painful satires in literature.

For some time after Gulliver's awakening to find himself the prisoner of the Lilliputians, it is the brilliant precision of the language and imagery which constitutes a large part of the narrative spell. Gulliver struggles to break his bonds, and is assailed by showers of tiny needle-like arrows. He demands food and is served by relays of Lilliputians, carrying joints of meat 'smaller than the wings of a lark'.

The first expression of the underlying satirical intention creeps up on the reader unawares and could easily be overlooked. The Emperor of the Lilliputians puts on various entertainments for Gulliver, which consist of tight-rope performances. The Emperor's Ministers are called upon to demonstrate their dexterity – and 'by contending to excel themselves and their fellows, they strain so far that there is hardly one of them who hath not received a fall, and some of them two or three.'

Another diversion is for the Emperor to hold out a stick, and whichever performer 'holds out the longest in leaping and creeping' over or under it is rewarded with a thread of purple silk. These bland descriptions most effectively lampoon the kind of careers Swift knew so well from his own experience of public life.

The Emperor's chief minister apprises Gulliver of the political situation – and, in the process, parodies contemporary English politics. The two main political parties in Lilliput are the Low Heels and the High Heels. There are also two warring factions, the Little Endians and the Big Endians (according to which end they crack their eggs). The Big Endians had just been defeated, and had fled to the neighbouring country of Blefuscu, which is about to launch a seaborne invasion of Lilliput. The purpose of the chief minister's visit is to try and enlist Gulliver as a kind of secret weapon.

There follows one of Gulliver's most famous adventures, when he wades across the channel separating the two countries, attaches lines to the enemy fleet, and drags it back with him to the Lilliputian capital. He is rewarded with a high title, but when he refuses to be 'an instrument of bringing a free and brave people into slavery' by making other forays against Blefuscu, the Lilliputian Emperor and his ministers are furious. His further service to the Emperor, putting out a serious fire at the palace by urinating on it, meets with a mixed reception.

Warned of a plot against him, Gulliver takes refuge with the Emperor of Blefuscu. A normal sized boat is washed ashore, and Gulliver eventually sets out to sea, is picked up by an English merchantman, and returns to England – where he makes enough money, by exhibiting the Lilliputian cattle he has brought with him, to finance another voyage and to leave his wife and family well provided for.

'A Voyage to Brobdingnag' begins in the same circumstantial way. This time Gulliver's ship is driven off course and anchors off an unknown coast. The long-boat, with Gulliver on board, is sent to fill the water casks. Wandering away from the party, Gulliver returns to find the long-boat rowing for dear life back to the ship, pursued by a giant. Taking refuge in a field, Gulliver is nearly killed by advancing reapers, until one of them discovers him crouching on the ground and hands him over to his master, who takes him home and gives him as a pet to his forty-foot high, nine-year-old daughter, Glumdalclitch. She calls him Grildrig (or mannikin) and cares for him devotedly, until her father sells him to the King and Queen. Gulliver is cosseted by the Court, provided with miniature furniture and utensils, and fashionably dressed in clothes of 'the thinnest silk' – which to him, however, are as thick as English blankets. He suffers a good deal from the wasps as big as partridges, and from the flies, the size of larks, who deposit their excrement on his food. Swift's preoccupation with bodily processes, which became increasingly morbid as he grew older, is more in evidence in this part of the book – a symptom perhaps of his deepening disgust with the human race.

Questioned by the King, Gulliver launches proudly into an account of eighteenth-century English political, social, and legal institutions. In the King's unexpected and disgusted reaction, the suave, reasonable tone of the earlier satire is replaced by the full savagery of Swift's anger and contempt. It is all the more effective because Gulliver is cast as the typical representative of his own culture. It simply does not occur to him that the King may have some justification for his outburst. Patronizingly, he tries to excuse the King and goes on, with amused contempt, to describe the King's own quaint ideas.

The passage is a superb instance of Swift's double-edged satirical technique. Obviously, the reader is supposed to subscribe to the King's ideals of common-sense, reason and justice; but the movement of Gulliver's argument is, conversely, to drive the reader to reject the ideals in practice. The pull between acceptance and rejection sets up an almost schizophrenic tension, and acts as a most powerful disruptive agency of conventionally accepted attitudes, and of the human conscience itself.

Eventually, Gulliver is carried off by a Brobdingnagian eagle, dropped into the sea, and picked up by an English ship.

Part Three of *Gulliver's Travels*, 'A Voyage to Laputa,

Luggnagg, Glubbdubdrib and Japan' is the least interesting to modern readers, partly because it lacks the unity of
structure of the others, and partly because the targets of
Swift's satire belong specifically, for the most part, to his
own age. This time, Gulliver's ship is boarded by pirates,
and he is set adrift, to be picked up by the remarkable flying island of Laputa, whose inhabitants are burlesque
figures through whom Swift attacks every kind of impractical scholarship, vain philosophy, and pretentious
economic scheme. The Laputans walk with their 'heads
... inclined either to the right or to the left; one of their
eyes turned inward, and the other directly up to the zenith.' All speculative thought, Swift is saying, is ultimately
ridiculous.

Gulliver now visits Lagado, the capital on the main-
land of Balnibarbi. There, he meets some inventors, including one who has been working for eight years on
extracting sunbeams from cucumbers; an architect who
advocates building houses from the roof down, and an
agriculturalist who is trying to propagate a breed of naked
sheep. The comedy here is of a more boisterous kind,
without much satirical subtlety.

Next, Gulliver visits Glubbdubdrib, a small island inhabited by sorcerers and magicians. These have the power
of summoning the dead to act as their servants. To entertain him they conjure up various famous historical personages, who soon alter his romantic ideas of the past.

Gulliver's visit to the island of Luggnagg is chiefly
memorable for his meeting with the Struldbrugs – rare
individuals who, by some freak of birth, are immortal.
But immortality does not alter human nature, for the
Struldbrugs '... had not only the follies and infirmities
of other old men, but many more which arose from the
dreadful prospect of never dying.'

Gulliver's next voyage is as captain of a ship. His crew
mutiny and set him ashore in unknown territory. There,
he encounters a number of ape-like creatures. 'I never
beheld in all my travels', Gulliver comments 'so disagree-

able an animal nor one against which I naturally conceived so strong an antipathy.' When one of these repellent creatures raises its forepaw as if to greet him, Gulliver drives it off with the flat of his sword. A swarm of the creature's companions come to its assistance, and several of them climb into a tree 'from whence they began to discharge their excrements on my head.'

A horse approaches and Gulliver's attackers flee, but when he tries to stroke the horse's mane, it shakes him off with an expression of great disdain. Gulliver soon understands why – for when the horse has taken him to his home, he produces another of the hideous ape-like creatures (a number of which he keeps to do simple field work) and compares it point by point with Gulliver, at the same time neighing something that sounds like 'Yahoo'. 'My horror and astonishment are not to be described,' Gulliver reports, 'when I observed in this abominable animal a perfect human figure . . .'

In this strange country it is the race of horses known as Houyhnhnms who are in command – and, not surprisingly, Gulliver learns their language as quickly as he can and sets out to convince them that, in spite of the physical similarities between himself and the Yahoos, he is a very different creature and that he, too, is endowed with reason and intelligence.

But the most the Houyhnhnms will concede is that he is cleaner, smoother, and more intelligent than the Yahoos. They insist that Gulliver is actually inferior because the various parts of his body are neither as strong nor as well adapted to the climate and terrain as those of the Yahoos.

A good deal of 'A Voyage to the Country of the Houyhnhnms' consists of conversations, debates, and general description of the Houyhnhnm view of life, and there is less circumstantial detail than in the other parts of the book. This helps to maintain the atmosphere of grave discourse which belongs naturally to the Houyhnhnms. It also sets the satirical tone: in this section there are no sallies into wit, comedy, or burlesque, and there are very few flashes of overt anger or savagery.

When Gulliver is asked to explain why humans go to war, he answers that the longest and bloodiest wars are 'those occasioned by difference in opinion, especially if it be in things indifferent.' The shocked Houyhnhnms' response is that it is fortunate that the Yahoos of Gulliver's race are so ill-equipped physically to inflict harm. So Gulliver goes on to boast of the numerous methods of destruction perfected by his fellow men, and the smugness and self-satisfaction with which he presents his case is a shocking indictment of humanity both in his age and, perhaps even more so, in our own, with its infinitely more terrible destructive powers. One of the positive aspects of Swift's satire, indeed, is that it dares to reveal those truths which most of us try to evade.

Gulliver's recital having had the opposite effect from the one he had intended, he now tries, just as unsuccessfully, to give a favourable description of human legal institutions and of the uses of money. But every question put to him by the Houyhnhnms elicits answers that inexorably reveal the evil uses to which humankind have put their much-vaunted faculty of reason. His final disillusionment comes when he is bathing naked in a stream and a female Yahoo, 'inflamed by desire', plunges in after him:

> ... now I could no longer deny that I was a real Yahoo
> in every limit and feature, since the females had a
> natural propensity to me as one of their own species ...

Eventually, Gulliver's complacency has been completely punctured and he resolves 'never to return to human kind, but to pass the rest of my life among these admirable Houyhnhnms,' whose conduct is governed by a universal and impartially extended 'friendship and benevolence and who have no conceptions of ideas of what is evil in a rational creature,' so that 'their grand maxim is to cultivate reason, and to be wholly governed by it ... not mingled, obscured, or discoloured by passion and interest.'

Although Gulliver is allowed to settle in the country, it is a short-lived paradise. The assembly of the Houyhnhnms fear that as he has 'some rudiments of reason added to the natural depravity of the Yahoos', he might eventually incite them to revolt. So Gulliver, with his Houyhnhnm master's help, builds a boat and 'with the utmost grief and despair' departs. When he is at last taken on board a Portuguese ship, he cannot bear the proximity of his own kind – though he particularly praises 'the great humanity' of the captain and crew (Swift is stressing that his indictment is not of individuals but of the human race collectively).

Whereas in the three other sections of the book, Gulliver's return to England occupies little space, his readjustment to the realities of his own world is far longer and more difficult this time, and the process is brilliantly conveyed by a multiplicity of almost drearily exact details. During the first year, Gulliver cannot bear being close to humans, even his family. His greatest pleasure is in conversing with the horses in his stable, who 'are strangers to bridle or saddle; they live in great amity with me and friendship to each other.' His aim in life is 'to apply those excellent lessons of virtue which I learned among the Houyhnhnms ...' – but he has not much hope for his own kind.

In 1727, Swift added to the book 'A Letter from Captain Gulliver to his cousin Sympson'. In it Gulliver complains that the reformations he had hoped to see as the result of the publication of his book have not been forthcoming – and the letter ends, in a voice clearly Swift's own:

I must freely confess that ... some corruptions of my
Yahoo nature have revived in me by conversing with a few
of your species, and particularly those of my own family,
by an unavoidable necessity, else I should never have

attempted so absurd a project as that of reforming the
Yahoo race of this kingdom; but I have now done with all
such visionary schemes for ever.

It is on this note of personal despair that *Gulliver's
Travels* closes.

Critical commentary

Some critics see misanthropy as the predominant element
in *Gulliver's Travels*. Others believe this view to be
exaggerated. Swift, it must be remembered, was reared in
a dialectical tradition which was in many respects more
mediaeval and Elizabethan than Augustan, as was his
near-contemporary Laurence Sterne, author of *Tristram
Shandy*. Like Sterne, though more seriously, Swift takes
up various propositions and follows them through all
their ramifications to see where they might lead. It is
doubtful, for instance, whether Swift seriously intended
the Houyhnhnms as a practical human ideal. George
Orwell pointed out that their life of reason results in an
essentially life-denying and dreary utopia. 'They are
exempt from love, friendship, curiosity, fear, sorrow, and –
except in their feeling towards the Yahoos, who occupy
rather the same place in their community as the Jews in
Nazi Germany – anger and hatred.' And F. R. Leavis has
said of the Houyhnhnms: 'they may have all the reason,
but the Yahoos have all the life ...'

The idea of the Yahoos, too, is one to be explored in all
its devastating implications, but not taken as the last word
about human nature. This is not to deny, however, that
both Houyhnhnms and Yahoos *do* convey terrible truths
about human cultures and civilizations which any Christian (or if it comes to that, any humanist) must be prepared
to confront. But the very fact that Swift was able to react
with so much horror in face of these truths, is a token in
itself that the message of *Gulliver's Travels* is not ultimately a purely negative one. It is rather a challenge to
all kinds of agonizing reappraisals. Above all, the richness

and variety of Swift's satirical resources, the toughness and resilience of his language and imagery, the vitality of his wit and imagination make the work the reverse of life-denying.

Does all this make *Gulliver's Travels* a novel? Obviously not in the usual sense of the term. However, it is not merely a string of loosely connected adventures. The various travels are arranged with a purpose; they are cumulative in their effect and could not be placed in any other order without damaging the total impact. *Gulliver's Travels* has its own organic unity. The central character changes and develops from the cocksure eighteenth-century European convinced of the superiority of his own age and culture to the shocked, sobered and disillusioned misanthrope (and here he merges with the personality of his creator). And all the narrative skills and devices that make great fiction are abundantly and brilliantly present.

Swift's purpose in writing *Gulliver's Travels* was predominantly satirical and reformative, but in adopting the new fictional techniques he also produced the prototype of the fable type of novel – with many descendants which include Samuel Butler's *Erewhon* (1872), Aldous Huxley's *Brave New World* (1932), George Orwell's *Animal Farm* (1945) and many others, and if *Gulliver's Travels* is not a novel in the sense we use the word today, it is certainly a brilliantly successful piece of imaginative fiction, and no account of the development of the English novel would be complete without it.

Pamela,
or Virtue Rewarded

Samuel Richardson

Samuel Richardson was born in 1689 in Derbyshire, the son of a London joiner who had migrated north. At school, Samuel was aptly nicknamed 'Serious and Gravity'. He wanted to become a clergyman, but his parents did not have the means to make this possible, and so when he was seventeen he was sent to London and apprenticed to a printer. He was the model apprentice, becoming successively compositor, corrector of the press, and printer on his own account – and marrying his master's daughter. He eventually became Printer of the Journal of the House of Commons, Master of the Stationers' Company, and Law Printer to the King.

There was little early indication that he possessed any literary talent, apart from a knack of writing elegant and well-phrased letters. Then, in 1739 (when Richardson was already fifty years old) two London printers commissioned him to compile a volume of letters which would serve as models for semi-educated country readers and at the same time inculcate sound moral and religious principles. Among these were to be a number of letters whose specific aim was 'to instruct handsome girls, who were obliged to go out to service ... to avoid the snares that might be laid against their virtue.' As Richardson worked on the letters, he remembered a true story he had once been told about a widowed country gentleman who, after repeated and unsuccessful attempts to seduce one of his pretty maid-servants, had ended up by marrying her. The outcome was that Richardson temporarily laid aside his collection of model letters (completed and published a little later) and wrote a novel instead, the first two volumes of which appeared in 1740, and two more in the following year. The close connection between the two projects, however, was made clear by this description which appeared on the title-page of *Pamela*:

> a series of Familiar Letters from a Beautiful Young Damsel to her Parents. Now first published in order to cultivate the Principles of Virtue and Religion in the Minds of the Youth of both Sexes ...

The success of *Pamela* was instant and spectacular. Two months after the appearance of the first volumes the *Gentleman's Magazine* reported that it was 'judged in Town as great a sign of want of curiosity not to have read *Pamela* as not to have seen the French and Italian dancers' – who were causing a fashionable stir at the time. One contemporary wrote that 'the person who had not read *Pamela* is disqualified for conversation, of which it was the principal subject for some time.'

It created just as big a sensation abroad. The contemporary French writer, Crébillon, declared that 'Without *Pamela* we should not know what to do or say here,' and within six years it had been translated not only into French but also into German, Dutch and Italian, becoming one of the most influential novels in the history of European fiction, with imitators as far afield as Russia. In fact, the prim, fussy, fifty-one year old printer had produced what was in effect the world's first bestselling novel.

Richardson went on to write the equally successful and even more prolific *Clarissa* (seven volumes, published 1747–1748) and followed that with his third and last novel, *The History of Sir Charles Grandison* (published 1753). He spent his remaining years contentedly anthologizing his own maxims and 'instructive sentiments', and in

endless correspondence with his very wide circle of mostly
feminine admirers. Some seven huge folios of his letters
still remain, largely unpublished. He died in 1761, and
was buried in London, close to his print shop.

Summary

The story which Pamela Andrews unfolds in her letters
to her parents begins just after her mistress, who had
employed her as lady's maid, has died. Squire B., her
mistress's son, taking advantage of Pamela's position, sets
out to seduce her. Although she is secretly in love with
him, she indignantly rejects his advances. Squire B. does
everything he can to force her to his will. He lures her to
one of his country houses, where she is practically imprisoned in the charge of two villainous and threatening
servants, Mrs Jewkes and Monsieur Colbrand. With the
help of Mrs Jewkes, he tries, unsuccessfully, to trap her
into a mock marriage. At one stage he is on the point of
raping her, but is scared off when she falls into a fit.
Eventually, he sends her away, but now, genuinely in love
with her, persuades her to return. After further attempts
to make her his mistress, which Pamela adroitly side-steps,
he decides, despite her humble birth and position, to make
her his wife.

The second part of *Pamela*, which was added in 1742,
shows Pamela and Squire B. ideally married, apart from
a short interlude when he becomes involved with a widowed countess at a masked ball, with Pamela dispensing
lengthy and pompous homilies in her letters on all sorts
of subjects. But this second part is of minor importance
and need not concern us here, though it was very popular
at the time, partly because of its high (not to say priggish)
moral tone.

Critical commentary

The importance of the moral and didactic purpose in *Pamela* must not however, be underestimated. It was an age in which volumes of sermons were eagerly read by large numbers of people, and one of the reasons for *Pamela*'s great popularity was undoubtedly the fact that it combined the attractions of devotional literature with those of fiction. It was no accident that a leading divine of the day openly commended the novel from the pulpit. It is important to bear in mind, too, that a strong moral purpose was to be characteristic of the English novel for many years to come.

The morality of *Pamela* seems somewhat dubious nowadays. There is a good deal of downright calculation in Pamela's fight for her virtue. Her chastity appears to be technical only, a commodity to be bargained for. From any truly moral point of view Squire B. shows himself, at any rate in the earlier part of the book, as a vicious, cruel and profligate bully: yet Pamela never considers whether he is really worth marrying, nor seriously questions his right to behave towards a woman in the way he does.

There are other unpleasant aspects of the novel. Richardson had a feminine streak in his own personality so pronounced that at times it led to a prurient inquisitiveness about women that came close to morbid identification. The sado-masochistic element in his nature, too, is very evident in the drawn-out, gloating descriptions of Pamela's fight for her virtue. There is in consequence a good deal of what D. H. Lawrence, nearly two hundred years later, described as a pornographic union of 'calico purity and underclothing excitements'. The poet and critic, Samuel Taylor Coleridge, reacted in a similar way:

> I confess that it has cost, and still costs, my philosophy
> some exertion not to be vexed that I must admire, aye
> greatly admire, Richardson. His mind is so very vile, a
> mind so oozy, so hypocritical, praise-mad, canting, envious,
> concupiscent.

The combination of stern moral rectitude and secret salaciousness in sexual matters was often symptomatic of the middle-class English Puritanism of the day – and indeed since. It frequently occurs in English novels of the nineteenth century, and one of the most striking features of Richardson's writing in this respect is the way it heralded the advent of attitudes we now label as 'Victorian'. In her steadfast refusal to admit the existence of any feelings of sexual attraction towards her pursuer until she is safely married, and in her exaggerated sensibility and delicacy, Pamela was the prototype of a new type of heroine who dominated the English novel for another hundred and fifty years at least.

In all these respects, as well as in the ways in which Richardson appealed to false romanticism, wishful thinking, and day dreaming, *Pamela* exhibits many of the worst features of the bestseller.

But there were other and more positive aspects to Pamela's fight for her virtue. It has been said that 'without the sex war the novel could not exist' and *Pamela* can be seen as a paradigm, within a particular social context, of the universal and, of course, fundamentally fruitful, conflict of the sexes. It was Richardson who first built this conflict into the centre of a novel. In addition, the sex war can frequently be regarded as part of another one – also considered essential to the health and vitality of the novel, and from which English fiction in particular has derived much of its strength – the class war.

There is never any doubt that however much Richardson may gloat over Pamela's predicament, he was fundamentally on her side; not only because he enjoyed acting as a champion of the 'fair sex', but also because, as a member himself of the new, rising middle class, he saw her (despite his political conservatism) as a typical victim of a still powerful and tyrannical aristocracy. As Walter Allen has said of Richardson:

Against an almost omnipotent authority, he pitted helplessness combined with virtue – and despite all hazards, helplessness combined with virtue triumphed, simply because it was virtue, and, what is more, forced authority to accept it on its own terms. It was this that the age applauded: Richardson was the spokesman of justice.

How good a spokesman can be seen in this extract from one of Pamela's letters:

> ... one may see how poor people are despised by the proud and the rich! yet we were all on a footing originally ... Surely these proud people never think what a short stage life is; and that, with all their vanity, a time is coming, when they must submit to being on a level with us. The philosopher said true, when he looked upon the skull of a king, and that of a poor man, that he saw no difference between them.

It was this aspect of *Pamela*, no doubt, that caused the villagers of Slough to ring the church bells for joy when they read that Pamela had triumphed in preserving her chastity and in imposing marriage upon Squire B.

The fact that Pamela grew out of a project addressed to 'handsome girls' in service, and that the heroine herself was a servant, was also of considerable importance from another point of view. An appreciable part of the new reading public in Richardson's day was in fact composed of the upper reaches of the servant class, in particular ladies' maids. Complaints from the more reactionary sections of the ruling class about the growing literacy of their higher servants were, indeed, frequent during the eighteenth century. Lady Mary Wortley Montagu, a notable letter writer herself, sarcastically observed that Pamela's success in holding on to her virginity in order to exact marriage from her would-be seducer had made her 'the joy of the chambermaids of all nations'.

Not that it was only the servant class, of course, to which *Pamela* appealed. The novel had a special relevance to eighteenth-century women in general. Their position was a very mixed one. On the one hand, the rise of economic individualism among the middle classes and the corresponding decline of the old patriarchial forms of social organization enhanced the status of married women, providing them with greater leisure and material comfort and, at the same time, placing the whole concept of romantic love firmly within the bounds of matrimony. On the other hand, the numerical predominance of women in the eighteenth century, and tne middle-class Puritan emphasis on the postponement of marriage until the man had attained economic success, made marriage increasingly difficult for women to achieve. In other words, Pamela's predicament was not merely one for morbid exploitation: a number of important social realities lay behind it.

It would be quite wrong, though, to regard *Pamela* as nothing more than an eighteenth-century social document, or, indeed, as a novel of merely antiquarian interest. It contains many elements of continuing and universal vitality. There is much in it for example, of the age-old Cinderella theme, and *Pamela*'s closeness to myth and fairy tale must not be overlooked. This aspect comes out with particular force in the scenes where Pamela is kept against her will, like a princess locked away in a castle, in Squire B.'s country house. The servants who guard her, too, are like the ogres of a fairy tale, and have the vivid reality of figures encountered in a nightmare. Take Pamela's description of Mrs Jewkes:

> She is a broad, squat, pursy, fat thing, quite ugly ... Her
> nose is fat and crooked, and her brows grow down over her
> eyes; a dead, spiteful, grey, goggling eye to be sure she has.

The technique of letter-writing which Richardson adopted in *Pamela* (and in his other novels) might seem at first awkward and restricting, though it was natural enough to his contemporaries. Stimulated by the spread of literacy and assisted by improved postal services, the cult of letter writing (especially among women) was one of the distinctive features of eighteenth-century literary history. But the method does have obvious disadvantages. In order to convey the plot, Richardson has to make Pamela write an unnaturally large number of letters, often of interminable length and larded with didactic and humourless passages. As an eighteenth-century servant girl – even a literate one – Pamela was hardly likely to have had the education to write such letters, while if she was as continually harassed and persecuted as she claims, she would hardly have had the leisure or opportunity to do so.

The technique was, however, an important advance as far as the novel was concerned. Inevitably it introduced the element of *control*, and therefore led to a tightening of plot. The very fact that Pamela had to be present practically all the time, busily describing what was happening to her, meant that the novel had what Henry James was to call a 'commanding centre', which provided a strong organizing principle mostly lacking in earlier works of fiction.

But the method had another merit. It enabled Richardson to achieve what he himself described as 'an immediate impression of every circumstance'. Even though this involved much wearisome detail, it is certain that, to quote Ian Watt, 'this very garrulity itself brings us very close to Pamela's inner consciousness ... the cult of familiar letter-writing provided Richardson with a microphone already attuned to the tones of private experience.'

What had happened with *Pamela*, in fact, was that a new dimension had entered the novel – the deliberate and detailed analysis of conduct, motive, action and reaction which was essential for further progress. The characters in *Pamela* have, in consequence, a new three-dimensional intensity. The long-windedness inherent both in the method Richardson had adopted and in his own personality was moreover, in many respects prophetic of the 'stream of consciousness' technique, as practised by such writers as James Joyce, Virginia Woolf and Marcel Proust, which was to come to full flowering in the twentieth-century novel.

For all these reasons, therefore, *Pamela* must hold pride of place for having achieved that crucial breakthrough which rightly confers upon its author the title of 'father of the English novel.'

The History of
the Adventures of Joseph Andrews and
his Friend Mr Abraham Adams

Henry Fielding

Henry Fielding was born at Sharpham Park in Somerset in 1707, the son of a General of aristocratic descent. He was educated at Eton, and then studied law at the ancient university of Leiden in Holland. Back in London, he became a prolific and successful playwright, mostly of farces and burlesques, often of a highly libellous nature in their political content, until the passing of the Licensing Act of 1737 imposed a crippling censorship and virtually closed the theatre to him as a career. He turned back to law and was called to the bar in 1740, later becoming a magistrate in Westminster and Middlesex, famous for his hard work, his humanity, and his advocacy of reforms designed to mitigate the savagery of eighteenth-century penal codes.

With the publication of *Joseph Andrews* in 1742 he began his parallel career as a novelist. At the same time he continued to do a good deal of miscellaneous writing, including political pamphlets and essays for the periodicals, as well as himself editing a periodical and a journal. He married in 1734 and his wife, whom he adored, served as the model for Sophia Western (the heroine of his most famous novel, *Tom Jones*) and for the heroine of his last novel, *Amelia* (1751). But she died ten years later, and in view of the themes of Richardson's *Pamela* and Fielding's own *Joseph Andrews* it is a piquant fact that in 1747 he married his late wife's maid, who had been acting as his housekeeper since her mistress's death.

In 1749 Fielding's health began to fail. He died in Lisbon, where he had gone with his family in the hope of recovering in a warmer climate, and he was buried there.

Samuel Richardson may be 'the father of the English novel', but many have considered Fielding the more important novelist. Perhaps the best way of looking at it is to see Richardson and Fielding as the two main pillars of the early English novel – at opposite ends of the building. They were, indeed, different in almost every respect. Richardson's *Pamela* seemed to Fielding so full of falsities, sentimentalities and hypocrisies that he wrote a skit of it entitled *An Apology for the Life of Mrs Shamela Andrews*. Whereas this was no more than a brilliant parody, *Joseph Andrews*, while continuing the attack on Richardson's novel, is a great work of fiction in its own right.

Summary

It is no accident, of course, that Richardson's Pamela and Fielding's Joseph share the same surname – they are sister and brother. For what Fielding did in his novel was to reverse the coin of Pamela's virtue by making Joseph, a handsome young footman, fight for *his* virtue against the assaults of *his* employer – who is none other than the aunt of Pamela's would-be seducer, Squire B.

This provided Fielding with a useful device for bringing out what he regarded as the priggish and calculating elements in Pamela's behaviour. The drollness and irony of the situation can be seen from this glimpse of one of Lady Booby's amorous advances on Joseph:

'Have you the assurance to pretend, that when a lady demeans herself to throw aside the rules of decency, in order to honour you with the highest favour in her power, your

virtue should resist her inclinations? That, when she has
conquered her own virtue, she should find an obstruction
in yours?' 'Madam', said Joseph, 'I can't see why her
having no virtue should be a reason against my having
any; or why, because I am a man, or because I am poor,
my virtue must be subservient to her pleasures.'

There is, however, another reason why Joseph resists the
blandishments of Lady Booby: in his home village he
has a sweetheart named Fanny to whom he has sworn
fidelity. Dismissed from Lady Booby's service, he sets out
on foot to join Fanny. On the road he is attacked by
robbers, stripped of all his clothing and possessions, and
left half-dead by the roadside. He is discovered by a passing stage-coach and carried to an inn. There, he meets his
old friend and mentor Abraham Adams, once curate in
the household of Lady Booby's former husband, and now
on his way to London to publish a volume of his sermons.
Adams generously provides for Joseph at the inn and,
finding that he is now short of cash and has absent-
mindedly left his sermons at home, he accompanies
Joseph on his journey. They meet with all kinds of adventures and encounter all kinds of odd characters on the
road – and Parson Adams gets into a number of hilarious
scrapes. At last they arrive, Joseph is reunited with Fanny,
and Adams makes arrangements for their marriage. But
Lady Booby has returned to her country seat in the same
village, and sets out to avenge herself on Joseph. She
manages to get him and Fanny arrested on a charge of
stealing a hazel twig, which Joseph had cut while out
walking in the fields with Fanny. They are on the point
of being sent to prison when Squire Booby arrives on the
scene – with his newly-wed wife, Pamela. The Squire
rescues his brother-in-law and Fanny from their predicament. It turns out that Joseph is really the son of gentle-
folk. The story ends with Joseph happily married to
Fanny, and living on a property given him by his new-
found parents, while Parson Adams is appointed to a

comfortable living by Squire Booby – and Lady Booby
returns to London where she finds solace in the arms of a
young captain of dragoons.

Critical commentary

It will be obvious that there could be no greater contrast
than that between the kind of novel written by Richardson and the kind written by Fielding. To some extent
this was a reflection of two utterly opposed temperaments
and ways of looking at life. It was also a cultural and
educational difference. Both Defoe and Richardson, in
common with other middle-class writers, were strongly
opposed to what they saw as the tyranny of the 'Rules',
deriving from the study of the ancient writers, which
dominated taste and criticism in the eighteenth century –
a period commonly known, indeed, either as the Augustan
(after the Roman Emperor Augustus, in whose reign
Virgil, Horace, Ovid, Tibullus and other famous Latin
authors flourished), or the Classical Age.

Fielding's classical education can be seen in the Preface
which he wrote to *Joseph Andrews*, in which he expounded a theory of comedy closely modelled on classical
precedents. Undoubtedly his main purpose in this was to
raise the status of the novel, which had fallen into low
repute among the aristocratic *literati*, but in some ways
it affected his own work adversely. Instead of the completely free flow of Defoe's or Richardson's narrative he
felt obliged to introduce into *Joseph Andrews* and his
other novels many similarities to the ancient classical
authors: for example in structure (the division into
Books), narrative method, arrangement of the incidents,
and in style (the use of mock Homeric similes). One of
the most important results was that Fielding's attitude
towards characterization was quite different from that of
either Defoe or Richardson. As he put it himself in *Tom
Jones*: '... I describe, not men, but manners; not an
individual, but a species.' Fielding was not practising

analysis of character as Richardson had done: indeed he was deliberately setting himself against it, believing that in Richardson's *Pamela*, analysis had been tantamount to over-indulgence, distortion and falsity. Consequently, as Ian Watt points out, 'Plot has priority, and it is therefore plot which must contain the elements of complication and development.' In approaching his task in this way Fielding was also drawing upon earlier works, themselves strongly influenced by the classical writers. Among these were the mediaeval satires on human folly and the morality plays (whose characters bore allegorical names like Pride or Avarice); the works of the sixteenth-century French humanist and satirist François Rabelais; the seventeenth-century French dramatist Molière and the seventeenth-century English playwright Ben Jonson. Fielding was also influenced by two earlier famous European novels: *Don Quixote*, by the great Spanish writer Cervantes, which was published in 1605, and the long picaresque romance, *Gil Blas*, by the Frenchman Le Sage, which was published between 1715 and 1735.

But the quality of Fielding's genius transcended all these self-imposed limitations. It possessed a breadth, a gaiety, a kind of insouciance that made it impossible for him to be hidebound by any theory. This is the quality which Byron had in mind when he declared that in Fielding: 'You see the man of education, the gentleman, and the scholar sporting with his subject – its master, not its slave.' The consequence is that *Joseph Andrews* is both less hampered by its classical machinery and less disorganized than it appears at first sight. In spite of his 'sporting' with theories and his classical analogies, Fielding keeps a firm grip of his main themes and always succeeds in somehow gathering up the loose ends. An important effect of Fielding's relaxed approach is that *Joseph Andrews*, in common with his other novels, has a well-ventilated, spacious quality – quite apart from the fact that a good deal of the action takes place in the open air.

To some critics, his demonstration of types as opposed

to the exploration and analysis of individuals, appears inimical to the spirit of the novel. His contemporary, the redoutable Dr Samuel Johnson declared:

> ... there is all the difference in the world between characters of nature and characters of manners; and *there* is the difference between the characters of Fielding and those of Richardson. Characters of manners are very entertaining; but they are to be understood by a more superficial observer than characters of nature, where a man must dive into the recesses of the human heart.

But flat characters can be as effective as round ones, provided they are infused with a broad and humane experience of life. It is impossible to read *Joseph Andrews* without feeling that the characters live vividly and abundantly. They are the reverse of mere caricatures. They may not develop much beyond the set of characteristics with which their creator endows them, but as Walter Allen has said: 'We feel that Fielding knows everything there is to be known about his characters even though he does not tell us all. They are so real to him ... that they become real for us.'

Joseph Andrews, in consequence, makes some significant contributions to the portrait gallery of great English comic characters. Besides Lady Booby and her hideous and amorous maid Mrs Slipslop, there are Mrs Towwouse, the sharp-tongued and skinflint landlady of the inn to which Joseph is taken after he has been robbed and wounded by Parson Trulliber, and many others. But above all, there is the eccentric, absent-minded but lovable Abraham Adams, a creation who in the view of Sir Walter Scott was in himself 'sufficient to stamp the superiority of Fielding over all writers of his class.'

Parson Adams is in many respects the real hero of Fielding's novel. Much of the comedy derives from the scrapes into which, in his innocence and gullibility, he is always blundering. But he is much more than a mere figure of fun. It was in creating him that Fielding was most influenced by Don Quixote, the hero of Cervantes' famous novel. Indeed, the title-page of the original edition of *Joseph Andrews* contained the words:

Written in Imitation of the Manner of Cervantes, Author of *Don Quixote*.

Cervantes' underlying purpose had been to show the contrast between the ideals to which Don Quixote selflessly devotes himself and the sordid and materialistic standards of the age in which he lived. In much the same way Fielding, through Parson Adams, sets out to demonstrate the vast difference between the ideals of Christianity and its practice in the England of his day.

This was also one of the main points in his criticism of Richardson's *Pamela*. It seemed to Fielding that Pamela's calculating defence of her virginity and the pious platitudes that accompanied it provided a typical example of routine adherence to the letter of Christianity, with little reference to its spirit. In contrast, Parson Adams is frequently seen by most of the other characters as a figure of fun *because* he naïvely adopts a truly Christian stance, as opposed to a merely formal, Pharisaical one. Time after time, Fielding uses Adams' simple Christian charity in order to satirize the essential coldness and hollowness of those who live by materialistic standards while paying lip-service to those of Christianity. A good example occurs when, encountering a bookseller in the inn, Parson Adams tries to get him interested in his volume of sermons by explaining that in his view strict adherence to the tenets of any particular dogma is not as important as true goodness. He declares that in his opinion '... a virtuous and good Turk, or heathen, are more acceptable in the sight of their Creator than a vicious and wicked Christian, though his faith was as perfectly orthodox as St Paul's himself.' Parson Adams just can't understand it when the bookseller hastily responds: 'I wish you success ... but must beg to be excused, as my hands are so very full at present; and, indeed, I am afraid you will find a backwardness in the trade to engage in a book which the clergy would be certain to cry down.'

Fielding makes it clear that there is always a serious purpose behind his comedy. In his Preface to *Joseph Andrews* he describes himself as the literary equivalent of 'the comic-history painter'. He was thinking specifically of his friend Hogarth, the *genre* painter of scenes of degradation, crime and debauchery, in both high and low society. As a magistrate, Fielding knew as much about the seamy side of contemporary life as Hogarth. No novelist had been closer to the social realities of his time, as Sir Leslie Stephen stressed:

> He has drawn the men and women of his land so faithfully that we learn more from him of the true character of his contemporaries than we learn even from a direct observation of the men themselves ... It is not merely that his portraits are faithful, but that his estimate of the actual forces at work impresses us as absolutely trustworthy ... he sees the real facts and the important facts.

Fielding was, in consequence, as much a moralist as Richardson, but one who worked within a wider social context and who was concerned with the health of society as a whole. Beneath the boisterous comedy of *Joseph Andrews* there is a constant preoccupation with charity and justice. Sometimes it takes the form of a sly, ironic dig – as when Squire Booby expostulates with the magistrate before whom Joseph and Fanny have been brought for stealing the hazel twig:

> 'Jesu!' said the squire, 'would you commit two persons to Bridewell for a twig?' 'Yes,' said the lawyer, 'and with great lenity too; for if we had called it a young tree, they would have both been hanged.'

At other times a whole scene is informed with the same ironic, and fundamentally Christian, comment. When the stage-coach finds Joseph lying badly wounded in the ditch, one of the so-called virtuous ladies exclaims: 'O

J-sus ... a naked man! Dear coachman, drive on and leave him.' Eventually she and the other occupants of the coach are persuaded that they ought to take Joseph, not out of compassion, but because a young lawyer argues that they might get into trouble if they left him. When Joseph himself refuses to get into the coach unless someone will lend him a greatcoat to cover his nakedness another heated argument takes place:

> Though there were several greatcoats about the coach, it was not easy to get over this difficulty ... The two gentlemen complained that they were cold and could not spare a rag ... and the coachman, who had two greatcoats spread under him, refused to lend either, lest they should be made bloody; the lady's footman desired to be excused for the same reason ... and it is more than probable poor Joseph who obstinately adhered to his modest resolution, must have perished, unless the postilion (a lad who hath been since transported for robbing a hen-roost) had voluntarily stript off his greatcoat, his only garment, at the same time swearing a great oath (for which he was rebuked by the passengers), 'that he would rather ride in his shirt all his life than suffer a fellow-creature to lie in so miserable a condition.'

This episode might be described as Fielding's version of the parable of the Good Samaritan. It is significant, that the only one in the stage-coach who emerges as truly virtuous in any real Christian or humane sense, is the postilion who was later to be designated, by the savage penal code of the day, as a criminal. It is as if Fielding is asking: 'What *is* virtue?' and attempting to show that it is a far less simple matter than Pamela's cut-and-dried, black-and-white precepts would suggest, and that what is needed is a broader and more humane view of morality.

At the same time, to set Fielding's *Joseph Andrews* and Richardson's *Pamela* in opposition in this way is not to deny the greatness of the latter. Between them, Fielding and Richardson had founded the two main traditions of the English novel. Richardson can be seen as the ancestor of moral and psychological novelists like George Eliot, Henry James and James Joyce; and Fielding as the ancestor of those like Thackeray and Dickens. Without either of them it is difficult to see how the new *genre* would have established itself. As Lionel Stevenson has said:

> Richardson and Fielding jointly achieved an immense enlargement of the readership of fiction. The moral middle class was finally convinced by *Pamela* that fiction was not a waste of time and a temptation to sin; the intelligentsia was convinced by *Joseph Andrews* that it was not a tissue of silly make-believe. Many people, of course, were able to enjoy reading both books and thereby to realise how wide a range of effects could be included in the genre.

Clarissa,
or The History of a Young Lady

Samuel Richardson

Richardson's second novel, *Clarissa, or the History of a Young Lady*, was published in seven volumes, the first two in 1747, the remaining five in the following year. In a superficial sense *Clarissa Harlowe* (as it is generally known), can be seen as a kind of pendant to *Pamela*. Richardson had not been altogether happy about his first novel. He was worried in case it should appear to have encouraged the idea that 'a reformed rake makes the best husband.' He was also upset by criticisms that the speech and behaviour of its heroine were vulgar.

In addition, in *Pamela* he had shown a virtuous girl successfully defending her chastity, and now he wanted to explore the possibilities of the opposite situation – an equally virtuous girl who loses the battle. At the same time he felt he had by no means said all he wanted to say by way of moral and religious exhortation on the relationship between the sexes. To some extent, therefore, *Clarissa Harlowe* is a series of extensions and corrections to *Pamela*.

Summary

Richardson counteracts the charge of vulgarity by placing his new heroine in a very different class. Clarissa is the beautiful and talented daughter of the wealthy Harlowes.

She is also 'of great Delicacy, mistress of all the Accomplishments, natural and acquired, that adorn the sex.'

She is wooed by the charming but profligate aristocrat, Robert Lovelace, who is genuinely attracted to her but has a grudge against women. Clarissa's family are determined to marry her to the elderly, ugly, mean-spirited – but extremely wealthy – Mr Solmes. When she refuses, her parents and her brother and sister are furious.

Her brother, losing a duel with Lovelace, insults him. Clarissa secretly corresponds with Lovelace, hoping to prevent him from taking the bloody revenge on her family which he has threatened. They suspect that she is really in love with Lovelace, but she promises to have nothing more to do with him or with any other man, provided she is spared the unspeakable Mr Solmes. But by now a very favourable marriage settlement has been drawn up, and Clarissa is confined to her room and subjected to every imaginable pressure. Lovelace continues to threaten vengeance, while presenting himself as her only means of salvation by offering unconditional sanctuary among the ladies of his own family.

When Clarissa is about to be physically forced to marry Solmes, she despairingly accepts Lovelace's offer of rescue, only to revoke her acceptance shortly after. But by various stratagems he manages to abduct her, and then she is in his powers. She expects immediate marriage, but Lovelace is vengefully determined to humiliate her by first making her his mistress, partly because of the demoniacal elements in his own nature and also because of his pride in his reputation as a rake. Continually promising and postponing marriage, he sets out by every means in his power to seduce her, and eventually takes her to London, to an apparently respectable lodging-house which is in reality a brothel. After further complications and attempts at more or less subtle seduction in the course of which Clarissa's complex feelings, veering between love and revulsion, are analysed in great detail, Lovelace adopts other methods. He arranges a mock fire which brings

Clarissa out of her bedroom in her nightdress. But she successfully repulses him, horrified now by his treachery. Lovelace professes repentance and offers marriage at last, but in terms which cause Clarissa indignantly to refuse him. When all else fails, he manages to first drug, then rape her.

Now, having vindicated his reputation as a rake, he is genuinely anxious to marry her. After an illness, however, Clarissa manages to escape from him and refuses to have anything more to do with him in spite of his appeals for forgiveness.

The final 'movement' of the book deals with Clarissa's vindication and ultimate sanctification. The truth begins to leak out, though not to her family who have condemned her out of hand. Her friend and correspondent, Anna Howe, and her cousin, Colonel Morden (her sole champion among her relations) are both prevented from reaching her. Clarissa remains in lodgings, befriended only by strangers, gradually wasting away from grief and shame, deaf to the by now frantic entreaties of Lovelace. Permanently disgraced by the harsh moral code of the day, she feels her only course is to turn her thoughts to the next world, and to vindicate her fundamental virtue by making her death a shining example to others. Her preparations for her own death and the actual dying itself, before an audience of new-found admirers, are dealt with in exhaustive detail. Her family learn the full truth about Lovelace's conduct in time to make public their grief and remorse at her funeral. Morden kills Lovelace in a duel, and all the other evil-doers in the book also meet their just deserts. However, Clarissa lives on in the memory of friends and relations as a saint and martyr.

Critical commentary

In this story, Richardson used the same epistolary form that he employed in *Pamela*, and it resulted in similar drawbacks. It encouraged Richardson's natural tendency to prolixity – no less than five hundred and forty-seven letters are exchanged in *Clarissa Harlowe* in order to narrate the events of eleven months. At over one million words it is easily the longest novel in the English language. His technique in *Clarissa Harlowe* nevertheless shows considerable improvements on that in *Pamela*. In the earlier novel, almost the whole correspondence is between Pamela and her parents, making Pamela's letters the major narrative vehicle. Accordingly, Richardson himself had to intervene as narrator to explain certain circumstances. In *Clarissa Harlowe*, however, there are two separate sets of correspondents. There was, of course, a danger of repetition and overlapping, but for the most part Richardson avoids this, either because the protagonists react to the same event in contrasting ways, or because he intervenes himself (solely as editor) to explain that some letters have been suppressed or shortened. Additional contrasts of tone and point of view are provided by the occasional introduction of new correspondents such as Clarissa's pompous uncle Anthony, Lovelace's semi-literate servant Joseph Leman, and the pedantic Reverend Mr Brand.

The massive correspondence is organized into several major blocks. The first two volumes, for example, concentrate on the letters between Clarissa and her friend Anna Howe. It is only when their characters and backgrounds (especially Clarissa's) have been fully established, and Clarissa is already in Lovelace's power, that the correspondence begins between Lovelace and his friend and fellow-rake Belford (who is, however, so affected by Clarissa's sufferings and virtue that he reforms). Thereafter, the various blocks are most effectively balanced against one another. A long section is devoted to the preparations for the rape, but the rape itself is reported quite briefly by Lovelace; and then there are another one hundred and fifty pages – during which the reader is kept in suspense – before Clarissa's side of the story is presented. When it becomes clear that Clarissa is going to die, the two-tier correspondence is broken into by a series of letters directly relating to her situation. Lovelace fades into the background and eventually his death is reported by a servant.

Obviously the construction of *Clarissa Harlowe* invites comparison with that of a play. Richardson claimed (perhaps with the criticisms of Fielding and others in mind) that he had conscientiously followed the principles of dramatic construction laid down by Aristotle. At times it seems that the term melodrama is more appropriate, and there is also a good deal of the same kind of prurience present in *Pamela*. V. S. Pritchett has said that Richardson was 'mad about sex', and *Clarissa Harlowe* has been described as being constructed on the principle of procrastinated rape. There is undeniably a strong sadistic element in what Walter Allen has described as 'the loving, lingering, horrified, gloating descriptions of Clarissa's long-drawn-out sexual humiliation.' Almost as morbid, too, is the detailed dwelling on Clarissa's preparations for death.

Yet none of this can detract from the undoubted power of *Clarissa Harlowe*. When he wrote it, Richardson was fully aware of the one outstanding advantage that the epistolary technique provided – that of immediacy. As he pointed out in his Preface:

All the letters are written while the hearts of the writers must be supposed to be wholly engaged in their subjects ... so that they abound not only with critical situations, but with what may be called *instantaneous* descriptions and reflections.

With few novels, indeed, does the reader feel himself so thoroughly caught up in the story. The French writer and philosopher Diderot expressed this sense of personal involvement when he described how, as he read Lovelace's soft words and specious promises when he was trying to seduce Clarissa, he found himself crying out: 'Don't believe him! He's deceiving you! If you go you'll be ruined!' It was this same sense of involvement that caused such an uproar when it eventually became clear that Richardson meant his heroine to choose death as the expiation of dishonour. Even the cool Fielding (who had enthusiastically reviewed the first two volumes) wrote to Richardson begging him to spare Clarissa's life.

Such an effect can only be produced by a writer of genius, and Richardson's command of language and dialogue in *Clarissa Harlowe* is of that order. Moreover, he can modulate his style to achieve widely contrasting effects. The scene in which Clarissa, confined to her room because she will not marry Solmes, is mocked and tormented by her unpleasant sister, is vastly different – with its air of refined feminine cruelty – from the scene of almost Zola-like realism and horror in which the hideous old bawd lies dying in her brothel surrounded by her equally revolting prostitutes.

Another variation is provided by the 'strokes of gaiety, fancy, and humour, such as will entertain and divert, and at the same time both warn and instruct,' which Richardson promised in his Preface as a relief to the pathos of the story. These really do result in some notable scenes of comedy – especially in connection with the ridiculous pedant, Mr Brand, who to some extent anticipated the Mr Collins of Jane Austen's *Pride and Prejudice*. This comic element in Richardson is often overlooked. The increased imaginative power in the set scenes is matched by a similar advance in the handling of the characters. As far as Clarissa herself is concerned, it is obviously not easy to make anyone humanly convincing who is meant to exemplify the highest moral perfection, but Richardson succeeds triumphantly. For one thing, he does not allow Clarissa to be a mere emblem on some religious text or medallion. At first, perhaps, she is too good to be true, but even then the details of her appearance, dress, opinions and manners are so numerous, and the background of family and home so solidly rendered, that she has a flesh-and-blood reality. Furthermore, we watch her change and develop under the stress of suffering. She grows into an awareness, for example, of her own hidden motives and evasions: thus at one point she taunts herself: 'So desirous to be considered an *example*! A vanity which my partial (i.e. 'partisan') admirers put in my head! And so secure in my own virtue ...'

Dr Samuel Johnson had every justification when he declared that *Clarissa Harlowe* was 'the first book in the world for the knowledge it displays of the human heart.'

Although to some critics Lovelace is a rather wooden figure, derived too directly from the 'gay seducer' of contemporary drama, to most readers he, too, comes over as a powerful and disturbing creation. He has a duality in his nature almost as horrifying as that of Robert Louis Stevenson's Dr Jekyll and Mr Hyde. On the one hand, he is (as his letters reveal) a man of considerable intellect, learning and wit, with a wild gaiety and charm. On the other, he is a cruel and rapacious profligate (though in that he is no worse than many of the real-life aristocratic rakes of the time) whose twisted code of honour is such that he has 'never lied to a man, and hardly ever said the truth to a woman.' He is also an embodiment of a universal type, the male who is so obsessed by his sexual pride that he is driven, inexorably and against his better nature (which does exist, Richardson makes clear) to humiliate women. Thus, in one of his letters to his friend Belford he declares:

> Caesar was not a prouder man than Lovelace ... I love, when I dig a pit, to have my prey tumble in with secure feet and open eyes; then a man can look down upon her, with an 'O-ho, charmer, how came you there?'

In creating Lovelace, it seems that Richardson tapped hidden springs in his own subconscious nature. He himself was surprised at the way in which his character developed, confessing to a friend, as he was writing his novel, 'my libertine in the next volume proves to be so vile that I regretted the necessity, as I may call it, which urged me to put the two former volumes to press.'

The 'necessity' *was* there, however. The truth is that his theme had got him by the throat, so that the creator took precedence over the moralist and the preacher. It was for this reason that he refused a contrived happy ending.

One other very important point must be made about *Clarissa Harlowe*. What Richardson does is to present a clash of irreconcilable opposites. It is impossible for Lovelace, hag-ridden as he is by his particular compulsions and obsessions, to change in his approach to Clarissa. It is equally impossible for her to go against the inner law of her being. Now this is the kind of clash out of which genuine tragedy is made, and most critics are agreed that the novel comes within this exalted category. Thus Richardson is not only the progenitor of the English novel, not only the first to introduce into it the tragic dimension.

The Adventures of Roderick Random

Tobias Smollett

Tobias George Smollett was born in Dunbartonshire in
1721, the grandson of a Scottish laird. His father died
when he was only two. He studied at Glasgow University
and was then apprenticed to a surgeon in that city. But
when he was eighteen he set out for London with a tragedy
he had written called *The Regicide*, of which he had
inordinate hopes and which was destined to become his
albatross. His repeated failures to get it staged embittered
him against the London literary establishment, and this
was a grievance from which he never recovered. He would
have starved had he not secured a position as surgeon's
mate in a British man-o'-war. He served in the disastrous
expedition against Cartagena in the Caribbean in 1741,
and had ample opportunity of experiencing at first hand
the horrifying conditions in the British navy of the day,
especially for the sick and wounded. He left the navy,
but remained for some time in Jamaica, where he married. In 1744 he returned to London, set up in medical
practice – and returned to the charge with his play, only
to meet with more disappointments. This further exacer-
bated his belligerency of temper, which found vent in
ferocious verse satires on contemporary literature and
politics. At the age of twenty-six he set to work to embody
his experiences and grievances in a novel, *The Adventures
of Roderick Random*, which was published anonymously

in 1748, the following year. It was translated into French as the work of Henry Fielding, but Smollett went to Paris in order to correct the misapprehension – and while there published his rejected play as 'by the author of *Roderick Random*'. Although he continued to practise medicine for some time (obtaining his degree of MD in 1750), he went on to achieve greater success with his second novel, *The Adventures of Peregrine Pickle* (published in 1751) and eventually became a full-time writer, pouring out a stream of histories, travel books, satires, essays and further works of fiction. In 1753 he settled in London and, among other activities, became editor of the new *Critical Review*. He travelled abroad for his health, and wrote an amusing but bad-tempered account of his journeys. He finally left England in 1769 and died two years later at Montenero near Leghorn.

Summary

Roderick Random is his most characteristic novel, and it is closely modelled on his own early experiences. The eponymous hero is a Scot of gentle birth, whose father had been disowned by his family because he had made a marriage of which they disapproved, and whose mother had died as a result of her poverty and privations. While Roderick is still an infant, his father, unhinged by his grief over his wife's death, disappears. Neglected and ill-treated by his grandfather, Roderick (with the help of his maternal uncle, a bluff naval officer named Tom Bowling) manages to obtain an education and to get himself qualified as a doctor. After losing touch with his uncle, who has been forced out of the navy following a quarrel with his captain, Roderick sets out for London accompanied by his old school-fellow, Strap. In London, Roderick meets with a series of adventures and misadventures in the course of which he is cheated by a succession of rogues. He tries to enter the navy as a surgeon's mate, but fails because he hasn't enough money to bribe the Admiralty clerks. He becomes assistant to a French apothecary until he falls into the hands of a press gang – and so joins the navy after all. He manages to establish his medical credentials and becomes a surgeon's mate. Like his creator, he is present at the siege of Cartagena. Other adventures follow thick and fast. He is shipwrecked, robbed, and left naked on the shore, but obtains employment as footman to an eccentric poetess with whose beautiful niece, Narcissa, he falls in love. Other misfortunes follow, however, and he is forced to run away because of the enmity of a more prosperous suitor for Narcissa's hand. He returns to England, is kidnapped by smugglers and taken to France, where he meets Tom Bowling again. He joins the French army and fights at the battle of Dettingen. Soon afterwards, his old friend Strap, now transformed into Monsieur d'Estrapes, helps to restore his fortunes. Further adventures follow, then the two of them return to London, where Roderick tries, unsuccessfully, to marry an heiress. At the fashionable spa of Bath he meets Narcissa again, but falls foul of her brother and has to return to London, where (having lost all his money gaming) he is thrown into prison for debt. He is rescued by the reappearance of his uncle Tom Bowling, and embarks as surgeon on a ship commanded by him. The voyage takes them to South America, where they meet a wealthy trader, Don Roderigo, who turns out to be Roderick's long-lost father. Together they return to Scotland where Roderick's father buys the family estates and helps his son to marry Narcissa, while the faithful Strap marries her maid.

Critical commentary

Now what, if anything did this novel contribute to the new genre? It will already be obvious that it is reminiscent of Defoe in its disjointed series of adventures among sailors, soldiers and various metropolitan scoundrels, and in its autobiographical form – though of course in Defoe's case the adventures related in the first person with such plausibility were mostly imaginary, while many of those in Smollett's novel were based on his own experiences. It is evident, too, that it is a 'large, diffused picture' (to quote Smollett's prescription for writing novels, given in the Preface of one of his later fictional works), a sprawling, rambling tale – with all kinds of ingredients, including even the story of Smollett's ill-fated play, told by one of the minor characters. In other words, *Roderick Random* belongs firmly to the old picaresque tradition. No novelist of the period, in fact, was more outspoken in acknowledging his indebtedness to the two classic examples of the picaresque mode, the *Don Quixote* of Cervantes and the *Gil Blas* of Le Sage. Smollett lauds both of them in his Preface to *Roderick Random* and Le Sage's hero in particular – an impoverished Spanish soldier's son, educated by his uncle and launched on a series of comic travels – influenced the hero of Smollett's novel.

This basic – and it might be said already archaic – pattern is present in all Smollett's novels. *Peregrine Pickle*, for example, relates the wandering adventures of a swashbuckling scoundrel who has little to his credit apart from wit and courage, and who meets with all sorts of adventures in England and on the Continent. His last novel, too, *The Expedition of Humphrey Clinker* (published in 1771), although it employs the epistolary technique and is also notably more genial in temper, is also fundamentally a picaresque novel. In addition, Smollett emphasized his discipleship to Cervantes and Le Sage by translating their novels, while another of his own, *The Adventures of Sir Lancelot Greaves*, written in prison and published in 1755, was an attempt to transpose Don Quixote to English soil.

There is no advance in structure or coherence of plot in *Roderick Random*, and Roderick himself must be approached – to quote Arthur Humphreys – 'In terms of the ... *picaro*, the rogue whose loosely-strung adventures do not call for characterization save as character prompts his escapades.' It is incident, in fact, that takes precedence over character, and Smollett does not dwell upon the reactions and emotions of his characters (as both Richardson and Fielding do) save for the limited and temporary purpose of making the action of the moment more immediate.

The action itself, on the other hand, is fast and furious and conveyed in terse, muscular prose. Here, for example, is part of the scene in which Roderick is tied to the deck during the naval battle:

> ... I concealed my agitation as well as I could, till the head of the officer of the marines, who stood near me, being shot off, bounced from the deck athwart my face, leaving me well nigh blinded with brains. I could contain myself no longer, but began to bellow with all the strength of my my lungs: when a drummer coming towards me, asked if I was wounded? and before I could answer, received a great shot in his belly, which tore out his entrails, and he fell flat on my breast. This accident entirely bereft me of all discretion: I redoubled my cries which were drowned in the noise of the battle ...

It is evident that Smollett is a born story-teller. His plotting may be slapdash, but the action is full of invention, and he can create splendid panoramic effects.

Another positive point emerges from the passage. Smollett was also breaking entirely new ground in his vivid and vigorous pictures of naval life. It is doubtful whether he has ever been excelled in this respect: and his fellow-countryman (and admirer) Sir Walter Scott declared that everyone who had written about the navy since seemed to have copied more from Smollett than from actuality. Smollett, in fact, was the progenitor of what may be regarded as a sub-species of the genre – the novel of naval life – which has had a vigorous line of descent down to our own times.

But the passage also establishes Smollett as the master of a new kind of ferocious realism accompanied by a grim humour and a sharp personal tang. It is a brand of realism which some readers have found difficult to stomach, depending as it does on brutal directness of language and incident, and concentrating on the most sordid and violent aspects of eighteenth-century life, especially conditions among the sick and wounded aboard ship. There are descriptions of Roderick's visits as surgeon's mate to the sick quarters below decks crammed with hammocks and all kinds of unmentionable filth, that do indeed turn one's stomach.

There is no doubt that like his contemporary Jonathan Swift, Smollett was morbidly obsessed by filth and decay. As with Swift, this was the result of susceptibilities that had been shocked by contact with actual horrors. At the same time, Smollett insists in his Preface to *Roderick Random* that his purpose was fundamentally a moral one: to show 'the contrast between dejected virtue and insulting vice', and to inspire 'that generous indignation which ought to animate the reader, against the sordid and vicious disposition of this world.'

The truth of the matter is that Smollett, more perhaps than any other contemporary novelist, ripped away the elegant façades of eighteenth-century life in order to expose the dirt, squalor and brutality beneath, and in this respect his work marks an extension of realism, pointing forwards in many respects to the later nineteenth-century English 'naturalists' such as George Moore in *Esther Waters* and Somerset Maugham in *Liza of Lambeth*.

Admittedly Smollett's realism is concerned only with exterior appearances: as David Daiches has said: 'The art is a surface one; there is no subtlety or complexity either of moral and psychological patterning or of structure.' The characters, in consequence, are flat and two-dimensional, either savage caricatures of living originals who had incurred Smollett's wrath, or exaggerated embodiments of character traits in the old 'humours' tradition, as exemplified in the plays of Ben Jonson, and stretching back to the personified 'vices' of the morality plays. Arthur Humphreys has applied to them such epithets as 'boneheaded automata' and 'inhuman puppets'. But if they are puppets, they dance with great gusto and vitality, and if they are caricatures, then they are like those of Rowlandson and Gillray, with a savagely satirical life of their own. Many of them have, too, the kind of ferocious joviality that we find in Dickens' characters such as Quilp in *The Old Curiosity Shop* – and it is not surprising perhaps that Smollett was one of Dickens' favourite authors.

For this reason alone, Smollett was an important link in the history of the English novel, and although he may have worked at a lower level of achievement than Defoe, Richardson or Fielding, he deserves to be counted among its founding fathers.

The History of Tom Jones, a Foundling

Henry Fielding

Henry Fielding's first novel, *Joseph Andrews*, did not receive anything like the acclaim accorded to Richardson's *Pamela*, the novel it had set out to satirize. However, *The History of Tom Jones, a Foundling* which appeared in 1749, quickly became so popular that 'Tom Jones' became a popular synonym for 'boyfriend', while the young gentlemen of the day took to calling their favourite dogs – or even their sweethearts – Sophia, after the novel's heroine. One of the reasons for its success was that whereas *Joseph Andrews* had been rambling and discursive, *Tom Jones*, in spite of the fact that it is three times as long, is remarkable for the ingenuity and coherence of its plot.

Summary

As an infant, the hero is mysteriously discovered in the bed of the wealthy and benevolent Mr Allworthy, who lives in a fine country house in Somerset with his unmarried sister Bridget. It is assumed that the baby's mother must be Jenny Jones, who had nursed Bridget through an illness. She is servant to Benjamin Partridge, the local schoolmaster, who is assumed to be the father. Both Jenny and Partridge separately leave the neighbourhood. Mr Allworthy takes a fancy to the infant and keeps him, giving him the name of Tom Jones.

Bridget Allworthy shortly marries the fortune-hunting Captain Blifil. She has a son by him, but the father dies a few years later. Young Blifil and Tom are brought up together, but not in amity: for whereas Tom is good-natured, easy-going and high-spirited, Blifil is cunning, hypocritical and mean, always on the look-out for opportunities of getting Tom into trouble. He ingratiates himself with their tutors – Square, the philosopher, and Thwackum, the parson – whereas Tom endures many beatings at their hands. However, later on Tom discomfits Square by finding him in bed with Molly Seagrim, the gamekeeper's daughter.

Tom now meets Sophia, daughter of Squire Western, the hard-drinking, hard-riding and hard-swearing owner of a neighbouring estate. Squire Western takes a liking to Tom because of his manliness. One day, while out hunting, Tom breaks an arm catching Sophia's runaway horse. He stays in the Westerns' house while recovering, and he and Sophia fall in love.

When Mr Allworthy falls seriously ill, Tom rushes back to his bedside where he finds Blifil in obsequious attendance. However his benefactor makes a miraculous recovery and Tom is so overjoyed that he gets drunk.

Blifil also has his eye on Sophia (and her father's estates) and she, playing for time, pretends to be interested in him. When her aunt arrives from London, she misunderstands Sophia's feelings and tells her brother to be prepared for a marriage between his daughter and Blifil. Squire Western is delighted at the chance of thus uniting the two properties.

So Blifil, plotting to remove Tom from the scene, makes Mr Allworthy believe that Tom's drunkenness when he was ill was the result of heartlessness, and that all he had been interested in was the reading of the will. This, combined with Tom's harum-scarum record and the news that he has fallen in love with Sophia, turns Mr Allworthy against him. He banishes Tom from his house, with a gift of five-hundred pounds, which in his grief Tom loses.

Sophia is also in disgrace for refusing to marry Blifil

and is locked in her room. She escapes and sets out for her aunt's house in London.

Tom, also on the road, quarrels at an inn with an ensign who has insulted Sophia's name and is laid out by a blow from a heavy tankard. His injury is treated by the local barber, who turns out to be Partridge, the one-time schoolmaster and employer of Jenny Jones. Partridge throws in his lot with Tom and becomes his companion on all his subsequent adventures.

Tom later rescues a lady named Mrs Waters from the assault of the ensign, and escorts her to an inn at Upton where she lures him to bed.

Unknown to Tom, Sophia arrives at the same inn with her maid. During the night an insanely jealous husband, Mr Fitzpatrick, arrives at the inn and bursts in on Tom and Mrs Waters, thinking that the latter might be his wife. In the course of the uproar that follows, Sophia learns of Tom's infidelity. She departs in a fury and falls in with Mrs Fitzpatrick who has fled from the inn in order to escape from her husband. Together they travel to London, where Sophia is introduced to various grand people, including the sophisticated and wanton Lady Bellaston, who takes the naïve young country girl under her wing.

Tom and Partridge also arrive in London and Tom, believing that Sophia will never forgive him, allows himself to be seduced and kept by Lady Bellaston, unaware that Sophia is living in her house. Eventually, though, he meets Sophia, assures her of his undying devotion, and promises to reform. The two lovers are reconciled.

When Squire Western arrives in London, Tom is in despair, knowing that he will never agree to his marrying Sophia. To add to his misery, Mr Allworthy also arrives with Blifil, determined to aid Squire Western in clinching the match between Blifil and Sophia.

Tom goes to Mrs Fitzpatrick for advice, but the jealous husband arrives on the scene, misinterprets Tom's presence, and challenges him to a duel. Fitzpatrick is wounded, mortally it is believed, and Tom is hauled off to gaol, where he receives visits from Mrs Waters – whom Partridge eventually identifies as none other than Jenny Jones, Tom's reputed mother. Tom is deeply shocked to discover that he has apparently committed incest. He sees it as a judgement on his former way of life, and resolves more fervently than ever to reform. Luckily, Fitzpatrick recovers from his wounds and acknowledges to Mr Allworthy that Tom was not to blame for the duel. Mrs Waters now reveals to Mr Allworthy that she was not Tom's mother – and that the real mother was none other than his own sister, Bridget.

Tom is released from prison and Mr Allworthy's former affection for him returns. He apologizes to Sophia for his part in attempting to force her to marry Blifil, and tells Squire Western that it is Tom who is now his heir. Squire Western consents to the match between Tom and his daughter. The odious Blifil is banished – though, at Tom's insistence, with a yearly stipend which Tom supplements from his own pocket.

All ends happily, with Tom and Sophia married and living on Squire Western's estate, the Squire himself retiring to a smaller house. Partridge is reinstated as schoolmaster and the story closes with him and the gamekeeper's daughter, Molly, about to marry.

Critical commentary

Even from such an over-simplified summary as this, it will be seen that the story depends to some extent on the stock theatrical contrivances of the day such as missing heirs, mysterious parentage, glaring coincidences and accidental meetings. But apart from this, the handling of the complex plot is in itself one of the outstanding features of the book. Coleridge went so far as to declare that 'the three most perfect plots ever planned' were the *Oedipus Tyrannus* of Sophocles, *The Alchemist* of Ben Jonson – and Fielding's *Tom Jones*. In much the same way, Thackeray described the novel as 'the most astounding production of human ingenuity', pointing out that 'there is not an incident ever so trifling but advances the story, grows out of former incidents and is connected with the whole.'

A consequence of this tightly-knit structure is that *Tom Jones* is as full of clues to the future action as any modern detective story. An example of the close hold Fielding keeps on his plotting is that during the events at the inn at Upton, which are crucial to the development of the novel, there is no direct confrontation between Mrs Waters and Partridge – who could, of course, have identified her as Jenny Jones – and there are scores of similar examples of what Thackeray called Fielding's 'literary providence' in *Tom Jones*. The result of this interlacing is that the links between the characters are always kept taut, and even the minor figures contribute directly to the unfolding of the plot.

In addition, the overall planning is also masterly. The novel is divided into eighteen books. These fall into three main sections. The first section, consisting of six books, deals with events in Somerset, on the estates of either Mr Allworthy or Squire Western, and in the neighbouring countryside. The second section, also consisting of six books, takes us on to the road, as Tom and Sophia make their separate ways to London. The third section, comprising the final six books, carries the action to London, apart from the last few pages which take the main characters back to Somerset. By adopting this division Fielding is able to provide a panorama of eighteenth-century life, both town and country, and this was one of his main objectives in writing the book.

To look at the structure from another angle: the first section of the novel deals with Tom's life from infancy to the age of twenty-one, but occupies only one eighth of the whole; the next year of his life is dealt with more fully; and then the bulk of the novel – about two-thirds of it – covers only a few weeks, with headings to the various Books like: 'Containing about three Weeks', 'Containing three Days', and 'In which the History goes forward about Twelve Hours', so that every day, and at times practically every hour, are accounted for. In this way Fielding draws a sharply-rising graph of his plot, achieving in the process a gradual tightening of the dramatic tension and a gradual broadening and deepening of his psychological, social and philosophical content.

The term 'classical symmetry' has often been applied to the structure of *Tom Jones*, and this is a reminder that the adherence to classical theories and models is, if anything, even more marked than in *Joseph Andrews*. Fielding was at particular pains to introduce into the narrative what he called 'sundry similes, descriptions, and other kinds of poetical embellishments', most of them derived from the ancient classics, and all of them rich in classical echoes and allusions. On several occasions, for example, he introduces a 'mock heroic' battle. The most famous instance occurs in a chapter entitled 'A Battle sung by the Muse in the Homerican stile, and which none but the Classical Reader can taste', in which Molly Seagrim is set upon by a crowd of villagers in the churchyard, to be rescued, after giving a very good account of herself, by Tom. The listing of the fallen and the recounting of their backgrounds and attributes are direct (but of course comic) imitations of the ways in which Homer describes his great battles and mighty heroes.

The French historian of English literature, Louis Cazamian, has expressed a common critical opinion in saying that 'All these trappings weigh heavily upon the work,' – though, as he also points out, they fail to crush it, because the work itself is so vigorous. Fielding's following of classical precepts was not, in any case, always detrimental. The revelation, towards the end of the novel, of the well-kept secret of Tom's birth, for example, is as inevitable and convincing as the *peripeteia* (sudden discovery or reversal of fortune) which formed the climax in Ancient Greek tragedy, and which the philosopher Aristotle prescribed in his *Poetics* (one of Fielding's critical bibles) as an essential element of plot.

In view of the greater concern for plot, it seems surprising that Fielding should have chosen to preface each of the eighteen books of the novel with a self-contained essay.

In addition there are frequent asides within the narrative itself. The presence of all these interventions by the author constitutes one of the main grounds of criticism, and here Fielding was going against his own classical masters. Inevitably the intrusions do hold up the action, and inevitably they have the effect of weakening the illusion, so that the reader is not always allowed to lose himself in the imaginary world of the novel – as he can, for example, in Richardson.

But this is exactly the point as far as Fielding was concerned: he was deliberately inserting his essays and asides in order to counteract what he regarded as the dangerous falsities and evasions of reality which belong to the kind of romantic illusion created by writers like Richardson. His was, in effect, a dual reality: a comprehensive picture of the contemporary scene in fictional terms, combined with a wide-ranging discussion of the philosophical and moral issues that arose from it. The characters he has chosen, he implies, may *illustrate* but could not be expected themselves to carry on this discussion – and so Fielding himself takes on the second task, becoming in effect a member of the *dramatis personae*.

This is contrary to the method inaugurated by Richardson, and to that practised by later advocates of the 'dramatic novel' such as Henry James, who believed that the art of fiction demanded that everything should be conveyed through the words and actions of the characters with the minimum of explanation from the author. In the view of Ian Watt, the fact that the moral commentary comes from Fielding himself 'is the result of a technique which was deficient at least in the sense that it was unable to convey the larger moral significance through the characters and action alone.' On the other hand, perhaps *Tom Jones* is simply a different kind of novel; one in which story, character, and author continually flow into, and out of, each other. Henry James came close to suggesting this when he wrote of Fielding's relationship to the hero of *Tom Jones* as having 'such an amplitude of reflection for him and around him that we see him through the mellow air of Fielding's fine old moralism.'

'Fine old moralism' is a phrase that would have surprised readers in the earlier part of the Victorian era, for the other major criticism of *Tom Jones* that was made then, and has been made since, is that its hero is immoral. It is certainly obvious enough that Tom is no paragon of virtue – indeed, in many ways he was an entirely new kind of hero – one who was quite *un*heroic by conventional standards. He is brave, generous, and well-meaning, and his heart is always in the right place, but he certainly has no heroic control over his impulses and his instincts. He is, in other words, an ordinary, weak human being.

This was Fielding's purpose in creating him, and he explicitly states in the opening chapter: 'The provision ... which we have here made is no other than Human Nature' – the choice of such an ordinary name as Tom Jones in itself helps to make him 'Everyman'. But while Fielding does not scruple to show Tom going to bed with Molly Seagrim, Mrs Waters, or Lady Bellaston he does not condone his behaviour, and neither does Tom himself, for he is perfectly well aware that he ought not to give way so readily to his appetites, and he is obviously genuine in his repentance and determination to reform. And after all, his liaison with Molly takes place before he has met Sophia, and his entanglements with Mrs Waters and Lady Bellaston after he believes he has lost her. When at last he and Sophia are married, the reader feels confident that Sophia will certainly have no further cause for complaint in this respect. In none of his escapades does Tom behave cruelly or meanly. What Fielding is suggesting, in fact, is that there are worse sins than those of the flesh, and that the generosity and kindness Tom consistently displays are virtues just as important as that of chastity – which, under certain circumstances, Fielding implies may not be a virtue at all. It was considerations such as these that must have made Coleridge exclaim: 'I do loathe the cant which can recommend *Pamela* and *Clarissa Harlowe* as strictly moral, while *Tom Jones* is prohibited as loose,' and caused him to add that he found in Fielding's novel 'a cheerful, sunshiny, breezy spirit, that prevails everywhere, strongly contrasted with the close, hot, day-dreamy continuity of Richardson.'

In practically all his work indeed, Fielding was conducting a battle against various forms of cant. In *Joseph Andrews* he condemned, in particular, religious cant. In *The Life of Jonathan Wild the Great*, which was published in 1743 and which told the story of a superman of crime who becomes king of the London underworld – and ends up on the scaffold – he dealt with another kind of cant, that which equates value with greatness or power. In *Tom Jones* he condemns an even wider range of hypocrisy, while his appeals for tolerance and Christian charity figure more powerfully than ever.

In conveying them he makes use of much the same kind of weapons that he employed in *Joseph Andrews*, though his irony is even more finely controlled. Often, too, moral and social criticism are combined, as in the account of Squire Western's behaviour towards his wife:

The Squire, to whom that poor woman had been a faithful upper servant all the time of their marriage, had returned that behaviour by making what the world calls a good husband. He very seldom swore at her (perhaps not above once a week) and never beat her: she had not the least occasion for jealousy, and was perfect mistress of her time; for she was never interrupted by her husband, who was engaged all the morning in field exercises, and all the evening with bottle companions. She scarce indeed ever saw him but at meals; where she had the pleasure of carving those dishes which she had before attended at the dressing. From these meals she retired about five minutes after the

other servants ... These, however, were the only seasons
when Mr Western saw his wife; for when he repaired to
her bed, he was generally so drunk that he could not see;
and in the sporting season he always rose from her before
it was light.

There could be no more telling description of a certain
type of masculine boorishness and insensitivity, and at
the same time Squire Western is also seen as a representative of the kind of arbitrary power Fielding so hated.

In this connection it is important to say something
further about Fielding's authorial intrusions. A passage
such as the one just quoted speaks for itself of course; but
the discussions which Fielding introduces on such subjects
as justice, compassion and charity always serve to rein-
force the point, and carry it onto a higher intellectual
and philosophical plane. Fielding conceived part of his
function as a novelist to be to *educate* his readers. This
educational or civilizing role is a dimension in Fielding
that must not be overlooked.

Something more must also be said about the characterization of *Tom Jones*. As in *Joseph Andrews*, there are
stock types derived from classical models. Blifil, for example, is 'the self-seeking hypocrite'; Squire Western 'the
irascible autocrat'; Partridge 'the loyal and comical servant'; and Mr Allworthy (whose name is a label in itself)
is 'the benevolent benefactor'.

Yet even in these type-cast characters there is more
elasticity and movement than in *Joseph Andrews*. For
one thing, many of them were based on real people whom
Fielding knew: for another, Fielding endows them with
the saving human grace of fallibility and inconsistency.
Thus, Mr Allworthy's magnanimity does not make him
immune to gullibility and tediousness, while Squire
Western, in spite of his boorishness, reveals occasional
flashes of rough kindliness and of genuine affection for
his daughter. Sophia herself, based as she is on idealized
memories of Fielding's first wife, is rather too good to

be true. Nevertheless, she is a flesh-and-blood character, showing determination in her refusal to marry Blifil, courage in her escape from her tyrannical father, and considerable tolerance and understanding in her dealings with Tom. Even the minor characters reveal unexpected facets: Thwackum and Square, for instance, are not merely mouthpieces for opposing religious dogmas, but display occasional glimmerings of intelligence and honesty.

One of the main reasons for the liveliness of all these characters is that Fielding has endowed each of them with his own individualistic idiom and tone of voice – and his use of dialogue in *Tom Jones* is both more natural and more extensive than in any previous novel. As a consequence, every one of the characters contains a vital spark: the cast, moreover, is so large and so varied that when spark is added to spark, the whole book seems ablaze with light and colour.

Whatever criticism there may be, *Tom Jones* remains one of the world's few truly great novels.

The History of Rasselas, Prince of Abissinia

Samuel Johnson

Samuel Johnson was born at Lichfield in Staffordshire in 1709, the son of a bookseller. He was educated at Lichfield Grammar School, and then at Pembroke College, Oxford, which he was forced to leave without taking a degree because of his poverty. After teaching for a time, and then (after his marriage in 1735 to a widow many years older than himself) unsuccessfully running a private school of his own, he set out for London in 1737 in the company of one of his pupils, David Garrick, who later became a great actor. Johnson had already written a good deal for the provincial press, and he now contributed a stream of essays, poems, biographies, and reports of Parliamentary debates to *The Gentleman's Magazine*. In 1738 he published *London*, one of his most considerable poems, which castigated the degeneracy of the times, the arrogance of the rich and the oppression of the poor. In 1744 he began a series of short biographies which later appeared in volume form as *The Lives of the Poets*. In 1749 his greatest poem, *The Vanity of Human Wishes* was published. Its title is characteristic of Johnson's outlook on life and foreshadows the general theme of *Rasselas*, written ten years later and published in 1759. In 1749, too, Garrick produced his former teacher's tragedy *Irene*. A year later Johnson launched, and almost entirely wrote, *The Rambler*, a twice-weekly periodical, which, together with

The Idler, a series in another periodical, contained most of his finest essays. In 1755 his famous *Dictionary* appeared, on which he had been toiling for eight years.

It was not until after 1762, when he was granted a state pension, that Johnson experienced anything approaching financial security. It was during this last phase of his life that he really emerged as the great arbiter ('The Great Cham' as Smollett called him) of eighteenth-century literary taste and morals, especially after the formation in 1764 of the select literary and artistic coterie known as 'The Club' which eventually included, besides himself, the portrait painter Sir Joshua Reynolds, the politician and writer Edmund Burke, the poet, essayist and novelist Oliver Goldsmith, his old friend and pupil David Garrick – and James Boswell, whose *Life of Samuel Johnson* is the most famous biography in the English language.

In 1773 Johnson and Boswell went on the tour of the Scottish Highlands and the Hebrides which resulted in Johnson's *Journey to the Western Islands of Scotland* (1775). Among his many other works, mention must be made of his 1765 edition of the works of Shakespeare, prefaced by an Introduction which still ranks as one of the masterpieces of Shakespeare criticism. The last two years of his life were saddened by the death of his friend Henry Thrale, and then by a quarrel with Thrale's widow. He himself died in 1784 and was buried in Westminster Abbey.

Rasselas was Johnson's only novel and the one-hundred and thirty odd pages were written at great speed (during the evenings of a single week, he told a friend). His immediate purpose in writing it was to defray the expenses of his mother's funeral. That at the age of fifty Dr Johnson, with some of his greatest work, including his famous Dictionary, behind him, should be reduced to such shifts shows how small the rewards of his genius and his superhuman labours had been. But Johnson's outstanding characteristics were honesty and integrity, and *Rasselas*, in spite of the circumstances attending its composition, could not fail to incorporate these qualities. Indeed, it is one of his finest works and the very fact that the most celebrated intellect of the age should have turned to the novel was in itself an indication of the extent to which the new genre had established itself as a serious form of literature.

Summary

Rasselas is not, however, a novel in the normal sense of the term, but rather a cross between an extended essay, a parable, and an oriental tale. Its underlying aim was a didactic one – to teach the essential futility of all human aspirations. The long opening sentence strikingly sets the tone and the theme:

> Ye who listen with credulity to the whispers of fancy, and pursue with eagerness the phantoms of hope; who expect that age will perform the promises of youth, and that the deficiencies of the present day will be supplied by the morrow; attend to the history of Rasselas prince of Abissinia.

In this respect *Rasselas* was intended to demonstrate the falsity of the current optimistic philosophy expounded by Rousseau in France and Leibnitz in Germany, a philosophy which was also refuted by the Frenchman Voltaire, whose celebrated fable *Candide* was, by a strange coincidence, published almost simultaneously with Johnson's tale, and was in some respects similar to it in tone and structure.

As *Rasselas* is fundamentally a parable it is not 'realistic' in the manner of most other eighteenth-century novels. Inevitably the moral argument takes precedence over all other elements: the characters are not so much individuals as embodiments of various ideas; the incidents are, in effect, diagrams designed to demonstrate their operation; and the language and imagery are simple and generalized with background scenery reduced to a minimum.

In attempting a summary of *Rasselas*, therefore, it is just as important to try and give some indication of the progression of the ideas as of the actual events. The story line, in any case, is very slender – whereas what might be called the idea line is very strong indeed.

Johnson takes as his starting-point an ancient custom supposedly practised by the Emperors of Abyssinia whereby the royal children were sent to Amhara, a remote fastness surrounded by unscalable mountains, for the rest of their lives – or until summoned to ascend the throne. Johnson had read that their lives there were harsh and unhappy, but for the sake of his story he drew on another old tradition which envisaged their captivity as an earthly paradise.

In his twenty-sixth year, the hero, Prince Rasselas, wearies of the joys of 'the Happy Valley'. He tries to explain his state of mind to his old instructor, who is completely bewildered:

'Sir,' said he, 'if you had seen the miseries of the world, you would know how to value your present state.' 'Now,' said the prince, 'you have given me something to desire; I shall long to see the miseries of the world, since the sight of them is necessary to happiness.'

But Rasselas can at first find no way of escaping. His hopes are momentarily raised when he hears a craftsman-artist discoursing on the possibilities of aviation (with some prophetic comments on its potential in warfare) but when the craftsman designs a pair of wings they fail to work.

Rasselas now commands the poet-philosopher Imlac to tell him the story of his life. It transpires that the end result of Imlac's many experiences had been that, unable to find true contentment, he had been glad to retire to the Happy Valley. However, when challenged he admits that although he is less unhappy than most because as a poet he has 'a mind replete with images', which he can 'vary and combine at pleasure', he too now finds his confinement irksome. Rasselas begs him to become his companion in escape, and his director 'in *the choice of life*'. This phrase, which Johnson originally intended using as his title, is from now on repeated at intervals (and always printed in italics) like a recurrent motif.

Eventually Rasselas and Imlac, joined by Rasselas' sister Nekayah and her maid Pekuah, succeed in getting away from the Happy Valley and into the great world beyond.

After enjoying the novelties and excitements of Cairo for a while, the serious search for *the choice of life* begins. At first Rasselas is puzzled because while he himself still experiences a mysterious inner sadness, everyone around him seems happy and carefree. But 'there was not one', Imlac assures him, 'who did not dread the moment when solitude should deliver him to the tyranny of reflection.'

Rasselas now joins a group of young men in their pursuit of youthful gratifications, only to find their pleasures merely 'gross and sensual'. He turns to a venerable sage, whose doctrine is that the only path to happiness is the conquest of the passions by reason. But when he visits the sage he finds him distracted by grief at the death of his daughter, utterly unable to practise the control and fortitude he had been preaching.

Rasselas and Nekayah now visit the countryside, quickly learning that the pastoral life, so lauded by the poets, is composed mostly of ignorance, poverty, squalor and envy. Entertained by the wealthy owner of a beautiful estate, who apparently lives in blissful rural retirement, they find that his prosperity puts his life in jeopardy from his envious enemies. They then visit a nearby hermit, only to be told that 'The life of a solitary man will be certainly miserable, but not certainly devout' – and that the hermit is on the point of returning to the Cairo fleshpots. Back in the city himself, Rasselas hears one of an assembly of learned men declare that the only way to happiness is to live 'according to nature, in obedience to that universal and unalterable law with which every heart is originally impressed.' When Rasselas begs him to explain how to put these precepts into practice, the philosopher can give no coherent answer. Johnson thus dismisses Rousseau's already widely discussed back-to-nature theories, which were to play such an important part later in the Romantic Revival.

Rasselas and his sister now decide to divide their search: Nekayah will enter 'the shades of humbler life', while her brother explores 'the splendour of courts'.

In the palace of the Bassa of Egypt, Rasselas at first feels that the exercise of power, with its opportunities of making thousands 'happy by wise administration', must represent the highest *choice of life*. Before long, though, the Bassa is deposed by the Sultan, and carried off to Constantinople in chains, while soon afterwards the Sultan himself is murdered.

Nekayah has been no more successful in her experience of ordinary domestic life. She has not entered a single home 'that is not haunted by some fury that destroys its quiet', and marriage 'has many pains, but celibacy has no pleasures'. But surely, Rasselas expostulates, the man who lives a virtuous life must be happy – to which Nekayah replies:

> All that virtue can afford is quietness of conscience, a
> steady prospect of a happier estate; this may enable us to
> endure calamity with patience; but remember that patience
> must suppose pain.

While visiting the Pyramids, Nekayah's much-loved attendant Pekuah is kidnapped by Arab marauders. In her grief, the princess sinks into a profound melancholy, though she is sufficiently aware of her condition to observe to Imlac that 'the unhappy are never pleasing, and all naturally avoid the contagion of misery.' Imlac offers her this advice, in language and imagery which is at once movingly simple and impressive:

'Our minds, like our bodies, are in continual flux;
something is hourly lost, and something acquired. To
lose much at once is inconvenient to either, but while the
vital powers remain uninjured, nature will find a means
of reparation. Distance has the same effect on the mind as
on the eye, and while we glide along the stream of time,
whatever we leave behind us is always lessening, and that
which we approach increasing in magnitude. Do not suffer
life to stagnate; it will grow muddy for want of motion:
commit yourself again to the current of the world ...'

Eventually Pekuah is found and her release secured by
the payment of a large ransom. She has been well-treated
in her captivity, and has acquired a great knowledge of
astronomy from the Arab chief, who had found her
society so superior to that of his mindless concubines that
he had fallen in love with her – but had been quite unable
to resist the size of the ransom.

Back in Cairo they decide to visit a learned astronomer.
Pekuah impresses him with her new-found knowledge,
and they become frequent visitors. But their company has
the effect of causing the astronomer to declare:

'I have passed my time in study without experience; in the
attainment of sciences which can, for the most part, be
but remotely useful to mankind.'

Rasselas sadly observes that variety seems absolutely
necessary to make life supportable, but Nekayah points to
the desert monks who 'support without complaint a life,
not of uniform delight, but uniform hardship.' Imlac
agrees that though mortification of the flesh is not virtuous in itself, the monks in their silent monastery are
less wretched than the Abyssinian princes 'in their prison
of pleasure', because their way of life 'is incited by an
adequate and reasonable motive', and so 'their toils are
cheerful, because they consider them as acts of piety, by
which they are always advancing towards endless felicity.'
The astronomer now takes them on a tour of the cata-

combs, which gives rise to an impressive dissertation by Imlac on the nature of the soul, and to Nekayah's encapsulation of Johnson's underlying religious message: 'To me ... the choice of life is become less important; I hope hereafter to think only on the choice of eternity.'

In the final chapter, '*The conclusion, in which nothing is concluded*', Pekuah resolves to retire to the convent of St Anthony, Nekayah desires to devote herself to knowledge and to found a 'college of learned women', and Rasselas hopes for 'a little kingdom, in which he might administer justice in his own person, and see all the parts of government with his own eyes.' Imlac and the astronomer are 'contented to be driven along the stream of life without directing their course to any particular port.'

But aspirations are one thing, their fulfilment another, and the book ends with a deliberate inconclusiveness:

> Of these wishes that they had formed they well knew that none could be obtained. They deliberated a while what was to be done, and resolved ... to return to Abissinia.

Critical commentary

The conclusion of *Rasselas* is as sombre as most of the other conclusions arrived at in the course of the search for *the choice of life*. Very little hope and encouragement is offered. The man with a well-stocked mind, and the man of virtue, may be in a better position than most; the former because he has a stock of images upon which to feed, and the latter because he has at least the comfort of a clear conscience. But none of this is any guarantee of happiness. Art, literature, romantic love, marriage, philosophical theories and scientific discoveries are all alike deceptive, because they stimulate false hopes and thus conceal the fundamental nature of the human lot. The only positive advice that emerges is a rational recognition of the futility of human wishes, and a Christian stoicism in the face of destiny, in expectation of the rewards of eternity.

The pessimism of *Rasselas* may in part be due to the mood in which Johnson wrote it, aware of his mother's inpending death. And yet it is not pessimistic in a morbid, life-denying sense. There is no indulgence in melancholy for its own sake, but rather a grave, courageous, and absolutely honest confrontation with reality, as Johnson saw it, and underlying it the solid rock of his own deeply-felt Christianity and his own moral probity.

The conclusion of *Rasselas* is also a reminder that the structure is intellectual rather than narrative, working to a climax of idea rather than to one of plot. But although the story itself may seem formless, the episodes are in fact excellently organized to illustrate the central theme.

The vitality of Johnson's genius prevents the tale – didactic parable though it is – from becoming nothing more than a tract. He uses sufficient narrative skill and suspense to hold the reader's interest in the characters and what happens to them. The very eagerness, for example, with which Rasselas and his sister approach their search for *the choice of life* and their distress at each disillusionment, generate a genuine emotion. And Imlac is endowed with something of his creator's own ironic acceptance of reality, his wit and compassion, and his steady wisdom and insight into human motives and behaviour.

The deliberately generalized backgrounds against which the characters move are not entirely bare. There are mountains, tree-shaded rivers, leaping fish, birds, browsing animals, gardens with flowers and fountains, and Johnson tempers his generalized approach to character and scene with sufficient concrete detail to give warmth and substance.

Above all, Johnson's language itself keeps the story alive. His style could be ponderous, but this seldom happens in *Rasselas* where the dignified prose is relieved by flashes of irony and wit and by a wealth of images which, besides being clear and impressive, are often of great beauty. The overall effect is of a subtle and varied orchestration, sonorous in its undertones and rising at moments (as in Imlac's moving discourse on the Pyramids) to a massive grandeur.

It is not surprising, therefore, to find that *Rasselas* has never been out of print and that it has been translated into many languages. In its own time it was a step towards the recognition of the new literary form as a fitting medium for intellectual exposition, and it proved that the novel could carry the most profound materials without sinking under the weight.

The Life and Opinions of Tristram Shandy, Gentleman

Laurence Sterne

Laurence Sterne was born at Clonmel in Ireland in 1713, where his father, an army officer, was stationed. The first ten years of his life were spent wandering with his parents from one barracks to another in England and Ireland. Then his uncle, Dr Jacques Sterne, Precentor and Canon of York Cathedral, took charge of Laurence, and sent him to schools near Halifax, and to Jesus College, Cambridge. When Laurence was eighteen his father died as the result of a duel. He had been an improvident, unreliable, mercurial sort of man, full of quirks and oddities.

After Laurence had graduated and taken Holy Orders, his uncle obtained a living for him near York. Twenty years of bucolic obscurity followed. He married for money, was unhappy with his wife, but adored his daughter. He was made a prebendary of York Cathedral. He performed his parish duties (or at any rate some of them), he preached his sermons, and he hunted – sometimes on Sunday mornings if the scent was particularly good. He spent much time with the more disreputable of the local gentry – particularly his old undergraduate friend John Hall-Stevenson, whose home at Skelton Hall was appropriately known as 'Crazy Castle' – and in their company indulged in some very unparsonical junketings. He quarrelled with his uncle Jacques and took sides in the interminable manoeuvrings and bickerings of ecclesiastical politics in a cathedral city.

When he was already forty-five, one of these ecclesiastical squabbles led him to compose a satirical pamphlet in the manner of his great contemporary, Jonathan Swift. The pamphlet was suppressed, but it had given him a taste for comic-satiric narrative – and he wrote the first two volumes of *Tristram Shandy*. The York booksellers would not print them, chiefly because of the near-libellous local references. They were, however, published in London in January 1760 – and when Sterne himself arrived in the capital he found that he was famous. Although *Tristram Shandy* was strongly disapproved of by some (including Samuel Richardson and Dr Johnson) on grounds of immorality, Sterne was thoroughly lionized and loved every moment of it. He was inundated with invitations; his portrait was painted by Sir Joshua Reynolds; he was written about by Horace Walpole, and a volume of his sermons proved almost as popular as the novel itself.

Nevertheless, it was Yorkshire that proved the best climate for Tristram Shandy-izing, and it was mostly at Coxwold, a new and lucrative living presented to him by Lord Falconburg, and in a house which he christened Shandy Hall, that he wrote the next four volumes. In 1762, however, the tuberculosis from which he had suffered intermittently since his undergraduate days drove him abroad. He was accompanied by his wife and daughter, and their home for the next two years was mostly in the region of Toulouse. Sterne found that he was just as famous in France: he was made much of in Paris, and eagerly sought out by Diderot and other leading French writers and philosophers of the day. He continued to work at *Tristram Shandy*, and Volumes Seven and Eight were published in 1765. The ninth and final volume did not appear until 1767, after his return to London, but in the interval he had made the seven-month tour of France and Italy which resulted (in 1768) in *A Sentimental*

Journey through France and Italy by Mr Yorick, and this book brought him a fresh access of European fame and influence. He also wrote further volumes of sermons, and *The Bramine's Journal* (published posthumously) addressed to Eliza Draper, his latest love, after she went to join her husband in India. He was by now permanently separated from his wife, and much distressed to be parted from his daughter. He died of pleurisy in his Bond Street lodgings in March 1768.

Summary

The best way of breaking into the bewildering maze which is *Tristram Shandy* is to pay heed to the author's own warning (with its refusal to adopt the usual eighteenth-century reverence towards the Latin poet Horace, whose *Ars Poetica* formed one of the critical bibles of the period):

> In writing what I have set about, I shall confine myself neither to (Horace's) rules, nor to any man's rules that ever ·lived.

Tristram Shandy, in fact, is a very eccentric book by a very eccentric man. Even the printing is freakish. Italics, capitals and Gothic type alternate with various typographical quirks and jokes such as a squiggle on the page to denote the pattern made on the ground by Corporal Trim's stick. Dashes, asterisks, and rows of dots (usually to hint at the omission of particularly indecent passages) abound. One chapter, of barely four lines, has a blank dedication space which the author offers to fill in with the name of the first person who will pay him fifty guineas. When Parson Yorick is reported dead a black page is inserted. Elsewhere, the reader is invited to write on a blank page his own description of Widow Wadman's charms. In another place there is a deliberate *non sequitur* and the marbled fly-leaf of a fresh volume, to suggest that a number of pages have been lost.

All these devices, besides being funny, are meant to make the reader aware of the book as a physical object (and most modern editions retain them). The construction of the novel is even more eccentric. There is so much of what Richardson called 'unaccountable wildness, whimsical digressions, comical incoherencies' that the hero isn't even born until Volume Four and after Volume Six disappears altogether. The story (if that is the word for it) flows on and on with no apparent pattern, so that Sterne was able to declare that there was no reason why he should not give his readers two volumes of what he called 'Shandyism' every year for the next forty years. And the ninth and final volume cannot be said to have come to the end in the ordinary way at all.

Not surprisingly, therefore, any attempt to summarize the plot of *Tristram Shandy* is bound to have an air of comic unreality – not to say desperation – which Sterne himself would undoubtedly have relished. Characteristically, the full title of the novel is of little help, for there is very little of the 'life' and even less of the 'opinions' of the nominal hero. Instead there is a gallery of the richest eccentrics in English literature. Notably there are Tristram's father, Walter Shandy of Shandy Hall (perhaps based on Sterne's own father), who is wrapped up in all kinds of fantastic, paradoxical notions which he defends with an astonishing parade of pseudo-scientific learning; his brother, Tristram's Uncle Toby, wounded in the groin at the siege of Namur, whose passion, in spite of the fact that he is a man of great 'sensibility', gentleness, and 'unparalleled modesty' is the science of attacking fortified towns, which he studies with fanatical zeal by means of miniature scarps, ravelins, and bastions on his bowling green (there are ambiguous suggestions that this innocence is connected with the anatomical area of his wound); the voluble Corporal Trim, wounded in the knee at Landen, Uncle Toby's devoted servant and assistant in his 'war games'; and behind these major figures, Yorick the parson, the bewildered and long-suffering Mrs Walter

Shandy, Dr Slop, the incompetent local quack, the redoubtable Widow Wadman, and many minor characters.

But, it cannot be too often emphasized, the main character is really the narrator himself. Sterne is the most
subjective of authors, and not only does he appear in the
story as the eccentric Parson Yorick, but all the other
characters are really vehicles for his own temperamental
quirks, his fantastic (and frequently indecent) sense of
fun – and for his serious satirical purposes.

The first three volumes of the novel are mainly concerned, amid numerous digressions, with the circumstances attending the forthcoming birth of the titular
hero – including the precise date and manner of Tristram's conception, pinpointed in Walter Shandy's diary.
Somehow or other the night of Tristram's birth is reached
– as his father and uncle are engaged in interminable discussions, largely at cross-purposes of course, and only interrupted long enough for Susannah the maid to inform
them of the impending birth, and for the midwife and
Dr Slop to be summoned.

When they arrive, Corporal Trim diverts the Shandy
brothers with the reading of a long sermon, while Dr
Slop goes about his work with characteristic incompetence. Mistaking the infant's hip for its head, he flattens
Tristram's nose with his forceps. Needless to say this leads
to much learned discussion on the effects of early experiences on later life, on noses in general, and the part they
play in determining human character and destiny, as well
as a reading by Walter Shandy of his translation from the
Latin of a ponderous treatise on noses by the (fictional)
German scholar Hafen Slawkenbergius. There is also an
inevitable connection between the accident to Tristram's
nose, and one some years later to another portion of his
anatomy, when, as a boy, he is relieving himself through
the window and the sash-cord breaks (an accident which
gives him a special fellow-feeling for his Uncle Toby).

Walter Shandy feels, in view of the accident with the
forceps and the sickly state of the infant's health, that

baptism must take place without delay. He wants the child christened 'Trismegistus', after one of his pet philosophers. Unfortunately, Susannah cannot carry the name in her head, and by the time she reaches Parson Yorick, she has transposed it to Tristram. Parson Yorick (also named Tristram) delightedly christens the infant accordingly, before the father (characteristically too late for the ceremony) can change matters – though he believes, for various erudite reasons, that the name of Tristram is exceptionally unfavourable. The only way this fresh misfortune can be counteracted is by a special education – to the devising of which he brings the full force of his ingenious, but hardly practical, intellect.

In time, Tristram's elder brother Bobby dies at Westminster School, followed inevitably by a whole variety of reactions, including exhaustive discourses by Walter Shandy on the nature of death and a long impromptu funeral oration by Corporal Trim, which occupies a good portion of Volume Five. Much of Volume Six is devoted to the breeching of Tristram.

Volume Seven and most of Volume Eight abandon the story altogether in order to describe the author's travels in France and to narrate the story of the King of Bohemia. Volume Nine is mostly concerned with Uncle Toby, and the Widow Wadman's advances to him. Uncle Toby, of course, is bewildered and unsuspecting, if mildly intrigued. Naturally enough, Widow Wadman is anxious to discover where exactly Uncle Toby *was* wounded and steels herself to ask the embarrassing question. To her consternation he promises to allow her to touch the exact spot – and, producing a map of Namur, lays her finger on the appropriate portion of the field of campaign. When, however, Corporal Trim enlightens his master as to the real nature of Widow Wadman's inquiry, he beats a hasty retreat from the danger of matrimony.

Critical commentary

In *Tristram Shandy*, Sterne had in effect written an anti-novel, a parody on the practice of his contemporaries. Tristram's innocent Uncle Toby (though the innocence has a characteristically bawdy explanation) is in part a skit on Richardson's heroine in *Clarissa*, while the designing Widow Wadman is partially a comic female counterpart of Clarissa's ravisher, Lovelace. But above all, Sterne's 'infinitely regressive hero' – as the philosopher and mathematician Bertrand Russell so aptly described him – is intended as a satire on the handling of the passage of time (the central problem for all novelists) by Defoe, Richardson and Fielding. It would be quite wrong, however, to see *Tristram Shandy* as nothing more than a protracted joke directed against the new form of the novel. It is, for one thing, a serious satire of various types of learning. Like Swift, Sterne turns back to many older conventions. The lengthy, deliberately frustrating digressions; the exhaustive and sometimes exhausting parsing and analysing of fanciful situations; the parade, half-serious, half-ironic, of recondite items of knowledge and pseudo-scientific lore; the elaborate verbal juggling – all have their antecedents in writers trained in the old Scholastic traditions, such as the sixteenth-century Rabelais, the seventeenth-century Robert Burton (author of that jumble of out-of-the-way learning and bizarre semi-medical theory, *The Anatomy of Melancholy*) and John Donne and the 'Metaphysicals'.

Part of the force of *Tristram Shandy*, indeed, derives from the subtle – and comic – tensions produced by the clash between the old methods and attitudes of philosophical investigation still surviving and the new rationalistic and more genuinely scientific approaches of the eighteenth-century 'Enlightenment', as it was called. There is, however, plenty of satire directed against contemporary scientists and philosophers as well. The theory of the 'association of ideas', expounded by the famous philosopher John Locke (whose pragmatic, rationalistic *Essay Concerning the Human Understanding* (1690) was one of the key contemporary books) lies behind the passages in *Tristram Shandy* describing Tristram's procreation. In these, it emerges that his father has made a rigid habit of both winding up the grandfather clock and performing his matrimonial duties on the first Sunday night of every month – with the result that:

> ... from an unhappy association of ideas which have no connection in nature, it so fell out at length, that my poor mother could never hear the said clock wound up – but the thoughts of some other things popped into her head – and *vice versa* ...

In consequence, on the night of Tristram's begetting, this is what happens:

> 'Pray, my dear,' quoth my mother, 'have you forgot to wind up the clock?' 'Good God!' cried my father, making an exclamation, but taking care to moderate his voice at the same time, 'Did ever woman, since the creation of the world, interrupt a man with such a silly question?'

Tristram's account continues, drawing upon other learned ideas about pre-natal influences:

> ... It was a very unreasonable question at least – because it scattered and dispersed the animal spirits, whose business it was to have escorted and gone hand in hand with the HOMUNCULUS and conducted him safe to the place destined for his reception.

Sterne's novel would not have survived as long as it has, though, if its author had not possessed to the full the great novelist's gifts of creating memorable scenes and characters. The people who inhabit *Tristram Shandy* may be a very odd bunch, but they are also human and endearing in their oddity. Outstanding among them, of course, is Tristram's Uncle Toby, described by the early nineteenth-century essayist and critic William Hazlitt as 'one of the finest compliments ever paid to human nature'. He was thinking in particular of the almost saintly simplicity and kindliness that lies behind Uncle Toby's eccentricities, a combination reminiscent in many ways of the Don Quixote of Cervantes' famous novel.

Uncle Toby appears at his most whimsical and appealing in the context of his passion for miniature fortifications. As D. W. Jefferson has said:

> There is a quality about Uncle Toby's hobby-horse which
> places it on a different level from other examples of
> make-believe and eccentric preoccupation. The difference
> is one of intensity ... A peculiar concentration and control
> of detail create the spell.

A notable example is the scene in which Corporal Trim devises a method of directing 'an incessant firing' and a satisfying volume of smoke:

> Upon turning it this way and that ... in his mind, he
> soon began to find out that by means of his two Turkish
> tobacco pipes, with the supplement of three smaller tubes
> of wash leather at each of their lower ends, to be tagged by
> the same number of tin-pipes fitted to the touch holes,
> and sealed with clay next the cannon, and then tied
> hermetically with waxed silk at their several insertions
> into the Moroccan tube, – he should be able to fire all the
> six field pieces together, and with the same ease as to fire
> one.

Sterne obviously possessed all the attributes of concreteness, particularly in the depiction of scene and character, required for the writing of a normal realistic novel. Instead he chose to write an abnormal one; and although this might at first sight seem to put him outside the mainstream of English fiction, with *Tristram Shandy* Sterne did, in fact, considerably extend and deepen the possibilities of the new genre. For one thing, he was the first exponent of internal and subjective characterization. The fact that he himself was so much *inside* the novel, through Parson Yorick and the general diffusion of his own personality, prevented him from being the aloof and god-like narrator present in Fielding and even to some extent in Richardson. Each of Sterne's scenes is created from the inside outwards. Instead of a single authorial point of view, there are the simultaneous actions and reactions of several characters at once, contrasted, grouped, individualized, interpenetrating – producing not a number of separate facets of experience, but its very texture. In many ways, too, Sterne's psychology marked an advance in sophistication. The waywardness of his characters may be irritating at times, but human beings *are* wayward and unpredictable, and much of his comedy was devoted to showing, under the influence of Locke, how much this is the result of both heredity and environment, and of the erratic and often irrational interplay of differing personalities. At the same time, he was the first to capture (in a way not so very different from that of Harold Pinter and other modern playwrights) the fragmentary, repetitive movement of everyday speech, and the ways in which it is often accompanied and interrupted by all kinds of physical gesture. Most momentous of all, though, as far as the future of the novel was concerned, was Sterne's handling of the chronological sequence. He eagerly adapted Locke's theory that time was purely subjective, governed by the succession, orderly or disorderly, of ideas, and therefore moving swiftly or slowly according to moods and the hundred and one random circumstances that affect them. Hence his introduction of variations of pace in his narrative, sometimes speeding it up, and sometimes slowing it down until it almost comes to a standstill. There is, too, the underlying assumption throughout that external matters have no real scale of importance in themselves but are significant only insofar as they happen to impress themselves on the observer's mind. Sterne had, in effect, evolved an impressionistic and relativist technique.

Although E. M. Forster complained of 'muddle' in the book, it is far more of a coherent work of art than its apparent formlessness would suggest. Sterne himself protested that his novel possessed an inherent unity:

> I fly off from what I am about, as far, and as often, too, as any writer in Great Britain; yet I constantly take care to order affairs so that my main business does not stand still in my absence ... By this contrivance, the machinery of my work is of a species by itself; two contrary motions are introduced into it, and reconciled, which were thought to be at variance with each other. In a word, my work is digressive, and it is progressive too – and at the same time.

Tristram Shandy in fact *does* have its own kind of form: but it is the form not of the normal chronological sequence, with a beginning, a middle and an end, but of a circle perpetually in motion.

It is obvious, therefore, why twentieth-century writers like Dorothy Richardson, Virginia Woolf and James Joyce (whose lying-in scene in *Ulysses* might almost have been lifted from *Tristram Shandy*) who also rebelled against the tyranny of the chronological sequence and adopted impressionistic techniques, felt a special kinship for Laurence Sterne. In obstinately remaining himself and standing to one side of the eighteenth-century tradition of the English novel, he had immeasurably widened its future potentialities.

The Castle of Otranto:
A Gothic Story

Horace Walpole

Horace Walpole was born in 1717, the fourth son of Sir Robert Walpole (later First Earl of Orford) the great Whig statesman who was Prime Minister from 1721 to 1742. Like his father, Horace was educated at Eton, and King's College, Cambridge. He, too, was a member of Parliament (though he retired early on) and he, too, on the death of his nephew in 1794, eventually became Earl of Orford. Horace Walpole, however, was not a born politician like his father, but a dilettante (in the best sense of the word) – a collector of books, manuscripts, and paintings; a friend and patron of scholars (including the poet, Thomas Gray); an amateur antiquarian and historian; a dabbler in various scholarly researches, arts and crafts (including printing); a notable wit and raconteur; and author of one of the most famous collections of letters in the English language which, together with his diaries, give a graphic and invaluable picture of eighteenth-century England. He also published the still important *Anecdotes of Painting in England* (1762–1780), and the *Catalogue of Engravers* (1765). After *The Castle of Otranto* (1764), he published, in 1768, a tragic play, *The Mysterious Mother*, and a treatise, *Historic Doubts on the Life and Reign of Richard III*. He had many and varied friends, including the actress Kitty Clive and the authoress Mary Berry and her sister Agnes (to whom, together with their father, Walpole left all his printed books and manuscripts). He never married and, although an uncomplaining sufferer from gout all his life, lived to a considerable age, dying in London in March 1797.

The most famous manifestation of Horace Walpole's attitudes and tastes was the conversion of his home at Strawberry Hill, Twickenham (where he settled in 1747) into what he described as 'a little Gothic castle', surrounded by a miniature forest containing a tiny hermit's chapel. The contemporary fashion, which quickly became a craze, for the Gothic, pointed-arch style of architecture was one of the symptoms of the growing interest in the Middle Ages. This was, in turn, symptomatic of the gradual break-away from the predominant Classicism of the eighteenth century and of the advent of Romanticism.

The Castle of Otranto sprang from a vivid dream Walpole had 'of which all I could recover', he wrote 'was that I had thought myself in an ancient castle (a very natural dream for a head filled like mine with Gothic story) and that on the uppermost bannister of a great staircase I saw a gigantic hand in armour. In the evening I sat down to write ...' The mock-Gothic atmosphere of Strawberry Hill provided exactly the right atmosphere for Walpole's novel, and the dream origin is responsible for much of the narrative spell.

Summary

The events which the story narrates are supposed to have occurred sometime in the twelfth or the thirteenth century, and although there is a real Otranto (on the Strait of Otranto, in southern Italy) the location is essentially dreamlike, while the names of Manfred, the Prince of Otranto in the story, and of Conrad, his ailing son, sound more German than Italian.

The story opens as Manfred is making hasty preparations for the marriage of Conrad to Isabella, daughter of the Marquis of Vicenza, whom he has secured in the castle with the connivance of her guardians and during the absence of her father. Manfred's servants attribute the haste to his dread of an old prophecy which declares *'That the castle and lordship of Otranto should pass from the present family, whenever the real owner should be grown too large to inhabit it.'*

Before the wedding can be solemnized, Conrad is crushed to death by a giant helmet which suddenly crashes into the courtyard. Afraid of being left without a male heir, Manfred determines to divorce his devoted wife, Hippolita, and to marry Isabella himself. Horrified by the proposal, Isabella escapes through an underground passage to the nearby church of St Nicholas and the protection of Father Jerome. She is aided in her escape by a handsome young peasant named Theodore, who bears a striking resemblance to the portrait of Alonso, the original Prince of Otranto (poisoned by Manfred's grandfather so that he could usurp the principality).

Theodore, already under suspicion of playing some part, through sorcery, in the death of Conrad, and now also suspected of helping Isabella, is imprisoned but secretly released by Manfred's daughter Matilda, with whom Theodore falls in love.

All kinds of complications follow, including the arrival of Isabella's father to demand the restoration of his daughter and to challenge Manfred to a duel; the flight of Isabella to a nearby cave, where she is protected by Theodore, who wounds her father when he mistakes him for one of Manfred's retainers; and a treaty between Isabella's father, who has recovered from his wounds, and Manfred whereby the former gives his consent to the match between Isabella and Manfred. Attending these complications are a number of mysterious and supernatural manifestations, all full of dire warning to Manfred.

Eventually Manfred, believing that Isabella and Theodore are in love, and hearing that Theodore and a lady are praying together before the tomb of Alonso, hurries to the church himself, and stabs the lady – only to discover that he has killed his own daughter, Matilda. The super-natural forces that have been at work in the background now bring matters to a climax. The ghost of Alonso, a gigantic figure (the owner of the helmet and of an equally outsize sword) has, in accordance with the prophecy, grown too big for the edifice and begins to break it asunder. Terror at last drives Manfred to admit that he is a usurper. Theodore turns out to be the son of Father Jerome and also the rightful heir to Alonso. Manfred and his wife Hippolita retire to houses of religion, while Theodore is established as prince of Otranto and, al-though still sorrowing for Matilda, marries her best friend Isabella 'persuaded he could know no happiness but in the society of one with whom he could forever indulge the melancholy that had taken possession of his soul.'

Critical commentary

It will be seen from the summary that supernatural ele-ments play as important a part in *The Castle of Otranto* as the mediaeval trappings, and contemporary readers were duly terrified. Gray, for example, wrote that he and his Cambridge friends were 'afraid to go to bed o'nights'. Besides the mysterious appearance of the giant helmet and sword accompanied by 'a hollow and rustling sound', there are a huge armoured hand on a bannister (as in Walpole's dream), a skeleton in a monk's habit, drops of blood that fall from the nose of Alonso's statue, and a portrait of Manfred's grandfather, the original usurper, that suddenly comes to life. This last device – which has, of course, grown stale over the years by constant repeti-tion – was long regarded as particularly horrifying – es-pecially as the portrait, with 'an audible sigh', steps down from the frame, causing Manfred to exclaim (with echoes of Hamlet when confronted by his father's ghost):

'Do I dream? ... or are the devils themselves in league against me? Speak, infernal spectre! Or, if thou art my grandsire, why dost thou too conspire against thy wretched descendant?'

Then, as the vision gestures him to follow:

'Lead on!' cried Manfred; 'I will follow thee to the gulph of perdition!' The spectre marched sedately, but dejected, to the end of the gallery, and turned into a chamber on the right hand ...

That gives something of the flavour of the novel, which was an important harbinger of certain aspects of the Romantic Revival, in which fondness for supernatural terrors was to some extent symptomatic of the desire to break out of the imaginative and emotional restraints imposed by the realism of Defoe, Richardson, Fielding and Smollett.

The contribution of *The Castle of Otranto* to the future of the English novel was twofold. First, it initiated the Gothic novel, which soon began to be called also 'the novel of terror', and which had a long progeny. There were a number of genuinely original works of fiction inspired by it, among them Mrs Ann Radcliffe's *The Mysteries of Udolpho* (1794), and Matthew Gregory Lewis's *The Monk* (1796) – which was so popular that its author was nicknamed 'Monk' Lewis. Later, famous writers of tales of horror and the supernatural who were indirectly influenced by Walpole's example included Charles Maturin, author of *Melmoth the Wanderer* (1820), Sheridan Le Fanu in *Uncle Silas* (1864) and the early nineteenth-century American, Edgar Allen Poe, as well as numerous later writers in the same genre – not to mention the makers of horror movies in our own times.

Second, the fact that Walpole had turned to the historical past, no matter how amateurishly, was of considerable importance in itself. At the height of the Augustan period, the past (except for that of classical Greece and Rome) was regarded as something dark and barbaric with little to teach a society which, to the Augustans, marked the highest possible point of cultural development – even Shakespeare was considered an 'untutored genius', several of whose plays had been 'civilized' by being put into heroic couplets.

The Castle of Otranto helped to shake a cultural confidence that showed signs of degenerating into complacency, and to point the way to that fruitful rediscovery of the past and of a sense of history, which was one of the most striking outcomes of the Romantic Revival. It was not surprising, therefore, that Sir Walter Scott should, in 1811, have praised *The Castle of Otranto* as 'remarkable not only for the wild interest of the story, but as the first modern attempt to found a tale of amusing fiction upon the basis of the ancient romances of chivalry.'

When *The Castle of Otranto* was reissued in 1964, to mark the two hundredth anniversary of its first publication, it was its hundred and fifteenth appearance at least – with many more editions still unaccounted for. It was obviously, in its day, very popular indeed. It still arouses sufficient interest to make the reader want to know how it works out, especially as, in marked contrast to most eighteenth-century novels, it is only about a hundred pages long. But its importance today is that it was a kind of bridging novel, published within the Age of Reason but inaugurating a number of developments usually associated with the period that followed it. As such, no account of the growth of the English novel would be complete without some examination of it.

The Vicar of Wakefield

Oliver Goldsmith

Oliver Goldsmith was born in West Meath, Ireland, in 1728, the son of a gentle and unworldly Protestant clergyman in the Church of Ireland, of English settler stock. He spent much of his childhood near the village of Lissoy – which was to figure largely in his imaginative world. After a spell at the village school he was educated at various grammar schools, where, undersized, ugly, and badly marked by smallpox, he was subjected to a good deal of bullying. At Trinity College, Dublin, he led a feckless and dissipated life, but managed – just about – to obtain his BA degree. He tried his hand at a number of professions, and failed at them all. He then studied medicine, in a very sporadic fashion, at Edinburgh and Leiden (in Holland) but failed at that too, though at some later stage he seems to have obtained medical qualifications of a sort. Still unable to find a settled job, he wandered on foot through Flanders, France, Switzerland and part of Italy, supporting himself by playing the flute. In 1756 he came to London. He applied for various medical appointments, but was considered incompetent to fill any of them. He spent a miserable period working as an usher (or assistant master) in a school. Eventually he turned to the no less wretched existence of a hack journalist, living in great poverty in a room with a single chair.

His first real success was a series of over a hundred

letters supposedly written by a Chinese mandarin visiting England to a friend in Peking, and clearly modelled on a similar series by his near-contemporaries, Montesquieu and Voltaire. Through his imaginary Chinaman, Goldsmith described, sharply but never maliciously, the coffee houses and brothels, the churches and law courts, the ladies of quality and the ladies of the town of contemporary England, every now and then also introducing adventures in Persia and Russia, and some enchanting fairy stories. This volume, published in 1762, was called *The Citizens of the World*.

Though all his works so far had been published anonymously, their grace, elegance and tolerant temper had been noted and admired, and by 1763 he was one of the nine original members of the select literary coterie known as 'The Club', dominated by the redoubtable Dr Samuel Johnson. Goldsmith's improvidence, fondness for flashy clothes, gambling and other dissipations, combined with his unfailing generosity towards those worse off than himself, still frequently reduced him to desperate financial straits however – and it was to this that we owe *The Vicar of Wakefield*. For in 1764, it appears, Goldsmith hastily disposed of the manuscript which had been lying about unregarded for some time, in order to pay arrears of rent to his landlady. The bookseller who acquired it showed no particular enthusiasm, and set it aside. It was only after the continuing success of Goldsmith's long poem *The Traveller* (the first work published, in 1764, under his own name) that *The Vicar of Wakefield* at last appeared in 1766. Following its success, Goldsmith published, in 1770, his greatest poem, *The Deserted Village*, and in 1773 his enormously successful play, *She Stoops to Conquer*, was first produced. Although success brought him fame and fortune, he overspent wildly and his gambling debts mounted. He fell ill and largely due to his own incompetent doctoring he died in London in April 1774. Although he was buried in the Temple churchyard, his friends of 'The Club' erected a monument to him in

Westminster Abbey, with a Latin epitaph written by Dr Johnson.

Summary

When the novel opens the narrator is Dr Primrose, Vicar of Wakefield (not a real place, though there have been attempts to identify it with the actual Wakefield in Yorkshire). He is kindly, charitable, whimsical – and utterly unworldly. Possessed of a private fortune, he devotes the whole of his stipend to good works, and lives in unpretentious comfort and contentment with his wife Deborah and his six children.

George, the eldest, has just come down from Oxford and is engaged to be married to Arabella Wilmot, daughter of Mr Wilmot, a wealthy neighbouring clergyman. Preparations for the wedding are far advanced when news arrives that the Vicar's fortune has been suddenly lost. Mr Wilmot breaks off the match and George goes to London to seek his fortune. Travelling to another and poorer living, the Primroses learn that its patron, Squire Thornhill, is a notorious womanizer. Sophia, the younger and more serious Primrose girl, is rescued from a fall by Mr Burchell, a dignified but apparently impoverished gentleman, who later points out Squire Thornhill's house and explains that the Squire is dependent on his reclusive uncle, Sir William Thornhill.

Visited by Squire Thornhill, Mrs Primrose and her elder daughter Olivia are particularly taken by his charm; and both daughters are dazzled by a later invitation to stay in London with two smart and sophisticated society ladies to whom he introduces them. Both the Vicar and Mr Burchell are against the idea but Mrs Primrose approves enthusiastically, and – anxious to impress these ladies – insists on exchanging the family's clumsy old horse for a smarter one. However Moses Primrose, the pompous, pedantic second son, is conned into swapping the creature for a gross of worthless green spectacles. The

Vicar himself is also conned by the same man when he tries to sell his remaining horse.

The London expedition falls through, the ladies having received a letter referring scandalously to the Primrose girls. This letter is apparently from Mr Burchell and he is banished from their company. Squire Thornhill remains attentive to the Primroses, and this gives rise to gossip. Hoping to force a proposal from the Squire, Mrs Primrose encourages a local farmer to court Olivia. This plan also fails when Dick, another Primrose son, brings news of seeing Olivia driving away with two strange men. Squire Thornhill disclaims all knowledge, Mr Burchell is suspected, and the Vicar sets off in pursuit of his errant daughter but is delayed at an inn by illness. Renewing his search, he meets Arabella Wilmot, still obviously in love with George, who turns up in the neighbourhood not long afterwards as a member of a group of strolling players.

Squire Thornhill, courting Arabella for her father's wealth, now arrives on the scene, is solicitous about Olivia and apparently helpful to George, for whom he buys an army commission in order to keep him away from Arabella. On his despairing way home, the Vicar finds Olivia destitute, and learns that it was Squire Thornhill and not Mr Burchell who had abducted her, and that the Squire's grand friends were in reality ladies of the town whom he employed to lure Olivia and Sophia to London for his own evil purposes. After a mock marriage to Olivia, the Squire had seduced her, introduced her to other women he had treated similarly, and eventually offered her to one of his equally dissolute friends. Ill and heartbroken, Olivia had run away.

Journeying home together, father and daughter see flames bursting from the vicarage. Dr Primrose is badly burned while heroically rescuing his youngest children, Dick and Bill, from the burning building.

The family have to set up home in an outhouse and Dr Primrose rallies them by his own unfailing patience and gentleness. Poor Olivia is further wounded on hearing of the impending marriage between Arabella Wilmot and Squire Thornhill, with whom she is still in love. The Squire calls and insultingly suggests that Olivia should be married off locally, thereby remaining available to him as one of his mistresses. When the Vicar indignantly turns him out, the Squire has him arrested for rent arrears, and Dr Primrose, after quelling the villagers' near-riot in his support, is thrown into a debtors' gaol. His three sons join him, and his wife and daughters take cheap lodgings nearby.

In prison, Dr Primrose meets Ephraim Jenkinson, the con man who had cheated Moses and himself, but who now, touched by the Vicar's Job-like patience, befriends him. Jenkinson persuades him to write to Sir William Thornhill, informing him of the injustices he and his family have suffered at his nephew's hands, but Dr Primrose receives no reply. News comes from Jenkinson that Olivia has died, and the heartbroken Vicar agrees to write to Squire Thornhill, informing him that now his daughter is dead he withdraws his objection to the Squire's marrying Arabella. The Squire returns an insulting reply. Tribulation is added to tribulation: Sophia is seized by an unknown man and carried off; then George, who has heard of the Squire's treatment of Olivia, is brought to the prison, wounded, in fetters and under sentence of death. He had challenged the Squire to a duel, but instead of facing him himself, the Squire had set his servants on George, and in the fight that followed George badly wounded one of them. The Vicar, enfeebled in body and spirit by all these blows, is roused out of his despair by George and addresses a moving sermon to the whole prison on the mysterious workings of Providence and the rewards waiting in the next world for the wretched of this earth.

Now the tide of fortune begins to turn. Sophia arrives at the prison with the Primroses' old friend Mr Burchell, who has rescued her from her abductors. Mr Burchell now reveals that he is in reality Sir William Thornhill, and that he had posed as Mr Burchell to make sure that Sophia would love him for his own sake. Jenkinson identifies Sophia's abductor as a ruffian named Baxter. Summoned by his uncle to answer the charges of the Primrose family, Squire Thornhill makes a plausible defence. Baxter, however, confesses that not only is he Sophia's abductor but also the man George was supposed to have wounded, and that the Squire had employed him for these purposes. Jenkinson reveals that the Squire had employed him also, to arrange the mock marriage to Olivia.

Arabella Wilmot and her father now arrive. Horrified to hear of her fiancé's infamies, Arabella is overjoyed to see George (now released from prison) and to learn that he had not, as the Squire had falsely reported, married and gone abroad. The Squire, however, has one last card – Arabella's fortune has already been assigned to him in the marriage settlement. Old Mr Wilmot is much annoyed by the news but, when Sir William promises financial backing, agrees to the dissolution of Arabella's engagement to the Squire and to her betrothal to George. Jenkinson now drops a bombshell. He reveals that it was not a bogus priest he had engaged to marry Olivia and the Squire, but a real one. He had kept the fact secret as a means of levying future blackmail on the Squire. What is more, he now produces Olivia herself, whose death he had announced to the Vicar as being the only way of inducing him to withdraw his objections to Squire Thornhill's marriage to Arabella, and so perhaps escape further persecutions. Olivia, therefore, is an honest woman after all, and the marriage settlement between the Squire and Arabella is, of course, invalid. The thoroughly routed Squire is dismissed by his uncle to a much humbler way of life. And, to cap it all, news arrives that the Vicar's fortune has been restored to him.

Amid great rejoicing on all sides, the Vicar and his family return home, Sir William Thornhill (alias Mr Burchell) is married to Sophia, and George to Arabella, while Olivia recovers her health and lives in hopes that one day Squire Thornhill, whom she still loves, will re-form and be restored to her. The Vicar ends his story with the words:

> I had nothing now on this side of the grave to wish for, all my cares were over, my pleasures were unspeakable.
> It now only remained that my gratitude in good fortune should exceed my former submission in adversity.

Critical commentary

Such is the plot of *The Vicar of Wakefield* and few would disagree with Lord Macaulay that:

> The fable is ... one of the worst that was ever constructed. It wants not merely that probability which ought to be found in a tale of common English life, but that consistency which ought to be found even in the wildest fiction about witches, giants and fairies.

Part of the trouble is that the novel is badly proportioned and too short for its dense, involved plot. Calamities come too thick and fast to be properly developed or make a proper impact. The denouement, with all the comings and goings, sudden reversals and startling revelations, is also rushed and perfunctory. (In his perennially fresh and lively comedy *She Stoops to Conquer*, however, Goldsmith showed how deftly he could handle complications of this kind.) It is clear, in fact, that the composition of *The Vicar of Wakefield* was scamped, and it has also been conjectured that at least one chapter must have been lost.

It cannot be said, either, that there is anything original about the plot and its characters. Seduction and abduc-tion formed the common fare of contemporary drama and fiction. Squire Thornhill's treatment of Olivia has obvious affinities to that of Squire B's treatment of Pamela in Richardson's novel, or that of Lovelace's behaviour in his *Clarissa Harlowe*. Even prison scenes had occurred before – as in Fielding's *Amelia* and Smollett's *Roderick Random*.

The characterization itself has no real depth, and no psychological subtleties. At the end of the novel the characters possess ·the same basic attributes with which they started: and, apart from the obviously sobering effects of misfortune, there is little tension or development. This is particularly the case with the Vicar himself. He changes least of all. His character seems, at times, to be a series of texts to which the misfortunes that befall him serve as illustrations – and as pretexts for some rather smug and wearisome sermonizing.

And yet – once one starts reading the novel it is practically impossible to put it down until it is finished, so absorbing are the lives and loves of the Primroses – and in particular, so lovable is the Vicar. Wherein lies the secret of the spell?

Quite simply, the style provides the fundamental answer to that question. Goldsmith expressed his own literary creed in this respect in his first book, *An Enquiry into the Present State of Polite Learning*, published in 1759:

Let us, instead of writing finely, try to write naturally: not hunt after lofty expressions, to deliver mean ideas, nor be forever gaping, when we only mean to deliver a whisper.

He consistently practised what he preached and the clarity and elegance of his style, to which his admirer Dr Johnson drew attention, makes him probably the most graceful and easily read of all the eighteenth-century prose writers. These were qualities that enabled him to obtain the maximum effect from the few basic characteristics he picked on in depicting the people of his novel. Thus he conveys the Vicar's whimsical kindliness and essential sunniness of spirit by means of a few simple words and a striking and delicately turned image:

... if we had not very rich, we generally had very happy

friends about us; for this remark will hold good thro'
life, that the poorer the guest, the better pleased he ever
is with being treated; and as some men gaze with admiration
at the colours of a tulip, or the wing of a butterfly, so I
was by nature an admirer of happy faces.

It is the style, above all, that helps to make the descriptions of countryside or domestic interiors so memorable,
and which have caused them to be compared with the
Dutch genre painters. Here is the humble home to which
the Primroses move after the loss of their fortune:

Our little habitation was situated at the foot of a sloping
hill, sheltered with a beautiful underwood behind, and a
pratling river before; on one side a meadow, on the other
a green ... Nothing could exceed the neatness of my little
enclosures: the elms and hedgerows appearing with
inexpressible beauty. My house consisted of but one
storey, and was covered with thatch, which gave it an air
of great snugness; the walls on the inside were nicely
white-washed and my daughters undertook to adorn
them with pictures of their own designing. Though the
same room served us for parlour and kitchen, that only
made it the warmer. Besides, as it was kept with the
utmost neatness, the dishes, plates, and coppers, being well
scoured, and all disposed in bright rows on the shelves,
the eye was agreeably relieved, and did not want richer
furniture ...

Typically Augustan in its coolness and good sense, that
passage also bears some obvious resemblances to descriptions in *La Nouvelle Héloïse* (1761) by Jean Jacques
Rousseau, the pioneer of Romanticism, and the Vicar
himself illustrates in many respects Rousseau's doctrine
of the innate happiness of the truly 'natural' man. *The
Vicar of Wakefield*, while firmly placed in the Augustan
mode, reveals, in fact, some of those elements which
would later contribute to the Romantic Revival.

It was Goldsmith's command of style, too, that gave the

two ancient and primitive strands upon which the novel is built – the riches-to-rags, rags-to-riches motif, and the theme of discomfiture of the rich and powerful by the humble and meek – so much narrative conviction. As the contemporary French critic De Buffon so rightly said 'Style is the man himself' – and the essential charm of *The Vicar of Wakefield* is, of course, the charm of Goldsmith. In spite of all his weaknesses, no-one ever doubted his essential goodness, and no misfortune could quench his innate optimism. The astonishing thing about Goldsmith's writings is that, in an age when harsh and bitter satire was so common, *The Vicar of Wakefield* is permeated by these qualities. The scenes and characters are, as the nineteenth-century American writer Washington Irving has said: 'seen through the medium of his good head and heart', and when Goldsmith says of his Vicar that he was 'an admirer of happy faces' he was also writing of himself.

It is impossible not to be attracted by this simple loving kindness in the novel. There are plenty of melodramatic elements in the plot itself but the characters are, in their essentials, the ordinary people of a family circle, with nothing extraordinary or strained about them. *The Vicar of Wakefield* has been called 'the first masterpiece of domestic fiction', and has in consequence always been regarded as an eminently sane and health-giving book. The great German poet and sage Goethe, related how, when he was a twenty-five year old student, he experienced the benign influence of 'that wise and wholesome book just at the critical moment of mental development', and he paid tribute to the 'high, benevolent irony ... the gentleness to all opposition,' and the 'equanimity under every change' which he had found in the novel.

It is not surprising that *The Vicar of Wakefield* has always been regarded as ideal family reading – and of course, to the Victorians, who found much to shock them in Fielding, Richardson, Sterne and Smollett, it was pre-eminent among eighteenth-century novels. What happened to Olivia, and what might have happened to Sophia, was shocking enough, but it could be regarded as something that took place beyond the charmed circle of family affections and loyalties which lies at the centre of the book.

The picture of family life is, admittedly, an idealized and sometimes sentimental one, viewed through the golden haze of Goldsmith's own memories. But what he did in *The Vicar of Wakefield* was to present a frankly idealized and utopian, but carefully controlled, picture of a way of life close to Nature and ruled by kindness and right relationships, as a contrast to the self-seeking, the scramble for riches, and the disruption of traditional social and religious ties which were already beginning to make themselves felt at the dawn of the Industrial Revolution. It is for this reason above all that *The Vicar of Wakefield* has survived. As Sir Walter Scott wrote:

> We read *The Vicar of Wakefield* in youth and age. We return to it again and again, and bless the memory of an author who contrives so well to reconcile us to human nature.

Evelina,
or The History of a Young Lady's First Entrance
into the World

Frances Burney

Frances Burney was born in 1752, the daughter of a
celebrated musicologist. From an early age Fanny (as she
was usually known) was surrounded by all kinds of artists
and writers, including Dr Samuel Johnson and David
Garrick. While in her early teens she wrote a number of
short stories, and then went on to a full-length novel, in
the then fashionable sentimental mode, which she called
The History of Caroline Evelyn. But her stepmother (of
whom she was very fond) disapproved of such frivolous
activities as novel writing, and persuaded her to burn the
manuscript. Fanny turned instead to keeping a voluminous journal, which provided her with excellent practice
in noting the minutiae of everyday behaviour and talk,
later her greatest strength as a novelist. She was also an
ardent theatregoer, especially when her friend David
Garrick was playing, and this helped to give her insight
into the handling of a complex plot.

In 1778, after the most elaborate precautions to preserve her anonymity, Fanny published her first novel,
under the title of *Evelina, or The History of a Young
Lady's First Entrance into the World*. It was instantly
successful, and when she was told that Dr Johnson had
commented that there were 'passages in the book which
might do honour to Richardson' (some readers in fact
wondered if Richardson was the author) she was 'almost

crazed ... with agreeable surprise'. When the real authorship of *Evelina* was eventually disclosed Fanny became a
celebrity, and she was appointed one of the keepers of the
robes to Queen Caroline until an illness forced her to
retire.

In 1793, Fanny married General D'Arblay, a refugee
from the French Revolution. In 1801, however, she and
her husband went to live in France, and Fanny remained
there until 1812 (during most of which time France, under
Napoleon Bonaparte, was at war with England). After a
spell nursing her father, until his death in 1814, she
returned to France, but after the final overthrow of
Napoleon following the battle of Waterloo, her husband
was allowed to settle in England with his wife. He died
in 1818, but Fanny lived on until the beginning of 1840.
Her other novels were: *Cecilia, or Memoirs of an Heiress*
(1782), *Camilla* (1796), and *The Wanderer* (1814). She
also published several volumes of her diaries (covering
the years 1768 to 1840), and an edition of her father's
memoirs.

Summary

In *Evelina*, she adopted the epistolary technique made
famous by Richardson, and the novel begins with an exchange of correspondence between Lady Howard and her
old friend the Reverend Mr Villars, which gives the necessary background information – and is in effect a summary
of Fanny's destroyed novel *The History of Caroline
Evelyn*.

The gist of it is that Mr Villars had once been companion and tutor to the wealthy young Mr Evelyn, who
had, most unsuitably, married a barmaid and had a
daughter named Caroline by her. Dying two years later,
Mr Evelyn had begged Mr Villars to take charge of
Caroline, though leaving his fortune to his wife, in the
expectation that she would, in turn, leave it to their
daughter when she grew up.

When Caroline was eighteen, however, her mother, now remarried to a Frenchman named Duval, had tried to force on her a suitor of her own choice. In order to escape, Caroline had secretly married the profligate Sir John Belmont with whom she had fallen in love. Sir John, discovering that his wife's fortune was dependent on her mother's goodwill, had burned the marriage certificate and repudiated his wife. Returning to the protection of Mr Villars in England, Caroline had died in giving birth to her daughter Evelina, whom Mr Villars had also brought up, wryly commenting to Lady Howard: 'the education of the father, daughter, and grand-daughter, has devolved on me.'

When Madame Duval begins to make inquiries about her grand-daughter, Mr Villars, not at all pleased at the prospect of the ex-barmaid entering Evelina's sheltered life, does his best to keep her safely in the country. Eventually, however, he reluctantly allows her to accompany Lady Howard and her married daughter, Mrs Mirvan, to London for the 'season'.

There the seventeen-year-old Evelina is enraptured by the giddy social round. Young and inexperienced, she is mortified by her *gaucheries*, particularly in the presence of the dignified and handsome young Lord Orville, with whom she finds herself falling in love. She is also much disturbed by the unwelcome attentions of Sir Clement Willoughby, as well as by the enmity of Mr Lovel, a fop whom she has inadvertently offended.

Madame Duval, as Mr Villars had feared, arrives in London, finds her long-lost grand-daughter, and tries to persuade her to return with her to France. She introduces Evelina to her nephew Mr Branghton, a silversmith, and he and his family, all of them impossibly vulgar in the eyes of the genteel and refined Evelina, are always pushing their way into her social engagements. What with this and the continued persecutions of Sir Clement and Mr Lovel, Evelina's enjoyment of London life is considerably clouded, although she is 'half pleased, and half pained' when she hears that Lord Orville has successfully dealt with Mr Lovel, so that he does not bother her again.

Madame Duval further agitates Evelina by announcing that she is going to take legal steps in order to try and force Sir John Belmont to acknowledge Evelina as his daughter and legitimate heiress. Mr Villars scotches this plan, but suggests that Lady Howard should address an appeal direct to Sir John. This she does, and receives a mysterious letter to say that Sir John will shortly be returning to England to reply in person.

Mr Villars also scotches Madame Duval's plan of taking Evelina back with her to France, but agrees that she can stay with her grandmother in London for a time – in the hope that this may lead her to bequeath her fortune (inherited, of course, from Mr Evelyn) to Evelina when she dies. The Branghtons (who hope to get Madame Duval's money for themselves) help her to rent a house in unfashionable Holborn, and take Evelina on excursions to the various London pleasure-gardens. In one of them she loses her party and is seized on by two ladies of the town who force her to walk with them – and of course runs into Lord Orville while in their company. When Lord Orville calls on her in Holborn she is able to explain her predicament, but the Branghtons involve her in a further embarrassing situation with him and she sends him a letter of apology. To cap it all, Madame Duval now suggests that Evelina should marry Mr Branghton's son.

Evelina is only too relieved to return to Mr Villars, but is shocked to receive from Lord Orville an insulting reply to her letter, and falls ill. Recuperating at the spa in Bristol, she meets Lord Orville, and is baffled to find him his old grave and courteous self. It transpires that he had not received Evelina's letter, which had been intercepted by Sir Clement Willoughby (still pursuing Evelina), and it was he who had written the insulting reply. Finally thwarted, Sir Clement goes abroad, and Lord Orville declares his love.

But now Evelina has another shock. Sir John Belmont arrives in the company of a young woman whom he declares to be his daughter – and repudiates Evelina as an impostor. Eventually, though, it is revealed that the nurse who had attended Evelina's mother when she died in giving birth to her, had passed off her own child on Sir John. He acknowledges Evelina as his daughter and heiress, and begs her forgiveness for the wrongs he had done to her mother. Evelina marries Lord Orville, and all ends happily.

Critical commentary

This rather complicated story is told with considerable narrative skill. Although the epistolary technique makes the novel a long one, there are few dull moments, plenty of variations of pace, and a wealth of subsidiary story-lines.

One of the narrative triumphs is that most of this material is presented through the eyes, mind and character of the youthful heroine, with exactly the kind of re-actions and responses to be expected from a girl of Evelina's age. The other characters, though sufficiently delineated for their purpose, do not have much substance to them, with the exceptions perhaps of Mr Villars, who reminds us in some respects of Oliver Goldsmith's bene-volent Vicar of Wakefield, and of the vulgar Madame Duval, who has moments of genuine vitality. The hero, Lord Orville, is obviously derived from Richardson's rather pompous and priggish Sir Charles Grandison. The gradual development of Evelina's character as she moves in society – her doubts, hesitancies and agonizing embarrassments, and above all the analysis of her feelings for Lord Orville, also suggest Richardson. And the influence of Fielding is very much in evidence in the scenes of social comedy.

In *Evelina*, Fanny Burney showed how the various approaches of her great contemporaries could be combined and refined to produce what was the first thorough-going 'novel of manners'. Few writers have had a sharper eye or ear for all the little pretensions, hypocrisies, affections, and cruelties in behaviour and speech of men and women in society. In addition, through the Branghtons, Fanny Burney was able to tilt at the middle-class manners of the day, and at the pretensions and vulgarities of the *nouveaux riches*. *Evelina*, indeed, marks the first appearance of class discriminations and snobberies in English fiction, and in many ways anticipates the work of Jane Austen, the greatest of the novelists of social manners.

Things As They Are,
or The Adventures of Caleb Williams

William Godwin

No-one could be more closely involved, both personally and intellectually, with the early Romantic Movement in England than William Godwin. He was the husband of Mary Wollstonecraft, author of *Vindication of the Rights of Women* (1792), the pioneer work in the struggle for the liberation of women, and he wrote a remarkable memoir of her, (published in 1798) as well as a telling portrait in his novel *St Leon* (1799). His daughter, Mary Wollstonecraft (whose mother died in 1797 in giving birth to her) became the author of the famous romantic novel *Frankenstein* (1818) and the wife of the poet, Percy Bysshe Shelley. By his second marriage he became stepfather to 'Claire' Clairmont, who was subsequently Byron's mistress and mother of his illegitimate daughter, Allegra. And his political and philosophical ideas made him a tremendous influence not only on his daughter and son-in-law, but also on the young Wordsworth, Coleridge, Southey and other ardent spirits of the day who saw in the French Revolution of 1789 the promise of a renovation of human society through truth, reason and love.

William Godwin was born at Wisbech, Cambridge-shire, in 1756, son of a Nonconformist minister of strict Calvinistic views. He was educated for his father's profession and became an even more extreme Calvinist. But while he was a minister at Stowmarket, a friend introduced him to the works of the 'Philosophes' – the name given to a group of eighteenth-century French authors, among them Diderot, D'Alembert and Condorcet, who were sceptical in religion, materialist in philosophy and hedonist in ethics, and who played a considerable part in creating the climate of opinion in which the French Revolution of 1789 took place.

As a result, Godwin left his pulpit and came to London to preach, with his pen, his essentially anarchistic doctrine that while man was innately good, laws and institutions were evil, and that by the use of reason, which naturally taught benevolence, men could live in harmony without them. In 1793 he expounded these ideas in his monumental work, *The Inquiry concerning Political Justice, and Its Influence on General Virtue and Happiness*, one of the most potent books of the age.

Godwin did not advocate revolution and was always opposed to violence. Nevertheless, he believed that both the American and the French Revolution heralded the advent of a new political society based on man's perfectibility. This, combined with the fact that *Political Justice* in condemning *all* political institutions inevitably condemned the British monarchy, aristocracy, legislature and court system, meant that Godwin was looked on with considerable suspicion by the government of the day. It is said that Pitt, the Prime Minister, only withheld prosecution of Godwin because he believed the price of *Political Justice* was too high for it to be bought widely and do much harm. In fact, the working men's clubs used their funds to buy copies and read the book aloud to their members, and in addition, Godwin went on to present his ideas in the more easily available and understood form of a novel.

As Godwin himself has said, *Caleb Williams*, published in 1794, 'was the offspring of that temper of mind in which the composition of my *Political Justice* left me,' and he made his ideological purpose quite clear in his Preface to the novel. As, at this time, a number of his close political associates were being prosecuted for treason, the frightened publishers insisted on omitting the Preface, though it was included in the second edition after the Treason Trials of 1794 ended in acquittal. In any case, the contents of the novel itself were just as inflammatory, and the epigraph on the title-page indicates its overall intention:

> Amidst the woods the leopard knows his king;
> The tyger preys not on the tyger brood;
> Man only is the common foe of man.

Godwin, who was running a bookseller's business, went bankrupt in 1822, but this did not prevent him in the following year publishing his still valuable *History of the Commonwealth*. In 1833 (a year after the passing of the Great Reform Bill) Earl Grey's Whig government conferred on him an apartment in Palace Yard where he died in April, 1836.

Summary

Caleb Williams is the self-educated son of humble parents. Mr Collins, steward to the wealthy and cultured local squire, Ferdinando Falkland, obtains for Caleb the post of secretary to his master. Mr Falkland proves a kind and considerate employer, but is obviously haunted by some secret grief. Caleb's curiosity (his overriding 'spring of action', he admits) is piqued, and he questions Mr Collins about his employer's earlier life.

Collins explains that in his youth Mr Falkland had based his life on the old ideals of chivalry, which had inculcated in him an extreme concern for personal honour and reputation. Some years later, he had come into conflict with a neighbouring landowner named Barnabas Tyrrel, a typical representative of the privilege of wealth and birth, and has done his best to help the victims of Mr Tyrrel's tyranny. Among these had been a sturdy yeoman farmer named Hawkins, who had offended

Tyrrel by refusing to allow his son to enter his service, and who, when Tyrrel had threatened to dispossess him, had declared that the law was the same for the poor as for the rich – a mistaken assumption with 'things as they are', to repeat the first part of the title of the novel. Tyrrel had found all kinds of ways of persecuting Hawkins, including blocking his access to the main road by erecting gates and fences, and then when Hawkins's son had pulled them down, having him thrown into prison.

By the time Mr Falkland had returned from a visit to another part of the country, he had been too late to help Hawkins who had been forced to sell up and leave the neighbourhood, while his son, fearing that Tyrrel would see to it that his fellow-magistrates had him transported or hanged, had escaped from gaol.

These, and other acts of tyranny had made Tyrrel hated, while Falkland continued to win golden opinions for his benevolence and charity. Then Tyrrel, after he had knocked down his hated rival in a quarrel, had been found dead. Falkland had been a melancholy recluse ever since. The blows he had received from Tyrrel, together with the fact that he had been suspected of the murder until Hawkins and his son had been arrested and, on strong circumstantial evidence convicted and hanged for the crime, had wounded his hyper-sensitive pride beyond repair, distorting his innate nobility.

Caleb, though, becomes convinced that the real reason for his employer's melancholy is that *he* was the real murderer, and a curious cat-and-mouse game develops, with Caleb continually dropping hints and by ingenious turns of conversation seeking to trap Falkland into damaging admissions.

At length, unable to endure the torment any longer, Falkland confesses to Caleb that he was indeed the murderer. But now the situation is dramatically reversed, and it is Caleb who becomes the victim, and Falkland the persecutor. For although Caleb protests his undying devotion to his master, and swears to keep his secret for ever, his every move is regarded with suspicion and he finds himself a virtual prisoner.

After several attempts to persuade Falkland to release him, Caleb runs away, only to be arrested on a rigged charge of having robbed his employer and put into prison – and the sufferings he endures there lead to some typically Godwinian comments on the iniquities of the English penal system.

Caleb manages to escape, however, and falls in with a band of robbers. He is badly wounded by one of them, named Gines, but the leader, a Robin Hood type of robber, not only protects him but also believes in his innocence. He is so patently a man of innate goodness that Caleb urges him to give up his life of crime, but is told:

'It is now too late. Those very laws, which by a perception of their iniquity drove me to what I am, preclude my return.'

With 'things as they are', that is, there is no room for mercy or forgiveness.

During the absence of the leader of the band, Caleb overhears some of the other members plotting to betray him in order to obtain the reward that is being offered. He escapes and after various other adventures, reaches London. There, he disguises himself as a young Jew and scrapes a meagre living by hack journalism. Before long he learns to his horror that the robber Gines is now employed by Falkland as an instrument of his vengeance, and is already on his trail. Adopting various other disguises, Caleb tries desperately to find alternative means of employment, but eventually his remorseless pursuer catches up with him. Caleb protests his innocence to a magistrate, and for the first time reveals the reason for Falkland's persecution. But he is sent back to the prison from which he originally escaped.

To his astonishment, however, Falkland does not proceed with his charge and he is released – to be immediately seized by Gines and his fellows and carried into the presence of Falkland himself. Caleb is told by his former master that his only chance of escaping his persecution is to sign a paper declaring that the story he had told the magistrate is a lie. But Caleb, who values his reputation every bit as much as Falkland does his (in many ways they are mirror images), refuses.

Though vowing vengeance, Falkland lets him go, and even has a small sum of money delivered to him. But this is only part of the cat-and-mouse game which he is now, in his turn, playing with his victim. Caleb retreats to an obscure market-town in Wales, but when he has settled down, made friends, and believes himself secure, the reputation he values so highly is blasted by the rumours spread by Gines, who has once again tracked him down. Shunned by all his new-found friends, he becomes a wanderer and an outcast as surely as Frankenstein's monster in the famous tale by Godwin's daughter – a very symbol of 'natural man' hounded by the tyrannies and injustices of an unnatural system.

In his wanderings (the remorseless Gines always on his heels) Caleb comes near to madness and suicide. He tries once more to leave England, only to be confronted by Gines and informed that, if he wishes to avoid further imprisonment or worse, he must be 'a prisoner within the rules' and the rules do not include escape from England. Still Caleb refuses to be defeated. He writes down the record of his tormented life, determined that it will one day see the light of day, and so vindicate him. At the same time he also resolves, as a last resort, to lay a formal charge of murder (as distinct from the mere verbal accusation he had made before) against Falkland.

Falkland, now consumed by both hatred and remorse to a shadow of his former self, appears before the magistrates to hear his accuser. Caleb makes an impassioned speech, in which he describes how Falkland had confessed to him that he was the true murderer of Mr Tyrrel, and has relentlessly persecuted him ever since. At the same time he reveals the agony of his soul in betraying the trust of a man he had loved and revered. When Caleb has finished, Falkland throws himself into his arms, confesses that he has treated him with cruel injustice, and confesses too that he was the murderer of Tyrrel. His nobility has at last reasserted itself. He is taken to prison but he dies a few days later.

But Caleb can feel no triumph. He has himself, he believes, now been guilty of murder. He should he feels, have made the 'just experiment' – that appeal to reason and the innate goodness of man that lies at the root of Godwinian philosophy. Things being as they are, the noble qualities of Falkland, and whatever potentialities for good he himself possesses, have been wasted. So it must always be in society as it is at present constituted, for:

> ... of what use are talents and sentiments in the corrupt wilderness of human society? It is a rank and rotten soil from which every finer shrub draws poison as it grows. All that in a happier field and purer air would expand into virtue and germinate into general usefulness, is thus converted into henbane and deadly nightshade.

In consequence Caleb knows that he will be haunted by Falkland, and the 'true' relationship he might have had with him, for the rest of his life.

Critical commentary

It is evident that Godwin's political philosophy plays a considerable part in *Caleb Williams*, and he never loses sight of his two main objectives. The first of these is to illustrate the various forms of despotism; the second is to demonstrate the *un*natural inhumanity of man to man, brought about by institutions but always susceptible to reason and truth (Godwin insists that a reversal of behaviour is possible even in someone so far gone in obsession as Falkland). But it would certainly not be true to say that these objectives turn *Caleb Williams* into a mere work of propaganda – as some of Godwin's later novels tended to be. Some of his critics urged him to omit the more ideological passages from later editions of *Caleb Williams*; but in fact very few of them, even the most rhetorical, fail to justify themselves in terms of plot or character, or to form an integral part of the novel as a whole.

Godwin was very much aware of the artistic challenge posed in the writing of a novel. He wanted to convey the ideas of his *Political Justice* in fictional form, but only when they were genuinely firing his imagination. In a preface to an edition of his novel *Fleetwood*, published in 1832 (four years before his death), he constantly refers to the unusual inspiration that accompanied the writing of *Caleb Williams* and says that he 'wrote only when the afflatus was upon me'.

At a period when most novels were still loose and rambling in structure, Godwin was unique in his detailed and careful planning. An unusual feature about its composition is that he began by concentrating on the climax, writing the third volume first, 'then proceeded to my second, and last of all grappled with the first.' The result is that the earlier volumes, pregnant as they are with the ultimate denouement, generate a disturbing tension, while the climax itself is remarkably powerful in its apparent inevitability. In addition, this method of composition led to various shifts in time, place, and narrator which are technically most effective, and it would perhaps be no exaggeration to say that Godwin was the pioneer in the 'point of view' approach to fiction, which was one day to be brought to perfection by Henry James.

Equally effective technically is the double-take, whereby Caleb is first the pursuer of knowledge about the murder, and then his victim's victim – himself the pursued and outcast. The relationship between Falkland and Caleb is psychologically a most subtle one, for Godwin was one of the first novelists to realize that characterization is a matter of inner processes rather than of visible peculiarities.

> The thing in which my imagination revelled most freely was the analysis of the private and internal operations of the mind, employing my metaphysical dissecting knife in tracing and laying bare the involutions of motive, and recording the gradually accumulating impulses ...

It was a most prophetic statement as far as the future of the novel was concerned. *Caleb Williams*, in fact, is not only the first genuine political-philosophical novel, it is also the first psychological thriller, the first crime-detection novel, and the first novel of pursuit of the type later produced by novelists like Victor Hugo in *Les Misérables*, Robert Louis Stevenson in *The Master of Ballantrae*, and Graham Greene in *Brighton Rock*.

Caleb Williams, therefore, although the conditions and speculations with which it deals are those of the 1790s, is a novel which refuses to become dated. What William Hazlitt wrote about it in 1825 still holds good today:

> ... no one ever began *Caleb Williams* that did not read it through; no one that ever read it could possibly forget it, or speak of it after any length of time but with an impression as if the events and feelings had been personal to himself.

Pride and Prejudice

Jane Austen

Jane Austen, it is generally agreed, is one of the greatest
of all the English novelists. Yet her life, at any rate on
the surface, was quiet and uneventful. She was born in
1775, one of eight children, at Steventon in Hampshire,
where her father was rector for thirty-seven years. She received some education in her childhood from tutors in
Oxford, Reading, and Southampton, and at home from
her father, who took in pupils. She knew French well, and
had some Italian. She was fond of playing the piano,
singing ballads, and of private theatricals, needlework
and dancing. She was a precocious reader of eighteenth-
century fiction, including the French romances, and was
particularly fond of the novels of Richardson, Fielding
and Fanny Burney. By the age of twelve she was writing
sketches and stories for the amusement of her family. She
wrote an adolescent novel in letter form, called *Lady
Susan*, and completed her first full-length adult novel
about 1795 (when she was twenty), also written in letter
form and entitled *Elinor and Marianne*. Its purpose was
to show up the absurdity of the craze for sensibility. She
then went on to write *First Impressions*, and in 1797 wrote
a third novel, *Susan*, which was intended to ridicule the
Gothic vogue. About the same time she rewrote *Elinor
and Marianne*, dropping the epistolary technique. Her
father now offered the manuscript of *First Impressions* to

a publisher, but it was such a contrast to the novels of the day that it was summarily rejected. In 1803 another publisher did accept *Susan* but then got cold feet about publishing a book that dared to satirize the Gothic romances, and put the manuscript away in his files.

In 1801, Jane Austen's father retired, and the family settled in Bath. After his death four years later, the widow and her two unmarried daughters, Jane and Cassandra, moved to Southampton, where they lived in genteel poverty. In 1809, the family moved back to the Hampshire countryside, to a house in the village of Chawton, given to them by Jane's brother Edward. It was not far from the country house which had been bequeathed to Edward by a wealthy childless couple who had adopted him and made him their heir.

For ten years or more Jane Austen had apparently written nothing except the beginning of an unfinished novel called *The Watsons*. But in Southampton she had come across the manuscripts of her two earlier adult novels, and when the family had settled again in the country, she began re-working them. In 1811, when she was thirty-six years old, Jane Austen at last appeared in print, with *Sense and Sensibility* (as she had re-titled *Elinor and Marianne*), ascribed to 'A Lady' and brought out at her own expense. It was sufficiently successful to justify the publication in 1813 of *First Impressions* (which now became *Pride and Prejudice*).

Encouraged by the reception of *Sense and Sensibility*, she had already started work on a new novel, *Mansfield Park*, which appeared in 1814. At last her work had begun to attract attention, and her next novel, *Emma*, was issued in 1816 by John Murray, the most influential publisher of the day. She began work on a new novel, *Persuasion*, and her brother also bought back the manuscript of *Susan*, which she now revised and re-titled *Northanger Abbey*. She began another novel called *Sanditon*, but failing health forced her to give it up. In 1817 her family took her to Winchester to be near medical attention, but she died some months later, at the age of forty-one. *Northanger Abbey* and *Persuasion* were published the following year.

Jane Austen never married, though there is some evidence that she had a suitor who died, and apart from the spells spent in Bath and Southampton and occasional visits to London, to seaside resorts on the south coast, and to the homes of various friends and relations, she spent most of her life in the country within the family circle.

Summary

It seems almost miraculous that out of such a background a novel as mature and artistically complete and satisfying as *Pride and Prejudice* should emerge. The note of assurance is struck in the very first sentence:

> It is a truth universally acknowledged, that a single
> man in possession of a good fortune, must be in want of
> a wife.

That precise, economical and ironic sentence leads to a masterly conversation between the rather vulgar Mrs Bennet and her sardonic husband – and to the crux of the novel. For a single man in possession of a good fortune *does* come into the neighbourhood, in the person of young Mr Charles Bingley, who, with his two sisters, has rented a house called Netherfield Park, and Mrs Bennet, insists that her husband call on the new arrivals.

Mr Bennet does so – and his eldest daughter, Jane, and Bingley fall in love. Bingley's friend, the proud and aristocratic Fitzwilliam Darcy, is also attracted to the second Bennet girl, the lively and intelligent Elizabeth, her father's favourite. But Darcy offends Elizabeth by his supercilious behaviour at a ball, and her dislike is increased by the account given her by a young officer in the militia named George Wickham son of Darcy's former steward of the unjust treatment he has (according to him) received from Darcy. The aversion is further intensified when Darcy and Bingley's sisters, disgusted with the vulgar behaviour of Mrs Bennet and her youngest daughters, set out to effect the separation of Bingley and Jane.

Darcy's pride is reflected in exaggerated form in his arrogant aunt, Lady Catherine de Bourgh. She is patroness to a pompous young clergyman, William Collins, who is awed to a point of grovelling ecstasy by her favour. Mr Collins is a nephew of Mr Bennet whose estate, in the absence of sons, is entailed to him. Lady Catherine advises Mr Collins to marry, and he decides to ask one of the elder Bennet girls to be his wife. Jane, he understands, is no longer free, so he settles on Elizabeth. The proposal scene that follows is one of the highlights of English comedy, besides counterpointing, with superb irony, the whole theme of love and marriage, true and false, on which the novel is based.

Elizabeth, of course, rejects her cousin's proposal, and Mr Collins marries her great friend Charlotte Lucas instead. This is an important link in the plot, for it is on a visit to the Collins couple that Elizabeth again meets Darcy who is staying with his aunt, the redoubtable Lady Catherine. Darcy is still attracted to Elizabeth, but he proposes to her in terms so full of pride and contempt for her inferior social station that she indignantly rejects him and accuses him of separating her sister Jane from Bingley, and of ill-treating Wickham. Darcy sends her a letter which proves the baselessness of the latter accusation, and reveals that Wickham is an unprincipled adventurer. On a trip to the north of England with her uncle and aunt, Elizabeth visits Pemberley, Darcy's country house in Derbyshire, believing its owner to be absent. However, Darcy appears, welcomes the visitors courteously, and introduces them to his sister.

Wickham now elopes with Elizabeth's younger sister Lydia. Darcy traces the fugitives, brings about their marriage, and generously provides for them. When Bingley returns to the Bennet neighbourhood, he and Jane become engaged – and Darcy woos and wins Elizabeth.

Darcy's pride and Elizabeth's prejudice have both been mitigated by experience, and because their feelings for each other are based on a realistic assessment of each other's characters, rather than on romantic illusions, they make a marriage of deep and genuine love. This process of realistic self-discovery is central to all Jane Austen's work.

Critical commentary

In reading *Pride and Prejudice*, it is perhaps the air of assurance, the easy but firm control of the material and the economy of means employed to achieve it, that more than anything else make it seem that the stage of experimentation and exploration in the novel has been left behind, and that the kind of fiction has arrived which the modern reader can enjoy without being unduly aware of the date at which it was written.

It has a maturity which was quite unrecognized at the time. By the beginning of the nineteenth century, the novel was showing signs of decline. The fashion for romantic 'sensibility' and Gothic thrills was resulting in unreal and melodramatic plots, and as the booksellers and circulating libraries tried to meet, and stimulate, the demand for fiction, there was a general lowering of standards. The six novels of Jane Austen, published between 1811 and 1818, marked a restoration of status for the form and also the achievement of its maturity.

There have been some critics, it is true, who have felt that the narrowness of her life inevitably imposed limitations on her work. G. K. Chesterton, for example, wrote:

> There is not a shadow of indication anywhere that this independent intellect and laughing spirit was other than contented with a narrow domestic routine, in which she wrote a story as domestic as a diary in the intervals of pies and puddings, without so much as looking out of the window to notice the French Revolution.

Certainly Jane Austen had little contact with the outside world. One of her nieces recorded that she could not recall 'any word or expression of Aunt Jane's that had reference to public events.' The limitations, however, have been exaggerated, and Jane Austen's life was not as remote from the outside world as these comments suggest. In 1797, for example, her brother Henry married his cousin Elizabeth, whose first husband, the Comte de Feuillade, had been guillotined during the Terror in France. Two other brothers were in the Royal Navy during the Napoleonic Wars, and both eventually became admirals.

Beneath the calm surface of Jane Austen's novels, moreover, the events of the day *do* make an impact – to a degree appropriate to the lives of ordinary middle-class country people of the time. This, in *Pride and Prejudice*, there is the advent of the militia, with its devastating effect on the lives of the local girls in general, and on Lydia and the Bennet family in particular. All her other novels have similar topical references, but they are so unobtrusively placed that they are easily overlooked. At the same time, it must be remembered that three of Jane Austen's novels (*Sense and Sensibility*, *Pride and Prejudice*, and *Northanger Abbey*) were written before the end of the eighteenth century, and the kind of social world she depicted was in essence an eighteenth-century one.

Much of Jane Austen's strength, indeed, lies in her acceptance of her limitations. She knew exactly what she could do, and what she ought to avoid. When the authorship of her novels became known and she achieved some modest fame, she received a message from the Prince Regent, through his librarian, that she was 'at liberty to dedicate any future book to HRH'. The librarian offered the suggestion that she might write 'an historical romance illustrative of the august House of Coburg'. Jane Austen's reply was:

I could no more write a romance than an epic poem. I could not sit down seriously to write a serious romance under any other motive than to save my life; and if it were indispensable for me to keep it up and never relax into laughing at myself or at any other, I am sure I should be hung before I had finished the first chapter. I must keep to my own style and go on my own way.

Her own way, she knew, was one of precision and carefully controlled economy. After a visit to a picture gallery she wrote that she had seen some paintings she liked, 'among them a miniature ... which exactly suited *my* capacity.' In another letter she described her fiction as 'the little bit (two inches wide) of ivory on which I work with so fine a brush ...' And again, in a letter to one of her nieces who was herself beginning a novel, she wrote:

You are now collecting your people delightfully, getting them exactly into such a spot as is the delight of my life; – three or four families in a country village is the very thing to work on.

At the same time it always seems, in reading Jane Austen, that the reduction in scale is not a matter of restricted experience or interest but of deliberate technique. R. W. Chapman has put it very neatly: 'She knows all the details, and gives us very few of them.' In consequence, there is always a sense of powers held in reserve and this creates a kind of tension which draws out the active imagination both in her characters and in her readers. The relegation of the great events of her time to the background – or rather just below the surface of her narrative – does not therefore lessen the scope of her art. Her world is as formal and stylized as one of the ballroom dances of her youth. Elizabeth and Darcy first meet in a ballroom and the changes in their relationship to one another thereafter have something of the formal movements of an eighteenth-century dance as they meet, circle cautiously round each other, then sharply retreat, to hover round each other again until, after further approaches and withdrawals, they unite as partners.

Some of the Romantics found this formal approach chilling – among them, another great woman novelist, Charlotte Brontë, born a year before Jane Austen died, who complained that 'Anything like warmth or enthusiasm, anything energetic, poignant, heartfelt,' was completely absent in Jane Austen's work:

> She does her business of delineating the surface of the
> lives of genteel English people curiously well. There is a
> Chinese fidelity, a miniature delicacy, in the painting. She
> ruffles her reader by nothing vehement, disturbs him
> by nothing profound ... What sees keenly, speaks aptly,
> moves flexibly, it suits her to study: but what throbs fast
> and full, though hidden, what the blood rushes through,
> what is the unseen seat of life and the sentient target of
> death – this Miss Austen ignores.

It is true that the conventions of the eighteenth-century society in which Jane Austen set her novels prohibited any open display of passion, but is the emotional life of *Pride and Prejudice* as thin as Charlotte Brontë maintained? It is important to remember, for one thing, that in all her novels Jane Austen insists that true love is the only possible basis for marriage. She is sympathetic and understanding towards Charlotte Lucas when she marries Mr Collins, on the grounds that even he is better than no husband at all; but she leaves her readers in no doubt that such a course would be unthinkable for Elizabeth, and indeed even for the more pliable Jane. Jane Austen is just as firm and consistent in her condemnation of marriage based on a mere infatuation that has not stood the test of knowledge and experience. That, after all, is the whole point of Lydia's elopement with Wickham. It should be noted, in this connection, that Elizabeth herself is for a time attracted to Wickham, while it later transpires that Darcy's sister Georgina had also been dazzled by him. Jane Austen, of course, is not explicit about this as most modern novelists would be, but it is obvious enough that the attraction of Wickham, in his dashing officer's uniform, is, quite simply, a sexual one. What Jane Austen is in effect saying is that this, by itself, is a dangerously inadequate basis for marriage. Indeed, there is always present the warning of Mr and Mrs Bennet's marriage, in which the wife has become sillier with the years, while the husband has retreated into his library and into a stultifying sarcasm, which makes him incapable of effective action when he hears of Lydia's elopement. The implication here is quite clear: that Mr and Mrs Bennet have only themselves to blame for their flighty daughter's behaviour. The Victorian critic, A. C. Bradley, described Jane Austen's novels as 'The Parents' Assistant, in six volumes'.

The whole point of *Pride and Prejudice* is that successful marriage can only be founded on deep love – and that depth can only be achieved through the genuine community of interests, mutual understanding and, above all, self-knowledge. The 'dance' in which Elizabeth and Darcy are engaged brings them closer and closer to these goals, and therefore to each other. They do not merely attract each other in the physical sense – they also bring each other out, force each other to radical reassessments of their individual characters, help to mould each other anew, and thus work towards their mutual fulfilment.

Elizabeth has to learn not only that her 'first impressions' were wrong in point of fact, in that Wickham's tale of Darcy's injustice towards him was a concoction, but also that she has areas in her character that are narrow and unyielding. She has to learn that she is her father's daughter, that she, too, is prone to make cleverness, witticism and irony a substitute for sound and humane assessment. The elopement of Lydia is the great crisis in her psychological development, shocking her into the realization that her whole family is tainted with a species of prejudice – in the extended sense of the term as lack of right judgement; that she herself is as much a Bennet as

Lydia; and that, as far as Darcy is concerned (he has already made his first unacceptably haughty proposal) 'every kind of pride' must revolt at the very idea of being connected to such a family, and of being a brother-in-law to Wickham.

Indeed, the elopement is the catalyst for the whole relationship between Elizabeth and Darcy. At the very point when Elizabeth thinks she has lost him, *he* has learned *his* lessons too. He has already admitted that his upbringing has predisposed him to haughtiness; he has already been shocked by his aunt's gross arrogance towards Elizabeth and her family; but, as his first proposal to Elizabeth had shown, he had not gone far enough in his self-purification. Elizabeth's indignant rejection, however, has forced him to further self-examination. He has grappled with the full extent of his pride and snobbery; he has come to realize that his own sister had behaved in a way not so very different from that of Lydia Bennet; and now the elopement gives him the chance, by the decisiveness and generosity of his actions, to prove to Elizabeth the full extent of his self-knowledge and so of his love. It is a redemption *through* love. Without this mutual testing of the hero and heroine, *Pride and Prejudice* would be little more than a kind of Cinderella story of a poor girl winning her prince. As it is, Elizabeth and Darcy prove their love in the fire of experience, and the hard shell of their egoism, their pride and their prejudice, is burned away.

Emma

Jane Austen

Emma, published in 1816, is usually regarded as the peak of Jane Austen's art. It was the novel she dedicated to the Prince Regent, because she felt she could hardly evade the strong hint conveyed to her from him. There is a touch of irony about this, for not only did she strongly disapprove of the Prince Regent for his notorious immorality, but *Emma* is as far removed from the kind of historical fiction about 'the august House of Coburg', which the Prince Regent's librarian had suggested, as could possibly be imagined. It is in many ways the quietest and least eventful of all Jane Austen's novels. The heroine is the only one who does not pass a single night away from home, and Jane Austen's younger contemporary and fellow-novelist, Susan Ferrier, complained: 'There is no story whatsoever.'

This is an exaggeration, but it is certainly true that in *Emma* Jane Austen deliberately reduced the usual 'machinery' of plot to a minimum. Nevertheless, *Emma* contains abundant vitality and interest, not so much in the external details of the plot as in the working out of the theme in terms of the heroine's inner life. Although she is subjected to the same process of self-discovery as Jane Austen's other heroines, and forced by it to the same kind of agonizing reappraisals in her pilgrimage from illusion to reality, Emma is more introverted than any of the others – as indeed the use of her name for the title (the only occasion Jane Austen does this) indicates.

Summary

This introverted quality in Emma Woodhouse is emphasized, as the novel opens, by the isolation in which she finds herself. Her mother died when she was a child, and her elder sister Isabella has been married for some years and lives in London, so that Emma, at twenty, is very much used to being mistress of Hartfield, her indulgent and valetudinarian father's country mansion near the village of Highbury. In addition, Emma's former governess and close friend, Miss Taylor, has recently married a local gentleman named Mr Weston and her departure has left a large gap at Hartfield and in Emma's life there. Her father can give her little real companionship and defers to her on all important issues. His hypochondria (he finds it impossible to believe that dishes that disagree with him might be acceptable to other people) is an exaggerated reflection of her own self-centredness. Emma is, in effect, locked up inside Hartfield as securely as any fairy-tale princess in her enchanted castle; moreover, she is not only the 'fair mistress of the mansion', but also of the whole novel. In Jane Austen's other books the heroine is paired with a sister or a brother, or at any rate with someone at a similar social level as herself, so that more than one point of view is available, but in *Emma* there is only the heroine. Not only does Emma's consciousness pervade the novel, but in a sense it also creates it, insofar as the plot concerns her subjective illusions and their effects.

While she was working on the novel, it was reported that Jane Austen said: 'I am going to take a heroine whom none but myself will much like.' This raises the interesting possibility that Emma is to some extent a self-portrait, a frank assessment of the disadvantages and dangers of the creative life. Certainly Emma is under the impression that she can mould those around her in accordance with her fantasies. When, in the first chapter, Mr Knightley, a thirty-eight-year-old widower and an old friend and neighbour, calls at Hartfield, Emma tells him that it was she who 'made the match' between Miss Taylor and Mr Weston. Mr Knightley sharply points out that the people concerned were quite capable of managing their own affairs.

It is evident that Mr Knightley belongs unequivocally to the real world, and that he sees the truth about Emma and is not afraid to speak it. 'Emma knows I never flatter her,' he says, and he points out to her at various stages in the story that she likes to be above 'sober facts'; that she is reluctant to submit to 'a subjection of the fancy to the understanding'; that she has a mind 'delighted with its own ideas' and therefore commits 'errors of imagination'; and that when she takes up an idea she seeks to make reality 'bend' to it.

In an attempt to fill the gap left in her life by the departure of Miss Taylor, Emma now takes under her wing a pretty but empty-headed seventeen-year-old girl, named Harriet Smith, the natural daughter of some person unknown.

Harriet accepts the role in which Emma has cast her. She enters into Emma's fantasy that her parentage must be an elevated one, and agrees accordingly to give up her 'bad acquaintance' with a young farmer named Robert Martin, whose proposal of marriage she rejects on Emma's advice – much to the annoyance of Mr Knightley who is Martin's landlord and who has a high regard for him. The fact that Emma sees Harriet as a projection of herself is revealed to the reader by all kinds of subtle touches. When Mr Elton, the young Vicar, praises Emma for the improvements she has wrought in her protegée, he says 'Skilful has been the hand' almost as if he were referring to a model in clay – or to the watercolour portrait of Harriet which Emma has in fact painted. It is Mr Elton whom Emma has decided upon as a proper match for her creation, but he refuses to conform to her scenario. When he proposes marriage, it is not to Harriet but to Emma herself. For the first time Emma has to admit that she has been wrong. She feels she has been 'disgraced by misjudgment', and resolves in future to repress her imagination and to be more humble. It is the formal declaration of error that Jane Austen demands of all her heroines, and the first step in Emma's salvation.

By a masterly stroke of irony, Mr Elton eventually marries a woman who in her outrageous conceit and self-satisfaction is a kind of blown-up caricature of Emma's own worst characteristics. Although Emma has been chastened by the fiasco of her first attempt in matchmaking on Harriet's behalf, she has by no means learned her lesson. Frank Churchill, the son of Mr Weston by a former marriage, who lives with a tyrannical old aunt who has made him her heir and whose surname he has adopted, now appears on the scene. His arrival has several times been announced and then postponed, and this has given Emma ample opportunity to create for herself a picture of what he ought to be like. Thus, she has the 'decided intention of finding him pleasant', and gives Mr Knightley a detailed list of Frank's supposed qualities which bears hardly any relation to the reality. Soon her fertile imagination is working in an old channel, although she struggles against the temptation. In other words she thinks of Frank as a substitute for Mr Elton and exhorts Harriet to forget her disappointment over him, hinting at the possibility of another suitor. At the same time an odd kind of flirtation develops between Frank and herself. He is gallant and flattering, though there is a teasing, rather mysterious element in his behaviour, and Emma is not really sure whether she is attracted to him or not. This ambivalent relationship seems to bring out in Emma a certain archness with rather unpleasant undertones. This shows itself primarily in relation to Jane Fairfax, a beautiful young woman who is staying with her aunt, Miss Bates, the impoverished, garrulous, but irrepressibly good-natured daughter of a former vicar of Highbury. Jane, the orphan daughter of an army officer, had been adopted by her father's general and brought up with his own daughter. This girl, who is very plain, has married the highly eligible Mr Dixon. Emma picks up various indications from Miss Bates's stream of chatter and, completely misinterpreting them, constructs out of them a guilty relationship between Jane and Mr Dixon. Knowing that Frank is acquainted with Jane, Emma makes all kinds of sly innuendoes about Jane and Mr Dixon to him, and he appears to join in the game.

Although she does not yet realize it, Frank Churchill is leading Emma in the direction of the one man who does possess the key which might release her from the prison of the self. This is conveyed in one of Jane Austen's most beautifully symbolic scenes, a ball at the Crown Inn given by the Westons and attended by all the main characters, including Jane Fairfax and Harriet. As in *Pride and Prejudice*, Jane Austen makes subtle use of the imagery of the dance. It is Frank who is Emma's first partner, but Frank is in an odd, distracted frame of mind. At the same time she is 'more disturbed by Mr Knightley not dancing than by anything else,' and she notices his 'tall, firm, upright figure' and tells herself that '... excepting her own partner, there was not one among the whole row of young men who could be compared with him.' Frank Churchill has taken her on to the dance floor, but it is Mr Knightley who leads her off it.

After the ball, Emma reverts to her plan for bringing Frank and Harriet together. Circumstances seem to conspire in favour of it. Frank rescues Harriet from a band of menacing gypsies. Surely such an adventure – 'a fine young man and a lovely young woman thrown together in such a way' – must, Emma feels, suggest 'certain ideas to the coldest heart and the steadiest brain.'

After an expedition to Donwell Abbey, Mr Knightley's home, where Emma is surprised to see him deep in conversation with Harriet, the party assembles for a picnic at Box Hill. This turns into another of Jane Austen's masterly symbolic scenes. Emma sits apart from the others, as if willing herself to cling to her old fantasy life, while Frank reports her wishes to the others – 'She requires something very entertaining from each of you', and so on – as if he were a magician's assistant. Emma is above being entertained by poor, gentle Miss Bates's chatter, which, if she had but realized it, is the very embodiment of the formlessness and inconsequentiality of real life. Instead she is rude to her, and when, as a result, Mr Knightley reprimands her, Emma's genuine mortification and regret mark another step on her way out of her prison.

Further steps soon follow. It is revealed that Frank Churchill has all along been secretly engaged to Jane Fairfax. The news has a profound effect on Emma. Frank has behaved badly in flirting with her, and pretending to join in her fantasies about Jane as a means of preserving his secret; but Emma realizes that he has only been playing her own game of fantasy. The fact, indeed, that he has outdone and outwitted her is the bitterest part of her humiliation. The revelation of the falsity of his make-believe is the final demonstration of the falsity of her own. At last she is able to confess openly that 'with common sense ... I am afraid I have had little to do.'

One further shock is necessary, however, before Emma can finally emerge into the reality of her own feelings. When she consoles Harriet on the loss of yet another potential suitor, Harriet confounds her with the announcement that the man she loves is Mr Knightley and that she has reason to believe that he returns her love. As Emma digests this information, she asks herself why she is so shaken by it – and then, 'It darted through her with the speed of an arrow, that Mr Knightley must marry no-one but herself!'

Now at last the walls of Emma's self-enchantment have fallen, and she knows she is ready for Mr Knightley and the world of reality he represents – now, when apparently it is too late. But in fact poor Harriet has been deluded – only too apt a pupil of Emma – mistaking Mr Knightley's kindness for love, while Mr Knightley himself has also had to undergo a minor purgation of his own by discovering, through his jealousy of Frank Churchill, the real depths of his feeling for Emma.

Emma now hears to her infinite relief that Harriet has recovered from her infatuation for Mr Knightley, and that she has received a second proposal of marriage from Robert Martin and accepted him. The secret of Harriet's birth also comes to light; she is the illegitimate daughter of a tradesman, not of some grand personage as Emma had imagined. And so, with her romantic edifice finally demolished, Emma can look forward with a clear conscience to her own marriage.

Critical commentary

In reading *Emma*, the plot, despite the paucity of incident, does not in fact seem at all thin, so rich is the texture and patterning, and so much 'felt life' (to use Henry James's phrase) does it contain. Emma herself is a subtle, and at times profound, psychological study, and Mr Knightley is the perfect foil for her: wise, solid, practical, yet tender and compassionate – probably the most likeable of all Jane Austen's heroes. Harriet and Frank Churchill, emanations of Emma's consciousness though they may in part be for much of the novel, nevertheless convince as personalities in their own right. The novel is notable, too, for the complete absence of mere 'type' characters: even the most minor of them – the tradespeople of Highbury, for example – register as individuals, while the valetudinarian Mr Woodhouse, the thick-skinned and conceited Mrs Elton, and the talkative Miss Bates, are among Jane Austen's most successful comic eccentrics.

Miss Bates is of particular interest, because her long, rambling discourses are so much at variance with Jane Austen's usual restraint and economy. She herself was a little uneasy on this score: 'Miss Bates excellent', she noted, 'but rather too much of her.' Nevertheless, Miss

Bates, besides being delightful in herself, fulfils a most important function in the novel. Buried in her rambling monologues about soups, baked apples, chimneys, ribbons, spectacles, carriages, visits, shops, errand-boys, and a thousand other things, are the simple truths about the outside world which Emma has to learn. It is largely through Miss Bates that the sense of Highbury as a bustling community is created. From her we learn, for instance, that Mr Abdy, once parish clerk to Miss Bates's father, is bedridden; that his son, an ostler at the Crown Inn, is consulting Mr Elton about parish relief for his father; that John Saunders mends spectacles; that Mrs Wallis keeps a bakery – and so on.

In direct description, too, *Emma* is frequently more graphic than any of Jane Austen's other novels, often with a detailed, almost documentary realism that is new to her work – as in the descriptions of the village shops, their proprietors and their customers. Other parts of the rural community are depicted with the same kind of particularity – Mr Knightley's Donwell Abbey, for example, and Robert Martin's Abbey Mill Farm.

All this adds to the richness of *Emma*, as well as affording, by the very vividness and sharp-edged nature of the detail, the most effective contrast imaginable to the insubstantial fancies that haunt Emma's brain. And Jane Austen also uses nature itself, to a degree unusual in her novels (suggesting that she was not altogether immune from the influence of the Romantics) as a means of drawing Emma out of her subjective fastness. Quite often she makes weather and season chime with mood in a manner that anticipates George Eliot and Thomas Hardy. Thus, the enclosed boredom of Hartfield is conveyed by the 'cold stormy rain' which is 'despoiling' the trees and shrubs. Similarly, when Emma hears that Frank Churchill is at last arriving, she thinks she can see signs that the elder is about to flower in the hedgerows and she detects 'a look of spring, a tender smile' even in Harriet.

It is significant, too, that the chapter in which the

misunderstandings between Emma and Mr Knightley are sorted out, and in which he makes his declaration of love, takes place away from the stuffy confines of Hartfield House and begins with a description of Emma as she runs out of doors to revel in 'the exquisite sight, smell and sensation of nature, tranquil, warm and brilliant after a storm' – and sees 'Mr Knightley passing through the garden door and coming towards her ...' The passage gives a special point and poignancy to the simple words with which, after the proposal scene, the next chapter opens: 'What totally different feelings did Emma take back into the house from what she had brought out!'

The Heart of Midlothian

Walter Scott

Walter Scott was born in Edinburgh in 1771, the son of
a prosperous attorney. As a result of an illness which left
him with a crippled leg, he spent much of his childhood
on his grandfather's farm in the Border country between
England and Scotland, where his imagination was fired
by the local history, legends and folk-songs. He was educated at Edinburgh High School and University, apprenticed to his father, and eventually called to the Scottish
Bar in 1792.

As a young man, Scott joined the thriving literary
coterie in Edinburgh and met many Scottish writers there,
including Robert Burns. When he was twenty-five, he
translated several of the ballads of the German Romantic
poets, then much in fashion. This led him to compose
ballads of his own, and also to collect and edit (with great
skill and scholarship) three volumes of the folk poetry he
had loved as a boy. These were published in 1802–1803,
under the title *Minstrelsy of the Scottish Border*.

At this stage, Scott had no thought of being anything
but a spare-time writer. In 1797 he had married the
daughter of a French Royalist refugee and two years later
he had been appointed Deputy-sheriff of Selkirkshire.
Then in 1805, the tremendous success of his long romantic
poem *The Lay of the Last Minstrel* (also based on legends
of his beloved Border country) made him think of turning

to literature as his main profession. He became partner, with his old school friend James Ballantyne, in a printing and publishing business, and invested heavily in it, especially after *Marmion* (1808) and *The Lady of the Lake* (1810) – both dealing with romantic episodes in Scotland's past and both in effect novels in verse – proved even more spectacular successes.

With part of the proceeds, Scott began to build a country home for himself at Abbotsford in the Border country on the banks of the Tweed. It was a typically Romantic baronial mansion and he filled it with all sorts of 'romantic' antiquities. He also helped to found the *Edinburgh Review* (but seceded because it was too Whig in its politics) and later the Tory *Quarterly Review*, and devoted himself to several massive enterprises of literary and historical scholarship.

About this time, Byron's narrative poems began to re-place Scott's as the bestsellers of the day, and his income rapidly dwindled. Determined not to change his way of life, he turned to the seven chapters of a novel which he had written some eight years before and thrown amongst his fishing tackle. He now completed the novel, which he called *Waverley*, but was so dubious about its chances that he published it anonymously in 1814. In fact *Waverley* was a tremendous success. Set at the time of the Jaco-bite rising of 1745 (the last armed attempt to restore the exiled royal house of Stuart to the British throne) it re-vealed qualities quite new to fiction. For one thing, it was set in the recent past and was based on careful his-torical research, including conversations with survivors of the rebellion. Its backgrounds, too, were absolutely authentic. In other words, it was utterly removed from the mock-mediaevalism of the Gothic novels. For another thing, *Waverley* revealed a genuine and profound histori-cal insight. It led Scott to concentrate on a moment of crisis in which two worlds confronted each other – the dying feudal world of the Gaelic clans of the Scottish Highlands, and the rising commercial and industrial world of Hanoverian England. At the same time it preserved a careful balance, for the hero, Edward Waverley, a young English soldier, falls in love with the proud Highland lass Flora MacIvor, but eventually marries a gentle girl from a Lowlands family opposed to the rebellion. Scott himself was a staunch supporter of the Hanoverian regime and believed that the social and economic changes in the prosperous Lowlands of Scotland that were destroying the last vestiges of the feudalism of the Highlands, were inevitable. In this he was a realist and an anti-sentimentalist. At the same time, he deplored the ugliness and inhumanity of the new industrialism as deeply as the most revolutionary of the Romantics. Furthermore, he was a patriot who was aware of the economic subjection of his country to England, and who understood to the depths of his being the pathos and tragedy attending the death-throes of the old Scottish way of life. These ambivalences underlie all the Waverley Novels – the term applied to the novels by Scott dealing with various periods of Scottish history – and provide the tensions which constitute their main strength.

These novels now flowed from Scott's pen at the astonishing rate of between two and three a year for the next ten years. They included *Guy Mannering*, (published in 1815 and composed, incredible though it may seem, in six weeks) which is set in the eighteenth century and is about the economic decay of an aristocratic Scottish family; *Old Mortality* (1816), which deals with the uprising of the fanatical Presbyterian Covenanters in 1679; *Rob Roy* (1817), whose hero is based on an actual Highland outlaw of the period of the earlier Jacobite rebellion of 1715; and then, in 1818, *The Heart of Midlothian*.

Other novels of Scottish history followed, but in 1819 came a change of direction with the publication of *Ivanhoe*, set not in Scotland, but in the England of the Middle Ages. Two further novels set in the period of the Crusades – *The Betrothed* and *The Talisman* were published in 1825.

In 1820, the new King, George IV, made Scott a baronet, the first time a professional writer had been thus honoured. All this time, Scott (who did not admit his authorship of the Waverley Novels until 1827) was leading an astonishing double life. In his *persona* of country gentleman he held open house at Abbotsford for a constant stream of guests, with whom he spent the days in fishing, shooting, and riding. At the same time, he somehow managed conscientiously to fulfil his official legal duties. As a rule, therefore, it was only at night that he was able to write, and, not surprisingly, his health suffered. Then, in 1826, Scott found himself involved in the financial ruin of the Ballantyne firm. Refusing to accept either bankruptcy or help from friends and admirers, and in spite of his grief at the death of his wife and the discovery that his much-loved grandson was incurably ill, Scott heroically stepped up his fantastic output, compiling a huge *Life of Napoleon* which involved the most onerous research, a long *History of Scotland* and other miscellaneous works, as well as keeping up his phenomenal output of fiction. Eventually he died of overwork in 1832, by which time he had paid off over half his debts, the remainder being cleared after his death by the sale of most of his copyrights. In seventeen years, he had written (quite apart from all his other voluminous publications) no less than twenty-nine novels.

Summary

The Heart of Midlothian is generally recognized as Scott's masterpiece. In it he is looking at his country a generation after the Treaty of Union of 1707, whereby England and Scotland were incorporated into the United Kingdom of Great Britain with a single parliament at Westminster. The historical background of the novel is that of the Porteous riot of 1736. This had been brought about by the action of John Porteous (Captain-Lieutenant of the Edinburgh City Guard) in causing the death of a number of citizens by ordering his men to fire at the crowd on the occasion of the hanging of a robber and smuggler named Wilson. This man had made himself popular by the brave manner in which he had earlier helped an associate named Robertson to escape from the Tolbooth, the old Edinburgh prison known ironically as 'the Heart of Midlothian'. Porteous had been arrested for the civilian shootings and tried and sentenced to death by the Scottish judges, but was reprieved by the English Secretary of State. Enraged by this apparent interference from London, at a time when many Scots felt that the Act of Union had imposed an alien rule on Scotland, the Edinburgh mob, headed by Robertson, stormed the Tolbooth, seized Porteous, and hanged him.

In the novel, there is in the Tolbooth at the time of the Porteous riot a young woman named Effie Deans, accused of infanticide. Effie is the younger daughter of 'Douce Davie Deans' a prosperous peasant farmer and a Cameronian – an adherent of an extreme Presbyterian sect formed in the previous century by Richard Cameron, one of the leading supporters of the National Covenant of 1638 which swore to defend the Protestant religion. Through Davie Deans, therefore, Scott introduces another strand into the historical texture of his novel.

Effie's lover (and the father of the child she is accused of murdering) is George Staunton, a young man of good family (roughly based on the real-life Robertson). During the raid on the Tolbooth he breaks into Effie's cell, but – sunk in shame at the disgrace of having borne an illegitimate child, and stunned by grief at its supposed death – Effie refuses to escape.

Meanwhile, Reuben Butler, a Presbyterian minister engaged to Effie's elder half-sister Jeanie, has been seized by the rioters and forced to administer the last offices to Porteous before he is hanged. Later, on his way home, Butler is accosted by a mysterious stranger who bids him tell Jeanie that, if she wants to save Effie, she must meet him at a remote spot near her home. Jeanie, who has been brought up in her father's stern religion, and believing that Effie's disgrace affects the whole family, breaks off her engagement to Reuben. But her conscience is soon confronted with an even harder trial. She keeps the appointment with the stranger, who turns out to be George Staunton. He tells her he has discovered that, by Scottish law, Effie would almost certainly be acquitted of infanticide if it can be proved that she did not seek to conceal her pregnancy. If, therefore, Effie confided her condition to Jeanie, she can be saved. Greatly distressed, Jeanie explains that Effie had told her nothing. Before their conversation is ended, Staunton is warned of the approach of officers of the law by a verse of an old ballad sung by Madge Wildfire, the insane daughter of Meg Murdockson, the old harridan who had attended Effie in her confinement.

Jeanie explains her predicament to her father, who tells her to follow her own conscience, but in ambiguous terms that reveal the agony of his mind. With the help of the taciturn and uncouth Laird of Dumbiedikes who is in love with Jeanie, counsel are engaged to defend Effie. But when Jeanie is called to the witness stand, she cannot – after taking the solemn oath to tell the whole truth on the Bible she has been taught to revere – break the training of a lifetime by telling the lie that would save her sister, and Effie is therefore condemned to death.

Jeanie now sets out for London on foot, determined to obtain a pardon for Effie. After many adventures on the road, including an encounter with Madge Wildfire, she manages to obtain an interview in London with the Duke of Argyle. Impressed by Jeanie's simplicity and honesty, the Duke obtains for her an audience with Queen Caroline. Jeanie's eloquent appeal on behalf of her sister touches the Queen's heart and she does indeed arrange for a pardon for Effie, which stipulates, however, that she must leave her native country for a period of fourteen years.

Back home, Jeanie, after a series of misunderstandings, is at last married to Reuben Butler as a result of the good offices of the Duke of Argyle who has returned to Scotland. The Duke also places Davie Deans on a comfortable farm on his estates. Effie, exiled in England, marries her lover who has now become Sir George Staunton.

Eventually, it turns out that the child whom Effie had been accused of murdering had in fact been carried off by Meg Murdockson, who had handed him over to a band of outlaws. Sir George and his wife come to Scotland to look for him. In an affray with a robber band, however, the boy kills Sir George (though without realizing he is his father), and then escapes to America. Effie, after 'blazing nearly ten years in the fashionable world and hiding ... an aching heart with a gay demeanour', becomes a Roman Catholic and retires to a convent on the Continent, while Jeanie and Reuben continue to live in peaceful domestic bliss.

Critical commentary

After reading that account of *The Heart of Midlothian,* and in view of the fact that Sir Walter Scott was in many ways the most complete embodiment next to Lord Byron of the Romantic Movement, it may come as a surprise to realize that he was an admirer of Jane Austen. The strangeness is increased, perhaps, by the fact that Jane Austen also admired Sir Walter Scott. But this mutual admiration serves as a warning against the inadequacy of such labels as 'Augustan' and 'Romantic', and the dangers of dividing literature into watertight compartments or periods. It also points to a genuine paradox: for Scott was *both* a Romantic *and* an Augustan.

His natural tastes were Augustan. The writers he most admired were eighteenth-century ones like Swift and Dryden (whose works he edited). He found the 'Lake Poets' – Wordsworth, Southey and their school – antipathetic, and the poet among his contemporaries he most approved of was George Crabbe, who is generally regarded as the last of the Augustans.

Then again, although many of Scott's novels are set amidst wild scenery, especially that of the Highlands of Scotland, Scott protested that he had no eye for the picturesque, and that for him human beings in society came first. He despised the Romantic cult of individualism, what he described as the age's 'desire, or rather rage, for literary anecdote and private history.' He was just as impatient with the cult of sentiment, as evinced for example in his fellow-countryman Henry Mackenzie's novel *The Man of Feeling* (1771), and he wrote to his friend Maria Edgeworth: 'Of all sorts of parade, I think the parade of feeling and sentiment most disgusting.'

However, to be both a Scot and a writer who loved Scotland was almost inevitably at that time to be a Romantic, in the sense that interest in Scotland, its history and culture was one of the most striking features of the English Romantic Revival, as people struggled to break free from the imaginative restraints of the London-centred Augustan culture. It was, in fact, the interplay between the Augustan and the Romantic elements that helped to give tension and significance to Scott's best work.

The Romantic elements are, of course, very much in evidence in *The Heart of Midlothian*, and some of them are of the crudest and most obvious kind. Midnight tryst, haunted ruins, wild scenery, a mysterious cloaked stranger, an eldritch unseen voice singing snatches of ballads – are all crammed into the scene in which George Staunton secretly meets Jeanie to tell her how she can save her sister. There are many stock romantic episodes, especially in the final sections, including the killing of Sir George Staunton by his own son. Sir George is, moreover, that conventional romantic figure, the aristocratic rake with good intentions, while his outlaw son has strong links with Rousseau's 'noble savage'. Effie, brooding over her husband's guilty past, is also a conventional romantic figure, and so is Madge Wildfire in many of her scenes. There is also a good deal of romantic indulgence in the depiction of the Duke of Argyle and of his idyllic country estate in Scotland – which embodies Scott's own romantic dreams of chivalry and aristocratic benevolence.

For the most part, though, it is the more positive aspects of Romanticism that are displayed in *The Heart of Midlothian*. Among these is the remarkable expansion of subject matter and social range. Scott's treatment of the Deans family is particularly important in this connection. An interest in the peasant, as a symbol of a more spontaneous way of life, close to nature, was one of the most characteristic symptoms of the Romantic Revival, and Scott helped to further this interest. But he does not idealize the Deans family, seeking rather to enter into their lives and to render them with understanding and objectivity.

Fundamentally *The Heart of Midlothian* is more of a realistic novel than a romantic one. And this brings one back to Scott's profound sense of history, which was the chief source of his realism and strength. As far as his own people were concerned, there was ample scope for the nostalgia which belongs to all transitional periods. Scott, in spite of his own modernism, had a deep sympathy for those Scots who still clung to the heroic traditions of the past, and he conveyed the sadness and inherent tragedy in their situation. At the same time he does it without sentimentality. The leaders of the rioters who hang Porteous, for example, though actuated in part by patriotic motives, are wastrels and robbers, far removed from the heroes of Scottish legend. The representatives of the old order are shown as inevitably declining into pathos, eccentricity or compromise. Thus, the decayed laird of Dumbiedikes is presented as struggling to preserve, by parsimony and a rather pathetic obstinacy, the long-vanished heroic traditions of his forbears. Even the old Covenanter, Davie Deans, eventually loses something of his fire as he is forced to come to terms with the realities of the present. It is Scott's understanding of these issues that makes him, in novels like *The Heart of Midlothian*, so notable a chronicler of historical processes.

Scott's use of the differences between English and Scottish law is another of his realistic devices in counterpointing the clash of opposing cultures. In *The Heart of Midlothian* he shows how these differences constituted a rallying point and a sense of national identity. The implication throughout is that London law is trying to impose itself on Scottish law – and also on 'gospel law' as preached by the Covenanters. The lively discussions on legal niceties, even among quite ordinary people, constitute one of the great strengths of the novel.

Much of its realism and vitality, in fact, derives from the horde of minor characters that throng its pages. And this is a reminder that Scott is also a novelist of 'social manners' in the Jane Austen tradition. Most important of all, it underlines the point that, for Scott, history and individual lives are inextricably mingled. In consequence, the history in *The Heart of Midlothian* is never remote and academic. It is the human beings caught up in the forces of historical change who matter. That is why Jeanie's morality and fortitude, which might otherwise seem false or priggish, are psychologically so convincing.

Needless to say, Scott could not have achieved such a subtle and complex synthesis unless he had been a writer of genius. The pressures under which he worked inevitably resulted in a good deal of carelessness in composition, and the long-windedness and apparent formlessness of his novels are a barrier to his popularity today. On the other hand, the type of novel he evolved was one that suited his genius, his multifarious interests, and his quick-moving but digressive mind, and there is a good deal of truth in his own statement:

I am sensible that if there is anything good about my poetry or prose, it is a hurried frankness of composition.

The loose, compendious type of novel which he wrote, moreover, though it may not be one which commends itself to the advocates of pure artistic form, has had many distinguished successors, among them Dickens and D. H. Lawrence, not to mention Dostoyevsky and the great Russians, and many American novelists from Fenimore Cooper onwards. In addition, Scott deployed remarkable resources of language in depicting his wide variety of characters and social classes. In this respect he has been compared to Shakespeare himself – though Scott bluntly disclaimed any such comparison: 'The blockheads talk of my being like Shakespeare – not fit to tie his brogues.' On the other hand, novels like *The Heart of Midlothian* do have certain genuine resemblances to the Shakespeare of the History Plays in their blending of different levels of society in order to present a particular historical event or situation in its totality.

In achieving this Scott created various types of language and dialogue. When he is trying to write formal Augustan English he can be stiff and heavy, but the narrative set-pieces, like the storming of the Tolbooth, are full of fire and tension. Above all, the same way as Shakespeare uses blank verse and prose to distinguish between his noble characters and his ordinary ones, Scott uses English and Scots dialect. In addition, he varies the Scots dialect to suit different purposes and levels of intensity. It is employed to great effect, for example, in his scenes of low life and in his comedy of Scots manners. But at other times it becomes highly poetic, as in the speeches of old Davie Deans with their biblical images and references, and in the dialect ballads sung by Madge Wildfire. Scott's use of song to heighten dramatic effect is also reminiscent of Shakespeare.

Scott also gives his main Scottish characters different levels of dialect according to the circumstances. This is especially so in the case of Jeanie. She can talk the broadest of Scots, but when she is deeply moved she uses a modified and easily comprehended form of the dialect –

as in her eloquent appeal to Queen Caroline on behalf of her sister, with its deep religious faith and its brave and simple humanity.

No reader of *The Heart of Midlothian* is likely to dispute the very modest claim which Scott advanced towards the end of his life:

> I have been perhaps the most voluminous author of the day; and it is a comfort to me to think that I have tried to unsettle no man's faith, to corrupt no man's principle.

The vast majority of his readers, indeed, would add that not only is he one of the most kindly and beneficent of English novelists, but also one of the greatest.

Nightmare Abbey

Thomas Love Peacock

The son of a wealthy London merchant, Thomas Love Peacock was born in Weymouth in October 1785. *Headlong Hall*, the first of his satirical romances, was published in 1816. *Melincourt* followed the next year, and, in 1818, *Nightmare Abbey* appeared. Peacock entered the East India Company, wrote three more novels: *Maid Marian* (1822); *The Misfortunes of Elphin* (1829), and *Crotchet Castle* (1831). In 1833 his mother died, and he wrote no more novels until his last, *Gryll Grange*, was published in 1861. He contributed papers to several periodicals, including reminiscences of the poet Percy Bysshe Shelley, whose friend and executor he was. He married Jane Gryffydh, the 'White Snowdonian antelope' of Shelley's *Letter to Maria Gisborne*, and their daughter was the first wife of the novelist George Meredith. In 1856 Peacock retired on a pension from the East India Company and died in Chertsey in January 1866.

Summary

Nightmare Abbey, like all Peacock's other novels, was written to a single basic formula. The first element of the formula is a remote country house – the Abbey is 'a venerable family-mansion in a highly picturesque state of semi-dilapidation' between the Lincolnshire fens and the sea. The second is to pack it with a miscellaneous bunch of odd characters (not unlike Sterne's in *Tristram Shandy*), with some very odd ideas – at any rate in Peacock's view. In *Nightmare Abbey*, two of the oddities are permanent inhabitants: Christopher Glowry, a gentleman with a very melancholy outlook on life, and his son, Scythrop. Their most frequent visitors are Mr Flosky, 'very lachrymose and morbid', who has lost himself in the 'transcendental darkness' of Kantian metaphysics; Mr Toobad, who believes that the Almighty has handed over the world to the dominion of the Evil Principle; and the local vicar, who is ready to adapt himself to any mood or shade of opinion for the sake of a good dinner. A third ingredient of Peacock's formula was the modelling of most of his main characters on well-known contemporaries. Scythrop, for instance is a caricature of the poet Shelley, and Mr Flosky of the poet and philosopher Coleridge.

During the absence of his father in London, and disappointed in love, Scythrop develops an equally romantic passion for reforming the world and publishes a treatise, at his own expense, which embodies it – but which sells only seven copies. He finds solace in madeira, a taste for which is the only positive result of his university education, and continues to lay 'deep schemes for a thorough repair of the crazy fabric of human nature' – just like his prototype, Shelley.

On his father's return, there are two additions to the company: Scythrop's old college friend, the Honourable Mr Listless, and the sprightly and coquettish Marionetta, Mr Glowry's orphan niece. Marionetta torments Scythrop unmercifully, but he is soon head over heels in love with her. She, however, has no fortune, and Mr Glowry intends his son to marry the daughter of Mr Toobad, who has.

Another feature of the Peacock formula are conversations, set out in semi-dramatic form, which reveal the characters' various quirks and conceits – as in this passage, which follows the delivery of some new books from London:

Marionetta Mr Listless shall recommend us the very newest new book, that every body reads.

The Honourable Mr Listless You shall receive it, Miss O'Carroll, with all the gloss of novelty; fresh as a ripe green-gage in all the downiness of its bloom. A mail-coach copy from Edinburgh, forwarded express from London.

Mr Flosky This rage for novelty is the bane of literature. Except my works and those of my particular friends, nothing is good that is not as old as Jeremy Taylor: and *entre nous*, the best parts of my friends' books were either written or suggested by myself.

The Honourable Mr Listless Sir, I reverence you. But I must say, modern books are very consolatory and congenial to my feelings. There is, as it were, a delightful north-east wind, an intellectual blight breathing through them; a delicious misanthropy and discontent, that demonstrates the nullity of virtue and energy, and puts me in good humour with myself and my sofa.

Mr Flosky Very true, sir. Modern literature is a north-east wind – a blight of the human soul. I take credit to myself for having helped to make it so. The way to produce fine fruit is to blight the flower. You call this a paradox. Marry, so be it. Ponder thereon.

Mr Toobad comes back from London with fresh cause for his belief in the diabolical nature of things. It seems that when he had informed his daughter Celinda that he had found a husband for her she had defied him, and when threatened, had disappeared.

A new visitor arrives, Mr Asterias, a cranky icthyologist, who believes in the existence of mermaids – and who shortly after is convinced that he has seen one on the seashore near the Abbey. This mermaid is, in fact, a beautiful girl who explains to Scythrop that she has been forced to flee from a tyrannical father. She tells him that she has read his treatise (which is entitled 'Philosophical Gas; or a Project for a General Illumination of the Human Mind') which has convinced her that they must be kindred spirits and inspired her to come to him for help and protection. Scythrop, delighted to find so unusual an admirer among his fan-club of seven, gives her a secret suite which he has constructed in the inner walls of his room. She tells him to call her Stella, and dazzled by her beauty, intellectual conversation and devotion to the ideals of 'total love', Scythrop makes no serious effort to find her alternative accommodation.

Mr Cypress (based on Byron) arrives, announcing that he is about to leave England (as Byron was forced to do after his wife divorced him) and uttering a prose parody of one of the most pessimistic sections of Byron's poem *Childe Harold*. The Company drink to Mr Cypress's imminent departure, and the celebrations end with a song from him (another neat parody of Byron) and a rousing drinking song from Mr Hilary and the Reverend Mr Larynx.

Mr Listless's valet announces that he believes the Abbey is haunted. This occasions a good deal of debate, with Mr Flosky taking the lead on the nature of the supernatural. Mr Glowry, however, his suspicions aroused by the valet's report, listens outside Scythrop's door, and is convinced he hears a female voice. He enters, and although to his astonishment Scythrop is alone, he taxes him with keeping a woman in his room. Scythrop denies it. Then, as Mr Glowry speaks of his son's forthcoming marriage to Marionetta (to which Mr Glowry has given his reluctant consent) the bookcase hiding the entrance to the secret suite swings back and a furious Stella appears, bursting into tears at Scythrop's perfidy. Marionetta also comes into the room – to swoon at the sight of Scythrop with another woman. And finally Mr Toobad arrives on the scene – to discover that Stella is his runaway daughter, Celinda.

Both Marionetta and Celinda renounce Scythrop, and

there is a general exodus from the Abbey. Scythrop, in despair, orders madeira and a pistol for his dinner – but only makes use of the former. His father asks which of the women he wants but (like Shelley in a similar situation) Scythrop cannot make up his mind. His father says he will go up to London to persuade one or other of them to change her mind. Scythrop tells him that if he does not return by a certain date and time with a favourable answer, he *will* make use of the pistol.

On the appointed day, Mr Glowry is in fact late, but fortunately Raven the butler (only servants with gloomy sounding names and melancholy natures are employed at Nightmare Abbey) has altered the clock. When Mr Glowry does at last arrive he brings back two letters; one from Marionetta announcing her imminent marriage to Mr Listless, and the other from Celinda announcing her engagement to Mr Flosky.

Father and son rail against the fickleness of women, but Mr Glowry comforts his son with the reflection that 'there are yet maidens in England' – advising him in future, however, to have only one string to his bow. Scythrop discovers the trick with the clock, summons Raven to reprimand him, but instead of doing so orders a decanter of madeira, without pistol.

Critical commentary

Obviously, *Nightmare Abbey* is not a normal sort of novel, and some critics have doubted whether it, or any of Peacock's other novels, merit the term at all. But it is at any rate a very enjoyable book. The dialogue is witty and sparkling, and the scattering of excellent songs gives it an additional effervescence. The satire is devastating, passionately felt, frequently very funny indeed, and not in the least vindictive. It deals with practically every aspect of the intellectual life of the age, in spite of being (like all Peacock's books) very short by the standards of the day.

Nightmare Abbey was published in the same year as Jane Austen's *Northanger Abbey*, and there is a certain rightness in the coincidence. Both novels satirized the vogue for Gothic gloom and mysterious mediaeval castles, and Peacock, like Jane Austen, may be regarded as a late survival of eighteenth-century rationalism. Like her, too, he deliberately confined himself to the limited range of subject-matter which he knew best and which genuinely engaged his sympathies. It was, however, a much narrower range than that of Jane Austen. His interests were scholarly, and he was more concerned with ideas than with the characters who embodied them. He was a satirist in a far more formal and deliberate sense than Jane Austen, modelling himself on such classical and neo-classical writers as Petronius, Rabelais, Swift and Voltaire.

To read *Nightmare Abbey* is to be given an intimate critique from the inside of all the ideas and theories so ardently bandied about by the Romantics. The most striking thing is that, in reading the book, these ideas and theories do not seem at all dated; the charm and sparkle of Peacock's manner cause them to spring to life again, like wilted flowers revived by a shower of rain. In addition, there is a kind of double effect; the reader finds himself intrigued by the ideas and theories themselves, and at the same time equally intrigued by what human minds do to them. In consequence, the satire seems to be just as relevant to the ideas and theories of our own age – or those of any other age.

In spite of the intellectual nature of *Nightmare Abbey*, it is not altogether lacking in sensuous life. The occasional flashes of natural description – the ivy-covered tower of the Abbey in moonlight, for example, a glimpse of the desolate fens, or the surf breaking along the shore – are fresh and vivid. The characters, of course, are meant to be predominantly types or 'humours', as many of the names indicate – Mr Toobad and Mr Listless for example – but oddly enough they do have some physical presence. In particular the women (as in all Peacock's novels) are surprisingly successful. There is no attempt at any depth or subtlety of characterization, yet Marionetta, with her lively pertness and coquetry, is no mere marionette, despite her name; and Celinda is not only a mouthpiece for 'advanced' feminist ideas: in some strange way both of them are convincing as women.

Nightmare Abbey, like Peacock's other novels, stands apart both from the fiction of its time and from the mainstream of the English novel in general. But it has had its influence on novelists of a similar cast of mind to that of Peacock, and of similar intellectual interests. Aldous Huxley is a notable example, especially in *Crome Yellow*, with its cast of eccentrics gathered in a country house and parading their pet intellectual obsessions; while the influence of Peacock's use of semi-dramatized dialogue is also apparent in the novels of Ivy Compton-Burnett. And in any case, *Nightmare Abbey*, 'rogue' novel though it is, deserves its place in any history of the genre for its own sake.

Ivanhoe

Walter Scott

Summary

Ivanhoe, published in 1819, is set in the England of the
twelfth century. As the novel opens, the arrogant Sir
Brian de Bois-Guilbert, Knight Templar (member, that
is, of the order founded in 1118 to protect Christian pilgrims to the Holy Land) is on his way to the great royal
tournament that is about to take place at Ashby-de-la-
Zouch in Leicestershire. He decides to spend the night at
Cedric's residence of Rotherwood, and is guided there by a
mysterious pilgrim. Cedric is passionately devoted to the
cause of restoring the Saxon line to the throne of England
(overthrown, of course, when the Normans invaded the
country in 1066) and sees the best chance of effecting this
in a marriage between his ward, the Lady Rowena, who
is a descendant of the great Saxon King, Alfred, and
Athelstane of Coningsburgh, also of the Saxon blood
royal. For this reason Cedric has banished his son, Wilfred
of Ivanhoe, because he and Rowena have fallen in love.
Ivanhoe joins King Richard 'the Lion-Heart' in his Cru-
sade in Palestine.

At supper, Bois-Guilbert boasts of the valour of the
Norman knights serving with King Richard in the Cru-
sade, and of his own exploits. Unexpectedly challenged
by the pilgrim, he admits that Ivanhoe the Saxon had

proved a doughty fighter for Richard, but declares that he would welcome the opportunity of meeting him in single combat. The pilgrim is Ivanhoe himself in disguise, and later that night he overhears a plot between Bois-Guilbert and his retainers to rob Isaac of York, a wealthy old Jew who is also sheltering at Rotherwood. Ivanhoe helps Isaac to escape, and in gratitude Isaac equips him with horse and armour for the forthcoming tournament at Ashby-de-la-Zouch, which takes place in the presence of Prince John, the King's evil brother who is plotting to usurp the throne in Richard's absence.

An unknown challenger enters the lists, defeats Bois-Guilbert and the other Norman knights, and is therefore called upon to name the Queen of Love and Beauty. He chooses Rowena, much to the joy of the Saxon section of the crowd. The following day, the main contest is a confrontation between two groups of fifty knights each. Bois-Guilbert heads one band, and the unknown champion the other. During the battle the latter is hard-pressed until another mysterious knight in black armour comes to his help, and between them they rout all their opponents. When the unknown champion removes his helmet in order to receive his prize from Rowena, she recognizes him as Ivanhoe. As he kisses her hand, he faints from the wounds he has received. Isaac of York and his beautiful daughter, Rebecca, carry him away and are joined by Athelstane and Cedric, who is still unaware of his son's presence. The Black Knight, however, (who is in fact King Richard himself, secretly returned to England) rides away.

The party carrying Ivanhoe is waylaid by Bois-Guilbert and his friends, Maurice de Bracy and Reginald Front de Boeuf, and taken off to Front de Boeuf's castle of Torquilstone. De Bracy wants to marry Rowena, whose royal Saxon blood would, he believes, further his political ambitions, while Bois-Guilbert becomes violently enamoured of Rebecca. He trieds to persuade her to become a Christian so that they may marry, but she scornfully rejects him.

Meanwhile, Gurth the swineherd has roused a band of Saxon outlaws led by Locksley (alias Robin Hood). Joined by the mysterious Black Knight, they storm Torquilstone, setting it on fire, and rescue the badly wounded Ivanhoe and Rowena. De Bracy, who has learned the true identity of the Black Knight, carries the news to Prince John, who resolves to capture his brother and throw him in prison. Bois-Guilbert also manages to escape, taking Rebecca with him as his prisoner. Isaac pleads with Lucas de Beaumanoir, the Grand Master of the Knights Templar, for the release of his daughter, but Bois-Guilbert, in order to salvage his pride, declares that Rebecca is a witch who had put a spell on him, and de Beaumanoir condemns her to be burned at the stake. She demands the ancient right of trial by combat, provided a knight can be found to defend her, and de Beaumanoir agrees.

Ivanhoe, still weak from his wounds, appears as her champion. In the desperate struggle that follows, Bois-Guilbert suddenly falls dead. Rebecca is released, and eventually, suppressing her love for Ivanhoe, leaves England with her father to seek a refuge from persecution in Spain. In the meantime, Cedric, who has also survived all his adventures (thanks largely to the heroic behaviour of his jester, Wamba) has invited the Black Knight to Rotherwood so that he can thank him for his intervention at Torquilstone. The Black Knight accepts, reveals himself as King Richard, and asks Cedric to pardon his son Ivanhoe. Cedric agrees, and Athelstane surrenders his claim to marry Rowena.

The Black Knight proclaims himself King again, punishing the Knights Templar for plotting against their lawful sovereign. Locksley and his Saxon outlaws affirm their loyalty to King Richard, and are pardoned. The King himself attends the wedding of Ivanhoe and Rowena, as do both Norman and Saxon nobles, and the novel ends on a note of reconciliation between Norman and Saxon, and in the hope that peace will once again return to a divided England.

Critical commentary

Sir Walter Scott has always been recognized as the 'father of the historical novel'. The earliest novels to be published in Russia, for example, were nearly all imitations of Scott, and later the Russian literary giants Lermontov, Pushkin, Gogol and Tolstoy, acknowledged their indebtedness to him. So, too, did Balzac and Stendhal in France, and so, indeed, did practically every writer of historical fiction throughout the nineteenth century, from Mickiewicz in Poland and Manzoni in Italy to Fenimore Cooper in America. When Scott died in 1832, Sainte-Beuve, the leading French critic of the day, summed up the European reaction:

> It is not only a loss to England, it should be one for the civilized world, for whom Walter Scott, more than any other contemporary writer, has been the prodigal enchanter, the amiable benefactor.

Scott's great international reputation, however, depended for the most part not on his Scottish masterpieces like *The Heart of Midlothian*, but on novels like *Ivanhoe* which were set outside Scotland, and reached far back in time. It was the publication of *Ivanhoe* in 1819 that first extended Scott's reputation to the Continent, thus making it into one of the key books in the history of literature.

Although *Ivanhoe* is far removed in place and period from the Scottish novels, its stress on reconciliation does nevertheless relate it to them in some degree. Scott always seeks to bring together the opposing claims of past and present, Highlander and Lowlander, Scotland and England. Ivanhoe himself, as both a Saxon and a follower of the Norman King Richard, has a foot in both camps (like Edward Waverley in Scott's first novel) while Cedric the Saxon has something in common with Scott's fanatical supporters of the 'grand old cause' of the exiled Stuarts. *Ivanhoe* resembles the Scottish novels, too, in its faith in the essential goodness of mankind.

In the Scottish novels, the richness and realism of the social and historic context add conviction to the characters. In *Ivanhoe* it tends to be less convincing because Scott has overlaid its characters with his own highly romantic interpretation of the mediaeval codes of chivalry. In addition, he makes them speak, for the most part, in a kind of chivalric rhetoric he invented for the purpose. Thus Cedric extends a welcome of high-flown courtesy to his Norman guests, which cannot but seem insincere in view of his bitter hatred of them; while Ivanhoe and Bois-Guilbert use the same kind of artificial rhetoric to each other, and fight according to the laws of feudal combat (or rather, Scott's idealized version of them) so that they seem more like ventriloquists' dummies than living men who hate each other and have real cause to do so. The least wooden characters in *Ivanhoe*, in fact, are those least affected by the chivalric mumbo-jumbo – Gurth and Wamba, Locksley and his outlaws, and Isaac and Rebecca. There is, in consequence, much that is stagey and stilted in *Ivanhoe* as there is in Scott's two other novels set in the period of the Crusades, *The Betrothed* and *The Talisman*, and as there is in varying degrees in all of the fiction in which the vital connection with Scott's native land has been severed.

However, a good deal of historical research went into *Ivanhoe*. Scott includes many scholarly details of twelfth-century English customs. Since these are not fully integrated into the lives and emotions of the characters, however, they tend for the most part to seem merely pedantic asides. This is another way of saying that the synthesis between realism and romanticism, achieved so triumphantly in novels like *The Heart of Midlothian*, is in *Ivanhoe* much less satisfactory. It is the unchecked romanticism that tends to take precedence. For one thing, in his desire for a richly varied panorama, as a substitute for the authentic local colour of the Scottish novels, Scott took far greater liberties with his history. Thus, he has shifted

Robin Hood and his outlaws two centuries back, and the Victorian mediaeval historian, Edward Freeman, criticized *Ivanhoe* on the grounds that there was no evidence in the contemporary records to support the existence, as late as the reign of Richard I, of the deep-seated enmity between Saxon and Norman which forms the basis of the novel.

How then, is the tremendous influence in Europe of *Ivanhoe*, and of Scott's other novels about the distant past, to be explained? At the simplest level, of course, the absence of Scottish dialect was an advantage as far as the European translator was concerned, while a greater degree of conformity to conventional Romantic expectations probably helped rather than hindered their popularity. But there was more to it than that. In the first place the stir, the colour and the narrative excitement of Ivanhoe, especially in the big set-pieces like the tournament at Ashby-de-la-Zouch, the storming of Torquilstone Castle, and the scene when Ivanhoe appears as Rebecca's champion, were far superior to anything of their kind that European readers had encountered before. These qualities were present, too, in later novels like *The Fortunes of Nigel* (1822), set in seventeenth-century London and containing a fine study of the paradoxical character of King James I; *Peveril of the Peak* (the longest of all Scott's novels, also published in 1822) which portrays King Charles II in a story of rousing melodrama, and *Quentin Durward* (1823), set in fifteenth-century France and considered by some critics to be the best of Scott's non-Scottish historical reconstructions, largely because of its notable portrait of King Louis XI – though the presence of a Scottish hero (a member of Louis's guard) may also have helped to engage Scott's more urgent sympathies.

It was impossible, moreover, for a writer of Scott's genius altogether to lose his grasp of the ways in which history acts upon human beings. The modern historian, G. M. Trevelyan, wrote of Scott's fiction as a whole:

To Scott a man is not so much a human being as a type produced by a special environment, whether it be a border-farmer, a mediaeval abbot, a cavalier, a covenanter, a Swiss pikeman, or an Elizabethan statesman. No doubt Scott exaggerated his theme as all innovators are wont to do. But he did more than any professional historian to make mankind advance towards a true conception of history, for it was he who first perceived that the history of mankind is not simple but complex, that history never repeats itself but ever creates new forms differing according to time and place.

Such a concern for historical processes in the service of fiction was something entirely new for the Continent. Most European historical novels at that time were a good deal more stilted and artificial, even closer to theatrical costume drama, than *Ivanhoe*. Also, they were almost entirely aristocratic in attitude and approach. If they introduced 'low' characters, it was in minor roles and by way of comic relief. Scott was the first major novelist to take them seriously, and the French novelist, George Sand, declared that he was 'the poet of the peasant, soldier, outlaw and artisan'. The fact that Scott began *Ivanhoe*, not with his grand characters but with a lively interchange between Gurth the swineherd and Wamba the jester, struck his European contemporaries as startlingly original. In spite of his own political conservatism, therefore, Scott was regarded on the Continent as fundamentally a democratic novelist. In all his fiction, Scott was aware that though men differ in externals from age to age, their essential reactions remain the same, and he himself wrote of:

Those passions common to men in all stages of society and which have alike agitated the human heart whether it throbbed under the steel corselet of the XV Century, the brocaded coat of the XVIII Century, or the blue frock and white dimity of the present day.

Although in Britain it may be considered that Scott's genius was best expressed in those novels dealing with his own country in the not-too-distant past, it is evident that *Ivanhoe* too must be regarded as one of the seminal works of European literature.

Mr Midshipman Easy

Frederick Marryat

Frederick Marryat was born in Westminster in 1792, the son of a Member of Parliament. At the age of fourteen he joined the Royal Navy as a midshipman. He took part in fifty naval engagements in various parts of the world, was wounded three times, was decorated, commanded a sloop off St Helena guarding against the escape of Napoleon Bonaparte, and rose to the rank of Captain. His blunt criticism of naval policy checked his further promotion and so, after the promising reception of his first two novels, *Frank Mildmay or the Naval Officer*, which was published in 1829, and *The King's Own*, which appeared a year later, Marryat retired from the Navy and took up a full-time literary career.

The best-known of the naval tales that followed are *Peter Simple* and *Jacob Faithful* (both published in 1834) and *Mr Midshipman Easy* (1836). *Snarley-yow or the Dog Fiend* (1837), the story of a waif-like hero named Small-bones and his persecution by a brutal Dutch captain and his dog Snarley-yow, is different in being set back in the year 1699, and is considered by some critics as Marryat's best novel. *Japhet in Search of a Father* (1836) is different again, being a picaresque story that takes place entirely on land – though its popularity among seafaring men can be gathered from the fact that while it was coming out serially, an American ship stopped a British merchantman in mid-ocean and ran up a signal asking 'Has Japhet found his father yet?'.

Marryat repaid the compliment rather churlishly by writing a *Diary in America,* following a stay in the USA and Canada between 1837 and 1839, which was highly critical of American manners, though on its publication in 1839 it made him even more money than *Mr Midshipman Easy,* his most popular novel. His best books after his return to England were written specifically for boys, and include three notable children's classics: *Masterman Ready* (1841), *The Settlers in Canada* (1844), and *The Children of the New Forest* (1847).

By 1843, Marryat had settled at Langham Manor in Norfolk, but the considerable profits from his writings were largely eaten up by costly experiments in farming and unfortunate investments. His death in 1848 was hastened by the news of the loss of his son in a shipwreck.

Summary

The first chapter of the book introduces Mr Nicodemus Easy, the hero's father, a well-to-do Hampshire squire, who is strongly reminiscent of the Walter Shandy of Laurence Sterne's *Tristram Shandy* in his devotion to a hobby-horse, and in his determination to bring up his son to ride in the same saddle. Mr Easy's obsession is with the Rousseau-esque doctrine that all men are born equal. As a result of his father's philosophical disquisitions and his mother's extreme doting, Jack Easy as a boy is pugnacious, argumentative, and utterly unruly. After he has got into various scrapes, Dr Middleton, the family physician, persuades Mr Easy to send his son to a school which, Mr Easy feels, must be run on sound egalitarian principles because it boasts of having abolished flogging. In fact Mr Bonycastle, the headmaster, has practised a fine verbal distinction: the word 'flogging' he argues, implies the birch – he has indeed abolished the birch – but substituted for it 'a series of canes, ranged up and down like billiard cues'. And so Jack learns his first painful lessons in the realities of obedience and inequality.

Other lessons, equally uncomfortable, follow. When he is fifteen, Jack insists on joining the Royal Navy, on the mistaken assumption that life aboard one of His Majesty's ships must be a close approximation to a truly egalitarian society. Fortunately for him, his father secures him a berth as midshipman to the kindly Captain Wilson of *HMS Harpy*, who treats Jack's aberrations with tolerance, trusting to time to cure him of them. Jack makes friends with Mesty, the ship's cook and a former Ashanti chief who had been sold into slavery in America and escaped, and also with a fellow-midshipman named Gascoigne. He also meets Vigors, the bully of the midshipmen's berth, and thrashes him when he finds him tormenting his favourite victim. Another of Jack's shipmates is Mr Joliffe, the master's mate, one-eyed and terribly disfigured from smallpox – one of the Smollett-like grotesques in the book, though also a good and kind man.

Jack naturally has a hard time practising his egalitarian theories, especially after a scoundrelly purser's steward named Easthrupp, professing the same views, behaves impertinently to him – and Jack has shamefacedly to admit to Captain Wilson that he has kicked Easthrupp down the hatchway and called him a 'radical blackguard'. Though he is still argumentative on matters of discipline, Jack's conduct in action is exemplary and during an attack on an enemy convoy he is given command of one of the boats, and Mesty is allowed to accompany him. But Jack disobeys orders, and goes off on his own in pursuit of a Spanish ship, successfully boarding her under cover of darkness. In one of the cabins, he finds three women passengers and treats them with great courtesy, putting them and their male relatives ashore with all their belongings. Jack and his men sail off in the captured vessel, but shortly after are blown off course.

Soon Jack has a mutiny on his hands. His men land on an island and settle down to a prolonged carousal. Jack and Mesty manage to capture their boat. Some of the men try to swim out to the ship, and are eaten by sharks. The horror-stricken Jack accuses himself of their murder. 'If I had not disobeyed orders,' he tells Mesty, 'if I had not shown them the example of disobedience, this would not have happened...'

  Eventually the mutineers, their provisions exhausted, beg to be taken back on board, and they set sail again. When at length they catch up with the *Harpy*, it is to find her engaged with a Spanish warship. They come to the *Harpy*'s assistance, and in view of the rich prize Jack has brought back and his part in the recent action, he is pardoned for disobeying orders. Jack manages, too, to secure lenient treatment for the mutineers, while on his recommendation Mesty is promoted to ship's corporal.

  At Malta, Jack is involved in a duel with Easthrupp and Biggs the boatswain. Jack and his friend Gascoigne pretend that they are frightened of being hanged for taking part in a duel so they can go off on a jaunt which eventually takes them to Sicily. There they rescue an elderly gentleman named Don Rebeira from an attack led by a young man named Don Silvio, whose family has a long-standing feud with that of Don Rebeira. When Rebeira introduces his wife and beautiful daughter Agnes, Jack recognizes them as the ladies he had assisted in the attack on the Spanish ship, and he falls in love with Agnes. When the two midshipmen reach Palermo they are welcomed by Agnes' two brothers, Don Philip and Don Martin, but are shortly afterwards arrested as deserters by the captain of a British ship. Don Rebeira, however, shoots the captain in a duel, and his second-in-command takes Jack and Gascoigne with him to Malta, where he hands them back to the *Harpy*. The British Governor of Malta, who is much entertained by Jack's stories, pleads for him and Gascoigne, pointing out they had only absconded because they thought they would be hanged for the duel, and the two midshipmen are pardoned.

By now Captain Wilson has been transferred to another ship, the *Aurora*, and takes Jack, Gascoigne and Mesty with him. After numerous other escapades, the two friends return to Malta where they run into a man they recognize as Don Silvio, Don Rebeira's bitter enemy. They unmask Don Silvio to the Governor, who has him sent back to Sicily under guard. The *Aurora*, too, sets sail for Sicily, and on the way fights a ferocious action with a Russian ship – one of the most exciting episodes in the book.

With the Russian prize in tow, they resume their voyage. Off the coast of Sicily they come upon a prison-galley which has run onto the rocks and been abandoned by her crew, though the galley-slaves have been left chained to their benches. Jack and Gascoigne are detailed to release the slaves. Among them is Don Silvio. When the *Aurora* reaches Palermo, Jack gets leave from Captain Wilson to go ashore with Gascoigne and Mesty to warn Don Reberia that Don Silvio is on the loose again. Agnes tells Jack that Father Thomaso, the family confessor, is firmly opposed to her marrying a heretic. When, however, Don Silvio and his fellow galley-slaves lay siege to the house, Agnes ardently confesses her love to Jack. They are rescued from their attackers in the nick of time by the arrival of a troop of soldiers, but Don Silvio again escapes.

Later, Father Thomaso tries to bribe Mesty to administer poison to Jack, but Mesty turns the tables on him by giving him the poison in his own supper. After disposing of the body and disguising himself in Father Thomaso's habit, Mesty is waylaid by Don Silvio's gang, but manages to escape, killing Don Silvio. Don Rebeira now gives his consent to the marriage between Agnes and Jack.

Back in Malta, Jack learns that his mother is dead, and that his father has been behaving in a very alarming fashion, inciting the local peasantry to revolt and throwing open his estates to poachers. Jack therefore resigns from the service and also buys Mesty's discharge. When he arrives home, he finds the house filled with insolent servants, loudly proclaiming the principles of liberty and equality, and his father (another Shandean touch this) absorbed in a machine he has invented for altering the bumps on people's craniums in order to induce mildness and benevolence. With Mesty's help, Jack, now thoroughly cured of his father's earlier indoctrination, restores order and persuades his father to sign a deed of attorney handing over to him the management of the estates. Not long afterwards, Mr Easy accidentally hangs himself in his phrenological contraption.

Jack now buys and fits out a privateer of his own, which he calls the *Rebeira*, in which he intends to return to Sicily in order to marry Agnes and bring her back home with him. In the Straits of Gibraltar the *Rebeira* comes to the aid of a British frigate beset by a swarm of Spanish gunboats. After the victorious action, Jack finds that Gascoigne is on board the frigate. Her Captain allows Gascoigne to join Jack on the *Rebeira* and the two friends decide that instead of proceeding straight to Palermo, they will first try their luck on the high seas. They capture several valuable prizes and after various other adventures finally reach Palermo; Jack and Agnes are married and return to England, Mesty is installed as a permanent major-domo, Gascoigne is promoted, and all ends happily.

Critical commentary

During the 1830s, novels of naval life, in the aftermath of the victory at Trafalgar and one of the most glorious periods in British naval achievement, came close to equalling the popularity of the historical romances. Most of these naval stories have now been forgotten, but a few survive – among them Michael Scott's *Tom Cringle's Log* and *The Cruise of the 'Midge'* (both published in book form in 1836), Frederick Chamier's *Tom Bowling* (1841), and in particular, the novels of Captain Marryat.

In novels like *Mr Midshipman Easy*, Marryat was the literary heir to the Smollett of *Roderick Random*.

Marryat's experience at sea was far more extensive than Smollett's, so the multiplicity and authenticity of the contemporary naval detail adds a kind of technical dimension which increases the realism and to some extent acts as a binding agent to the sprawling mass of incident. But his naval novels, like those of Smollett, abound in the cruelty and degradations of contemporary naval life; in grim scenes of carnage and violent death, and in grotesque 'humours'-type characters. As with Smollett, his young heroes are naïve, plucky, and addicted to frequently callous horseplay and practical jokes. And like Smollett, he was a masterly narrator.

Mr Midshipman Easy is obviously a straightforward adventure yarn of the kind that appeals to 'the young of all ages'. The main characters are uncomplicated, and the love interest, though involving plenty of exciting incident, is conventional and devoid of anything approaching passion. At the same time, the various oddities among the characters are presented with considerable power, and Marryat has been described as a bridge between Smollett and Dickens. It will also be obvious that Marryat was a staunch patriot and conservative, devoted to his old service and passionately opposed to egalitarian principles in any shape or form. Yet at the same time he was (unlike Smollett) sunny and good-natured by temperament. He was able to sympathize with the harsh lot of the ordinary seaman of the day, and also to present, with considerable tolerance, opinions with which he violently disagreed. This applies even to Mr Easy, whom he endows with a genuine generosity of spirit, and who, in fact, inspires in the reader more than a sneaking sympathy. It was these qualities that, later in the century, were to impress another and greater novelist of the sea, Joseph Conrad. In several ways, therefore, *Mr Midshipman Easy* plays a small but honourable part in the history of the English novel.

The Posthumous Papers of the Pickwick Club

Charles Dickens

Dickens is so generally recognized as the great genius of the English novel, and is still so much of a living classic, that it is sometimes difficult to realize that *The Posthumous Papers of the Pickwick Club*, his first novel, was published less than a hundred years after the appearance of Richardson's *Pamela* initiated the genre. Dickens was, indeed, close to the eighteenth-century world in a number of ways, and *Pickwick* reveals a high degree of nostalgia for it. In order to appreciate the reasons for this, it is necessary to examine some of the circumstances of his early life – leaving later biographical details to the other chapters on Dickens.

Charles John Huffam Dickens was born in 1812, the second of eight children, at the naval station of Portsea where his father, John Dickens, was a minor clerk in the Navy Pay Office. Before Charles was ten, his family had moved from Portsea to London, from London to Chatham, and then back again to London. This semi-nomadic existence was attended by a continuous state of anxious poverty, greatly increased by the incompetence and improvidence of Dickens's father – the prototype of Mr Micawber in his semi-autobiographical novel, *David Copperfield* (published in 1849–1850) – and there is little doubt that the tension and insecurity of his early years affected him permanently.

The most traumatic experience of Dickens's whole life came when he was twelve years old. His father was arrested for debt and sent to the Marshalsea, one of London's debtors' prisons, where (according to the practice of the day) his wife and younger children joined him. But Dickens himself was considered old enough to live in lodgings on his own, and to be sent to work sticking labels on bottles at a small blacking factory. Some idea of the anguish which the highly-strung, sensitive child endured at this time can be gathered from this sentence from a fragment of autobiography written twenty-three years later for his friend and first biographer, John Forster:

> That I suffered in secret, and that I suffered exquisitely,
> no one ever knew but I. How much I suffered it is ...
> beyond my power to tell. No man's imagination can
> overstep the reality.

These sufferings were in part the result of his father's disgrace – which, he confesses, made him feel that he had 'prison taint' – in part that of the long hours of uncongenial work in the roughest company, but above all because of his isolation and bitter sense of abandonment. As he recalled later:

> I lounged about the streets, insufficiently and unsatis-
> factorily fed. I knew that, but for the mercy of God, I might
> easily have been, for any care that was taken of me, a
> little robber or a little vagabond.

He might, in other words, have become like the Artful Dodger and the other child criminals whom he depicted in *Oliver Twist*, the very different kind of novel which followed shortly after *Pickwick*.

After a few months in the Marshalsea, something 'turned up' for John Dickens (as it so often did for Mr Micawber) in the form of a small legacy, and after paying his creditors he was released. Even then, it was several months before Dickens was taken away from the hated blacking factory and sent to a cheap school where he remained until he was fifteen.

He had previously received some schooling during the family's more settled period at Chatham, which he supplemented by voracious reading, especially of *The Arabian Nights*, translations of the old picaresque novels *Gil Blas* and *Don Quixote*, Fielding's *Tom Jones*, and the works of Smollett. When he left school, Dickens became an office boy in a legal firm as a first step towards being articled to a solicitor, an experience which further increased his contempt for the machinery of justice, which he had already seen in operation when his father fell into debt.

Then 'The Prodigal Father' (as his son called him), having left his job with the Admiralty, found employment as a newspaper reporter. In order to qualify himself for the same profession, Dickens taught himself shorthand and worked for three years as a court stenographer – thereby storing up further knowledge of the workings of the legal system. He tried unsuccessfully to go on the stage, and then, in 1835, he became a newspaper reporter of debates in the House of Commons (and of political meetings in various parts of the country) – gaining in the process much information about parliamentary politics. At the same time, he was also writing a series of short narrative and descriptive sketches, under the pen-name of Boz, for his own newspaper and various popular magazines, working into the small hours of the morning. The *Sketches by Boz, Illustrative of Every-Day Life and Every-Day People* were published in book-form in 1836, when Dickens was twenty-four, so his first approach to fiction was a by-product of his journalism.

After an abortive romance with the daughter of a bank manager, who did not at all approve of the suit of a mere newspaper reporter, Dickens fell in love with Catherine Hogarth, daughter of one of the principals of his newspaper, *The Morning Chronicle*. The marriage, in April, 1836, was a happy one to begin with and was a help both to his literary and social ambitions. It took place in an aura of sudden and spectacular success. A few months previously, a popular humorous artist named Robert Seymour had conceived the idea of an illustrated serial in monthly parts, in the manner of Pierce Egan's *Tom and Jerry* (to shorten the very long title) which had been published in the same way between 1821 and 1824, illustrated by the artist George Cruikshank (later to become one of Dickens's illustrators). This had been highly popular because of its racy depiction of the life of Regency 'bucks', especially their devotion to sports such as racing, coach-driving and boxing. Seymour probably also had in mind another very popular series of sketches about a London grocer who wanted to be a fox-hunter, by Robert Smith Surtees, which ran serially from 1831 to 1834, and was published in book-form in 1838 as *The Jaunts and Jollities of that Renowned Sporting Citizen, Mr John Jorrocks* (usually known as *Jorrocks' Jaunts*).

Seymour's plan was to portray a 'Nimrod Club', composed of town-dwellers who would meet with all kinds of ludicrous adventures in their pursuit of various country sports. The enterprising new publishing firm of Chapman and Hall accepted the idea, and looked round for someone to write the letterpress, at that time regarded as quite subordinate to the drawings. When several professional authors had rejected the commission, it was offered to the unknown Boz. The twenty-four year old Dickens accepted, and so committed himself to the rapid and improvised kind of composition demanded by serialization. As it happened, it was exactly the method that, despite its inevitable drawbacks, best suited his frantic, helter-skelter kind of genius.

He began writing the first number of his assignment only eight days after he received the publisher's offer – but by then he had persuaded a reluctant Seymour to allow him to choose his own story-line, to expand the text, and to deal not just with sporting material but with anything that might strike him as comic in contemporary life. It was thus, in 1836, that *Pickwick* was born.

The original plan of collaboration, however, lasted only through the second number, at which point Seymour committed suicide. Unable to find an established artist to fill his place, the publishers engaged a twenty-year-old youth just out of art school as illustrator, and from then on Dickens was in complete control.

All these circumstances combined to make the first few numbers awkward and undistinguished, and it looked as if the project were about to fail. Then something happened which was to be a common experience for Dickens: he invented a character who kindled his imagination and demanded a vigorous life of his own. This character was Sam Weller, Mr Pickwick's Cockney servant, and when he appeared in the fourth number, the circulation suddenly soared and Dickens was assured of fame and fortune.

Summary

The book begins with an entry from the transactions of the Pickwick Club, describing the setting up of a Corresponding Society, consisting of Mr Samuel Pickwick, Chairman and founder of the Club, and Messrs Tracy Tupman, Augustus Snodgrass and Nathaniel Winkle, 'which shall from time to time report back to the Club the observations of character, manners, local customs, and any other interesting matters,' gathered on a series of journeys they are about to undertake. This forms the basis on which the novel is constructed, and the Club serves as an occasional connecting link for the series of adventures which follow.

The members of the Corresponding Society begin these adventures by taking a cab – and becoming involved in a fracas with the cabbie, from which they are rescued by a shabby young man carrying a brown paper parcel, named Mr Alfred Jingle, who joins them when they board the coach to Rochester.

On the journey, Mr Jingle entertains the Pickwickians with a stream of anecdotes and a variety of tall stories about his apparently very varied and colourful career, as well as helping them very substantially to quaff a number of alcoholic beverages and to consume several barrels of oysters. Arriving at the inn in Rochester, they learn that a ball is taking place there that evening. Jingle fires the romantically inclined but shy Mr Tupman with promises of all the beautiful damsels he would be able to introduce him to – if only he had his evening dress with him. But unfortunately his vast and compendious luggage has been lost, and all he has with him at that moment is the contents of his brown paper parcel. Mr Tupman therefore 'borrows' for Jingle the evening dress of Mr Winkle, who has dined and drunk too well to notice what is happening. At the ball, Jingle offends an army doctor namer Slammer, and the next morning the innocent Mr Winkle, identified by his evening coat, is challenged to a duel by Dr Slammer – until the mistake is revealed and the two shake hands. One of the doctor's companions recognizes Jingle as a strolling player.

The following day, the Pickwickians (without Jingle, who is unaccountably absent) attend a military display, and are caught between the opposing lines of soldiers conducting a mock battle. Beating a hasty retreat, they are invited into the carriage of jovial Mr Wardle. There they meet Mr Wardle's spinster sister, Rachel, and his two daughters Emily and Isabella, devour a gargantuan picnic – with the help of Mr Wardle's attendant, the fat boy Joe – and are invited to visit Mr Wardle's home at Dingley Dell.

They are received there with lavish hospitality. Mr Winkle falls in love with Arabella Allen, one of Mr Wardle's guests, and, in order to prove his reputation as a sportsman, goes out shooting – but only succeeds in winging Mr Tupman in the arm.

The annual cricket match between Dingley Dell and Muggleton takes place the next day. While Mr Tupman stays behind in the care of the ladies – much to his delight because it gives him a chance to flirt with Rachel Wardle – the rest of the party attend the match. In the refreshment tent they run into Mr Jingle again, and Mr Wardle invites him back to his home. Jingle, coming to the conclusion that Rachel has money of her own, manages to blacken Mr Tupman's reputation, and persuades her to elope with him. Mr Wardle and Mr Pickwick set off in pursuit.

They arrive at an inn in London where Sam Weller is working, and with his help track down the runaway couple. Jingle is bought off, and the tearful Miss Wardle taken back to Dingley Dell. Meanwhile, the disconsolate Mr Tupman has departed to 'The Leather Bottle' at Chobham to nurse his sorrow. Mr Pickwick finds him there and talks him out of his melancholy mood.

Mr Pickwick, returning to London, tells his landlady, Mrs Bardell, that he has come to an important decision which will be to her advantage, and she – utterly misunderstanding him and thinking he is about to propose marriage – falls swooning into his arms. In fact the decision Mr Pickwick had been talking about was to engage Sam Weller as his servant.

Attended now by Sam, the Pickwickians proceed to Eatanswill, where the Hon. Samuel Slumkey and Mr Horatio Fitzkin are the parliamentary candidates. As Slumkey's agent proves more efficient in the business of bribery and corruption, it is not surprising that his candidate, after a boisterous campaign, gets elected. While at Eatanswill the Pickwickians attend a fancy-dress breakfast party given by a local poetess, Mrs Leo Hunter. One of her honoured guests is a Mr Charles Fitz-Marshall – who is in fact none other than Mr Jingle. He disappears as soon as he catches sight of the Pickwickians, but Mr Pickwick discovers that he is staying at the Angel Inn, Bury St Edmunds, and follows him there. Jingle's 'servant', Job Trotter, tells Sam that his 'master' is going to elope that night with a young heiress from a nearby boarding-school for young ladies and persuades Mr Pickwick to climb over the school wall in order to catch Jingle red-handed. But in fact the story of an elopement is a fabrication, invented by Jingle and his accomplice in order to give them time to escape. Mr Pickwick is suspected of breaking into the school, but is rescued from his predicament by Sam and Mr Wardle – who is in the neighbourhood on a shooting trip.

Mr Pickwick now receives a letter from a firm of solicitors named Dodson and Fogg, informing him to his amazement that Mrs Bardell has instituted a breach of promise action against him. After various other adventures, the indignant Mr Pickwick returns to confront Messrs Dodson and Fogg. He tries to explain that Mrs Bardell was utterly mistaken as to his intentions, and accuses the rascally solicitors of attempting to swindle him. He is led away by Sam to a local tavern to recover his composure and is there introduced to Sam's father, a stage-coach driver. Sam tells him of their adventure with Jingle and Job Trotter. Mr Weller Senior recognizes the description of two well-known con-men who were recently his passengers on the Ipswich coach. After engaging a solicitor to defend him in the breach of promise action, Mr Pickwick and Sam board Mr Weller Senior's coach for Ipswich. On the way, Mr Pickwick makes the acquaintance of a Mr Peter Magnus. At an inn where they all spend the night, Mr Pickwick goes to bed in the wrong room, which he has to vacate hastily when its rightful occupant, a middle-aged lady, arrives. This lady turns out to be one on whom Mr Magnus has set his heart, and, refusing to listen to any explanation, Mr Magnus threatens Mr Pickwick with vengeance. The lady, frightened that a duel is about to take place, appeals to a local magistrate Mr Nupkins. Mr Pickwick and his fellow-Pickwickians are brought before him. Sam, however, has discovered that Jingle – alias Captain Fitz-Marshall – has been accepted by Mr Nupkins as a suitor for his daughter, and is staying in the Nupkins's house. While Jingle, still quite unabashed, is being unmasked upstairs, below stairs Sam is falling in love with Mary, one of Mr Nupkins's maids.

There is a Christmas reunion at Dingley Dell, during which Isabella Wardle is married, Mr Winkle kisses Arabella Allen under the mistletoe, and the poetical Mr Snodgrass becomes enamoured of Emily Wardle. Needless to say, they shift vast quantities of food and drink, ably assisted by the fat boy Joe. They also make the acquaintance of Benjamin Allen (Arabella's brother) and his friend Bob Sawyer, two young medical students. Mr Winkle is not at all pleased to see that Bob Sawyer has his eye on Arabella, and is further discomfited when Benjamin tells him that he intends to cut the throat of anyone, except his friend Bob Sawyer, who aspires to his sister's hand.

Mrs Bardell's breach of promise suit is heard. Her barrister, the redoubtable Serjeant Buzfuz, manages, among other manoeuvres, to convince the judge and jury that various innocent notes which Mr Pickwick had written to Mrs Bardell, including one requesting chops and tomato sauce for his dinner, are of a highly suggestive nature. The outcome is that judgement is found for the plaintiff, with damages and costs.

The Pickwickians proceed to Bristol, and discover that Benjamin Allen and Bob Sawyer have set up in medical practice there, and that Arabella, closely guarded, is staying nearby in Clifton. Sam discovers her whereabouts, and in the course of his search also meets Mr Nupkins's servant Mary again. He and his master assist Mr Winkle, with the help of a somewhat erratic dark-lantern, to keep a secret assignation with Arabella.

Back in London, Mr Pickwick refuses to pay the damages and costs awarded to Mrs Bardell and is sent to the Fleet Prison for debtors. There he meets Jingle and Job Trotter again, and moved by their extreme want, comes to their assistance. When Mr Pickwick insists that he cannot allow Sam to spend his days inside a prison, Sam, helped by his father, gets himself imprisoned for debt too, so that he can remain near his master.

The Pickwickians pay their respects to their chairman in the Fleet Prison and Sam receives a visit from his father, his step-mother, and the latter's friend, a pious humbug named Mr Stiggins who is both a drunkard and the deputy shepherd of the Ebenezer Temperance Association.

Dodson and Fogg, who had taken on Mrs Bardell's case in the confident expectation of Mr Pickwick's paying up, now have Mrs Bardell arrested because she cannot pay their fees, so she and her son Tommy also land up in the Fleet. Mr Pickwick's solicitor urges his client to accept the court's unjust ruling against him, for the sake of a lady in distress and her innocent child. Mr Winkle also arrives with Arabella, whom he has secretly married, and assures Mr Pickwick that he is the only one who could possibly reconcile Arabella's brother and Mr Winkle's wealthy father to the runaway match. This combination of circumstances persuades Mr Pickwick to discharge his debt, while Sam's father, of course, promptly withdraws his own concocted summons against his son. Before leaving the debtor's prison, Mr Pickwick makes arrangements for the release of Mr Jingle, who, with further assistance from Mr Pickwick, emigrates to the West Indies accompanied by his faithful friend Job Trotter.

Arriving in Bristol, Mr Pickwick manages to persuade Benjamin Allen and Bob Sawyer to accept the marriage of Arabella and Mr Winkle with a good grace. To begin with, though, he fails to placate Mr Winkle Senior, who threatens to disinherit his son. Sam receives news that his step-mother, Mrs Weller, has died and hastens to comfort his father, who tells him that his wife, repenting of her attachment to Mr Stiggins, has left her money to himself and Sam. When Mr Stiggins arrives to see if there are any pickings for him, old Mr Weller kicks him out. He also asks Mr Pickwick to take charge of his legacy (wisely invested, it eventually allows old Mr Weller to retire to a public house of his own) and discusses Sam's future with him. Mr Pickwick reveals that Sam has been courting Mary, and proposes setting them up in a little business. Sam, however, refuses to quit Mr Pickwick's service.

Meanwhile, it has also been revealed that Mr Snodgrass and Emily Wardle have been in love ever since the Christmas party at Dingley Dell. Mr Pickwick is instrumental in overcoming Mr Wardle's objection to the match, and old Mr Winkle, after calling incognito on Arabella and falling captive to her charms, gives his blessing to her marriage to his son. The Pickwick Club is wound up, and Mr Pickwick settles in a house at Dulwich, cared for by Sam and, after their marriage, by Mary, who becomes Mr Pickwick's housekeeper.

Critical commentary

It will be evident from this necessarily imperfect summary that *Pickwick* retains some vestiges at least of its original purposes. There are, for instance, the sporting episodes such as the cricket match at Dingley Dell, and the various shoots in which the Pickwickians take part. In many of these Mr Winkle is cast for the role (similar to that of the hero of *Jorrocks' Jaunts*) of the townsman revealing his clumsiness and ignorance. Many of the incidents also fulfil Dickens's first intention of reporting on matters of topical interest and all manner of social types and oddities, hence the descriptions of the election at Eatanswill, of the various solicitors' offices, of the law courts in action, travellers in stage-coaches or in inns, of newspaper editors, country squires, and so on, all of them very similar in style and approach to the *Sketches by Boz*.

To begin with, indeed, it seems as if *Pickwick* is going to be no more than a miscellany of loosely connected sketches. To a large extent, of course, this was the result of serialization, and it was only when he became thoroughly accustomed to this method of publication that

Dickens was able to impose shape and coherence upon his story as a whole. Such qualities can hardly be expected in the special circumstances attending the writing of *Pickwick*. But what is astonishing is the way in which, after the first few episodes, which remain as more or less isolated units, Dickens instinctively realized what was needed in the composition of a novel, and made determined efforts (as at top speed he produced one number after another) to draw his material together. He makes excellent use, for example, of the engaging scoundrel Jingle as a kind of sub-plot and as a link between a cluster of key episodes, and most of the minor characters (of whom only a proportion have been mentioned in the synopsis) play some part in the development of the various story-lines. From the moment too, that Mrs Bardell appears on the scene a central plot does emerge, involving suspense and tension, and working towards a recognizable climax and denouement.

At the same time, *Pickwick* remains the most diffuse and episodic of Dickens's novels. It is in this respect that it most obviously resembles the eighteenth-century picaresque novels, especially *Joseph Andrews* and *Tom Jones*, which also deal with a string of loosely-connected adventures in coaches, inns, and on the open road, and which introduce separate short stories – a practice which Dickens also adopted in some of his other novels.

Dickens's attachment to the eighteenth century in *Pickwick*, however, was emotional as well as technical. He hankered after it as a world less ugly and inhumane than that of the England of the Industrial Revolution, and, as has been pointed out, whenever he could he placed his tale some twenty years back, when the stage-coach was a recognized means of transport. At the time *Pickwick* was written, the railway revolution in Britain was still in its infancy. It was to figure powerfully in some of Dickens's later novels (notably in *Dombey and Son*, published in 1848) but he always looked back upon the passing of the stage-coach with nostalgic regret. There is no doubt that this was closely connected with his persistent yearning after what he always regarded as the golden age of his childhood – when the stage-coach was still a common sight – and before he was plunged into the horrors of his father's imprisonment, his abandonment, and his experience in the blacking-factory. Dickens always associated this lost Eden of imagined childhood innocence and bliss with the Chatham and Rochester area of Kent which figures so prominently in *Pickwick*. It was there that he and his family had lived during one of their rare spells of comparative financial stability, from about 1816 (when Dickens was four) to 1823, and his imagination was stirred whenever he turned back to those 'lost years': even the names of some of his characters come from tombstones in the churchyard he used to visit as a child.

There are many ways in which *Pickwick* conforms to this picture of an idealized past. There is what G. K. Chesterton called 'that everlasting sense of youth'. There are the feasting, drinking and jollity, the typically Dickensian Christmas at Dingley Dell, the frequent air of kindliness and goodwill; and above all, the benevolence of Mr Pickwick himself. It is to some extent an idealized world. Dickens had a special affection for *Pickwick* himself, and in many respects he was always yearning after the vision it represented.

It would be quite wrong, though, to regard *Pickwick* as a uniformly jolly, Christmas-card kind of novel. The shadows of a harsher world are present, even in the sunny early chapters. Jingle, for instance, is not just a funny man: with his ancient green coat whose 'soiled and faded sleeves scarcely reached to his wrists', and his 'scanty black trousers' with their shiny patches, and his brown-paper parcel, he is also an emanation of a London far removed from jolly well-fed Pickwickians. Similarly, Sam Weller is not just the lovable, comic Cockney servant. He is also the man who tells Mr Pickwick how at one time he had been forced to take 'unfurnished lodgings' under 'the dry arches of Waterloo Bridge', among 'the worn-out, starving, houseless creatures as rolls themselves in the dark corners o' them lonesome places.'

Many of the interpolations, too, are grimly realistic stories of poverty, deprivation and crime. These shadows in the Pickwickian sunshine prepare the reader for their gradual deepening when Mr Pickwick is imprisoned in the Fleet, amidst scenes of misery and want that are far from jolly – and which make the return to the sunshine in the final chapters almost intolerably poignant by contrast.

It is easy to see that the sombre intensity of some of the scenes in the Fleet derived from Dickens's memories of his own father's imprisonment in the Marshalsea. It is from the same source that his passionate reformism proceeds. This element is not as powerful in *Pickwick* as in the later novels, largely because at this stage, before disillusionment had set in, he believed that a universal Pickwickian benevolence was the best way of curing social ills. It is present in *Pickwick* nonetheless, particularly in the exposure of a corrupt and inhumane legal system, and also in the equally savage indictment (in the chapter on the Eatanswill election) of a corrupt parliamentary system – and it must be remembered that *Oliver Twist*, with its demonstration of the grim consequences of the Poor Law of 1834, followed closely after *Pickwick*.

None of this alters the fact, of course, that *Pickwick* is a very funny book. The flow and variety of the comic invention are astonishing, especially in view of the author's youth and the fact that it was his first novel. There are dozens of episodes which by themselves would rank as masterpieces of comedy – the cricket match at Dingley Dell, Mr Pickwick's adventures at the girls' boarding school, and his escapade with the dark-lantern at Clifton, to take some of the more obvious examples. The proliferation of comic characters is truly amazing. It is as if Dickens only had to lift his hand for them to come tumbling out of the walls and ceilings. They may be flat humorous-type characters, and some of them indeed have semi-allegorical names, like Angelo Bantam, the strutting Master of Ceremonies, and the fatuous Lord Mutanhead. But each of them, even if he only appears for a few moments and speaks no more than a couple of sentences, registers his own unique brand of comic vitality.

But these minor characters are only side-shoots. Those into whom Dickens pours the whole of his creative energies expand into quite other dimensions of imaginative fantasy. This is especially the case with Mr Pickwick himself. In part he is an idealized father-figure, with Sam often in the role of son, especially when he cares for his master in the debtors' prison, a service which the child Dickens had no doubt often dreamed of performing for his father. In part, he is a product of earlier literary influences. Thus he is frequently reminiscent of Goldsmith's Vicar of Wakefield, and even more so of Parson Adams in Fielding's *Joseph Andrews*. He recalls, too, the great universal comic character who also lies behind Parson Adams, the Don Quixote of Cervantes' famous classic – the Russian novelist Dostoyevsky described Mr Pickwick as 'pure Don Quixote'. This is not quite correct insofar as Mr Pickwick is by nature jovial and full of a sense of schoolboy fun, which can hardly be said of 'the knight of the doleful countenance': but Mr Pickwick does resemble Don Quixote in his consistent courtesy and gallantry, his old-fashioned notions of chivalry, his extreme innocence and gullibility, his proneness to romanticize people and situations, and in the ludicrous predicaments into which this tendency frequently leads him – and, above all, in his readiness to endure ridicule and suffering for the sake of a principle.

Like Don Quixote, too, Mr Pickwick, as his character gradually deepens under the stress of experience and his rather conventional benevolence of the earlier chapters changes into a deeply felt care and concern for others, reveals qualities that can without exaggeration be described as saint-like; so that Sam Weller can fervently declare to Job Trotter in the debtors' prison:

> I never heard, mind you, nor read of in story books, nor
> see in pictures, any angel in tights and gaiters, nor even in
> spectacles, as I remember ... but mark my words, Job
> Trotter, he's a reg'lar thoroughbred angel for all that.

With a character like Mr Pickwick, the reader cannot help feeling with G. K. Chesterton that:

> Dickens was a mythologist rather than a novelist ...
> He did not always manage to make his characters men, but
> he always managed, at the least, to make them gods.

The Posthumous Papers of the Pickwick Club in consequence remains, in spite of the faults of youthful inexperience and hasty composition, one of the funniest, most inspiriting and truly 'good' novels in the history of literature.

Sybil,
or The Two Nations

Benjamin Disraeli

It is shortly after the accession of Queen Victoria in 1837, and only a few years, therefore, before 'the hungry forties', perhaps the most wretched period for the poor in the whole of English history, and one in which England came close to revolution. A young generous-minded aristocrat named Egremont has met two strangers in the churchyard of the ancient Abbey of Marney and they get into conversation:

'... say what you like, our Queen reigns over the greatest nation that ever existed.'

'Which nation?' asked the younger stranger, 'for she reigns over two.'

'You speak of—' said Egremont, hesitatingly.
'THE RICH AND THE POOR.'

This immediately explains the subtitle of *Sybil*. It also pinpoints the fact that *Sybil* is a political novel, the first genuine specimen of its kind. This is, perhaps, hardly surprising, considering that its author was one of England's greatest statesmen, though what may seem surprising, in view of the radical tone of the extract just quoted, is that he was also a Conservative.

Benjamin Disraeli was born in London in 1804, the son of Isaac D'Israeli, a noted scholar and literary historian. Although he attended various private schools, he was to all intents and purposes educated in his father's very comprehensive library, and he never went to a university, though in 1824 he entered Lincoln's Inn with a view to making the law his career. When he was thirteen, the whole family had been received into the Church of England, then essential to any kind of public career, though Disraeli, proud to be a Jew, always insisted on the continuity of the Hebrew and Christian religions, proclaiming that he 'believed in the whole Jewish religion ... in Calvary as well as in Sinai.'

As a youth he was a dandy who delighted in wearing extravagant clothes and adopting melodramatic Byronic poses. He gave up his legal studies and, as a result of unwise gambling on the Stock Exchange, got badly into debt. He had already shown a precocious interest in politics, eagerly studying the writings of Viscount Bolingbroke, Edmund Burke and other exponents of philosophical conservatism, and the careers of the great Conservative statesmen, William Pitt the younger and his brilliant pupil, George Canning.

One of the literary phenomena of the late 1820s was a species of fiction nicknamed 'silver fork'. These were novels set in high society, taking their lead from *Tremaine, or The Man of Refinement* which was published in 1825 and ascribed by the enterprising publisher to some mysterious public personage of renown, though in fact its author, Robert Plumer Ward, was a successful but little-known lawyer and Member of Parliament. The aristocratic characters who figured in the 'silver fork' novels were aptly described by the German poet Heinrich Heine as 'wooden butterflies that flutter in the salons of the West End of London', though they were more realistic than many of those in the Gothic romances of the period, and the novels are of some value for their meticulous recording of the dress, food, etiquette and conversation of the fashionable circles of the day.

It was under the influence of *Tremaine*, that Disraeli –

before he had reached his twenty-first birthday – wrote his first novel, *Vivian Grey*. It was published anonymously in 1826 by the publisher of *Tremaine*, and with the same hints as to the eminence of its author and the identification of its characters with famous contemporary personages.

Vivian Grey is derivative, disjointed, melodramatic, and its flamboyant and epigrammatic hero is obviously an idealized self-portrait. But what is significant about it is that the first part of the novel deals not only with the hero's meteoric career in politics but also with his attempts to organize a new faction to compete with the old traditional political parties. A second novel, *The Young Duke*, followed in 1831, and again, though ludicrous in many ways, it contained many perceptive comments on political theories and issues. After a 'Grand Tour' of Europe and the Near East, in 1832 Disraeli published *Contarini Fleming*, a very Byronic story of a rootless young man who gets into trouble for writing a novel of political satire and becomes the leader of a band of brigands, then wanders gloomily about the East before finally deciding to enter politics.

A number of other novels followed, among them *The Wondrous Tale of Alroy* (1833), a historical romance set in the twelfth century about a heroic Jewish prince who leads a revolt against the Moslems; and *Venetia* (1837), interesting because of its fictional representations of Byron and Shelley. And in the same year, Disraeli was elected a Member of Parliament. Two years later he made an advantageous and eminently happy marriage to the wealthy widow, Mrs Wyndham Lewis, to whom he was to dedicate *Sybil*.

After making a disastrous start in the House of Commons, chiefly because of the florid style of his oratory, Disraeli began to make headway. In 1839 he horrified the older Tories by expressing sympathy in Parliament for the aims of the Chartists, the massive popular movement whose leaders had drawn up a petition, or charter, with a million and a half signatures demanding electoral and parliamentary reforms, in the hope of achieving some amelioration of the growing distress among the working classes, especially those in the new urban and industrial centres.

In 1841, Disraeli, along with a number of other like-minded young men, founded the New England movement. This opposed not only the Whig oligarchy, which in Disraeli's view was a political faction rather than a genuine party and representative only of vested interests, but also the cautious compromising Tories who represented the new capitalist class and who took their lead from Sir Robert Peel, himself the son of a factory-owner. Disraeli and his New England group appealed for an entirely new type of Conservatism ('Tory Democracy' as it was later called), based on what was in their view the natural alliance between the old aristocracy (recalled to their ancient traditional duties) and the peasantry; an alliance supported by the Established Church and with the Throne at the apex of the system. Only by the restoration of this natural harmony, they argued, could the welfare of the country be assured, and the exploitation of the urban workers by the factory owners be prevented.

It was a highly romantic concept, but it had a genuine emotional appeal, and the movement demonstrated that it had teeth by sympathizing not only with Chartism (though not with the Charter itself or with the revolutionary extremists) but with the new Trades Unions and with the agitation for a ten-hour day. In order to present these policies to a wider public, Disraeli now composed a trilogy of novels. The first of them, *Coningsby, or the New Generation*, was published in 1844. As in his earlier novels, many of the characters were based on living originals, but his overriding purpose was no longer satire or fashionable gossip, but the analysis of social and political forces, and in effect the novel is the story of English political administration in the twelve years following the passing of the Parliamentary Reform Bill of 1832. *Sybil,* published in 1845 and the most powerful of the three novels, was designed to come to grips with the evils of the new industrialism. *Tancred*, the third of the trilogy, published in 1847, sends its aristocratic young hero on a tour of the Holy Land in search of the origins of his Christian faith. It was designed to convey the message that in order to achieve ideals of the New England kind a genuine spiritual revival was also necessary.

By now, politics were driving literature into the background as far as Disraeli was concerned. He became the acknowledged spokesman of the Tory squires in their revolt against Sir Robert Peel, and was largely instrumental in bringing about his political downfall and a split in the Conservative Party. He then devoted his energies to rebuilding the party more in accordance with the ideals of Tory Democracy. He was Chancellor of the Exchequer in Conservative administrations in 1852 and in 1858. In 1866, again as Chancellor of the Exchequer, he introduced and carried through the House of Commons a far-reaching Reform Bill which extended the franchise to large sections of the population hitherto excluded – thus meeting some of the crucial demands of the Chartists. He was Prime Minister in 1868, but his party was defeated in the first election under the extended franchise. In 1874, however, his belief that the new working-class voters were by no means hostile to Conservatism of the kind he preached was vindicated. His Party was returned to power, and during the next six years he proved to be one of Britain's greatest and most successful Prime Ministers. Highly regarded by the Queen, he was created Earl of Beaconsfield in 1876. He died in April 1881.

During all these years at the forefront of the nation's affairs, literature had not been altogether abandoned. In 1870, while the party he led was in opposition, Disraeli published *Lothair*, about a wealthy nobleman and his involvement in the cause of Garibaldi and Italian liberty, which some critics regard as his best book next to *Sybil*.

Then after another interval of ten years, in his retirement he wrote his last novel, *Endymion*, the subject of which is the rise to political eminence of a young man, and which is full of striking pictures of life in elevated social and political spheres, and of cleverly drawn portraits of some of the leading political figures of the period between 1834 and 1841. Nevertheless, it is in *Sybil* that Disraeli the novelist and Disraeli the political theoretician most successfully join forces.

Summary

Charles Egremont, the hero, is the younger brother of Lord Marney, whose family originally derived their lands and wealth from the spoliation of the monasteries under Henry VIII. In the centuries since, 'the Egremonts had never said anything that was remembered, or done anything that could be recalled,' nor shown the least understanding of the duties and responsibilities involved in true aristocracy. It was such families, Disraeli argues in a long passage which belongs rather to a political treatise than to fiction, that had brought the nation to its present parlous condition.

Egremont agrees to seek election to Parliament, though he is in complete disagreement with his brother's support of the hated Poor Law of 1832 (which Dickens inveighed against so powerfully in *Oliver Twist*), and of other measures like it, and deplores the state of affairs allowed to exist in the village of Marney. It is after the burning of some ricks by the starving peasantry that Egremont meets two strangers in the churchyard and one of them makes his point about the two nations. The strangers are joined by a girl wearing the habit of a religious order and Egremont is much taken by her beauty and mystic appearance – which are presented in Disraeli's most floridly romantic manner. Before he can learn the names of the strangers, however, they leave for the nearby town of Mowbray. Shortly afterwards, Lord Marney tells his brother that he wishes to marry one of the daughters of Lord Mowbray, who is descended from an Indian nabob – someone who has made his fortune in India and bought his way to ancient aristocratic titles. Egremont agrees to go with his family on a visit to Mowbray Castle.

At the town of Mowbray, Egremont meets the strangers again. They are Stephen Morley, editor of a radical newspaper, Walter Gerard, an ardent supporter of the movement of popular protest and the man who had made the two nations speech, and Gerard's daughter, Sybil, who has been educated in a convent and is considering taking the veil. Gerard, who is an overseer at the factory of a Mr Trafford, one of the rare owners who care for the welfare of their workers, is descended from a very ancient family, and their present visit to Mowbray is to trace the whereabouts of an antiquarian named Hatton, thought to have important documents relating to Gerard's lineage.

The visit is also used to introduce a scene in the market place, in which factory workers at Shuffle and Screw's Mill are unable to buy meat for the Sunday meal because their employers have stopped most of their meagre wages in ridiculous fines. Various individual factory workers also appear, among them the clever young 'Dandy Mick' Radley and the nameless orphan known as 'Devilsdust', who has managed to give himself some education and who has 'read and pondered on the rights of labour, and sighed to vindicate his order.'

At Mowbray Castle, Egremont listens approvingly to an impassioned plea made by the vicar, Mr St Lys, for an improvement in the lot of the poor in both towns and villages. St Lys, who tells Egremont that in his view the Church has deserted the people in their hour of greatest need, takes him on a visit to the family of a starving hand-loom worker named Philip Warner. There, Egremont again meets Sybil, who has arrived on an errand of mercy to Warner's sick wife.

There are further scenes depicting the state of affairs among the poor. One of them presents the colliers leaving the pits, among them women who 'naked to the waist, an iron chain fastened to a belt of leather ... between their legs' have been hauling tubs of coal on their hands and knees, up steep and muddy paths below ground 'for twelve, sometimes for sixteen hours a day'; and boys and girls of four and five who, in darkness and solitude, have been operating the ventilation-doors for even longer stretches. The conversation of the miners in the nearby public house reveals the iniquitous system whereby they are forced by the mine-owners to accept unwanted articles (in this case, waistcoats) as part of their wages. Another scene shows the women jostling in long queues in order to get basic necessities at highly inflated prices in the 'tommy' shops run by the factory owners.

After quarrelling with his brother, Egremont – posing as Mr Franklin, a freelance journalist – takes lodgings near the cottage where Walter Gerard and his daughter Sybil are living. Gerard takes him to see the factory-village of his employer Mr Trafford, who has proved that humane treatment of his workers, including the provision of various welfare arrangements, is by no means at variance with profit for himself. On his way back to his lodgings one night, Egremont is waylaid by a mysterious assailant, but rescued by Sybil's bloodhound, Harold. Eventually, at his mother's entreaties, Egremont joins her in London for her wedding to Lord Deloraine; and afterwards he takes his seat in the House of Commons.

Walter Gerard, Stephen Morley and Warner address a great torch-light meeting of Chartists, while Dandy Mick, introduced by his friend Devilsdust, goes through the secret ritual of initiation into a trades union. Gerard and Morley, with other delegates of the People's National Convention, now come to London to get support from those members of the ruling classes they have reason to believe are not unsympathetic to their cause – and so discover that one of these, the Honourable Charles Egremont, is the man they had known as Mr Franklin.

Through them, Egremont meets Sybil again. He tries

to convince her that by themselves the people are not strong enough to achieve the changes they seek, and that they must turn for help to the 'new generation' of aristocrats whose consciences have at last been awakened. Eventually, too, he declares his love for her, but Sybil, proud of her father and his cause, declares that 'the gulf is impassable' between them.

In the meantime, Hatton the antiquarian, deeply attracted to Sybil, encourages Gerard to institute legal action for the restitution of his ancient lands and titles.

The Chartists present their petition to Parliament in the midst of growing unrest. Egremont makes a speech in which he declares that 'the results of the Charter' can be obtained by Parliament and the ruling classes it still represents taking the initiative themselves.

Sybil reads Egremont's speech in the newspapers and is impressed by it. Egremont himself warns her that the Government are preparing action against the Chartist leaders, and urges her to try and persuade her father to leave London. Stephen Morley, too, is alarmed by Gerard's increasing association with the extremists, who are now preaching open insurrection. But Gerard insists upon attending another meeting of the Chartist leaders. While Sybil is waiting anxiously for his return, Morley arrives to warn her that the police have been ordered to raid the meeting. He also pours out his love for her – and it emerges that it was he who had been Egremont's unseen assailant on the occasion when the dog Harold had come to his rescue.

Sybil alerts the Chartist leaders, but before they can escape, the police arrive and arrest the delegates – and Sybil herself. She succeeds, however, in sending a note to Egremont and the following morning, disguised as a coachman, he arrives with a warrant from the Secretary of State for Sybil's release, and drives her away. In the coach, he reveals his identity and takes her in his arms.

But, after her father has received a comparatively light prison-sentence thanks to Egremont's intervention and influence, Sybil returns to the convent at York. On his release from prison Gerard finds employment as a skilled artisan in Mowbray. Sybil is allowed to visit him at weekends, and the Mother Superior of the convent dissuades her from taking her final vows.

The conditions of the working classes, however, have considerably worsened. Morley, the advocate of moral force as opposed to violence, has fallen into the background and younger leaders, among them Dandy Mick and Devilsdust, are coming to the fore in Mowbray. Nevertheless, Gerard is still their hero, and he terrifies Sybil by his talk of future revolutionary actions, though he is opposed to violence.

Near Mowbray is Wodgate, one of the ramshackle towns thrown up by the Industrial Revolution, and inhabited chiefly by master-craftsmen who treat their apprentices even more tyrannically than the mine and factory owners treat their employees. The unacknowledged 'king' of Wodgate is 'Bishop' Hatton, brother of the antiquarian. Hatton leads his 'hell-cats' through the district, calling on miners and factory workers to come out on strike until Parliament has accepted the Charter. The violence grows and the hated 'tommy' shop in Mowbray is burned to the ground, with its proprietor inside it.

'Bishop' Hatton and his men march on Mr Trafford's works, but before they can break in, they are stopped by Gerard, who reminds them that Mr Trafford has always been a good employer who respects the rights of labour. Baffled in this attempt, the 'hell-cats' now turn their attack on Mowbray Castle. This exactly suits the plans of Hatton the antiquarian and Stephen Morley, who hope in the confusion to extract from Lord Mowbray's muniment-room the documents that will prove Gerard's title to his property.

Sybil, who has taken refuge at the Castle, confronts the rioters, and her father's followers among them rally to her. She is aided in her efforts by St Lys, who has thrown open his church to the rioters, assuring them of his support for their just demands, but at the same time preaching against violence. Thanks to the efforts of Sybil and St Lys, Lady Mowbray and her family leave the castle unmolested, but in the confusion Sybil is separated from them. While this is happening, Morley, assisted by Dandy Mick and Devilsdust, are searching for the documents. At the very moment they discover them a detachment of yeomanry, commanded by Egremont, arrives on the scene. Morley draws his pistol and is shot dead by one of the troopers. Dandy Mick manages to escape with the documents.

Egremont returns to the park in time to rescue Sybil, but the castle goes up in flames. Meanwhile, Lord Marney, at the head of a larger troop of yeomanry is also hurrying towards the castle. They encounter a crowd headed by Walter Gerard, who are in fact on their way to restore law and order. Without waiting for explanations however, Lord Marney orders his men to attack. Gerard resists, and is shot down. His enraged supporters fight back with stones and cudgels, and Lord Marney is killed too.

Dandy Mick delivers the documents safely to Sybil. With the help of Mr Hatton the antiquarian, who accepts the dashing of his own hopes in relation to Sybil, her claim (as Gerard's daughter) to the Mowbray estates is established, and shortly afterwards, Lord Mowbray dies. As a reward for his share in securing the documents for Sybil, Dandy Mick is set up in business by Egremont (now Lord Marney) and takes Devilsdust as his partner. Good harvests and wise measures introduced by Sir Robert Peel have mitigated the worst distresses of the people and the Chartist agitations have receded. And needless to say, the new Lord Marney and Sybil are happily married, thus symbolizing the true union of aristocracy and people.

Critical commentary

The novel would have been a good deal more effective if Disraeli had not made Sybil and her father aristocrats. Indeed, the whole business of mysterious antecedents and missing documents is one of the more overworked themes of the Gothic romance. Most of the love passages between Egremont and Sybil are also full of romantic clichés. Sybil first appears to Egremont as 'a seraph, that had lighted on this sphere, or the fair phantom of some saint haunting the sacred ruins of her desecrated fane.' There are numerous purple passages of this kind, and others couched in the kind of stilted rhetoric that caused Lord Balfour to comment that to know how Disraeli spoke in Parliament 'it was only necessary to imagine a bronze mask speaking his novels.' The unreality of much of *Sybil* is summed up by these words of the later Victorian novelist, Anthony Trollope.

> A feeling of stage properties ... and that pricking
> of the conscience which must be the general
> accompaniment of paste diamonds.

At the same time, Disraeli's taste for the flamboyant and the grandiose could fire both his wit and his imagination. The false glitter of high society; the inanities of club life; the brittle excitement of noble ladies in the game of politics as an alternative to cards or racing; the intrigues of professional political manipulators – all these are often brilliantly rendered. The picture of Society with a capital 'S' that Disraeli presents is both satirically sharp and remarkably comprehensive.

It must be remembered, too, that Disraeli's portraits in *Sybil* include a wide variety of working-class types, all of them possessing a degree of authentic vitality. With the major characters the overriding preoccupation is, admittedly, with the various political attitudes they represent. All the same, they are not entirely puppets, and each of them has some individual form of behaviour or discourse.

Egremont *does* convince as a gentleman in the best sense of the word; while his brother really *is* a most unlikeable specimen of upper-class insensitivity. As for Disraeli's female characters, they form a refreshing contrast to the sentimentalized, doll-like women of the majority of Victorian novels. All of them, including Sybil (preposterous though she is in many respects) have brains, and show it in their talk and behaviour.

Disraeli's florid style, moreover, can sometimes achieve impressive *chiaroscuro* effects, as in his descriptions of the Chartist torch-light procession and of the firing of Mowbray Castle. The latter is reminiscent of the storming of the Tolbooth in Scott's *The Heart of Midlothian*, and Disraeli possesses some of Scott's skill in the handling of crowd scenes, as well as a good deal of his narrative force. These echoes of Scott, moreover, have a profounder significance. Disraeli, of course, is dealing not with the past but with events he has himself lived through. Nevertheless, his depiction of the period of Chartist agitation is not, on the whole, a simple matter of contemporary *rapportage* but comes close to genuine historical reconstruction of the kind practised by Scott.

Disraeli's use of living originals for his characters has already been mentioned. In *Sybil*, for example, St Lys is based on Ambrose Phillips de Lisle, a Roman Catholic member of Disraeli's original New England group; Stephen Morley derives in part from William Lovett, leader of the 'Moral Force' Chartists; the benevolent factory-owner, Mr Trafford, is probably a composite portrait of Sir Robert Peel and Robert Owen, the pioneer Socialist and owner of the model factory-village at New Lanark and several of the grand ladies are modelled on famous political hostesses of the day.

The topography of *Sybil* is also carefully related to actual localities in the North of England, mainly in Yorkshire. Thus Marney is Ripon, and Mowbray a combination of Skipton and Huddersfield, and most of the country houses, villages, and natural features described in the novel have been identified. In addition, Disraeli took considerable pains with his varieties of north-country dialect.

The details of the Chartist torchlight rallies and of the 1842 riots in Yorkshire and Lancashire are also painstakingly accurate. The initiation of Dandy Mick into a trades union is a faithful transcript of the rituals of initiation – largely derived from those of Freemasonry – revealed at the time of the trial of the Tolpuddle Martyrs in 1834 (at this period trades unions were still illegal). The descriptions of conditions in the factories and mines were based on personal observation and on the various Royal Commissions and Parliamentary Reports of the day.

Some of the passages in *Sybil* read *too* much like Government blue papers, but, on the whole, Disraeli preserves sufficient artistic detachment to give his novel permanent human and historical value. The fictional scenes, incidents, and characters embodying the various issues outnumber the purely journalistic or propagandist passages. The reader remembers not only the 'two nations' speech, but the man who made it, and the context to which it belongs. Similarly, the use of heartless Utilitarian and Malthusian doctrines (which argued the existence of self-regulating mechanisms in the movements of wages, products, and population) by the more selfish sections of the wealthy classes to justify a policy of *laissez-faire* (or non-interference), is not merely stated but demonstrated in the behaviour, habits and speech of Lord Marney and his friends.

All this means that *Sybil* deserves to rank as a social novel as well as a historical one, and in this respect it can be seen as an influence on later social novels such as those of Dickens, Mrs Gaskell, and Charles Kingsley. At the same time, it is obviously a pioneer political novel, in the sense that it is basically concerned with political ideas and that its main characters are absorbed in the theory and practice of politics. As a political novelist Disraeli has had his descendants, but it is doubtful if anyone has equalled him. Some of the books in Trollope's Palliser sequence, such as *Phineas Finn* (1869) and *The Prime Minister* (1876), perhaps come closest to him in this respect, but their author is primarily interested in the social background to politics and reveals no interest in political theory and Trollope did not possess Disraeli's intimate inside knowledge of the day-to-day workings of the Parliamentary and governmental system.

Although, therefore, there are many obvious flaws in *Sybil*, it survives not only for the politics but also for the degree to which it succeeded in expressing them in fictional terms.

Jane Eyre

Charlotte Brontë

Next to Shakespeare's Stratford-on-Avon, the most visited literary shrine in England is the old parsonage at Haworth, on the edge of the Yorkshire moors, once the home of three remarkable women novelists – Charlotte, Emily and Anne Brontë. This is not only the result of the books the Brontës wrote, but also of the strange circumstances of their lives.

It was in 1820 that the Reverend Patrick Brontë arrived at Haworth with a sick wife and six small children. The son of an Irish peasant named Prunty, he had by dint of heroic efforts got himself to St John's College, Cambridge, where he had obtained his MA degree and taken holy orders. He had also changed his name to Brontë, after the Duke of Brontë, which was one of Nelson's titles.

A year later, Mrs Brontë died of cancer. Her unmarried sister, Miss Branwell, came to keep house. But it was not long before tragedy struck again. In Charlotte's eighth year (she was born in 1816) she and Emily, together with the two elder girls, Maria and Elizabeth, were sent as boarders to a school for poor clergymen's children at Cowan Bridge, much against their will, as they were already attached to their home and to each other with an almost abnormal intensity. Maria and Elizabeth, weakened by the spartan and unhealthy conditions, harsh discipline and bad, inadequate food at Cowan Bridge caught typhus during an outbreak of the disease, and were brought home to die. Soon afterwards, Charlotte and Emily were removed from the school, to be thankfully reunited with their brother Branwell (a year younger than Charlotte), and Anne, the youngest of the family.

None of the Brontë children ever fully recovered from these successive shocks. As so often happens with precocious and sensitive children in such circumstances, the tragic deaths in the family were accompanied by irrational secret agonies of self-blame and guilt. These were accentuated by the harsh Calvinistic doctrines that had been directed at them at Cowan Bridge and, to a lesser extent, by their aunt. At the age of twenty, Charlotte declared in a letter to a friend that she was still frequently 'smitten ... to the heart with the conviction that ghastly Calvinistic doctrines are true, darkened in short by the very shadow of spiritual death!'

Their home life became even more precious to them. Their father discussed literature and politics with them as equals, making his library fully available. Although later, Charlotte was to read many contemporary books and to be particularly interested in Thackeray and Tennyson, it was her early reading of the Bible, Shakespeare, Bunyan, Scott, Byron and the eighteenth-century essayists that exercised the greatest influence on her. The Brontë children also delighted in the tales of village and country life retailed to them by Tabitha Ackroyd, the rough but kindly Yorkshirewoman who came to work at the Parsonage when Charlotte was nine and remained until she died in 1855, only a few months before Charlotte herself – and who was the prototype for Nelly Dean in Emily's novel *Wuthering Heights*.

But it was in each other's company that the Brontë children found the most complete escape from the haunting memories of the past, in long hours wandering over the moors, or playing together in the Parsonage – and above all, in the invention of a whole fantasy world of their own; or rather, two fantasy worlds, called Angria and Gondal, each with its own geography, history and politics. All imaginative children indulge in daydreams, but what was unique about those of the Brontë children was that they were shared simultaneously by four minds, and that in addition they were set down in microscopic writing on tiny pages and bound in miniature volumes with wrapping paper from the shops in Haworth. The stories and characters in these sagas were Byronically romantic and melodramatic, surprisingly adult (seductions and adulteries are common, for example) and with a strong unconscious erotic element. These juvenile writings were to some extent rehearsals for the adult works to come, but they were also obstacles that had to be overcome if maturity was to be reached. They were in many respects dangerously introverted and escapist. They heightened the Brontës' dependence on each other and on their remote, isolated home, so that one of their friends commented that they were 'like growing potatoes in a cellar'. The problem that faced all of them, in consequence, was how to adjust themselves to the reality outside the confines of Haworth and the spell of their shared romantic imaginings. All of them found it painfully difficult. When Charlotte was fifteen, for instance, and went to Roe Head (a humane and well-run school very different from Cowan Bridge) for eighteen months, she was only too relieved to return to that 'web of sunny air', as she described the old spell of childhood intimacy and fantasy.

Charlotte, though, was the most determined of them in her efforts to escape. Reality, in any case, had to be faced. The family were poor, and Branwell, with his Byronic good looks and behaviour, already exhibiting signs of emotional instability, had to be launched on a career. Accordingly, in 1835 Charlotte returned to Roe Head to qualify as a teacher there. Emily went with her as a pupil but was so homesick that she fell ill and after two months had to return to Haworth, to be replaced by Anne. Charlotte struggled on as a teacher at Roe Head, and then as a governess. Anne, too, became a governess. Then Charlotte conceived the idea of the three sisters running a school of their own. In 1842, in order to improve their qualifications, she took Emily with her to Brussels to study languages at a boarding school run by a married couple named Héger, and Charlotte also taught there for a spell. This period was crucial for Charlotte's development, not least because she fell passionately but hopelessly in love with M. Héger, an experience which deepened both her feeling of being doomed to unhappiness and her strong sense of moral independence and integrity.

Reunited in Haworth in 1844, the sisters had to accept the fact that Branwell, after failing as a portrait-painter, a clerk on the railways, and a tutor, was rapidly deteriorating under the influence of drink and drugs. They sent out prospectuses for their school, but the Parsonage was too remote to attract pupils. In 1846 the sisters published – under the male pseudonyms of Currer, Ellis, and Acton Bell, and at their own expense – a volume of their poems. In spite of the genius so evident today in Emily's contributions, the volume sold only two copies. But the sisters had also been working on novels, and in 1847 Anne's *Agnes Grey* (based on her experiences as a governess) and Emily's *Wuthering Heights* were accepted, though not immediately published. Charlotte's *The Professor* (which drew on her experience in Brussels) was rejected (and did not appear until 1857, two years after her death), but by then she had completed *Jane Eyre*, which was accepted by another publisher and issued in October 1847. The success had the effect of stimulating her sisters' publisher to bring out their novels shortly afterwards. Anne's second novel, *The Tenant of Wildfell Hall* also appeared the following year. Their publisher hinted that Emily's and Anne's novels were by the author of *Jane Eyre*, and this led to the revealing of the true identities of Currer, Ellis, and Acton Bell.

In the September of the same year, Branwell ended what Charlotte described as his 'brief, erring, suffering, feverish life'. His sisters had succeeded in surviving the shocks of their early lives and in rising above their escapist dream-world to reach a genuinely creative expression of their innate genius, but Branwell was in some respects the presiding spirit in all their novels. This is particularly the case with Anne's *The Tenant of Wildfell Hall*, which is the study of the effects of a charming young man's gradual degradation through drink and debauchery; and Branwell, in his earlier Byronic aspects, is also present to a lesser extent in the Heathcliff of Emily's *Wuthering Heights* and in the Rochester of *Jane Eyre*.

Perhaps it was the shock of Branwell's tragic end that finally loosened Emily's and Anne's hold on life, always weaker than that of Charlotte. It was at Branwell's graveside that Emily caught the chill which, after repeated refusals to see a doctor, led to her death a few months later. Anne, who had long been in delicate health, died the following May – and Charlotte was left alone in the Parsonage with her ageing father and the faithful 'Tabby' Ackroyd. With her usual fierce determination and independence, she went on writing. In 1849 *Shirley* appeared, her novel about the lives and loves of a proud, beautiful and clever heiress named Shirley Keeldar – a portrait, Charlotte confessed, of Emily as she might have been in different circumstances – and of the gentle and retiring Caroline Helstone, against the background of the Luddite riots, in which the distressed Yorkshire weavers attacked and destroyed the new machines which were robbing them of their livelihood. *Villette*, her last novel, was published in 1853, and in the following year Charlotte married her father's curate Arthur Bell Nicholls. After a brief period of happiness (during which she became pregnant), Charlotte, too, caught a chill, and died in March 1855, only thirty-nine years old.

Summary

The sorrows, tragedies, intensities and courage of Charlotte's own pilgrimage are strongly present in *Jane Eyre*. The sense of isolation, frustration, and defiance is immediately captured. Jane is a plain, penniless orphan. Mr Reed, her mother's brother, had taken her into his home, Gateshead Hall, as an infant and treated her tenderly, begging his wife on his deathbed to bring her up on an equal footing with his own children. But Mrs Reed has an antipathy for Jane and treats her with great harshness, allowing her own children to torment and insult her. After John Reed, a hulking schoolboy of fifteen, has bullied her beyond endurance, Jane, in the extremity of her pain and fear, strikes out at him and is locked in the 'red room' – the room in which her uncle had died. Alone in the darkness Jane imagines that his ghost is coming to haunt her, and she falls unconscious in a fit. She is nursed back to health by Bessie, one of Mrs Reed's servants and the only member of the household to show Jane any kindness. When Jane has recovered, Mrs Reed sends for Mr Brocklehurst, the grim Calvinistic clergyman who is responsible for the running of Lowood Orphan Asylum – clearly modelled on the ghastly Cowan Bridge school. Mrs Reed presents Jane to him as a rebellious and deceitful liar who needs strict discipline if she is to escape hell-fire. The description of the cold, bad food, insanitary conditions and harsh discipline at Lowood closely follows Charlotte's own experience at Cowan Bridge. Jane makes friends with a gentle girl named Helen Burns. Like Charlotte's sister Maria at Cowan Bridge, Helen is mercilessly bullied by the French teacher at the school; and, like her, she succumbs when typhus sweeps through the school. Jane herself is tormented by Mr Brocklehurst, but is befriended by a kind teacher named Miss Temple, under whose supervision she makes rapid progress in her lessons. After an investigation by the authorities, conditions improve and Jane stays on as a teacher. But when Miss

Temple marries and moves to another part of the country, Jane advertises for a post as governess.

She receives a favourable reply from a Mrs Fairfax of Thornfield Hall. Before leaving Lowood, she has a visit from Bessie who tells her that some years back a Mr Eyre had called at Gateshead Hall, announcing himself as Jane's uncle and inquiring for her; but as he had been *en route* for his business in Madeira he had been unable to make the journey to Lowood.

Arriving at Thornfield Hall, Jane finds that Mrs Fairfax is housekeeper to the absent owner, Mr Edward Rochester, and that her pupil is a precocious, French-speaking little girl named Adèle Varens, apparently a ward of Mr Rochester. While Mrs Fairfax is showing her over the house, Jane is startled by a spine-chilling laugh from a locked room, and is told that it is Grace Poole, the sewing woman.

While out walking later on, Jane comes upon a stranger who has been thrown from his horse, and helps him to remount. He is a Byronic-looking figure – dark-visaged and brooding – with a distinct resemblance to one of the heroes of Charlotte's childhood 'Angria' saga.

Back at Thornfield, Jane discovers that the stranger is the curt and masterful Mr Rochester. He is much taken by Jane's quiet, composed manner, her frankness and spirit, and her intelligence. He confides that Adèle is the illegitimate daughter of a worthless French opera dancer, who, after claiming that he was the father, had abandoned the child. It is clear to Jane, who is by now falling in love with Rochester, that he is haunted (in true Byronic fashion) by other dark secrets. One night, Jane is awakened by strange sounds, and finds smoke billowing from under the door of Mr Rochester's bedroom. She discovers him asleep in a blazing bed and succeeds in putting out the flames. He tells her that the fire must have been caused by Grace Poole, and forbids Jane to mention the incident to anyone else in the house.

Rochester leaves Thornfield on a visit to one of his

neighbours, and Mrs Fairfax tells Jane that the beautiful and aristocratic Blanche Ingram will be one of his fellow-guests. Jane bitterly upbraids herself for indulging in foolish day-dreams about her employer, and by the exercise of her habitual self-discipline regains her composure; but she is sorely tried when Mr Rochester returns with a party which includes Blanche Ingram and commands Jane to attend in the drawing-room in the evenings, where she is treated with condescension by his guests.

A Mr Mason from the West Indies arrives at Thornfield. That night, Jane is roused from sleep by screams coming from the upper floor of the house. Rochester summons her to help him attend the mysterious caller, Mr Mason, who has been badly wounded with a knife – attacked, as Jane supposes, by the maniacal Grace Poole. During the night Mr Mason is spirited out of the house. Rochester now confides in Jane that he hopes to seek release from a sinful past by marriage to Blanche Ingram, and he begs Jane to give him her blessing.

Shortly afterwards, Jane receives the news that Mrs Reed has had a stroke and has asked to see her. She gets leave from Mr Rochester to visit her aunt. Mrs Reed is as cold and unforgiving as ever, but is obviously vexed by a guilty conscience. Before she dies, she gives Jane a letter she had received years before from Jane's uncle in Madeira requesting Jane's address because he wished to make her his heiress. Mrs Reed, hating the very thought of Jane receiving a benefit of any kind, had told Mr Eyre in her reply that his niece had died during the epidemic at Lowood. After attending Mrs Reed's funeral, Jane returns to Thornfield. She is surprised to find no sign of preparations for the wedding of Mr Rochester and Blanche Ingram – and Rochester reveals that it is not Blanche Ingram he wishes to marry – but Jane herself. Rochester is an impetuous wooer, but Jane insists upon keeping him at arm's length and continuing her duties as a governess until the marriage. She also writes to her uncle in Madeira, in the hope that through him she might achieve some degree of financial independence. Nevertheless, she is uneasy at the excess of her adoration for her future husband. 'I could not, in those days,' she says, 'see God for His creature, of whom I had made an idol.' Two nights before the wedding, Jane receives a visitation from a horrible-looking creature who tries on her bridal veil. Rochester suggests that perhaps Grace Poole had entered her room in the night and that the other details were supplied by a nightmare, but Jane finds her veil on the floor, torn in two. On the wedding day the ceremony is interrupted by Mr Mason and his solicitor, who produce evidence that Rochester is already married, and that his wife is living in Thornfield Hall. Rochester takes the wedding party to the locked apartment at the top of the house and shows them a mad woman who immediately attacks him with maniacal fury until she is overpowered with the help of Grace Poole, her attendant. This mad woman, Rochester admits, is indeed his wife: many years ago, when he was in Jamaica, he had been trapped into marrying her, although her father and her brother, Mr Mason, knew that there was insanity in the family. It was the mad Mrs Rochester whose terrible laugh Jane had overheard from time to time, who had tried to set fire to Mr Rochester's bed, and who had torn Jane's wedding veil. It also transpires that Mr Mason had been staying in Madeira with Jane's uncle when Jane's letter arrived. Mr Eyre himself had been too ill to travel to England to prevent his niece's bigamous marriage to Mr Rochester, and had despatched Mr Mason instead.

Rochester pleads with Jane to stay with him, passionately assuring her of his love and devotion, but profound though her own love and pity are, Jane refuses to live as Rochester's mistress and leaves Thornfield Hall secretly by night. She spends all her savings on a coach-journey that takes her far from Thornfield Hall, tries unsuccessfully to find work, and is on the verge of death from starvation and exposure when she calls at a house and begs for food and shelter. She is taken in by a clergyman named

St John Rivers, and is cared for by his sisters, Mary and Diana.

Calling herself Jane Elliott, she wins the warm affection of Mary and Diana. Their father has recently died, leaving them in straitened circumstances, and they have also been disappointed in their expectations of an inheritance from an uncle, so they are about to leave their old home, Moor House, and go to work as governesses. Their brother obtains for Jane the post of mistress at the school he is starting at nearby Morton (where his parsonage is situated) with the financial help of a young heiress named Rosamond Oliver. It is soon evident to Jane that St John Rivers is in love with Rosamond, and she with him, but he is resolved to become a missionary and has come to the conclusion that marriage to Rosamond would be inimical to his vocation.

St John Rivers discovers Jane's true identity and tells her that there have been advertisements in the papers asking for news of her because her uncle in Madeira has now died and left her his fortune. It turns out, moreover, that Mr Eyre was also the uncle of whom the Rivers family had had expectations. Jane insists on sharing her fortune with her new-found cousins. Mary and Diana are thus able to return to their old home, and Jane joins them. She hopes that St John's share of her fortune will induce him to give up his intention of going to India as a missionary, and to propose marriage to Rosamond Oliver. But he is unbending in his resolve and not long afterwards Rosamond becomes engaged to another man. Before he sets out for India, St John Rivers asks Jane to marry him – not, she knows, because he loves her, but because he believes she would make an excellent missionary. Jane still loves Rochester, but the force of St John's personality begins to wear her down. She finds herself 'tempted to cease struggling with him – to rush down the torrent of his will into the gulf of his existence', and there lose her own. And then, suddenly, she hears a voice calling 'Jane, Jane, Jane'. It is the voice of Rochester.

Jane sets out for Thornfield Hall, but when she arrives she finds nothing but a blackened ruin. She learns that after her departure Mr Rochester had sent Adèle away to school, retired Mrs Fairfax and thereafter lived the live of a recluse. One night his insane wife had again escaped from the custody of Grace Poole, had set fire to the house and then climbed on to the roof. Rochester had followed her in an attempt to save her, but she had plunged to her death. Rochester himself had been trapped and when he had been dragged clear it had been found that he was blind, and that one hand had to be amputated. He had now retired to another of his properties, the remote manor-house of Ferndean.

Jane goes to Ferndean and Rochester is overjoyed to see her. He tells her that four days previously he had, in an access of loneliness and despair, called out her name. It had been the exact date and time at which Jane had heard the voice. Jane and Rochester are married and live in blissful devotion to each other. Rochester recovers the partial sight of one eye in time to see his first-born son. Jane continues to be close friends with Mary and Diana Rivers. From time to time she also receives letters from St John Rivers in India, where he has devoted himself, body and soul, to his missionary labours, and where, as his health fails, he views the early death he anticipates with true Christian resignation.

Critical commentary

A summary of *Jane Eyre*, divorced from the urgency of Charlotte Brontë's style and tone of voice, tends to throw the cruder elements into prominence – and that these exist cannot be denied. The stock devices of the contemporary Gothic romance – lord of the manor haunted by a mysterious past; sinister mansion hiding its guilty secret; innocent girl trying to fathom the mystery – are all present. In addition, there are the Gothic horrors of Mrs Rochester's madness and various supernatural manifestations such as the white light that shines in the red room where Jane is locked up as a child and which she supposes to be the ghost of her uncle. The melodramatic plot depends often, too, on the grossest of coincidences, especially that whereby Jane, after her flight from Thornfield to a part of the county completely unknown to her, chances upon the very house where her unknown cousins live.

There are also aspects of the love story between Rochester and Jane which are at the level of the novelette. The whole idea of the plain, poor girl eventually capturing the rich, bear-like but deliciously attractive aristocrat has obvious affinities with fairy tales like Cinderella, the Ugly Duckling, and Beauty and the Beast.

Rochester himself is a stock Byronic figure, close to the heroes of Charlotte's childhood fantasies. The taming of the dominant male by eventually making him blind and maimed has a large element of romantic dream-fulfilment about it, as well as undertones of a morbidly erotic nature.

Nevertheless, *Jane Eyre* does succeed as a work of art. The very intensity with which even the most escapist and over-romanticized elements are presented makes them convincing, and these elements, after all, were close to the personal experience of the four Brontës – it could, indeed, be said that in many respects the situation at Haworth really *was* a Gothic one.

But a more important reason is that the struggle which Charlotte conducted against the insidious spell of the old day-dreaming in her own life is part, too, of her creative life, so that in her novels she and her heroines, although at times they yield to this spell, also recoil from it. Intense and passionate struggle lies at the core of all Charlotte Brontë's novels. When, for example, Rochester in wooing her addresses her playfully as Mrs Rochester, she replies:

'It can never be, sir; it does not sound likely. Human beings never enjoy complete happiness in this world.
I was not born for a different destiny to the rest of my

    species; to imagine such a lot befalling me is a fairy
    tale – a daydream.'

This is partly an expression of the mood of depression
and unworthiness, caused by the tragic circumstances of
her life, that often assailed Charlotte. But it is also symptomatic of her heroine's instinct (a very sound one, as it
turns out) that there is something make-believe about
Rochester's first courtship – when he lavishes presents on
her her reaction is that 'the more he bought me, the more
my cheek burned with a sense of annoyance and degradation.'

    This is a good instance, too, of the way in which practi-
cally everything in the book is filtered through the consciousness of the heroine. The other characters, for
example, *appear* to have abundant life of their own, but
to look more closely at the text is to realize that even the
vital and masterful Rochester exists primarily by virtue
of Jane's observations and reactions.

    Jane Eyre marks a considerable advance in the hand-
ling of first-person narrative. One of Charlotte Brontë's
innovations in this respect is the subtle use she makes of
her time-scale. As the final chapter makes clear, Jane is
telling her story years after her marriage to Rochester.
This enables her every now and then to assess the agonies
and joys through which she passed long after they are
over. But there are also short-term assessments. Some of
them take place immediately after the particular experience that has just been narrated, as when Jane reflects on
the unlikelihood of Rochester preferring her to Blanche
Ingram; others occur some months after, as when Jane
looks back from her new life at Moor House at her experiences at Thornfield; and there are other occasions
when she compares the present with the quite distant
past, as in the chapter describing her return to Gateshead
Hall, the scene of so many of her formative childhood
sufferings. There are also occasional appeals to the reader
to join in the assessment on the basis of the facts pre-

sented. These shifts of narrative viewpoint help to give texture to the novel as a whole.

At the same time, each of Jane's agonies and joys is presented with an astonishing immediacy, as if she were living through it at the moment of writing. It is the degree of this immediacy that distinguishes the novels of Charlotte and Emily Brontë (and to a lesser extent those of Anne) from all that had gone before. There is the feeling of being in direct contact with the very essence of basic human passions. The language and imagery of *Jane Eyre* are permeated with this quality, not only in the romantic scenes but also in those where Jane is in iron control of her feelings – for instance, when, from her corner in the drawing-room, she watches Rochester in the company of Blanche Ingram and the other grand ladies who are visiting Thornfield. The same quality also enters the description of Jane's feelings about men and marriage in general. At that period, of course, it was impossible to be explicit about such matters, but there are passages in *Jane Eyre* which convey the reality of passion in all its rawness with remarkable concentration. It is significant in this connection that Jane rejects St John's offer of marriage because she knows he cannot bring 'a husband's heart' to her, and that she could not 'receive from him the bridal ring, endure all the forms of love (which I doubt not he would scrupulously observe) and know that the spirit was quite absent.' It is true that Jane believes with every fibre of her being that the spirit must be predominant in any real marriage, but it is quite clear that she, like her creator, knows that body and spirit must both be present, and that it is the union of the two she seeks.

It was, no doubt, the frankness and emotional intensity with which these issues were conveyed, at a time when it was the convention to ignore them, that made some contemporary critics describe *Jane Eyre* as immoral. It was a criticism that caused Charlotte much pain, for the novel is nothing if *not* moral and Christian, a probing into the whole problem of right behaviour in the situation in which God has placed each individual. *Jane Eyre* is in essence an emotional and spiritual pilgrimage which seeks to discover the right balance between the demands both of the body and of the soul, and of society and the individual. Each stage of the story is attended by revelations of self-discovery and self-adjustment. In the wretchedness of her life at Gateshead Hall Jane learns the limitations of mere defiance and thirst for revenge. At Lowood as a pupil, starved in body, she learns that Helen Burns's meek self-abnegation is not for her. Later, as a teacher at Lowood, starved now in mind and emotions, she learns something of the reality of her own selfhood and its just demands and expectations. At Thornfield she faces two temptations: first, that of a love which she knows is somehow not 'right' in terms of her deepest instincts; and then, when the existence of the mad Mrs Rochester is revealed, that of becoming Rochester's mistress (and it is made quite clear that she is by no means insensible of the appeal) and thus committing herself to the passionate and worldly in defiance of God's laws as she sees them. Then, at Morton, she is confronted with her third major temptation, that of marrying St John Rivers and so turning to the spiritual and other-worldly in defiance of the laws of her own nature. She has to overcome all these temptations before she can feel she has purified herself, and is thus ready for a true marriage to Rochester ('No woman was ever nearer to her mate than I am,' she tells us, 'ever more absolutely bone of his bone, and flesh of his flesh') – just as Rochester himself has had to go through a purgation by fire, physical suffering and deprivation before he can learn the true nature of his feelings for Jane.

In its insistence that these were problems that concerned women as much as men, *Jane Eyre* was far in advance of its time. For Jane's pilgrimage takes place within a specific social context, one in which women were still denied the most elementary of political, educational, emotional and physical rights. In presenting the humiliatting and limited scope which a male-dominated world sought to impose on a spirited and intelligent girl like Jane, the novel includes a passionate plea for justice for all women. Time after time, Jane insists that love and passion must not involve a swamping of individual independence. It is significant, for instance, that when Rochester proposes marriage to her, she tells him that she wishes to go on working in order to maintain her economic independence and also insists that they must maintain a certain emotional distance and detachment for their mutual benefit. In other words she, like her creator, was demanding for women an emotional, and by implications, a sexual, independence. It was a revolutionary demand at the time.

Part of the strength of *Jane Eyre* lies in its close personal involvement with these contemporary and continuing issues. At the same time they are also universal issues in the sense that the cry (uttered by Jane in her time of testing at Thornfield) for the emergence of the individual spirit from the strains and stresses imposed by society or fate, is valid for everyone, irrespective of time, place, or sex:

'Who in the world cares for *you*? or will be injured by what you do?' Still indomitable was the reply: '*I* care for myself. The more solitary, the more friendless, the more unsustained I am, the more I will respect myself ...'

It is the powerful personal integrity of Charlotte Brontë's genius in *Jane Eyre* that makes it one of the living classics of English fiction.

Wuthering Heights

Emily Brontë

The account of the lives of the Brontës in the chapter on *Jane Eyre* will have indicated that one of the reasons for the uniqueness of Emily Brontë's great novel *Wuthering Heights* (1847) is that she was the most isolated and self-sufficient of all the sisters (even Charlotte admitted that she could not be sure whether she really understood her). It was Emily who suffered most when she was away from Haworth, and who, after her few absences, returned most thankfully to it. It was she who was most thoroughly steeped in the history, traditions and legends of the district, and in the wild life of the moors, which she knew in intimate detail and which provided her with some of her deepest satisfactions. The word 'wuthering', used in Yorkshire to describe wild, tempestuous weather, indicates both the mood of the novel and its local ambience.

Nevertheless, if the bare bones of the plot are extracted from the poetic imagination, language and imagery that give them substance, *Wuthering Heights* does not appear as the mere product of a particular locality, but with its wild scenery, primitive passions, supernatural events, and its Byronically 'Satanic' hero, can also be seen to derive from the Gothic tale of terror. One of the means by which Emily Brontë cancelled out the adverse effects of this now old-fashioned form in *Wuthering Heights* was by the unusual structure she adopted. To her contemporaries this seemed muddled and confusing, but in fact she anticipated the methods of later novelists like Henry James and Joseph Conrad, who were particularly concerned with new approaches both to chronology and to narrative method in the art of fiction.

Summary

Like Conrad (in his novels *Lord Jim* and *Chance*), Emily Brontë begins towards the end of the story. The novel opens with a date – 1801. A Mr Lockwood, who has recently become tenant at Thrushcross Grange, is recording his first visit to his landlord, Mr Heathcliff, who lives at Wuthering Heights. He describes his surly reception by the grim, powerfully built, gipsy-like Heathcliff. He describes, too, the savage isolation of the ancient farmhouse, a savagery matched by that of the dogs which attack the visitor. Mr Lockwood, however, is fascinated by Heathcliff, and pays him a second visit. On this occasion he meets Heathcliff's aloof and haughty daughter-in-law, Catherine, and a boorish, unkempt young man named Hareton Earnshaw – both of them treated by Heathcliff with bitter hatred and contempt. It begins to snow heavily and Lockwood, reluctantly obliged to stay overnight, is shown into a bedroom by the housekeeper, which, she explains, is not normally used. There, Lockwood finds a number of books inscribed with the name 'Catherine Earnshaw' and dated twenty-five years earlier. On the blank spaces in these books, the first Catherine had kept a diary. It describes how as children, Catherine and Heathcliff, after many hours of joyless Calvinistic preaching by Joseph, the Earnshaws' servant, had thrown their religious books at him, and the harsh treatment meted out to them as punishment, especially to Heathcliff, by Catherine's brother, Hindley.

When Lockwood eventually falls asleep, he is visited by a nightmare in which he hears the knocking of a branch against the window. When he puts his hand out of the window to seize the branch, he touches instead 'the fingers of a little, ice-cold hand', while a child's voice wails that she is a waif, lost on the moors for twenty years, and begs to be let in.

Lockwood's cries arouse Heathcliff who enters the room and is himself greatly agitated as Lockwood emerges from his nightmare. When Lockwood leaves the room and lingers for a moment in the corridor outside, he hears Heathcliff crying out at the window:

> 'Come in! come in! ... Cathy, do come! Oh! my heart's darling! hear me *this* time, Catherine, at last!'

Later, when he has recovered his composure, Heathcliff guides Lockwood back across the snowbound moors to Thrushcross Grange.

This brilliantly conceived first section of the novel establishes straight away the nature of the inhabitants of Wuthering Heights, their relationship to each other, and the strange atmosphere that surrounds them, but all filtered through the curiosity of a stranger with a practical, even pedantic, turn of mind, so that the details of the moor and its vegetation, of the appearance of the house without and of its structure and furnishings within are all clear-cut, as if seen for the first time.

It is the palpable quality of Lockwood's nightmare that saves the suggestion of an actual haunting from being merely another piece of Gothic spookiness. Everything has been so 'real', including the unnatural behaviour of most of the inhabitants of Wuthering Heights, that it does not demand too great an imaginative leap on the part of the reader to accept also the possibility of the supernatural – as Lockwood does when he tells Heathcliff, after his nightmare, that the room is 'swarming with ghosts and goblins! You have reason in shutting it up, I assure you.'

But what has also been established is that this is a story in which normal chronological order is irrelevant. For the events of twenty-five years ago recorded in the diary seem to be just as much a part of the present as far as Wuthering Heights is concerned as those in which Lockwood himself is involved in 1801; more so, indeed, in that Lockwood is merely the bustling intruder from the outside world of clocks and calendars into one in which time stands still, or rather flows in a perpetually circling motion. What is more, the reader is made to feel that the Catherine who haunts the nightmare of Lockwood and the waking hours of Heathcliff is as 'real' as they themselves are. And it is essential that this feeling should be conveyed early on because the whole point about the relationship between Catherine and Heathcliff, which forms the substance of the novel, is that while it is solidly and concretely placed, nevertheless it belongs to a plane quite outside that of normal time.

When he arrives back at Thrushcross Grange, Lockwood asks Nelly Dean, the housekeeper (who stayed on when he rented the house) to tell him the story of his strange neighbours. Her narration (with occasional interjections from Lockwood) forms the bulk of the novel. She begins at a point some time before the events recorded in the diary Lockwood had read at Wuthering Heights. The Earnshaw of that date has brought back with him from a visit to Liverpool a filthy, dark-visaged waif whom he has found starving in the slums. Mr Earnshaw calls the boy Heathcliff (after a son who had died in infancy), which serves as both his surname and Christian name, and tells his son Hindley and his daughter Catherine (or Cathy) that they must treat him as a brother. Cathy soon takes to the newcomer, but Hindley, jealous of the affection lavished on Heathcliff by his father (especially after the death of Mrs Earnshaw), bullies him unmercifully whenever he has the chance.

When Mr Earnshaw dies, Hindley, now married, inherits Wuthering Heights, promptly puts an end to the schooling Heathcliff has, in company with Cathy, been receiving from the local curate, and sets him to work as a farm labourer, seizing every opportunity to torment, degrade and humiliate him. Cathy, however, refuses to give up her comradeship with Heathcliff, and in spite of harsh punishments from both Hindley and the sanctimonious, Bible-thumping servant Joseph, the two continue their long rambles over the moors.

On one of these Cathy and Heathcliff creep up to the lighted windows of Thrushcross Grange, the home of the wealthy and cultivated Lintons, and look in on the pampered Linton children, who, hearing noises outside the window, rouse the household. In making their escape Cathy is set upon by the Lintons' bulldog. She is taken inside to have her wounded ankle seen to, but Heathcliff is contemptuously dismissed. Cathy stays five weeks at Thrushcross Grange, and when she returns to Wuthering Heights, she has been transformed into an elegant young lady. Hindley and his wife entertain the Lintons, while Heathcliff, though still stoutly championed by Cathy, is more firmly excluded from the family circle than ever. A year passes. Hindley's wife gives birth to a son, who is christened Hareton, but she dies not long after and Hindley takes to drinking heavily. At the same time, Edgar Linton starts courting Cathy. Eventually she confides to Nelly that he has proposed and that she has accepted him, because it would now 'degrade' her to marry Heathcliff. At the same time, she passionately assures Nelly, she will not marry Edgar Linton unless he agrees to her continuing her friendship with Heathcliff, and she tries to define the contrast between her feelings for him and those for Edgar:

'My love for Linton is like the foliage in the woods; time will change it, I'm well aware, as winter changes the trees. My love for Heathcliff resembles the eternal rocks beneath: a source of little visible delight, but necessary. Nelly, I *am* Heathcliff! He's always, always in my mind: not as a pleasure, any more than I am always a pleasure to myself, but as my own being.'

This passage is perhaps the crux of the whole novel, conveying as it does the unique nature of the love between Cathy and Heathcliff which is in essence non-corporeal, above and apart from finite time and space, and therefore reaching back to the apparently supernatural manifestations of the opening section – and forward to the ultimate climax.

The immediate aftermath, however, is that Heathcliff disappears from Wuthering Heights. Cathy searches for him over the moors in a storm, and falls ill as a result. The Linton parents take her to Thrushcross Grange to nurse her back to health, but both of them catch her fever and die of it. Back at Wuthering Heights, Cathy waits in vain for news of Heathcliff, and eventually, nearly three years later, marries Edgar. To begin with, Cathy, in spite of her uncertain temper, is happy with her gentle and adoring husband. Then Heathcliff returns, well-dressed, well-spoken, and obviously prosperous. Cathy, overjoyed to see him again, persuades her husband to receive him courteously. They are astonished to learn that Heathcliff is staying at Wuthering Heights, and paying Hindley Earnshaw a handsome rent, which he badly needs for his drinking and gambling. Edgar continues to allow Heathcliff access to Thrushcross Grange, but when his sister Isabella becomes infatuated with Heathcliff, Edgar turns him out. Shortly afterwards, Cathy falls ill with a brain fever, and in the confusion Isabella elopes with Heathcliff. Cathy, who is pregnant, makes only a partial recovery. Isabella's life at Wuthering Heights – where Hindley, encouraged by Heathcliff, has sunk deeper into drink and debt while his son Hareton has been turned by Heathcliff into a young savage, and where she is treated with cold hostility by her husband – is wretched in the extreme. It is clear that Heathcliff has married Isabella (who by the terms of her father's will is to inherit Thrushcross Grange in the event of her brother's death) as an act of revenge and in the hope of eventually getting her brother, too, into his power.

Heathcliff now informs Nelly that he must see Cathy

again. Nelly points out the risk to Cathy's precarious state of health that such a meeting would entail. But Heathcliff knows more than anyone else the true reason behind Cathy's illness – that in marrying Edgar and adopting the Linton way of life, she had gone against her deepest instincts.

The meeting takes place (with Nelly's help) while Edgar and the servants are at Sunday service. It is one of the most moving love scenes in English fiction, yet nothing could be farther removed from the conventionally romantic or sentimental. Even while clasped desperately in each other's arms, each accuses the other of cruelty and betrayal. That same night Cathy dies, two hours after the birth of her daughter, who is also named Catherine. When Nelly takes the news to Heathcliff, she finds that he has already sensed it. When she tells him that Cathy died peacefully and expresses the conventionally pious hope that she will 'wake as kindly in the other world', Heathcliff's response is the reverse of conventional:

> 'May she wake in torment! ... Catherine Earnshaw, may you not rest as long as I am living! ... Be with me always – take any form – drive me mad! only *do* not leave me in this abyss, where I cannot find you!'

It is not yet half way through the book and, a most unusual feature in any novel, the heroine is already dead. But in what sense *is* Cathy really dead? She is certainly not so as far as Heathcliff is concerned, as the opening section has made clear, and it is now that Emily Brontë's original structure and narrative approach triumphantly vindicate themselves. For they have enabled her to transfer the novel to another plane – or rather, to establish the plane on which Cathy now has her being side by side with the terrestrial one, and from now on the reader is always aware of the possibility of interaction between the two. This, indeed, is symbolized by the fact that Catherine, by her own request, is buried neither in the Linton family vault nor beside the Earnshaws, but in a remote corner of the churchyard 'where the wall is so low that heath and bilberry plants have climbed over it from the moor, and peat mould almost buries it.' It is as if an easy way had been left open for her spirit to escape on to the moors where, in the past, she had so often wandered with Heathcliff.

At this point, though, by a subtle change of rhythm and in effective contradiction to the kind of expectations raised by the opening chapter, it is the terrestrial world that takes precedence. The events that belong to it come thick and fast, and the whole action is speeded up. Isabella arrives at Thrushcross Grange with a gash in her cheek. Heathcliff has been behaving like a madman, and Hindley has made an ineffectual attempt to kill him, only to be battered into unconsciousness. When Isabella had taunted her husband with being the real cause of Cathy's death, he had thrown a knife at her, and in terror she has escaped across the moors. Pausing only to collect some clothes, she continues her flight and eventually settles somewhere near London, where she gives birth to a son who is christened Linton. A few months later, Hindley dies and it is found that he has mortgaged the whole of his property to Heathcliff, so that from now on Hareton Earnshaw can only live at Wuthering Heights, his ancestral home, by Heathcliff's patronage.

Twelve years pass. Isabella is dying and begs her brother Edgar to care for Linton, her sick and ailing son; but Heathcliff insists on removing him from Thrushcross Grange to Wuthering Heights. Young Catherine, rapidly growing into a beautiful young woman and showing a combination of her father's gentleness and her dead mother's wilfulness and fire, secretly gets to know her cousin Linton, and Heathcliff conceives the plan of a marriage between them. Edgar, learning of this meeting, forbids Catherine to have any further contact with Wuthering Heights, actuated by anxiety for his daughter's future in view of his own failing health, and the fact that on his death Linton, as Isabella's son, will inherit Thrushcross Grange.

Eventually, Heathcliff lures Catherine and Nelly Dean into Wuthering Heights and imprisons them there until Catherine, desperate to get back to her dying father, promises to marry Linton. Even so, after the marriage she has to escape through a window in order to reach her father's bedside. He tries to alter his will so that some of his money will be secured to his daughter in her own right, but the lawyer, who is in Heathcliff's pay, deliberately delays, and Edgar Linton is dead before he arrives.

It is only now, when all these violent events are over and Heathcliff's revenge is nearly complete, that the first Catherine again comes into the story. Heathcliff confides to Nelly that just after Catherine died he had been visited by her spirit, and that ever since he has been longing in vain for another visitation – cursing her the while for her cruelty in failing to appear to him.

When the young Catherine returns to Wuthering Heights, she devotes herself to nursing her husband, Heathcliff refusing to allow any of the household to help her or to summon a doctor. Before Linton dies, Heathcliff forces him to make a will leaving Thrushcross Grange and Edgar Linton's fortune to him. Young Catherine, embittered and penniless, but still defiant, stays on at Wuthering Heights, to receive from her father-in-law the same brutal treatment he metes out to his other dependents.

The narration now switches back to Mr Lockwood. He rides over to Wuthering Heights, to inform Heathcliff that he will shortly be giving up his tenancy of Thrushcross Grange. Before he leaves, Lockwood overhears Heathcliff muttering that, in spite of himself, he feels a stirring of affection for Hareton because of his likeness to the dead Catherine.

Now there is another precise date – the year 1802. Lockwood has returned to the moors on a grouse-shooting expedition and visits Wuthering Heights. As he arrives, he is surprised to overhear through the open window young Catherine teaching her cousin Hareton to read, the two of them apparently on the most affectionate of terms. Lockwood seeks out Nelly, and her narration carries the story back to the point at which Lockwood had departed for London.

To Nelly's surprise, she had been summoned to Wuthering Heights to keep young Cathy company. She witnesses the gradual change in the relationship between her and Hareton – and trembles at the thought of the effect it may have on Heathcliff. But he, too, is gradually changing. He has become curiously distracted and remote. He is still subject to outbreaks of violence, but they tend to tail off. His will to carry his vengeance into the second generation, against Hareton and young Cathy, has inexplicably slackened. For one thing they remind him more and more forcibly of the dead Catherine – and of his boyhood relationship with her. For another, he is finding it increasingly difficult to adapt himself to the terrestrial world at all.

He returns to Wuthering Heights one morning after wandering all night on the moors, with 'a strange joyful glitter in his eyes'. He believes he has at last met Catherine again, and longs for a closer union. During the next four days he deliberately starves himself. When he dies, he tells Nelly he must be buried between Catherine and her husband (as he has already arranged with the sexton) but he wants no minister of religion at his funeral:

'... I tell you I have nearly attained my heaven; and that of others is altogether unvalued and uncoveted by me!'

He locks himself in Cathy's old room, and the next morning Nelly finds him dead.

Heathcliff is buried according to his wishes, and young Catherine and Hareton make plans for their marriage and removal to Thrushcross Grange. Ordinary, terrestrial life reasserts itself: but the country folk are convinced that the ghosts of Catherine and Heathcliff still roam the moors. As E. M. Forster has said of the two lovers:

They cause the action by their separation: they close
it by their union after death. No wonder they 'walk'; what
else could such beings do? Even when they were alive
their love and hate transcended them.

Critical commentary

It must be stressed once again that within the terms laid
down by the novel, the hauntings in *Wuthering Heights*
are not supernatural in the usual sense of manifestations
against the laws of nature. On the contrary, given the
circumstances of the novel, it could be said, paradoxically,
that they are essentially *natural*. That is why the country
people, and even Lockwood when he has become sufficiently imbued with the spirit of the place, accept them
naturally. They are solidly based in the folklore of a
particular district, and Emily Brontë is at pains to introduce a number of references to other traditional supernatural phenomena such as fairies, elves, goblins, and
demons.

But there is a sense, too, in which the supernatural
elements can also be seen as firmly rooted in a specific
historical and social context, to which Heathcliff and
Cathy inevitably belong, and of which they are the tragic
victims. Much of the special affinity that exists between
them for example, is the product of a mutual rebellion
against the harsh regime of Hindley and Joseph, and
against the kind of adult tyranny exercised against children at that period, largely by means of religion, which
had also evoked Blake's passionate indignation in his
Songs of Innocence and *Songs of Experience*. It is this
rebellion, so patently justified, that arouses sympathy for
Heathcliff in the earlier part of the book, a sympathy
which is not entirely destroyed by his monstrosities later
on.

The potentialities of tragedy are present from the
moment when Cathy seeks to break this special bond –

and it is made quite clear that social and economic motives enter into her decision. Heathcliff, the nameless product of the Liverpool slums, has been reduced by Hindley to the condition of an illiterate serf, whereas Edgar Linton represents all that is socially desirable. In spite of her deep instinctive reaching after freedom of quite another kind, Cathy is still the prisoner of her class and upbringing. How, indeed, given the social and economic powerlessness of women of her period, could she be otherwise? The situation is further complicated by the fact that with one part of her nature, as she makes clear time after time, Cathy genuinely loves Edgar and genuinely *needs* the kind of life he represents – but she is telling an unalienable truth when she says that her love for Heathcliff 'resembles the eternal rocks beneath', and since he is the very condition of her being, she is bound to know and feel that she has been guilty of a betrayal. For a time she hopes to have the best of both worlds by marrying Edgar and retaining Heathcliff as a friend, but such compromises are inevitably doomed to failure. She is in an impossible situation, caught between irreconcilable forces – and this is the very stuff out of which tragedy is made.

Heathcliff, of course, is also in an impossible situation. All that he has is his revenge. When he first comes back, rich and successful, it is difficult for the reader not to feel a surge of sympathetic exultation. He still represents something freer, more vigorous and more fully human than either the drunken Hindley or the Lintons – and Emily Brontë leaves us in no doubt that the way of life represented by the Lintons, in spite of Edgar's charm, is in some way soft, effete and corrupt. The glimpse through the window of Thrushcross Grange young Heathcliff and Cathy had of Edgar and Isabella as spoiled and pampered children told the fundamental truth. But Heathcliff, too, is guilty of a betrayal. In order to avenge himself against his enemies, he has to adopt their traditional methods of financial pressures, land deals (it has been shown that

Emily Brontë had carefully studied the legal complexities in this connection), and 'advantageous' marriages. He, too, is corrupted in the process; he, too, tramples on the special affinities that bound him and Cathy so closely together, so that they have become distorted into bitterness and hatred, and the reunion with Catherine's spirit for which he longs is denied him. It is only towards the end, when he becomes aware of the similarity between the situation of Hareton and young Cathy, united in rebellion against him, and that of himself and the first Catherine when they were oppressed by Hindley, that some human rightness reasserts itself, and Catherine can be released from her torment and the relationship between herself and Heathcliff re-established.

It is only through death, it is true, that this can take place. It is, indeed, the actual manner of their dying, with first Cathy and then, many years later, Heathcliff, bravely facing the reality, that provides the necessary first condition for the ultimate union. The dissolution of terrestrial bodies is of no particular import to Emily Brontë. There is nothing unnatural to her in the idea of a relationship having to wait until after death in order to achieve consummation. The whole crux of the matter, indeed, lies in the fact that owing to the special circumstances of Cathy's and Heathcliff's lives, including the social and economic pressures of the time, compounded by their own mistakes and failures of understanding, it was impossible for this to take place during their lifetimes. The novel is full of references to frustrated longings, unfulfilled desires, and an agonizing spiritual hunger – which Heathcliff eventually has to starve his body to satisfy. Most of these references imply that the conditions of this earthly life are such that it is only after death that the fulfilment of the soul, so ardently yearned after, can be achieved. Thus Cathy, on her deathbed tells Nelly that she is 'tired of being enclosed here ... wearying to escape'.

Similarly, Heathcliff exclaims after Catherine's death:

'I *cannot* live without my life! I *cannot* live without my soul!' And just before his own death, when he has met Catherine's spirit again, he cries:

> 'I'm too happy; and yet I'm not happy enough. My soul's bliss kills my body, but does not satisfy itself.'

There are, however, two ways of looking at this suggestion that fulfilment of the soul is only possible after death. On the one hand, it can be envisaged in a purely religious sense – what Derek Traversi has described as:

> an awareness ... of the necessary incompleteness of all the elements that go to make up human nature in its time-conditioned state.

Or on the other hand, it can be regarded as expressing the extension or overflow of unusually powerful human passions subjected to a quite intolerable frustration, and symbolizing overwhelmingly just human demands for fulfilment which, at that particular time and place, were denied their true correlatives. Either way, *Wuthering Heights* emerges as one of the world's few truly great tragic novels.

Vanity Fair

William Makepeace Thackeray

William Makepeace Thackeray was born in 1811 near Calcutta, where his father was an official in the East India Company (which administered British India until the Crown took over in 1858). After the death of his father and the remarriage of his mother, Thackeray, still only six years old, was – according to the custom among the British in India – sent home to England to be educated. Through one of his characters, he later described the time he spent at a preparatory school and then at Charterhouse as 'Ten years banishment of infernal misery, tyranny, arrogance.'

After leaving Charterhouse, he went to Trinity College, Cambridge. He left without taking a degree, and travelled in France, Italy, and Germany, meeting the great German sage and writer Goethe at Weimar (which features in *Vanity Fair* as Pumpernickel). He read law for a spell and ran a weekly paper. He studied drawing and painting in Paris, and in 1836 he published a number of his own cartoons of ballet dancers. The loss of the family fortune he had inherited caused him to turn to journalism as a career, and his artistic training and his fondness for the medium of caricature played a part in his development as a writer. He was unsuccessful in his application to become illustrator of Dickens's *Pickwick Papers*, but he illustrated many of his own works, including *Vanity Fair*, to which in its first edition, he gave the subtitle 'Pen and Pencil Sketches of English Society'; and this is a significant pointer in itself both to the moral-satiric intention behind the novel, and to the 'humours' or allegorical elements in the characterization.

In 1837, accordingly, Thackeray returned to England and began contributing a stream of humorous and satirical sketches and stories (under various pseudonyms) to the magazines and periodicals of the day. He had married in 1836, and his wife bore him three daughters, but in 1840 she became permanently insane, a blow from which Thackeray never recovered.

In 1842 he began a long series of contributions to the humorous magazine *Punch*, which had been founded the previous year. The most considerable of these was published in volume form in 1847 as *The Book of Snobs*, which anticipated *Vanity Fair* in a number of respects, especially in its satire of the English gentry of the period.

Thackeray was already thirty-six and still comparatively little known when, in 1847, *Vanity Fair* began to appear in twenty monthly parts (followed by publication in volume form in 1848). To begin with it looked as if this, too, was going to be a series of loosely connected sketches, but Thackeray quickly realized that he had a major novel on his hands.

Summary

The title derives from the Fair in the town of Vanity, in which Christian and Faithful are tempted on their journey to the Celestial City in John Bunyan's *The Pilgrim's Progress*. This association is important in a number of ways.

In the first place the fairground imagery is itself appropriate. Someone once called Thackeray's novel 'The Greatest Show on Earth' and this aptly describes one of the sensations it creates – that of having wandered for hours through a giant fairground, full of glittering tableaux and side-shows, and populated by swarms of jostling, chattering humanity. It is an impression that Thackeray himself is at pains to create. In an introduction to the novel, entitled 'Before the Curtain' he introduces himself as 'the Manager of the Performance', looking out into the Fair and surveying 'the bustling place', just before he himself opens a puppet show, which he promises will be 'accompanied by appropriate scenery and brilliantly illuminated with the Author's own candles'.

But the association with Bunyan's Vanity Fair has a deeper significance. In his novel, Thackeray not only sets out to exhibit the actions and fortunes of a particular group of people in the early years of the nineteenth century, but also to reveal certain truths about the human condition itself. As G. K. Chesterton said: 'In *Vanity Fair* the chief character is the World.' On the very last page of the novel Thackeray quotes the Latin tag *Vanitas Vanitatum*, or, as expressed in the Book of Ecclesiastes: 'Vanity of vanities, all is Vanity' – and it is this universal concept that underlies the whole work.

This means that *Vanity Fair* is, like Bunyan's *The Pilgrim's Progress*, basically a moral fable or allegory. In reading it, therefore, it is necessary always to bear in mind that the characters and incidents, however vividly they may live in their own right, are also representatives or symbols of wider entities.

Basically, *Vanity Fair* is the chronicle of the parallel careers of two strongly contrasted women; the gentle and self-effacing Amelia Sedley, daughter of a wealthy London stockbroker, and the strong-willed, self-seeking and courageous Becky Sharp, orphan daughter of a penniless artist and a French opera-dancer.

As the novel begins, in the early years of the nineteenth century, Amelia and Becky are close friends at a genteel Academy for young ladies at Chiswick, run by the majestic Miss Pinkerton, aided by her good-natured sister, Miss Jemima. Amelia is a favoured pupil because of her docility and her father's wealth, while Becky, who has been paying her way by teaching French, and who is by no means docile, is treated by Miss Pinkerton with evident disdain.

When they both leave school, Becky is invited to stay for a time at the Sedley's fine house. Here she meets Amelia's brother, Jos (or Joseph) Sedley, the grotesquely fat, foppish, and conceited Collector of Boggley Wallah in India – a lucrative post under the East India Company. The penniless Becky sets her cap at Jos. His vanity is flattered, and Becky has high hopes of clinching matters during an expedition to the pleasure grounds of Vauxhall Gardens. George Osborne, a handsome young officer engaged to Amelia, disapproves of the idea of having Becky as a sister-in-law, and gives Jos (when he has sobered up) a lurid account of his drunken misbehaviour and persuades him to leave London. George's fellow-officer, Captain William Dobbin, has also been at the Vauxhall party, in order to be near Amelia, whom he worships from afar. The disappointed, but by no means defeated, Becky obtains a post as governess at the home of the miserly old baronet, Sir Pitt Crawley. She sets out to captivate him and his rich spinster sister Miss Crawley, whom she nurses through an illness. As a second string to her bow, she also pays attention to Sir Pitt's second son, Rawdon, a spendthrift cavalry officer, gambler and duellist, partly because she is genuinely attracted to him – and partly because she knows that, as the favourite of Miss Crawley, he is to inherit her fortune. When Sir Pitt's downtrodden wife dies, he proposes marriage to Becky. But Becky has overreached herself. She has to reveal that she is already secretly married to Rawdon. Both Sir Pitt and Miss Crawley are furious. The latter, willing to make much of Becky while she was in an inferior position, cannot tolerate her as a member of the family, and she cuts Rawdon out of her will in favour of his elder brother, Pitt. Meanwhile, the worthless George Osborne is enjoying his reputation in the regiment as a rake too much to be in any hurry to marry Amelia. Dobbin, unable to bear the sight of Amelia meekly pining away, lets out the news of the engagement in the regimental mess, so that George, though furious at Dobbin's interference, feels in honour bound to admit it and to pay Amelia a little more attention. But a more serious obstacle to the marriage intervenes. Amelia's father is ruined by speculations on the Stock Exchange and forced into bankruptcy. George's father, although he owes his own rise in business to Sedley, forbids George to have anything further to do with the now penniless Amelia. George promptly obeys him, and Amelia is heartbroken. Once again Dobbin comes to the rescue. He manages to make George realize the shabbiness of his conduct, and George performs what is probably the only unselfish act of his life by marrying Amelia in defiance of his father. The couple honeymoon in Brighton where they meet Rawdon and Becky, who are now up to their necks in debt as a result of living handsomely on 'nothing a year'. Dobbin in the meantime has been acting as mediator between George and his father, but when the old man hears of George's marriage, he repudiates him and cuts him out of his will. Dobbin hurries to Brighton to announce the failure of his mission, and the even more momentous news that the forces of Napoleon (following his escape from Elba) are on the move, and that he, George, and Rawdon have been recalled to their regiments. Becky and Amelia accompany their husbands to Brussels, and Jos Sedley also joins the party. They take part in the social whirl of the capital and George, tiring of Amelia, begins an intrigue with Becky. Then, as the news of the unexpectedly rapid advance of the French forces arrives, the British army marches out of Brussels to meet them. When the sound of the cannon is heard in Brussels, there is panic and many of the British civilian residents hastily decamp. Becky is among them, securing a place in the carriage of her grand acquaintances, Lord and Lady Bareacres. Jos Sedley, after pleading in vain with his sister to accompany him, joins in the exodus, leaving Amelia, who is prostrate with anxiety for George but determined to stay in Brussels, in the charge of Mrs O'Dowd, wife of a major in George's and Dobbin's regiment. And meanwhile, some miles away, the Battle of Waterloo has taken place.

> No more firing was heard at Brussels – the pursuit rolled miles away. Darkness came down on the field and city; and Amelia was praying for George, who was lying on his face, dead, with a bullet through his heart.

Rawdon and Dobbin are both promoted after the battle, Rawdon also receiving a decoration for his outstanding bravery. He and Becky are reunited in Paris, joining to the full in all the celebrations indulged in by the occupying powers after Napoleon's final banishment to St Helena. They maintain themselves in style on the proceeds of a lucky streak in Rawdon's gambling, while Becky, as usual, is surrounded by a host of admirers. She also finds time to bear Rawdon a son, named after his father and adored by him, but soon neglected by his mother. Amelia, too, has a son and she also christens him after his father, and dotes on him with the same blind adoration she had given to George to whose memory she is utterly devoted. She lives with her parents in penury, which Dobbin secretly does his best to alleviate. Her father-in-law, though secretly deeply moved by the death of his son, is unrelenting towards Amelia in spite of further attempts by Dobbin to soften his heart. Eventually, however, when Amelia can no longer afford to support the young George, old Mr Osborne takes him into his home, but he will not admit Amelia and makes it almost impossible for her to see her son.

After two years of living beyond their means in Paris, Rawdon and Becky return to London, where they set up house in their usual style, and amass their usual debts. Becky wins her way into the grandest society. There she catches the practised eye of the vicious old Regency buck, the Marquis of Steyne, and she reaches the zenith of her social climb when Lord Steyne introduces her at Court. Without her husband's knowledge, Becky receives jewels and large sums of money from him. When Rawdon asks Becky for money, she pretends that she has none to spare. Rawdon is arrested for debt and writes to Becky explaining his predicament. But in her reply she ignores his request for the money needed to pay off his creditor. He appeals to his brother who reluctantly settles the debt and secures his release. When Rawdon unexpectedly arrives home, he finds Becky and Lord Steyne in incriminating circumstances. Rawdon cannot stomach this final revelation. After a furious scene with Lord Steyne, who leaves the house incensed against both Rawdon and Becky for having landed him in a situation so damaging to his pride, Rawdon breaks with Becky. He challenges Lord Steyne to a duel, but interested parties on both sides are determined to prevent a scandal, and eventually Rawdon is manoeuvred into accepting the Governorship of remote Coventry Island, while Lord Steyne slips out of the country. After entrusting his son to the care of his brother and sister-in-law (now Sir Pitt and Lady Crawley), Rawdon sets out for his tropical island, where he dies a few years later of yellow fever. After a ten-year absence in India, both Dobbin and Jos Sedley return to England. By now Mrs Sedley has died and Amelia is keeping house for her father. Jos rescues them from their poverty and Dobbin declares his love for Amelia. But the memory of her dead husband still stands between them. Dobbin and Jos call at the Osborne's house, where they find little George tyrannizing over his now doting grandfather, and when old Mr Osborne dies he leaves most of his fortune to his grandson.

Mr Sedley by now has also died and Jos and Dobbin take Amelia and young George on a holiday to the Continent. In the capital of the little German principality of Pumpernickel, they meet Becky again, living in very reduced circumstances. She succeeds, however, in once again captivating Jos Sedley who intercedes on her behalf with his sister. Although Dobbin warns Amelia and Jos against Becky, Amelia insists upon taking her away from her sordid garret and having her to live in her own house. After quarrelling with Amelia on the issue, Dobbin leaves Pumpernickel and returns to England. Amelia, Jos and Becky move to Ostend. There two of Becky's shady friends, Major Loder and Captain Rook, attach themselves to the party in order to share in the pickings. Both of them have designs on Amelia and terrify her by their attentions. Eventually, Becky herself takes a hand. She reveals to Amelia that her beloved George was making advances to her at Brighton within a week of his marriage, and shows her a note which George had written to her on the eve of Waterloo, begging her to elope with him. Her idol shattered, Amelia is at last free to admit to herself that she loves the long-suffering Dobbin, who hurries back to Ostend where they are married before returning to England.

Jos Sedley remains with Becky, now completely under her thumb. At her suggestion, he takes out a large life insurance policy, and dies three months later, with Becky as his main beneficiary, under circumstances so suspicious that the insurance company are at first reluctant to pay up. Becky's son, however, has now inherited his uncle's estates and title. Although he refuses to see his mother again, the young Sir Rawdon Crawley makes her a generous allowance, and in addition she is apparently well supplied with money from other mysterious sources. She spends most of her time at Bath or Cheltenham, creating for herself a respectable reputation by ardent church-going and good works.

Critical commentary

A summary of this kind inevitably makes *Vanity Fair* look like a straightforward realistic novel. But there are a number of ways, apart from the title, in which Thackeray shows his underlying allegorical intention. Many of the names of his characters are intended to denote their circumstances or moral attributes. This is particularly the case with the minor ones. Thus the name Bareacres suggests the possession of large but barren estates, while a notorious gambler and card-player is named Deuceace. Many of the fictitious French and German names are also of this kind. But this element is present, too, in the names of some of the major characters. The Crawleys, for example, belong to the type of small gentry who long to join the rank above and are prepared to 'crawl' to them in order to be admitted. Lord Steyne is most appropriately named, both because of the suggestion of moral 'stain' and because there is a district in Brighton, the seaside resort which became fashionable among the licentious high society of the Regency period, which is called The Steyne. Then again Dobbin, the name used by children for a rocking-horse, neatly fits the decidedly wooden character of that name – who is also a 'willing horse', frequently put upon in one way or another. As for Becky Sharp, there is no doubt that she is sharp by nature as well as by name.

These are not allegorical names, however, in the same direct way as those of Bunyan, for there is a fundamental difference between Thackeray's allegory and that of Bunyan. Whereas Bunyan was primarily concerned with the heavenly kingdom, Thackeray's main interest was very much in this world. It is man in society that concerns him rather than man in relation to God, and this relates him even more closely to the eighteenth-century satirists, as well as to the 'humours' tradition of seventeenth-century dramatists like Ben Jonson.

In the hands of a great writer satire is basically moral and corrective. At the same time, combining allegory and moral satire in a novel the size of *Vanity Fair* involved special difficulties and resulted in a number of distinctive features. The most obvious of these is the author's running commentary. Sometimes this takes the form of brief first-person asides – as when, relating the hardships

Amelia had to endure before the return of her brother and Dobbin from India, Thackeray says 'I hope she is not to suffer much more of that hard usage!' At other times it is a matter of direct address to one of the characters. After Amelia, reunited with Becky in Pumpernickel, has kissed her, Thackeray says of Becky 'Ah, poor wretch, when was your lip pressed before by such pure kisses?' Sometimes, too, there are questions addressed in confidence to the reader. Thus, when Rawdon leaves Becky after discovering her alone with Lord Steyne, Thackeray demands 'what were her thoughts when he left her?' and a little later, 'What *had* happened? Was she guilty or not?' Some of these interpolations, however, are (after the manner of Fielding, whom Thackeray regarded as his master) short essays in themselves.

Many critics have found these interventions irritating: they resent having the author breathing down their necks and catching hold of them by the coat-lapels in order to force upon their attention the moral of this scene or that. On the other hand, it can be argued that such passages form an integral part of the whole and that they are in large part responsible for the remarkable unity and consistency which Thackeray manages to impose on his welter of material. Given the particular form and approach he had adopted, it was not unnatural for the showman-moralist to comment upon the various tableaux of the cautionary tale he is presenting. Moreover, his commentary helps to illuminate the action, and at the same time to propel it forward. In addition, it helps to create atmosphere and to set the story firmly in its social and historical context. Thackeray's frequent references to fashions, entertainments, popular songs and many other details of the period make the story more realistic and vivid; at the same time they also distance it and make it more poignant. There is in fact a good case for claiming that far from being an aesthetic monstrosity, Thackeray's commentary in *Vanity Fair* is, on the whole, justified and effective.

But although Thackeray took such pains with the historical detail of the novel, and although there is a good deal of history in it, *Vanity Fair* is not, properly speaking, a historical novel – as was *Henry Esmond* (published in 1852) in which he brilliantly recreates the life and times of Queen Anne. The whole point about a novel of that kind is the historical setting, and the actions of the characters must be related to it. This was not Thackeray's purpose in his greatest novel: there the setting is not history, but the Fair called Vanity. It is to Vanity Fair and not to history, therefore, that the actions of the characters had to be related. In consequence, Thackeray deliberately restricts himself as far as historical narrative and description are concerned. The battle of Waterloo takes place offstage and there is no description of it, apart from the one vivid but deliberately brief passage in which George Osborne's death is described. As Thackeray himself says in one of his interpolations just before the battle: 'We do not claim to rank among the military novelists. Our place is with the non-combatants.'

The same principle applies to the action itself. There is very little narrative for its own sake. Thackeray in *Vanity Fair* is not the kind of storyteller who sets out to exercise his powers of invention and to astound his reader by all kinds of unexpected twists and turns of the plot. There is none of the machinery of the conventional romance: no implausible coincidences, missing heirs, unexpected legacies, no gratuitous violence, and no supernatural manifestations. The incidents all bear upon and are explicable in terms of the central moral thesis.

If the plot is deliberately limited in this way, it follows that so are the characters. The centre of the stage is occupied by the rising (or falling) merchants and financiers, and by the class above them, the aspiring small gentry – the classes, that is, which in a materialistic and acquisitive society are most exposed to the temptations of vanity and least likely to resist them. All the other characters are grouped round them. For the most part they belong either to the nobility (with brief glimpses of royalty) or to the hangers-on of various degrees – doctors, lawyers, professional soldiers, tradesmen, and servants – those, that is, who cater in one way or another to the appetite for vanity. The cast of the novel is so large that it is easy to overlook the fact that Thackeray's social range in *Vanity Fair* is far narrower than that of many of his contemporaries. It does not include, for example, representatives of the new industrial working classes, or of the factory owners, for the simple reason that their aspirations and strivings, at that period, were of an entirely different nature.

Thackeray originally subtitled *Vanity Fair* 'A Novel without a Hero', though this does not mean that there are not good characters in it, who may even on occasion be capable of heroic actions. Mrs O'Dowd is 'a good natured Irishwoman;' Lady Jane Sheepshanks (who becomes the younger Sir Pitt's wife) is all 'sweetness and kindness'; the Marchioness of Steyne is depicted as a near-saint; and there are the two humble clerks who buy some of the silver at the forced auction of Mr Sedley's possessions in order to give it back to his wife. None of these is corrupt. There is, of course, also Dobbin who is undoubtedly a 'good' character. He performs acts of great kindness and unselfishness which raise him head and shoulders, Thackeray says, above 'the great struggling crowds' of Vanity Fair. He is certainly the nearest approximation to a hero. But his creator makes it quite clear that the plain, clumsy Dobbin is not cast in the heroic mould (any more than Amelia is). Thackeray was not writing an epic or a tragedy; he was not trying to show how unusual characters can triumph over evil, or go down in tragic defeat before it – but that in Vanity Fair most people are permeated by its values. It is they who constitute the very unheroic norm – the chosen subject of his study – and to have focused too much admiration and sympathy on any one of the 'good' characters would have distorted his intention. On the other hand, the picture would have lacked realism and conviction if there had been no counterweights at all to the prevailing selfishness and greed; and so Thackeray created a few virtuous characters – Dobbin in particular (though on the evidence of the original manuscript notes of the novel he was probably a late addition to the story) who would redress the balance, but who would not detract from the main impact by rising to any heroic heights.

In discussing the characters of *Vanity Fair* it is important to bear in mind that it is *not* a psychological novel in the usual sense of the term. That is not to say that it lacks shrewd and penetrating psychology – for example in the handling of Amelia's protracted mourning for the worthless George which degenerates into a morbid obsession, and in Dobbin's sudden realization, after he has quarrelled with Amelia over Becky at Pumpernickel, that there must be a limit even to his dogged devotion. But Thackeray relates these and other psychological events himself: they are not seen to be happening *inside* the characters. It could hardly be otherwise when Thackeray, in his preamble, has introduced his characters as puppets with simple labels attached – for instance, 'the famous little Becky Puppet ... uncommonly flexible in the joints, and lively on the wire', 'the Amelia Doll' and 'the richly dressed figure of the Wicked Nobleman' (Lord Steyne, that is) 'on whom no expense has been spared'. There is also the fact that the more obvious denizens of Vanity Fair – a blustering merchant like Osborne, a pompous administrator like Jos Sedley, or a 'big, heavy dragoon with strong desires and small brains, who had never controlled a passion in his life' like Rawdon, *have* no mental life to speak of and live almost entirely by instinct and appetite. As for Amelia, her inner life was said to be 'continuous and deep', but there is little evidence to support such a statement – and indeed it is hard to credit.

The workings of Becky's mind, it is true, are much more fully displayed: naturally enough, because she is the only really clever person in the novel. Her conversation in consequence is often brilliant and witty; but even here it is usually Thackeray who tells us so, and when Becky does talk it is not merely to illustrate her wit but nearly always to convey in addition some moral or satirical point.

In *Vanity Fair*, therefore, there are hardly any of the devices upon which many modern novelists rely – such as the 'stream of consciousness' or the 'interior monologue'. Thackeray's novel is fundamentally a series of moral illustrations to a set text: the characters and situations change at the showman-novelist's manipulation – as they may be said to do in the series of paintings by the great eighteenth-century artist Hogarth which demonstrate the stages of *Marriage à la Mode* or *The Rake's Progress*. None of these methods constitute defects: they are limitations voluntarily accepted in order to preserve the unity of purpose, and the marvel of *Vanity Fair* is that so much life bursts through in spite of them.

Most critics, however, are agreed that there are two major faults. The first of these is that although Thackeray was aware of the more universal applications of his allegory, these are inadequately represented. It is here, above all, that his novel cannot stand comparison with Bunyan's *The Pilgrim's Progress*. In that novel, one is always aware of witnessing a cosmic battle between Good and Evil: the great issues at stake are never lost sight of for a moment. By comparison, Thackeray's scale of values seems trivial. It is difficult to feel with any conviction that it ultimately matters what happens to the souls of his characters, if indeed they possess them. Vanity in Thackeray's hands becomes less a universal, spiritual issue than a continuous jockeying for position within a soulless, materialistic society by soulless, materialistic people or – as Thackeray's contemporary, the critic and historian Walter Bagehot put it in rather an extreme form – the accumulation of 'petty details to prove that tenth-rate people were for ever striving to be ninth-rate'.

The second and closely related defect is a kind of timidity that seems to make Thackeray draw back at the point when he should be committing himself most decisively. His fellow novelist Anthony Trollope, for example, wrote of 'a touch of vagueness' in Thackeray's work, 'a failure of nerve', which, he believed, indicated that 'his pen was not firm while he was using it.'

This timidity is particularly apparent when Thackeray is dealing with the relationship between the sexes. His evasiveness in this respect struck even some of his contemporaries as excessive. In spite of the prudery of the age, other Victorian novelists (among them Charlotte and Emily Brontë and George Eliot) managed, if only by implication, to convey a good deal of powerful sexual passion. It is an element that is almost entirely absent in *Vanity Fair*, as elsewhere in Thackeray's work, and inevitably this introduces an element of falsity in his handling of the two central characters, Amelia and Becky. It is true that Amelia is nothing like as mawkishly presented as many of Dickens's heroines, and in calling her a 'tender little parasite' with 'silly romantic ideas', Thackeray makes it quite clear that he is at times exasperated by her. At the same time she figures in some grossly sentimental scenes – and it is the impossibly goody-goody aspect which is meant to be taken most seriously.

Clearly it is the 'wicked' Becky who really engages Thackeray's creative love. It is she who dominates not only the novel, but also the whole of his work. But Thackeray does not have the courage to present her completely in the round. Although the only logical conclusion on the evidence is that Becky becomes the mistress of the Marquis of Steyne and of Jos Sedley, and probably of Major Loder and half a dozen others, Thackeray sidesteps the issue. In addition, he is so muddled in his attitude towards her that in a number of respects he does not play fair by her. One of Becky's outstanding characteristics, in spite of all her self-seeking, is – on Thackeray's own showing – her underlying good nature, which reveals itself, for instance, in her refusal to entertain any resentment towards Dobbin in spite of his efforts to thwart her plans, and in her decision to take a hand in bringing him and Amelia together. And it is difficult to reconcile this characteristic either with her unkindness towards her son or with the melodramatic suggestion towards the end of the novel that she may have murdered Jos Sedley. It is as if Thackeray found himself reacting too strongly towards Becky's vitality, and so savagely invented damning incidents in order to prevent his sympathy getting out of hand, and in order to conform to conventional Victorian standards.

In the view of some critics, this evasiveness of Thackeray's is, in essence, social snobbery. He does, it is true, make occasional efforts to do justice to Becky in this respect – on her visit to the younger Sir Pitt's home, he has her musing:

'It isn't difficult to be a country gentleman's wife ...
I think I could be a good woman if I had five thousand
a year.'

And Thackeray adds the comment: 'Who knows but Rebecca was right in her speculations – and that it was only a question of money and fortune which made the difference between her and an honest woman?' But he makes no real attempt to face up to the question posed by the modern critic, Arnold Kettle: What is a young woman of spirit and intelligence to do in the polite but barbarous world of bourgeois society? It is obvious, of course, that she should not behave as Becky did, but Thackeray did not make it sufficiently clear that in a society as wicked and materialistic as that of Vanity Fair there was little else that a young woman of spirit, placed as Becky was, could do but live by her wits. He had touched on the central dilemma which faced many women of the period – whether to submit and become doormats like Amelia, or to rebel as Becky did – but he lacked the insight or the courage to present the dilemma fairly and squarely.

Nevertheless, Becky Sharp is one of the great women characters of English literature, one of the very few who can be placed side by side with Chaucer's Wife of Bath. She may be unprincipled and even downright wicked, but it is difficult (as Thackeray himself knew) not to forgive her: for her intelligence, which brings her to despise High Society at the very moment she is achieving her most brilliant triumphs in it; for her gaiety and courage; for her resilience and cheerfulness in adversity – and above all, for her abundant vitality. She is one of those characters who run away with an author's intention. It has often been said that the real hero of *Paradise Lost* is Satan. And there can be no doubt that Becky is the real heroine of *Vanity Fair*. Thackeray the moralist meant to put her in a booth marked 'Awful Warning' – but Thackeray the artist had to let her steal the show.

But although the characterization of Becky is one of the main reasons why *Vanity Fair* is a great novel, it is not the only one. There are few novels to equal it as a sustained and realistic study of men and women as they actually behave in society, and few that convey more vividly or in such exact and concrete detail the day-to-day concerns, sorrows, joys, and aspirations that make up the stuff of living. The very scale of this enterprise is one of its triumphs. Because of his unified moral vision, Thackeray was able for the first time in the history of fiction, to impose an organic unity upon a vast mass of heterogenous material.

Occasionally, owing to the difficulties of serial publication, the organization of the novel does falter – there is some confusion over the chronology of Dobbin's and Jos Sedley's return from India, for instance. But on the whole, *Vanity Fair* is one of the most closely-knit novels in the English language. Its main construction is masterly. Its lynch-pin is the double story of Amelia and Becky, and not only do those two balance each other psychologically, but their careers are plotted in contrasting curves of development, with Becky's fortunes rising half-way through the book, then sinking, while Amelia's decline then pick up again. At the same time the other characters are grouped round these two in a subtle system of balanced opposites. The method does not allow any lowering of tension from beginning to end, and few works of fiction are richer in scenes of the most brilliant comedy and drama.

Thackeray was also an innovator in the handling of time. The actual chronological span of the novel, as far as the direct action in concerned, is quite short – from about 1813 to 1839. But by a skilful narration of past events in the lives of the characters, and by the presence of a remarkably succinct and satisfactory final chapter (where so many writers of long novels go astray), Thackeray creates the illusion of watching the characters grow and develop by almost imperceptible degrees from childhood through youth and on into middle age. The example of Tolstoy (who greatly admired *Vanity Fair*) inevitably comes to mind, and perhaps only *War and Peace*, so often described as the greatest novel in the world, surpasses Thackeray in the handling of time and the changing generations. That in itself is a measure of Thackeray's achievement in *Vanity Fair*.

The History of Pendennis:
His Fortunes and Misfortunes, His Friends and His Greatest Enemy

William Makepeace Thackeray

The great success of *Vanity Fair* changed Thackeray's life. 'All of a sudden,' he wrote in one of his letters, 'I am a great man. I am ashamed of it, but yet I can't help seeing it, being elated by it and trying to keep it down.' He had no intention, however, of resting on his laurels. The last serial number of *Vanity Fair* appeared in the July of 1848 – only a month later he was hard at work on *Pendennis*, and the first instalment appeared in the November of that year. There was a three-month interruption when Thackeray fell seriously ill, but the last instalment was issued in the January of 1850, although Thackeray never completely regained his health. In 1851 he delivered a series of lectures on *The English Humourists* (published in book form in 1853), first in England and Scotland, and afterwards in the USA. In 1852 *Henry Esmond*, his novel set in the reign of Queen Anne, was published. In 1853 he travelled on the Continent and fell ill again, but his next major novel, *The Newcomes*, was issued serially from October 1853 to August 1855. In the October of the same year he went on his second lecture tour to the States, choosing as his subject *The Four Georges* (the four English Hanoverian kings of that name) which was published in book form in 1860. In 1857 he unsuccessfully stood for Parliament at Oxford, and in the same year the first numbers of another of his large novels,

The Virginians (a sequel to *Henry Esmond*) began to appear, and ran until 1859. Although he had resigned from the staff of *Punch* in 1854, from 1860 to 1862 he was editor of *The Cornhill Magazine*, in which he published several of his less well-known novels, as well as a long series of sketches. He died suddenly in December 1863 when he was only fifty-two. His output may not have reached the gigantic proportions of his great contemporary Dickens, and he did not display the same ceaseless and frenetic energy, but Thackeray, too, can be said to have burned himself out.

Most critics would probably agree that, next to *Vanity Fair*, *Pendennis* is the novel of Thackeray's that deserves most consideration. It ran its serial course side by side with Dickens's *David Copperfield*, a strange coincidence because each novel was the most obviously autobiographical of its respective author's books, each was its creator's favourite, and each was bathed in a kind of golden glow of affectionate and humorous recollection. Each of them in addition, recorded a young man's education, successive love affairs leading eventually to the 'right' marriage, and his adoption of authorship as a career, and in both cases many of the characters can be identified with real people who figured in the author's life.

As so many of the novels of the nineteenth century were written for serialization in the first instance, this inevitably affected their composition. The first readers of Thackeray and Dickens followed the fortunes of a group of characters over a period of two years, and they had to wait for a whole month to know what happened from one instalment to the next. A number of consequences followed. To begin with, readers expected both to get full value from each separate number, and to have their curiosity aroused at its end. But they did not in the least object – provided these conditions were fulfilled – to the introduction of fresh episodes and characters to give the number 'meat'. At the same time they grew as attached to the main characters as to their own friends and relations, never tired of their doings, no matter how small or apparently irrelevant to the main plot, and waited in a fever of expectation to know what would happen to them next. And at the end, while indifferent to loose ends in minor matters, they expected the lives of these characters to be satisfactorily rounded off, preferably with appropriate rewards for the 'goodies' and punishments for the 'baddies'. They were, in fact, not at all unlike the followers of the modern mammoth radio or television serials.

Thackeray found the episodic, improvised serial method of composition ready-made to his own tastes and temperament, and was therefore perfectly content to go along with it. He was the sort of writer (except in *Henry Esmond*, which was not written for serialization and is his best-constructed novel) who starts off with a rough idea of the theme and overall plot, and with a group of characters to whom he allows a good deal of latitude to wander in or out of the novel as they please. In addition, his tendency to diffuseness and looseness of structure was accentuated by his fondness for the eighteenth-century novelists, and especially for Fielding, which is evident even in the long original title of *Pendennis*. Even if this kind of approach does not always make for artistic unity, it *is* remarkably like life itself in its untidiness and apparent inconsequentiality. Thackeray was not so much a creator in the sense that Dickens with his fertile imagination and flow of comic invention was, as a shrewd and sensitive observer of men and manners. Although *Pendennis* is a very long novel, a great deal of it is taken up with evocations of a wide variety of social milieus and types, and the basic plot is fairly simple.

Summary

The novel opens with Major Pendennis, an elderly bachelor officer on half-pay, reading an agitated letter from his widowed sister-in-law, Helen, imploring him to come to Clavering St Mary's, because her seventeen-year-old son Arthur (to whom the Major is guardian) has got himself most unsuitably engaged to an actress a good many years older than himself. The Major complies, even though it means refusing invitations from several grand friends – for the good Major is a great diner-out and tuft-hunter.

Mrs Helen Pendennis lives with her son at a small estate named Fairoaks. Also living at Fairoaks is Laura Bell, the daughter of a former lover of Helen's, whom she had been unable to marry because as a very young man he had been trapped into another engagement. This helps to explain Helen's extreme panic when her son shows signs of making a similar mistake, and in addition her wish has always been that he would one day marry Laura, whom she had adopted as a child.

While at school, Arthur had made friends with Harry Foker, son of a wealthy brewer. It is Foker who has introduced him to a wild, tipsy Irishman, Captain Costigan, father of the actress with whom Arthur has fallen in love. Arthur's infatuation for Miss Fotheringay (Emily Costigan's stage name) is encouraged by her father who believes Arthur is much richer than he is, but discouraged by the kindly little musician Mr Bows who is devoted to her himself. The diplomatic efforts of Major Pendennis, however, result (after the revelation of the true nature of Arthur's purse and prospects) in the breaking-off of the engagement.

The Major, having obtained work for Emily in a London theatre, persuades his nephew to go to his own old college, St Boniface's, in the university of Oxbridge. There Arthur, or Pen as he is called, spends lavishly on wines, dinners, cigars, fine clothes, and all kinds of diversions. He mixes with a set far wealthier than himself, and gets hopelessly into debt. To make matters worse, when he sits for his final examinations, he is 'plucked' – that is, he fails. The self-centred egotism of Pen's despair, in which he imagines the whole world must be holding its breath because of his disgrace, so typical of that of any very young man in the same kind of situation, is rendered with great compassion and humour.

Pen is in despair, but when he slinks back home, he finds that his academic failure and his financial scrapes alike are accepted with loving forgiveness by the two devoted women in his life. Laura insists upon paying his debts out of the small sum she had inherited from her father, and Pen returns to Oxbridge, gives up (for the time being) his bad habits, works hard, and obtains his degree.

When Pen returns home again, there is great excitement in the neighbourhood because Clavering Park, the local 'great house', is about to be occupied again. Its owner, the spendthrift and despicable Sir Francis Clavering, had been forced to live abroad, but he has recently married an extremely wealthy widow. The family, which includes Blanche Amory, Lady Clavering's daughter by her previous marriage, move in with a host of retainers, among them Captain Ned Strong, Sir Francis's jovial confidential factotum, and Alcide Mirobolant, the dandified French chef who nurses a secret passion for his employer's stepdaughter (a notable comic creation, based on a famous chef of the Reform Club, of which Thackeray was a member and assiduous *habitué*).

Both Pen and Laura become close friends with the beautiful but selfish and self-willed Blanche, though Laura's friendship is tinged with jealousy because of Blanche's flirtatious behaviour towards Pen. At a public ball in the nearby seaside resort of Baymouth, Laura gets her own back on Pen by dancing with a college acquaintance of his. Pen, on the other hand, makes a fool of himself by falling down while dancing with Blanche, and by getting into a ludicrous altercation with Monsieur Mirobolant, from which he is extricated, after the latter has challenged him to a duel, by the tactful intervention of Captain Strong. Also at the ball is a stranger whom Captain Strong introduces as Colonel Altamont, formerly Commander of the bodyguard of the Nawab of Lucknow.

It is now decided that Pen should go to London to train as a barrister, and Laura provides the money to launch him on his career. Before he goes, Pen proposes to her in a very youthfully pompous speech, in which he gives, as his main reasons for wanting to marry her, his indebtedness to Laura, and that this is what his mother would like. But Laura is much too independent and high-spirited to accept a proposal couched in these terms.

In London, Pen shares chambers with George Warrington, an eccentric solitary whose life has been blighted (though Pen is unaware of this) by a disastrous youthful marriage – this theme of the dangers of premature attachments is one that frequently recurs in the novel. In spite of the good influence of Warrington (perhaps the finest character in the book) the good-hearted but spoiled and self-indulgent Pen soon relapses into his old habits. A large proportion of the sum Laura had advanced him goes on his subscription to his uncle's smart West End club – for the Major wishes his nephew to mix with the best society. But Pen mixes in low society too, where he again meets the raffish Captain Costigan, now subsidized by Emily who has married the wealthy Sir Charles Mirabel, to the sorrow of the still devoted Mr Bows. When Pen is down to his last guinea he confesses to Warrington (who has supposed from his way of life that Pen is well provided for) the true state of affairs and his indebtedness to Laura. Warrington, who supplements his meagre income at the Bar by journalism, encourages Pen to write, and introduces him to various editors and publishers. Pen, though in fact less talented than Warrington, is very successful, especially after the publication of a daring, 'Byronic' novel, and is thus able to repay Laura.

He now resumes his connection with the Claverings who have come up to their town house for the Season. Captain Strong takes lodgings nearby, which he shares, at Sir Francis Clavering's request, with the mysterious Colonel Altamont, who is obviously blackmailing Sir Francis. But when Altamont, fighting drunk, bursts in on a dinner party at the Clavering's house, and is unexpectedly confronted by Major Pendennis, he is oddly discomfited and leaves in a hurry. Also at the dinner party is Pen's old friend, Harry Foker, who falls head over heels in love with Blanche.

Major Pendennis has been assiduously cultivating the kindly but vulgar Lady Clavering because he has come to the conclusion that it might be advantageous to his nephew's prospects to keep up his relationship with Blanche. True, the Claverings have a son and heir who already shows promise of following in his dissolute father's footsteps, but obviously the Major has an idea (not yet revealed to the reader or to Pen) that events might modify this situation. Pen goes along with his uncle's wishes, and when he confides to Foker that he is thinking of marrying Blanche, poor Foker is racked with jealousy.

Pen, though, is soon caught up in a fresh entanglement. On a visit to Vauxhall Gardens, he meets Captain Costigan, who is escorting Mrs Bolton, the lodge keeper at Shepherd's Inn where he has rooms, and her very beautiful young daughter Fanny. Pen is captivated by Fanny, and takes to calling on Captain Costigan as an excuse for seeing more of her. Old Mr Bows, who also lodges at Shepherd's Inn and who, balked in his love for Emily Costigan, now lavishes a paternal and protective love on Fanny, charges Pen with having dishonourable designs on his protegée, though Pen is able to convince him to the contrary, and assures him that, now he realizes how seriously Fanny has been taking the affair, he will eschew further temptation.

Unfortunately Pen snubs Sam Huxter, an apothecary and old acquaintance from Clavering St Mary's, who has himself been smitten by Fanny's dazzling looks – and Sam writes home with lurid accounts of Pen's amorous activities in London. The rumours reach Pen's mother, causing her and Laura much distress. When Pen falls seriously ill and Helen and Laura, hurrying to his bedside, find Fanny in attendance, they put the worst construction on her presence, and haughtily dismiss her, though in fact the poor girl is guilty of nothing but the most devoted nursing with the knowledge and approval of the doctor who is attending Pen. While they are staying in Pen's chambers, his mother and Laura meet Warrington, who falls in love with Laura – and she in turn is much attracted to him.

Eventually, after Pen has recovered from his illness and discovers the treatment meted out to Fanny, he angrily upbraids his mother, announcing that the only way he can make up for her unkindness to Fanny is to marry her. Warrington, however, is able to reassure Helen that there is no truth in the scandalous rumours she has heard about her son's conduct – while for Pen's benefit (and indirectly for Laura's, too) he now reveals his own disastrous marriage and explains that his wife, who had run away with a lover, is still living. Pen and his mother are completely reconciled, but not long after Helen dies, leaving a small legacy to Fanny and a letter begging her forgiveness for having misjudged her. Fanny realizes sadly that she has no future with Pen and gradually grows fond of the uncouth, but honest and devoted, Sam Huxter. Laura goes to live with old Lady Rockminster, a lifelong friend.

Meanwhile Colonel Altamont, after a spectacular win at the Derby, has gone to the continental casinos, where his phenomenal lucky streak continues. But although relieved of the extortions of his blackmailer, Sir Francis Clavering has sunk deeper and deeper into debt. His wife once more pays his creditors, on condition that he will confine himself to the generous allowance she makes him. But before long he is at his old tricks again, and it is now that Major Pendennis's plan is revealed. He had recognized Colonel Altamont at their first meeting as Amory, Lady Clavering's first husband (whom he had met in India), reputedly dead in the Australian bush after he had escaped from a convict settlement. Major Pendennis promises Sir Francis not to reveal the secret – on condition that he accepts the fact that it is Blanche who, as Amory's daughter, is now the legitimate heir to Lady

Clavering's fortune; that he makes his parliamentary seat at Clavering St Mary's available to Pen; and that he eventually retires to the Continent with his allowance.

Pen, dazzled by the prospects of worldly success (though he knows nothing of his uncle's bargain with Sir Francis) pays court to Blanche. Not long afterwards, she herself meets Altamont again and learns that he is her father, though he swears her to secrecy. As for Pen, his conscience is troubled by his gross careerism, and he goes to see Laura. He tells her that he is contemplating marriage to Blanche, and Laura gives him her blessing. She also confesses that she would have married Warrington if he had been free. She and Pen are reunited in their old childhood intimacy, but each is moved, too, in a way they cannot yet recognize.

Major Pendennis's rascally valet, Morgan, now enters the story. He has been enriching himself for years on the proceeds of blackmail levied against various gentlemen whose guilty secrets he has wormed out of their servants. He has now discovered the identity of Colonel Altamont, and, knowing Major Pendennis's grand plans for his nephew, attempts to blackmail the Major too. But his employer turns the tables by threatening to declare that various presents he has given his valet were stolen. The discomfited Morgan, however, tells Pen the secret about Altamont, who has by now returned to England with the proceeds of his successful gambling.

Both Pen and Laura have begun to realize the real nature of their feelings for each other. But they agree that Blanche cannot be blamed for her convict father, and that it would be dishonourable for Pen to abandon her in her trouble. Pen realizes, too, what his uncle has been up to and that it would be dishonourable for him to accept a parliamentary seat in the circumstances.

He now goes to Blanche to tell her that he wishes to marry her, but finds that he has been forestalled by his old friend Harry Foker, who has inherited his father's fortune. Pen hurries back to Laura with the news that they are now free to marry. Lady Rockminster wins Major Pendennis round by hinting that Laura will eventually inherit her fortune. In the midst of their joy, Pen and Laura do not neglect to smooth the way for Fanny and Sam Huxter by reconciling the latter's father to the match.

Colonel Altamont's secret is finally revealed, and when he comes down to Clavering St Mary's, Morgan (who is now putting the screws on Blanche) tries to have him arrested so that he can collect the reward attached to Altamont's capture as an escaped convict, but Altamont evades him. In the course of these events, however, Madame Frisby (one of the minor characters) has recognized Altamont as *her* long-lost husband, Johnny Armstrong. Lady Clavering had been one of his many bigamous wives, and so she really is Lady Clavering after all. She and Sir Francis are more or less reconciled. Harry Foker, disillusioned by Blanche's deceit, breaks off the engagement, and Blanche eventually marries a French count of grand but dubious titles. Pen and Laura marry, of course, and Warrington becomes godfather to their first child. Pen prospers by the advantageous sale of some of his land to a railway company and by his continuing success as a writer; and when Sir Francis Clavering dies, it is Pen who becomes the new Member of Parliament for Clavering St Mary's. Thackeray says goodbye to his hero with the words:

> ... knowing how mean the best of us is, let us give
> hand of charity to Arthur Pendennis, with all his
> faults and shortcomings, who does not claim to be a hero,
> but only a man and a brother.

Critical commentary

Thackeray intended *Pendennis* to be a truthful portrait of a typical young man of good heart but healthy appetites, somewhat in the manner of Fielding's *Tom Jones*.

This intention was clearly expressed in the allegorical cover design for the novel, (drawn by Thackeray himself) which shows his hero standing irresolute between on the one side a voluptuous looking mermaid, attended by baby fauns, and on the other a respectable wife and children. But in the event Pen's dissipations are only hinted at, and while his teenage infatuation with Emily Costigan is convincingly rendered, his adult involvements with Fanny and Blanche are so carefully guarded and camouflaged that they become evasive and unreal. This made Pen more morally acceptable by Victorian standards but it also tends to render him colourless, insipid, and priggish.

That Thackeray himself felt bitterly frustrated in this respect is borne out by this passage from a preface which he added to the novel in its volume form:

> Since the author of 'Tom Jones' was buried, no writer
> of fiction among us has been permitted to depict to
> his utmost power a MAN. We must drape him and give
> him a certain conventional simper. Society will not
> tolerate the Natural in our Art ...

Nevertheless, it was not only society that was to blame. The same timidity that was present in *Vanity Fair* also weakens the impact of Pendennis, and Thackeray's concern with the 'purity' of his hero is at times downright obtrusive. There is, too, the same uncertainty in his handling of the women as there was in *Vanity Fair*. M. R. Ridley has pointed out that 'with Blanche Amory, Thackeray plays the same cat-and-mouse game that he does with Becky Sharp, now condemning, now excusing.' Although Laura in *Pendennis* is a much more satisfactory heroine than the doll-like Amelia of *Vanity Fair*, it is on the whole Blanche who is the really vital character – and once again Thackeray is unable to make up his mind about her. As for Pen's mother, her doting on her son is sometimes pushed to the point of imbecility, and one can sometimes detect a jeering, almost savage note in

Thackeray's portrayal of her. J. Y. T. Greig is probably right when he says Thackeray was 'dominated and controlled by the tutelary spirit' of his own mother – and interestingly enough, Thackeray makes one comment on Helen Pendennis and her attitude towards Blanche Amory's earlier flirtation with Pen that is quite startlingly explicit at a time long before the advent of Freud and psychoanalysis: 'I have no doubt there is sexual jealousy on the mother's part.' But that revealing flash does no more than indicate the potential depth of Thackeray's insight and understanding, and confirms the feeling one so often has in reading him that he could have been a far greater novelist than he allowed himself to be.

A similar withholding of power is evident in his satire. There is no question as to the warmth of Thackeray's heart, of the liberal nature of his opinions, or of the soundness of his fundamental values. Few writers have so thoroughly exposed the shams, pretences, snobberies and hypocrisies that beset the career of a young man like Arthur Pendennis in a materialist society. But as those last sentences of the novel demonstrate, the tone that attends the exposure tends to be one of world-weary disillusionment and therefore is almost too forgiving and indulgent, which may explain why Thackeray was, often much to his distress, accused by his contemporaries of cynicism. He was, in fact, far too good-natured and perceptive to be merely a cynic, but one cannot help feeling sometimes that if he had allowed himself to be angrier in his satire, it would have been much more effective. To take an obvious instance, the worldly schemings of Major Pendennis, although they are undertaken with the best motives and out of genuine affection for Pen, should surely have been condemned more roundly than they are rather than dismissed with an indulgent shrug of the shoulders.

When all the reservations have been made, however, *Pendennis* remains a notable fictional achievement, and (in spite of Thackeray's misgivings) one of the few that really does recapture something of the freshness and spaciousness of Fielding's *Tom Jones* itself.

Alton Locke, Tailor and Poet

Charles Kingsley

Charles Kingsley is usually remembered either for his exciting novels of adventure like *Westward Ho!* (1855) and *Hereward the Wake* (1865), or for his children's classics: *The Water Babies*, about a boy chimney-sweep transported into a happy aquatic life as a water-baby, published in 1863, and *The Heroes* (1856), a charming re-telling of some of the legends of Ancient Greece. But in *Alton Locke* he also produced a 'condition of England' novel which, if lacking the fictional mastery and subtlety of Mrs Gaskell's *North and South* and the imaginative brilliance of Disraeli's *Sybil*, is nevertheless something more than a mere tract of the times.

Charles Kingsley was born in 1819, in his father's vicarage on Dartmoor in Devon. As a boy he reacted strongly against his parents' conventional piety, devoting himself instead to geology and athletic sports. As an undergraduate at Cambridge, however, he met (and eventually married) a young woman who restored his Christian faith. He took holy orders and in 1842 became curate, and afterwards rector, of Eversley, an impoverished country parish in Hampshire, which was his main home for the remaining thirty-three years of his life.

Kingsley's Christianity was neither High Church like that of his wife, nor Evangelical, like that of most of the Victorians. It grew out of the combined influence of two of the most original social thinkers of the period. One of them was Thomas Carlyle (1795–1881) who, although he had no patience with democratic processes and believed in a return to the kind of social organization practised in the Middle Ages, was one of the most vigorous opponents of the Industrial Revolution which, he argued, had sought to subordinate all human values to the 'cash nexus'. The other was John Frederick Denison Maurice (usually known as F. D. Maurice), a gentle and compassionate clergyman who preached (both in the pulpit and in books and pamphlets) that Christ was 'the actual representative of Humanity', and that 'a true socialism is the necessary result of a sound Christianity' – although he also believed that the social revolution could only come about by religious and moral means, by a change in men's hearts.

Kingsley had read F. D. Maurice's writings while still an undergraduate, and when the two men met in 1844 they became firm friends. Kingsley's contact with the ignorance, vice, and squalor he found at Eversley confirmed him in his views, and he became a convinced Christian Socialist. In 1848 under the pseudonym of Parson Lot, he contributed a series of sympathetic 'Letters to the Chartists' to the penny weekly *Politics for the People* which had been launched by F. D. Maurice and his group, thereby earning for himself a reputation as a firebrand.

It is to this context that Kingsley's two important 'social-problem' novels belong. The first of them was entitled *Yeast, or The Thoughts, Sayings and Doings of Lancelot Smith, Gentleman*, and was published anonymously as a serial, also in 1848. *Yeast*, the shortened title by which the novel is generally known, and which was intended of course to suggest the social ferment of the times, was largely directed to dispelling the notion that misery, dirt, and disease existed only in the industrial towns. Disraeli had made this point too in his description of the squalid village of Marney in *Sybil*, but *Yeast* was the first novel wholly devoted to the subject. Its attack on the vested interests of the landlords and on the game laws, and its idealization of the peasantry in the form of a manly verse-writing gamekeeper, frightened the publisher so much that he begged Kingsley to bring the serial to a hasty conclusion, and it did not appear in volume form until three years later.

In the meantime, *Alton Locke, Tailor and Poet* (published anonymously in 1850) had switched the main attack to the conditions prevailing among the London poor. This novel was largely based on the real-life career of Thomas Cooper, who, while working as a shoemaker's apprentice, had managed to teach himself Greek, Latin and Hebrew. He became a schoolmaster and then a journalist, took part in Chartist agitations, served a two-year prison sentence for organizing a strike (during which he wrote a political verse epic), and later, as his revolutionary enthusiasm waned, turned to lecturing on history and educational theory. It was at this stage in his life that Kingsley came to know him and set out to convert him from his religious scepticism.

Kingsley's enthusiasm for Christian Socialism began to wane after the publication of *Alton Locke*. Though he was always a strong advocate of improved living conditions for the poor, he became something of an Establishment figure, accepting appointments as Chaplain to Queen Victoria in 1859 and as a canon at Westminster Cathedral two years before his death in 1875.

Summary

Alton Locke is the son of a failed small shopkeeper, brought up by his widowed mother, a strict Baptist who suppresses her own tender feelings in order to inculcate in her son the merciless Calvinistic doctrine of predestination. For a time Alton entertains the idea of becoming a missionary, until a Baptist minister assures him that 'Jesus does *not* love one and all', but only those few 'elected' at birth for grace and redemption.

After obtaining some rudimentary schooling, Alton, at fifteen weakly, undersized and consumptive, is apprenticed to a tailor, in whose workroom he meets a Chartist, John Crossthwaite, who introduces him to the eccentric old Scottish bookseller, Saunders Mackaye (modelled on Carlyle). Mackaye detects Alton's latent literary talent, supplies him with the books for which he craves, and when Alton, no longer able to tolerate his mother's narrow views, quarrels with her and leaves home, takes him into his own house.

Interested by reports of his impoverished nephew's cleverness, Alton's well-to-do uncle sends for him, and his son George, a Cambridge undergraduate, takes Alton to the picture gallery at Dulwich. There, his evident excitement attracts the attention of the kindly Dean Winnstay, his beautiful daughter Lillian and her cousin Eleanor Staunton. Alton falls in love with Lillian and begins writing romantic poetry about her.

Alton's master dies, and his son takes over the business. Determined to get rich as quickly as possible he announces that he is going into the 'show trade', which means that he will be closing the workshop and giving out the work for the men to make up in their own homes. Crossthwaite warns the men against 'the infernal system of contract work', but when he asks them to sign a protest, only Alton complies. Crossthwaite takes him to a Chartist meeting and he becomes a convert to the Chartist cause.

Mackaye advises Alton to take his volume of poems to Cambridge in the hope that his cousin will help to get it published. He sets out on foot, enraptured by his first experience of the countryside. He is given a lift by a farmer named Porter, who tells him that he has a lost son who is, he believes, working as a tailor somewhere in London, and Alton promises to try and find him. When he reaches Cambridge, Alton is hospitably, if patronizingly, received by his cousin. He burns with indignation, however, at the treatment meted out to him by some of the 'young gentlemen'. The courteous and liberal-minded young nobleman, Lord Lynedale is a notable exception. Through Lord Lynedale, who is engaged to Eleanor Staunton, Alton again meets her uncle, Dean Winnstay and his beautiful daughter Lillian. They invite him to visit the deanery at the nearby cathedral town. Lord Lynedale interests the Dean in Alton's poems, and he promises to try and get them published and also to explore the possibility of obtaining for him a sizarship at Cambridge. But there is a condition: Alton must remove the fiery political passages which are 'the very pith and marrow of the poems'. His deepest instincts tell him to refuse; but since to do so would, he feels, take him for ever out of the sphere of Lillian, he agrees. To his surprise, Eleanor Staunton is disappointed by his decision.

Back in London, Alton scrapes a living by hack journalism for one of the Chartist papers. He has not forgotten his promise, though, to Farmer Porter, who himself comes to London to join in the search for his son. Eventually, they find him in a tailor's sweat-shop run by Jemmy Downes (a former workmate of Alton's) among a number of exhausted, half-starved and half-naked wretches, who for months past have not been allowed out of doors because of the debts they have incurred for their miserable food and lodging. Farmer Porter is joyfully reunited with his son, and Alton uses the ten pounds which the farmer has insisted on giving him to redeem the other inmates of the sweat-shop.

Alton's cousin George is about to take holy orders and Alton is shocked by his worldly attitude to his intended vocation, and by his professed intention of exploiting his acquaintance with Lord Ellerton (formerly Lord Lynedale and now married to Eleanor) in order to forward his ambitions. He is even more shocked to learn that marriage to Lillian is among these ambitions. When Alton reveals his own feelings for Lillian, George warns him off in terms which cause Alton a good deal of worry because he is in debt to George – until he discovers that some unknown benefactor (perhaps Lillian herself, Alton romantically imagines) has paid the debt for him. Alton's volume of poems is published and proves successful. He is invited to a reception given by the Winnstays in their London house, where he sits at Lillian's feet. He also meets Eleanor again for the first time since her marriage to Lord Ellerton, and learns something of the far-reaching reforms and improvements she and her husband have been introducing on his estates. But when Alton calls at the house the following morning, he learns that Lord Ellerton has been killed in a riding accident.

Alton's joy in his volume of poems is short-lived, for one of the radical papers gets hold of the fact that he had emasculated his work in order to please his upper-class backers and pillories him as a time-server and a traitor to the working-class cause. Even his loyal friends Sandy Mackaye and Crossthwaite are disappointed in him, the latter affectionately but bluntly accusing him of veering 'between flunkeydom and the Cause, like a donkey between two bundles of hay.' Anxious to reinstate himself in the eyes of his comrades, Alton begs to be given some dangerous mission, and is sent to represent the Chartists in a country area where there is serious unrest among the agricultural labourers. His heart sinks when he learns that it is near the cathedral town where Dean Winnstay and his daughter live. He attends a meeting of farm workers and listens to a tally of wrongs, injustices and miseries as bad as anything he has encountered in the East End of London. After he himself has made a fiery speech, the unruly elements in the crowd lead a march on a nearby farm in search of food, and rioting takes place. When the yeomanry arrive on the scene, Alton is among the six rioters who are arrested. Mackaye and Crossthwaite organize their defence. The money has been provided by the same mysterious benefactor who had earlier paid off Alton's debt to his cousin – and again he entertains the romantic notion that it is Lillian. When witnesses testify to his attempts to prevent violence, Alton receives the comparatively light sentence of three years imprisonment, though two of the other rioters are sentenced to transportation and, with savage irony, thank the judge for rescuing them from starvation.

When Alton emerges from prison, he finds that the Chartists, encouraged by the 1848 revolutions on the Continent, are compiling a huge petition to be presented to the House of Commons. If the MPs accept the demand for electoral reform, so that working men can vote and sit in Parliament, the Chartists are convinced that sweeping social and economic reforms will quickly follow. If it is rejected, then, the extremists argue, they too must take to the barricades.

Before the monster petition is presented, old Mackaye dies, a staunch champion of the people to the end, but increasingly critical of the course of events. Eleanor (Lady Ellerton) appeals to Alton to give up his part in the insurrection that is now expected, passionately assuring him that there is another path of deliverance, but Alton is in no mood to listen to her when she reveals that his cousin George has been blackening his reputation with the Winnstays – and that George is engaged to be married to Lillian. But there is no insurrection. Thousands of special constables are enrolled, troops stand by and the people are intimidated. But the Chartist leaders quarrel among themselves, the rally they have organized is poorly attended and soon breaks up, while the petition is contemptuously rejected by Parliament.

After the break-up of the rally, Alton catches sight of George among a group of well-heeled special constables and follows him to the London home of the Winnstays, where he sees him and Lillian locked in an embace. George discovers him and knocks him down. Alton makes his way to Waterloo Bridge, with the idea of committing suicide. But when another man leaps on to the parapet with the same intention, Alton instinctively prevents him. The man is Jemmy Downes, now himself a sweater. He takes Alton back with him to a ghastly shack, inside which lie Downes's wife and two children, dead of typhus, their bodies gnawed by the rats and covered with the coat on which they had been working up to the moment of death. As a result, Alton himself catches typhus. He owes his life to the nursing of Eleanor, aided by Crossthwaite and his wife. He learns from the Crossthwaites that it was Eleanor and not Lillian who had been his unknown benefactor and that she is now running a home, on co-operative lines, for the 'fallen women' among the needlewomen of the East End. It also emerges that in his will, Sandy Mackaye had left Alton and Crossthwaite two hundred pounds apiece, on condition that they 'cool down across the Atlantic' for a period of seven years.

While Alton is convalescing, Eleanor (the chief mouth-piece of Kingsley's Christian Socialist ideas) exhorts Alton and Crossthwaite to turn to Christ 'the great Reformer ... the true demagogue' as their leader. When they ask whether she is demanding that they should give up all they have struggled for as Chartists, she tells them to keep their faith, provided they recognize it as belonging to the kingdom of God. Alton also learns from Eleanor that his cousin George is dead of typhus from an infected coat, as well as the valet who had brushed it and the shopman who had sold it to him – the very coat Alton had seen covering the corpses of Jemmy Downes's wife and children. Alton sees in this the hand of God, 'the consistent Nemesis of all poor George's thrift and cunning, of his determination to carry the buy-cheap-and-sell-dear commercialism, in which he had been brought up, into every act of life!' The realization that the beautiful but shallow Lillian is free causes him no more than a passing pang; he knows now that she had been a false idol and it is Eleanor who em-bodies his hopes of redemption. The Charter was 'a self-willed idol', so God's blessing had been withheld from it. Alton and his comrades had not realized that they could not succeed without the cooperation of the nation as a whole, and had in consequence neglected to turn to their natural allies, those truly Christian clergy who alone could bridge the gulf between the classes.

Eleanor rejoices that Alton has come round to her way of thinking. She sends him to America (in company with Crossthwaite and his wife) so that, his health restored, he will on his return be fit to devote himself to the cause he believes in – but permeated now with Christian principles. She herself will not be there to see it, because, she reveals, she is mortally ill and has not much longer to live. Her last request to Alton is to write his history as an example to others.

It is to this task that Alton devotes himself on his transatlantic voyage. Then, within sight of land, he himself dies, and the book ends with a letter from Crossthwaite (who has been Alton's fellow-passenger) expressing his determination eventually to return to England to 'assist in the Emancipation of Labour, and in establishing a fraternal union of all classes'. He quotes the poem which Alton had written just before he died, addressed to all those who sympathize, in a true Christian spirit, with the sufferings and just aspirations of the English workers.

Critical commentary

Alton Locke is in many ways even more overtly propagandist than Disraeli's *Sybil*. The style frequently recalls that of Kingsley's 'Parson Lot' polemics, with their rather hectoring pulpit-rhetoric. *Alton Locke*, indeed, was in many respects no more than a fictionalized version of one of Kingsley's tracts, entitled *Cheap Clothes and Nasty*, which appeared in 1850 (while he was still working on his novel) and which was based upon the researches of the Victorian sociologist Henry Mayhew, exposing the horrors of the sweat-shops in the tailoring trade.

The chief fault of *Alton Locke*, therefore, is one common to most propaganda fiction – the propaganda becomes more important than the novel. In his eagerness to preach the cause of Christian Socialism, Kingsley too often forces plot and character alike to fit his thesis. The most striking example is the way in which the life goes out of the novel after Alton has caught typhus. Up to this point Kingsley has for the most part allowed his hero to tell his own story with desperate and convincing sincerity, and has given ample evidence of his lively and inquiring mind. Now Kingsley turns him into the almost completely passive recipient of a series of sermons on Christian Socialism from Eleanor. It is true that Alton is a captive audience in the sense that he is lying in bed convalescing, but this cannot excuse the fact that he seems to have become an altogether different person. For the sake of his Christian Socialist propaganda Kingsley has suddenly reduced his hero to a mere cipher.

Some of Eleanor's sermonizing is certainly eloquent, moving and convincing. But much of it is also woolly and tendentious. Although Kingsley took a double first degree in Classics at Cambridge and was professor of Modern History at his old university from 1860 to 1869, he was never a consistent or very logical thinker, had a number of religious prejudices (including a virulent hostility to Roman Catholicism), and was subject all his life to emotional fits and starts.

In reading *Alton Locke*, it is not difficult to see why the Christian Socialism of the period as preached by Kingsley made so little impact on the working-class movement. There is nothing really socialist about the overall intention of the novel. Though there is plenty of sympathy for the social and economic grievances of the Chartists, their political aim of throwing open the franchise and membership of the House of Commons to the working classes (which was of course eventually achieved) meets with little approval. The Christian Socialism of the novel never for a moment implies anything approaching a radical change in the actual structure of society, and Kingsley makes it quite clear that in his view the natural leaders and initiators of reform must be liberal-minded aristocrats like Lord Ellerton, high-minded ladies like Eleanor, and the more enlightened clergy. If Alton is to better himself it can only be, as both the Dean and Alton's self-seeking cousin impress upon him, by abandoning his working-class self and completely identifying himself with the established social structure. Even so, Kingsley does not approve of such attempts, for in a letter to a friend, not long after the publication of *Alton Locke*, he wrote:

> The moral of my book is, that the working man who tries to get on, to desert his class and rise above it, enters into a lie, and leaves God's path for his own ...

In other words, while the condition of the working classes must be improved, it must be achieved from above and within the existing social order. The working classes must continue to know their place.

Nevertheless, *Alton Locke* does succeed as a novel. Kingsley had imagination, and he simply could not prevent himself pouring it into the creation of his hero. In view of the author's own class and background, Alton himself really is a remarkable achievement. He is, until those last few preachifying chapters, and apart from some stilted conversations (Kingsley is much better at analysis of feeling than at dialogue) undoubtedly convincing as the brilliant, self-educated working man. The rather strained, rhetorical style of the earlier chapters, for example, is exactly what one might have expected from someone not accustomed to ease of expression, and who has modelled himself on contemporary writers like Carlyle. The fierce hunger for books, ideas, beauty, and the almost unbearable joy on each occasion that it is satisfied, have seldom been better conveyed. Through Alton's eyes, for example, the reader sees Guido's 'St Sebastian' in the Dulwich Gallery; is with him when he exultantly reaches the open countryside on his way to Cambridge and enters a wood for the first time in his life; and experiences with him, too, the poignant blend of awe and frustrated longing with which he gazes at the Cambridge colleges and breathes in the atmosphere of antiquity and learning – an evocation not to be equalled until, later in the century,

Thomas Hardy in *Jude the Obscure* has his stonemason hero visit Oxford in a very similar frame of mind.

Even more remarkable, perhaps, is the way in which Kingsley has captured the shyness and pugnacity, the prickly pride and readiness to take offence, the raw feelings so easily hurt, and the burning sense of injustice experienced by someone in Alton's situation, and with his innate sensitivity and intelligence. It was the first time that class-consciousness, from the point of view of Alton's social level, had been so thoroughly explored, and it was not to be done so well again until the advent of H. G. Wells and D. H. Lawrence. Particularly effective, for example, is the scene where Dean Winnstay and Lord Lynedale (both of them good and benevolent men) discuss Alton's poems in his presence – but as if he weren't there – pointing out to each other their deficiencies, their lack of cultural background and their derivativeness from the few obvious models Alton has had the chance to study. The sense of a yawning social and cultural gap could not be conveyed more vividly.

Kingsley writes from inside Alton's skin, too, in describing the development of his hero's political consciousness. The unforgettable evocations of the East End slums and sweat-shops, for instance, are not those of an outside observer, but of someone who knows only too well, as Alton does, the thinness of the partition that divides the respectable poor from the abyss of utter destitution. An edge of anxiety makes them even more vivid, and at the same time makes Alton's indignation and growing political extremism seem not only understandable but inevitable. The reader in consequence finds himself participating to the full in the exultations and excitements of Chartism (the accounts of meetings and rallies are among the best passages in the book) and in the hopeless bitterness of defeat and disillusionment.

There is, therefore, a genuine imaginative identification between Kingsley and his hero. So much so that he became uneasy, and in the later edition of his novel he found it necessary, in describing Alton's reactions to Cambridge as an institution reserved for the privileged, to insert a footnote explaining that his views '... are not my own. They are simply what clever working men thought ... from 1845 to 1850; a period at which I had the fullest opportunities of knowing the thoughts of working men.'

Alton, in other words, had come too much alive for Kingsley's comfort, and taken on an existence independent of his creator's intentions. That is why towards the end of the novel, as he suddenly realized that it was time he got down to his own theorizing, Kingsley decided to smother him. But *Alton Locke* remains as yet another example of the truth, proclaimed by D. H. Lawrence in our own century, that where the creative imagination is genuinely at work 'a didactic purpose ... cannot put to death the novel.'

Villette

Charlotte Brontë

Summary

Lucy Snowe, the heroine of *Villette* (Charlotte Brontë's last novel published in 1853) is, like Jane Eyre, an orphan. When the story opens she is visiting her godmother, Mrs Bretton. The six-year-old Paulina Home, whose mother has recently died, also comes to live with the Brettons. This strange, elfin-like child is 'adopted' by sixteen-year-old John Graham Bretton, who teases her mercilessly but whom she comes to adore.

Eight years elapse. For much of this time Lucy has been working as companion to an elderly invalid. With the death of her employer she is now in London, utterly alone, with very little money, and craving for a new life. On an impulse she boards a cross-Channel steamer. There she meets a flighty seventeen-year-old girl named Ginevra Fanshawe, who explains that her godfather, the Comte de Bassompierre, is sending her to a school in Villette run by a Madame Beck. Lucy too goes to Villette. She loses her way and finds herself outside a school, the brass plate of which announces that the proprietress is Madame Beck. She goes in, and Madame Beck – advised by her cousin M. Paul Emanuel, a teacher at the school who likes the look of Lucy – employs her as a nursery governess to her children. Impressed by the skill with which

Lucy handles them, she appoints her to the teaching staff.

Lucy does well and quickly learns the language. She renews her acquaintance with Ginevra Fanshawe, who confides in her that she has a mysterious suitor, though she admits that she prefers the dandified Colonel de Hamal, whom she has met at a ball.

When one of Madame Beck's children breaks an arm, she is attended by 'Dr John' (as he tells the child to call him), whom Lucy feels she has met before. It transpires that it is Dr John who is Ginevra's mysterious suitor, and before long Lucy has fallen in love with him herself. She also becomes more closely acquainted with the irascible but kind-hearted M. Paul Emanuel as the result of a school play he produces and in which he persuades Lucy to take part.

When the long vacation arrives and Lucy is left alone at the school she sinks into a deep depression. In her despair she enters the confessional-box of a church she passes in her lonely wanderings through the city, and tells the kindly priest something of her distress. On leaving the church, she collapses and the priest entrusts her to the care of Dr John, who happens to be passing. He takes her to his home where his mother recognizes her – and Lucy now reveals that she had realized some time ago that Dr John was none other than the grown-up John Graham Bretton.

The Brettons look after Lucy and take her with them on a number of expeditions. At the theatre, Ginevra's contemptuous treatment of his mother begins to wean Dr John from his infatuation. Paul Emanuel, who is also in the audience, disapproves of the pink dress (a present from Mrs Bretton) which Lucy is wearing. However, he comforts her in her distress over her feelings for 'Dr John', but shows symptoms remarkably like those of jealousy when she receives a letter with the Doctor's seal on the envelope.

While in the garret, where she has gone in order to read her letter in privacy, Lucy is terrified by the ghostly figure of a nun, but – after seeing the apparition for a second time – agrees with the Doctor that it must be the product of a disordered imagination. She receives other letters from Dr Bretton (as he is now called), and though she knows in her heart that they are no more than the expressions of kindness – accompanied by a certain enjoyment in the effect they produce – she cherishes them and the dream they represent.

One night, when she is at the theatre with him, there is a fire and in the panic that ensues a young girl is knocked down. Dr Bretton treats the girl's injured shoulder. It turns out that she is Ginevra's cousin and the daughter of the Comte de Bassompierre. Not long afterwards, on a visit to Mrs Bretton, Lucy meets Mlle de Bassompierre again – and learns that she is in fact the Paulina Home she had met years ago while staying with the Brettons in England. Paulina's father had inherited a large fortune, on condition that he adopted his mother's maiden name of Bassompierre. It soon becomes apparent to Lucy that the childhood attraction that had existed between Dr Bretton and Paulina is by no means dead.

When Lucy finds that Madame Beck has been reading Dr Bretton's letters to her, she buries them in the garden, and in so doing again encounters the mysterious nun. Meanwhile, Paul Emanuel continues to annoy Lucy by his sharp comments on her frequent absences with her grand friends, and they have many quarrels. Gradually, however, Lucy finds her feelings softening towards him. On his birthday, she presents him with a watch-guard she has made for him, and while they are in the garden together they both see the mysterious nun. During an outing organized by Paul Emanuel for the pupils and staff, he pays special attention to Lucy. On their return, Lucy sees him and Madame Beck in earnest conversation, and senses that some crisis is impending.

A few days later, Madame Beck sends Lucy on a concocted errand to the house of a grim, hunchbacked old woman named Madame Walravens. There she meets again Père Silas, the old priest whom she had once visited. He tells her that Paul Emanuel has for years been supporting Madame Walravens, because he had once been engaged to her grand-daughter who, when her family had disapproved of the match, had entered a convent where she had died. According to the priest, Paul Emanuel has sworn eternal fidelity to the memory of his dead fiancée.

Although it still causes Lucy great pain to hear Paulina rhapsodizing over Dr Bretton, she agrees to intervene on behalf of the lovers with Paulina's father, and he gives his blessing to their union.

It is announced that M. Paul Emanuel will no longer be teaching at the school because he has to go on a voyage to the West Indies – on behalf of Madame Walravens who has a plantation there which urgently requires honest supervision. The day before that fixed for his departure, Lucy receives a note from him to say that he must see her before he goes. But Madame Beck mixes an opiate in Lucy's drink when she retires to bed with a headache. The drug, however, has the opposite effect to that intended, producing a state of feverish excitement in which Lucy leaves the school and, drawn by the sounds of a military band, makes her way in a kind of trance to the municipal park where a fête is taking place. In the park, Lucy, concealed in the shadow of some trees, is astonished to see a party consisting of Madame Beck, Madame Walravens, Père Silas and a young girl, closely attended by Paul Emanuel. From their conversation Lucy gathers that Paul Emanuel has postponed his departure because he has important business to complete – and she jumps to the conclusion that this concerns the girl. The sight of the two of them together, apparently on the most affectionate terms, brings home to Lucy the realization that she is now in love with him. When she gets back to the school she finds the habit of a nun on her bed and the following morning Ginevra Fanshawe is missing. She has eloped with Colonel de Hamal – it is he who had adopted the disguise of the ghostly nun in order to keep his assignations with her. The Comte de Bassompierre pursues the runaway couple, but they are already married when he catches up with them.

The day before he does finally sail, Paul Emanuel arrives at the school to see Lucy, sternly dismissing Madame Beck when she again tries to interfere. He then takes Lucy to see a house he has rented and equipped as a school for her to run during his absence. This was the uncompleted business of which Lucy had heard him speak in the park, and the girl she had seen him with is his ward and already engaged to be married. When eventually they part, Lucy and Paul Emanuel have declared their love for each other.

Secure and happy in this knowledge, Lucy makes a success of her school during the three years of her lover's absence. As the novel ends she is anxiously awaiting Paul Emanuel's return, amidst ominous reports of Atlantic tempests and shipwrecks – and the reader never knows whether he survived them.

Critical commentary

When George Eliot finished reading *Villette*, she wrote to a friend:

> I am only just returned to a sense of the real world about me, for I have been reading *Villette*, a still more wonderful book than *Jane Eyre*. There is something almost preternatural in its power.

Most critics would probably agree with this assessment. One of the chief reasons lies in the fact that whereas the earlier novel is only partially derived from situations and emotions the authoress had actually lived through, *Villette* is from beginning to end a grappling with the realities of her personal experience, with very little indulgence in escapist fantasy or daydreaming for their own sakes.

Whereas, too, in *Jane Eyre* the main areas of experience

Charlotte was struggling to come to terms with – the traumas of her early life and the ingrown world of the Haworth parsonage – both belonged to childhood, her last novel grew out of the central experience of her adulthood, her years in Brussels (Villette in the novel) and her frustrated love for M. Héger, husband of the proprietress of the school which Charlotte and her sister Emily had attended.

In addition, *Villette* has the advantage of being in some respects a second go at the same basic material. For Charlotte's rejected novel, *The Professor*, had also been set in Brussels, and its re-creation of people and places, particularly of the school and its surroundings, is sometimes as vivid as anything in *Villette*. At that stage, however, Charlotte had not yet sufficiently recovered from her unhappy infatuation to trust herself to deal with it head-on in fictional, and objective, terms. She had also been very much aware of the romantic temptations to which she was subject. These two factors combined to make her over-determined in *The Professor* to hold emotionalism sternly in check and to be as 'realistic' as possible. This weighed too heavily on the novel, preventing it from catching fire, whereas in *Villette* she had reached that degree of detachment that enabled her to release the full flow of her emotions and at the same time subject them to artistic control.

Not that the novel is without quite serious flaws. The Gothic elements, for example, are still in evidence, as in the ghostly nun (though this, of course, has a rational explanation), and in the grotesque figure of Madame Walravens and her sinister house. There are, too, far too many contrived coincidences, such as the reappearance in Villette of both the Brettons and of Paulina and her father; while the account of Paul Emanuel's devotion to his dead fiancée smacks of the romantic novelette. But these elements are less obtrusive than in *Jane Eyre* and they do not seriously detract from the impact of the novel as a whole. In spite of it defects, *Villette* is the most successfully integrated of Charlotte Brontë's novels, and, on the whole, all the elements that compose it are caught up in a single and powerful act of creativity.

This overall sureness of touch sprang from a fuller command of herself and her experiences, and therefore, of her raw materials. In *Villette* she was able to turn back to her thwarted love for M. Héger and treat it at last with full artistic detachment. The whole episode had become fully real to her and, therefore, fully available. It was no longer necessary for her to disguise or distort any part of it, either by fantasy or by a purely personal resentment.

The unified vision behind the novel enables Charlotte Brontë, in drawing upon her own vivid memories, to endow the most commonplace scenes of Lucy's daily life at the school – the classrooms, the tiled hall, the long dormitory, the secluded garden, the humdrum details of a teacher's routine – with a hypnotic intensity. Their concreteness, moreover, provides a firm base from which the fictional creation can extend outwards. In *The Professor*, the reader sometimes feels hemmed in by the narrow, somewhat austere ambience of the characters; in *Villette*, in spite of the grimly claustrophobic nature of many of Lucy's experiences, there is a sense of extension and even spaciousness. The world beyond the walls of the school is as fully created as that within them. The reader is made vividly aware of the capital itself: the bustling streets, boulevards, and squares; the churches, theatres, art galleries; the parks and festivals, and the countryside beyond. One is, aware, too, of the foreignness in customs, dress, habits, speech, politics – and religion. The religious debate which is present in all Charlotte Brontë's novels receives in *Villette* a particularly satisfying and concrete rendering, and the church bells which Lucy hears from the school serve as a kind of chorus to her psychological and spiritual struggles.

The range of characters in *Villette* is also wider than in Charlotte Brontë's other novels. It takes in not only the world of the school, but those of the Brettons, the Bassompierres, Paul Emanuel – and the city of Villette itself. At the same time none of the characters, with the possible exception of the Gothic Madame Walravens, is merely a type. All of them are fully realized, endowed with a life of their own that exists quite apart from the heroine and her consciousness. Even the frivolous Ginevra Fanshawe, a type which Lucy (like her creator) particularly disapproves of, is presented with objectivity and tolerance, while Madame Beck, largely drawn from Madame Héger (a woman who must have inspired much resentment in Charlotte) is a truly memorable creation, with her calmness, practicality, and the apparent amiability which masks a cold and ruthless nature. However, she is presented without rancour and with full justice paid to her good points.

Dr Bretton is depicted with considerable psychological subtlety. There is no doubting his charm, his sunny temperament or his genuine kindliness – but at the same time there is in him an unconscious streak of cruelty. There is something distinctly unpleasant, for example, about his teasing of Paulina both as a child and a young woman, and of Lucy herself.

Equally successful is the characterization of Paul Emanuel. Here, if anywhere, one might have expected Charlotte Brontë's pen to have faltered, for clearly he derives from M. Héger. Clearly, too, he is the old masterful male and his relationship with Lucy is still very much that of master and pupil. But none of the obsessive elements that had marked Charlotte's unhappy devotion to M. Héger remain. Paul Emanuel is presented with realism, objectivity, and affectionate humour (though humour is not a quality usually associated with the Brontës) so that his endearing qualities emerge naturally and convincingly, and at the same time his essential goodness is conveyed without falsity or sentimentality. He is seen, moreover, not only through the heroine's eyes (as happens for the most part in *Jane Eyre*) but in a whole series of concrete scenes and situations. In these he acts, reacts and, above all, talks as his own man, not as a projection of Lucy's ideas about him. His talk, half French and half English, is particularly vivid and characterful. It is notable, indeed, that whereas even in *Jane Eyre* the dialogue is often forced and stilted, in *Villette* it is nearly always vigorous, natural, and perfectly adapted to character and situation. The lively exchanges between Paul Emanuel and Lucy form the most obvious example, but there are others, including the conversations between Lucy and Ginevra, and between Dr Bretton and his mother.

The impression of lively and varied dialogue is all the more remarkable in view of the fact that *Villette* is as fully a first-person novel as *Jane Eyre*. Much of it, indeed, is in the form of an interior monologue; for Lucy Snowe is not simply the narrator, but solidly placed as the central character, the very embodiment of the novel's inner meaning. Some contemporary critics found Lucy too gloomy, too obsessed by the craving for love. It is true enough that through her Charlotte Brontë expressed the furthest reaches of her own frustration and despair. When Lucy describes herself as 'tame and still by habit, disciplined by destiny', or when she says of her life 'I found it but a hopeless desert', it is undoubtedly Charlotte speaking as well. Her own feeling that she had been dogged by an adverse fatality is echoed by Lucy. So is her bitter and indignant sense of the precarious nature of what small chance of real happiness and fulfilment was available for women in her kind of society. This, in fact, is the artistic justification for the section about Paulina as a child – which brings out the contrast between her openness and vulnerability and the deliberate suppression of the emotional self which Lucy has already learned to practise, and which Charlotte knew from personal experience was the safest form of adaptation for a woman of her time. Paulina and Lucy, however, are not only contrasted, their lot as women is also compared; for when they meet again it is evident that Paulina, despite her beauty and wealth, is the same sensitive and vulnerable creature she was as a child; still dependent, therefore, in a male-dominated world on her adored lord and master, and with no more guarantee of meaningful fulfilment in the future than the isolated Lucy herself.

In *Villette* the blackest, most negative elements are handled with a firm artistic purpose. The slow, detailed unfolding of the various stages of Lucy's loneliness and despair during the long vacation at the school and the certainty that her love for Bretton is doomed to frustration, is one of the most terrible pictures of near mental breakdown in the whole of literature. In facing the kind of devastating depression she herself had known at first hand, and rendering it in fictional terms, Charlotte Brontë triumphed as an artist over her innermost sufferings as a woman.

And Lucy does not break down; the stasis is not permanent. The novel is not one of surrender to suffering and destiny. It is, on the contrary, one of courageous progress – slow and painful but nevertheless certain – towards the inner tranquillity that comes from self-acceptance. It is significant that early in the first chapter of the novel, Lucy compares her visits to Mrs Bretton to 'the sojourn of Christian and Hopeful beside a certain pleasant stream, with "green trees on each bank, and meadows beautified with lilies all the year round".' References to and quotations from Bunyan's *The Pilgrim's Progress* are frequent throughout the novel, for it is a pilgrimage that Lucy, too, is describing. To begin with she is seeking to escape from too much consciousness, from a life which she feels will inevitably bring her nothing but pain and disappointment. 'The negation of suffering,' she says, 'was the nearest approach to happiness I expected to know.' But negation is exactly what she is not allowed to have. She must live and suffer until full consciousness is in fact achieved, whatever the cost.

Lucy's decision to chance her fate abroad is the first major step in this pilgrimage. Her reluctant acceptance of the teaching job at Madame Beck's school is the second.

Even then, much of her self has to be locked away – '... in catalepsy and a dead trance,' she says, 'I studiously held the quick of my nature.' She comes out of the trance to feel the pangs of love for Dr Bretton, and to endure the ordeal of the long vacation. But her emergence from that Valley of the Shadow (there are references in this part of the novel to Christian's struggle with Giant Despair in *The Pilgrim's Progress*) is with her spirit and her will to live intact, and she is able to contemplate Dr Bretton's marriage to Paulina without bitterness.

It is only when she has undergone all her trials and come through them with heart and spirit purified that Lucy can discover, as her relationship with Paul Emanuel gradually matures, that she, too, may be blessed with human love. Her hope may end in tragedy, but Lucy knows that she has now acquired the inner resources to enable her to meet whatever lies ahead. She knows that she can never again be a mere looker-on. She has given herself to life, and to her surprise learns that it can bring not only pain but also peace.

It is important, though, to realize that although Lucy's winning through to acceptance of life is a projection of Charlotte Brontë's own experience, in a sense this is irrelevant as far as the novel as a work of art is concerned. It is to the novel that Lucy belongs, and fundamentally she, like all its other elements, is the product of poetic truth. Of all Charlotte Brontë's novels, *Villette* is the nearest to poetry, and in this respect it joins company with her sister Emily's *Wuthering Heights*.

This pressure of the poetic imagination results in an exactness of language and imagery superior to anything that she had achieved before. The whole of the first part of the novel powerfully reinforces the theme of deliberate withdrawal from life and hope both in tone and language, with the ironic use of words like 'clean', 'quiet', 'calm', 'smoothly' and 'blandly'. The choice of the symbolic surname Snowe for the heroine ('a cold name she must have', Charlotte Brontë told her publisher) is symptomatic of the same poetic faculty. So is the air of mystery that surrounds Lucy's early life and which is echoed in the ambiguous ending. A type of imagery closely akin to symbolism occurs, too, at the most dramatic points in the story, when Lucy's emotions and destiny are set against the background of natural and, one is made to feel, supernatural forces. In moments such as these, Charlotte Brontë's own religious preoccupations, and the sense of oneness with Nature which all the Brontës shared, come forcefully together, conferring on the novel a cosmic dimension. In *Villette*, therefore, Charlotte Brontë had at last succeeded in fusing the world without and the world within. The weaknesses that derived from the fantasy world of her girlhood had finally been eradicated, and she had arrived at the complete truth of her own destiny through the medium of her art.

North and South

Elizabeth Cleghorn Gaskell

One of Mrs Gaskell's most famous books is her *Life of Charlotte Brontë* (published in 1857) which is generally acknowledged to be one of the best of the Victorian biographies. In many respects, though, it would be difficult to imagine a greater contrast than that between the two women. Charlotte Brontë was a rebel against the limitations, expectations, and stereotypes imposed upon her sex, but, to quote David Cecil:

> 'In an age whose ideal of woman emphasized the feminine qualities at the expense of all others she (Mrs Gaskell) was all a woman was expected to be ...'

This is, admittedly, something of an exaggeration. Mrs Gaskell was too intelligent and imaginative to accept unquestioningly the subservient role women were called upon to play in Victorian society. The comments she made on the subject were not without irony. She was not unsympathetic to some of the feminist causes of the period. Her novel *Ruth* (1853) was severely criticized for its boldness in making the heroine a girl who bears an illegitimate child, in refusing to condemn her unreservedly and in apportioning the blame equally between her and her seducer, thereby showing up the prevailing double standard of the day. Nevertheless, it is by and large true that Mrs Gaskell's philosophy was one of acceptance rather than of rebellion.

One of the consequences is that the texture of her novels is not scored and fretted by personal passions and frustrations, as are those of Charlotte Brontë. If she had personal problems, crises, or rebellious impulses, she did not normally use her fiction as a means of grappling with them. As she herself said in a letter of 1853:

> The difference between Miss Brontë and me is that she puts all her naughtiness into her books, and I put all my goodness. I am sure that she works off a great deal that is morbid *into* her writing and *out* of her life; and my books are so far better than I am that I often feel ashamed of having written them and as if I were a hypocrite.

Elizabeth Cleghorn Stevenson was born in Chelsea in 1810, daughter of a Unitarian minister. (The sect of Unitarians assert that the Godhead is a single being and not a trinity.) Her mother died not long after her birth, and she was brought up by her aunt at Knutsford in Cheshire, which is the original of the little town in *Cranford*, her gently humorous and idyllic novel which was published in 1853, and which is the most popular of her works. From 1826 she attended a school at Stratford-on-Avon for two years, and developed into a singularly beautiful young woman noted for her sweetness of disposition. In 1832 she married William Gaskell, minister at the Cross Street Unitarian chapel in Manchester, and their married life was one of calm and affectionate harmony. It was her husband who urged her to undertake her first novel, as a distraction from grief over the death in infancy of her only son; and to this extent *Mary Barton*, which was published in 1848, contradicts the general rule that she did not allow her personal life to intrude into her fiction – in fact she later decided that she had written the novel for 'a wrong motive'. The theme, however, was a social not a personal one – the appalling distress suffered by the industrial workers in the Manchester area during the 'hungry forties', which, as the wife of a minister, Mrs Gaskell had ample opportunity of seeing for herself, and the novel provoked a good deal of indignation among some of the critics by its condemnation of the un-sympathetic attitude of the factory owners towards their workers.

Mary Barton also attracted the attention of Charles Dickens, and it was to his magazine *Household Words* that Mrs Gaskell contributed *North and South*, published in 1855. The best-known of her later fictional works are *Sylvia's Lovers* (1859) and *Wives and Daughters*, which was not quite finished when she died, still only fifty-five, in 1865.

Summary

North and South begins in fashionable Harley Street, London. The heroine, Margaret Hale, has been living there for some years with her well-to-do aunt, Mrs Shaw. Mrs Shaw's amiable but rather flighty daughter, Edith, is about to be married to the somewhat bone-headed Cap-tain Lennox, whose clever lawyer brother shows interest in Margaret. But Margaret is not really suited to smart London life, and she is longing for the imminent reunion with her parents in the quiet parsonage at Helstone in the New Forest.

When she returns home, however, she does not find it as idyllic as she had anticipated. There is the austere poverty of the parsonage and the careworn appearance of her parents, still grieving over the absence of their son, Frederick, and the disgrace of the circumstances – as a young naval officer he had been involved in a mutiny against a tyrannical captain and forced to seek refuge abroad for fear of being hanged if he returns to England. Margaret's father, too, obviously has some new worry, while her mother is full of complaints of the restricted social life they are obliged to lead in Helstone. Margaret's vague sense of unease is not relieved by a visit from Henry Lennox with a proposal of marriage which some instinct, undefined but imperative, causes her to reject. Shortly after, the reason for her father's anxiety reveals itself. He has been having serious doctrinal doubts. On grounds of conscience he can no longer continue as a minister in the Church of England and has in fact already resigned his living. They must leave Helstone for Milton-Northern, the manufacturing town in Darkshire (Manchester, in Lancashire, that is) where Mr Bell, his old tutor at Oxford and a native of Milton-Northern, can get him work as a private tutor, in particular to John Thornton, an up-and-coming young manufacturer who wants to improve himself, and who rents the lease of the Marlborough Mills in Milton from Mr Bell.

When they reach the dark and gloomy northern city, Mr Thornton calls at the hotel where they are temporarily staying. Thornton is struck by Margaret's beauty and by her ladylike self-sufficiency, but nettled by her haughty manner. Nevertheless, he helps her parents to find a reasonably comfortable house, while his intelligence and application to his studies impress Mr Hale, and the two men soon become friends.

Margaret finds the bold, independent behaviour of the working people of Milton-Northern utterly different from anything she has encountered before. She is shocked by the 'loud spoken and boisterous girls', who comment on her dress, 'even touch her shawl or gown to ascertain the exact material' – until she realizes that this 'rough freedom' is by no means unfriendly, and that there is 'such a simple reliance on her womanly sympathy with their love of dress, and on her kindliness' that she quickly learns to respond.

She finds it far more difficult to get used to the workmen who, in the same open, fearless manner comment not on her dress, but on her looks. But here, too, she eventually comes to understand that 'the very out-spokenness marked their innocence of any intention to hurt her delicacy.' These details may seem small and unimportant, but they add together to make a remarkably fresh and human picture of the contrast between northern and southern behaviour – and one that has not fundamentally dated.

Margaret gets to know one of the neighbouring work-men named Nicholas Higgins, and his daughter Bessy, who is seriously ill from the effects of inhaling cotton fluff because the owner of the factory where she used to work has not installed a wheel to disperse it. Higgins sets the central theme when he says: '... yo see, North and South has both met and made kind o' friends in this big smoky place.' North and South meet, too, when Mr Thornton comes to tea with the Hales, and Margaret notices the contrast between her father's face, with its 'soft and waving' almost feminine lines, and that of his visitor, with its lines 'few but firm, as if they were carved in marble', though they can relax from time to time in a 'rare, bright smile'. Although Margaret likes the smile, she thoroughly dislikes Mr Thornton's criticisms of the 'old worn grooves of life' in the South, his elevation of the factory owner as a man dedicated to a certain 'grandeur of conception', and his unsympathetic attitude towards the workers. Margaret's indignation against Thornton is increased by her visits to the dying Bessy, and hardly alle-viated by a visit from Thornton's formidable mother and affected sister, Fanny.

On a return visit to the Thorntons' house, which is within the walls of the Marlborough Mills, Margaret and her father learn that a strike is imminent. Margaret and Thornton again clash over the latter's uncompromising attitude towards the workers whom he is determined to crush. Thornton is stung by Margaret's accusation that he is being inconsistent in praising north-country inde-pendence of character at the same time that he is advocat-ing ruthless despotism. For the Hales these matters are soon overshadowed by the realization that Mrs Hale is ill with what is obviously incurable cancer. She confides in Margaret her desperate wish to see her son Frederick, who is now living in Cadiz, before she dies.

Margaret continues to hear a good deal about the strike from Nicholas Higgins, who is one of its leaders, and who explains that the reason for it is that the masters have banded together to impose a reduction of wages. He tells her that Thornton is the most formidable of them, but speaks of him with grudging respect as a master with whom he and his fellow-workers can expect 'an honest up and down fight', and who would scorn to adopt the slippery tactics advocated by some of the other masters, such as pretending to offer the old wages and then eroding them by a system of unjust fines. At Higgins's house Margaret also meets John Boucher, a weak and improvident worker, whose sick wife and eight children are now in desperate straits because of the strike, and who accuses Higgins and the Union of being 'a worser tyrant' than the masters themselves. Higgins, convinced that the masters are near breaking-point, urges Boucher to hang on and gives him what money he has to spare, and Margaret adds her contribution.

When Margaret calls at the Thornton's house to borrow a water-bed for her mother, whose condition has deteriorated, a mob arrives, enraged by Thornton's importation of unskilled labourers from Ireland. Thornton boldly goes out to face the mob, but when it is obvious that they are about to attack him, Margaret warns them that the soldiers have been sent for and shields Thornton with her own body. Thornton has misunderstood Margaret's action and when he calls to thank her he also begins to make a declaration of love, but is deeply hurt when Margaret coldly interrupts him with the assurance that her behaviour had no personal motive. All the same, after Thornton has gone, Margaret 'shrank and shuddered as under the fascination of some great power, repugnant to her whole previous life.'

The leaders of the riot, among them John Boucher, are arrested. Bessy dies and Margaret takes Higgins, distracted by grief for his dead daughter and by anger against the strikers for having resorted to violence against the union's orders, to see her father. The three of them argue about the strike, which has now collapsed, and Margaret attacks the action of the union in forcing a man like Boucher to join. Higgins retorts that trade unionism is '... a withstanding of injustice, past, present, or to come' to which Mr Hale replies with a sigh:

> Oh ... your union in itself would be beautiful, glorious – it would be Christianity itself – if it were but for an end which affected the good of all, instead of that of merely one class as opposed to another.

Higgins is unmoved, but at the end of the scene consents to kneel in prayer with the others.

It is perhaps too easy a conclusion to the debate and one that would hardly satisfy a revolutionary. But at least Mrs Gaskell has tried to state the terms fairly, and much of her argument has a remarkably modern ring.

Meanwhile, Margaret, yielding to her mother's entreaties, has summoned Frederick from Cadiz. He arrives in great secrecy in time to see his mother before she dies. But it is not safe for him to remain in Milton. There is a reward for his capture, and a man named Leonards, who was on the same ship as Frederick when the mutiny took place, has been seen in the neighbourhood. On their way to the station Margaret and Frederick are seen by Thornton. On the platform Leonards tries to seize hold of Frederick. Frederick pushes him aside and causes him to fall heavily, then gets away on the train.

Next day, a police inspector calls on Margaret. Leonards has died after his fall. The medical cause of his death is an internal disorder caused by his drinking, but as the inspector has received a vague account of the scuffle at the station from someone who thinks he saw Margaret there, he is obliged to investigate. In order to shield Frederick, Margaret is forced to deny her presence. The inspector consults Thornton, who is a magistrate. Thornton does not reveal that he had seen Margaret and Frederick on the way to the station, and though he is racked with jealousy because he thinks Frederick must be Margaret's lover, he prevents an inquest and the investigation is closed. When Margaret learns what Thornton has done, she is moved and deeply distressed at the thought of the conclusion he must have drawn from her conduct, and she realizes that his good opinion means a great deal to her. Shortly afterwards she receives a letter from Frederick informing her that on Lennox's advice he has left London and is already on his way back to Cadiz, and after Lennox has reported that there is little chance of the Admiralty reversing its decision, Frederick marries and reconciles himself to permanent exile.

Higgins is now out of work because the masters are refusing to take back union men. He harshly reprimands Boucher, who has tried to get work by promising to reveal the union's secrets, only to be turned away because of his part in the riot – though Thornton, who has no vindictiveness in his nature, has not bothered, once the strike was over, to press charges against him. Soon afterwards, neighbours arrive with the news that Boucher has drowned himself.

Higgins decides that it is his duty to provide for the Boucher family, but, disillusioned with Milton, he announces that he is going to take them south, where he will look for work as a farm labourer. To her surprise, Margaret finds herself urging him to abandon this plan: such a life, brutalized by hard and badly paid labour in the fields, would be 'eternal fretting' for a man like Higgins, a workman proud of his skill and accustomed to voicing his opinions. She insists that, in spite of all its drawbacks and in spite of the deadlock between masters and men, there is more of the spirit of independence to be found in the industrial north than in the south she loves so much.

She and her father persuade Higgins instead to apply to Thornton for a job. At their first interview there is a clash of wills and Thornton bluntly refuses to employ a troublemaker. But he has been secretly impressed by Higgins's spirit, and when he discovers that he was telling the truth when he said that he wanted to work in order to support the Boucher family, he seeks him out, begs his pardon, and persuades him to come back to work for him. In a man-to-man confrontation the two come to a grudging respect for each other.

Mr Hale's old Oxford tutor, Mr Bell, pays them a visit and takes a great liking to Margaret. He also shrewdly deduces that Thornton is in love with her and she, although she does not realize it, with him. Mr Hale, accustomed only to his daughter's criticisms of Thornton, scoffs at the idea, but realizes that she is unhappy and, on a return visit to his Oxford college, begs Mr Bell to look after Margaret if anything should happen to him. The request has been premonitory, for the next morning he is found dead in his bed. Mr Bell travels north to break the news to Margaret. Thornton is on the same train. He is distressed by the news, and deeply concerned for Margaret; but when Mr Bell tells him about Henry Lennox's interest in her, Thornton concludes that Lennox must have been the man he had seen with Margaret on the night of Leonards's fall. Margaret's aunt, Mrs Shaw, takes Margaret back with her to London. She no longer takes any pleasure in the social round, however, and hoping to restore her spirits, Mr Bell takes her on a visit to Helstone. Margaret is enraptured to be back again in the village which she had dreamed about so often in the smoky wilderness of Milton. But the reality does not at all live up to the dream. This is brought home to her in a startling and most effective fashion when one of her father's former parishioners calmly relates how, in accordance with 'one of the savage country superstitions' designed to influence 'the powers of darkness', a cat had been roasted alive. So this, Margaret reflects, was the place which had seemed to epitomize the softer, more civilized atmosphere of the south.

Not long after this, old Mr Bell also dies, leaving his fortune to Margaret – part of which consists of the Marlborough Mills of which Thornton is the tenant. Henry Lennox acts for Margaret in connection with the will –

and sets out to woo her all over again. Meanwhile, at Milton there is a slump in the cotton trade and Thornton is hard pressed. His difficulties date from the strike, because the Irish labourers he had imported had proved inefficient workers and he had in consequence fallen behind in his orders. In addition, he had bought expensive new machinery and built a dining hall for his workers. In the meantime Higgins had told him of Frederick's visit at the time of his mother's death, and Thornton realizes that he was the man he had seen with Margaret.

Eventually Thornton, after resisting the temptation of a financial gamble which is contrary to his principles, pays off all his creditors honourably and has to go out of business. He resists the offer of a partnership with a man of whom he disapproves, preferring to look for a job as manager which will give him greater opportunities of implementing his new ideas for improving relations in industry.

During a visit to London in connection with his tenancy of the Marlborough Mill, Thornton meets a prominent Member of Parliament who is interested in labour relations. The MP is much impressed when Thornton explains that his ambition in life now is to find 'the opportunity of cultivating some intercourse with the hands beyond the mere "cash nexus" ...' He does not suggest that this would prevent the recurrence of strikes, but he does believe that it might 'render strikes not the bitter, venomous sources of hatred they have hitherto been.' This is another instance of the fact that the novel, published in 1855, has not fundamentally dated. Before he leaves, Thornton tells Margaret that he had received a round-robin from his men, organized by Higgins and stating their wish to work for him if he were ever in a position to employ labour again.

Margaret explains to Thornton the plan she has worked out with the help of Henry Lennox, whereby she will invest part of her money in the Marlborough Mills so that

Thornton can continue to run them. She tries to represent it as a purely business arrangement, but her voice falters, she loses her way in the legal documents – and suddenly she and Thornton are in each other's arms.

Critical commentary

It will be evident that *North and South*, like Disraeli's *Sybil*, belongs on one level at any rate to the category which has been called 'the condition of England novel'.

In many respects, however, *North and South* is superior to Disraeli's novel. It is true that Mrs Gaskell's analysis of the social, political, and economic malaise of the times is not as profound and comprehensive as his. Neither are her conclusions as radical: on the whole she accepted unquestioningly the *laissez-faire* laws of the contemporary economists as forming the essential basis of the social order. Her conscious aim was to advocate the application of Christian principles as a means of mediating between the conflicting interests of the classes. In addition, the two nations with which Mrs Gaskell deals in *North and South* are the two main regions of England, with their different attitudes and cultures, rather than the two nations of rich and poor in Disraeli's *Sybil*. But, as Arnold Kettle has pointed out, Mrs Gaskell's pictures of working-class life are less abstract than those of Disraeli, and she is informed with a respect for her working-class characters quite different 'from the social worker's interest or the responsible intellectual's effort of sympathy.' In consequence, they are never mere demonstration pieces designed to illustrate a theory. They proceed from heart and imagination combined, and characters like Higgins, Boucher, and their families are present not only as representatives of a class but as human beings in their own right. As such, what matters most is their human ambience, and from this point of view the intrusion of positive ideological conclusions would have been artistically damaging.

Perhaps this is really another way of saying that *North and South* is a genuine novel. It does possess its faults, of course: for example the episode of Frederick's visit and Leonards's intervention smacks of Victorian melodrama, while the unexpected legacy which helps to bring about the happy ending was one of the most hackneyed fictional devices of the day. As Mrs Gaskell herself complained, the exigencies of serial publication resulted in undue compression in the final sections, with Mr Bell's death following too closely on that of Mr Hale – and though she introduced fresh material when the novel was published as a volume, the weakness remains. Nevertheless, in its gentle, unobtrusive way, the structure of *North and South* is both subtle and sophisticated. The first introduction of the heroine is neither at Helstone, with which all her childhood dreams are associated, nor at Milton, which is at first to form so grim a contrast to it, but on the neutral ground of London where she does not really feel at home – and in this way she is most effectively poised in a kind of limbo between the two ways of life, and on the threshold of her own development.

In some respects the theme of the novel is not unlike that of Jane Austen's *Pride and Prejudice*, the working through of a number of illusions in order to reach reality and that degree of emotional openness and self-knowledge which is necessary for the admission of true love. The first of the illusions Margaret has to surrender is that represented by Helstone: the dream of an idyllic pastoral family life with herself in the privileged position of only daughter. What in fact she finds is a mother full of complaints and a father about to resign his ministry, and neither of them much aware of the other's problems. In addition, although they are prepared to lean heavily on their daughter, Margaret finds that she has by no means displaced Frederick at the centre of her parents', and especially of her mother's, concern.

Nevertheless, Margaret clings to the Helstone dream. She has to, if she is to endure the move to Milton and at the same time sustain her parents. She clings resolutely to the particularly narrow kind of snobbery that belongs to a place like Helstone – it is significant, for example, that it is Margaret and not her mother, who turns up her nose at their neighbours and who (when they move north) is most upstage towards the Thorntons. But Margaret is much too sensitive and intelligent to maintain prejudices that are belied by her observations, experiences, and feelings. When Higgins starts talking about moving south, influenced as she knows by her own rapturous accounts, she realizes that she has been guilty of presenting him with an illusion instead of a reality. It is at that moment, too, that she realizes where the reality does lie, and her visit to Helstone with Mr Bell serves both as a confirmation and a final farewell. When Thornton, after the failure of his business, travels south and collects a bunch of roses from Helstone to present to Margaret on his arrival in London, it is as if, in a most delicate gesture of love and respect, he were laying a wreath on a childhood now fully relegated to the past.

But Thornton himself has also had to abandon an illusion as romantic in its way as Margaret's – that of the perfect self-sufficiency and autocracy of the self-made man. Thornton, too, is much too intelligent and sensitive not to come to the realization that a system that involves human beings, yet pretends that human beings do not exist, simply cannot work. It is Margaret, of course, with her purely instinctive and humane response to the situation she finds in Milton, who first opens his eyes to these realities, just as he helps her to see that the north has virtues which she was not originally prepared to admit. It could be said, in fact, that a deep or lasting love was not possible between them until her south was ready to yield to his north, and his north open to influence from her south. North and south, in other words, are not merely regional terms: they also have spiritual and psychological connotations.

At one time, critics tended to overlook these deeper

implications of Mrs Gaskell's work, and to dismiss her talent as a charming but slight one. David Cecil, for instance, while paying tribute to her tact, good taste, and delicacy as well as her charm, argues that she was so typically 'feminine' that she was incapable of creating satisfactory male characters. It is difficult, though, to see how this view can be maintained in the presence of Thornton, who so effectively combines the personal and industrial issues of *North and South*, and is, surely, the perfect foil for Margaret. He is also the perfect foil in another way to Mr Hale, subtly bringing out the latter's kindly, ascetic but not very positive nature, so that he, too, becomes a fully rounded fictional creation. Equally successful is the characterization of Nicholas Higgins, and, as it has been pointed out, Mrs Gaskell's handling of working-class characters (except in her first novel, *Mary Barton*) is free from simplification and caricature. One has only to turn to Dickens's portraits of Stephen Blackpool, the good artisan, and Slackbridge, the evil union agitator, in his novel *Hard Times* (which immediately preceded *North and South* in 'Household Words') to see how convincingly alive Higgins is by contrast.

It is only recently that critics have come to realize that, as a psychological novelist, Mrs Gaskell in many respects anticipated the methods of George Eliot and Henry James. A careful reading of *North and South* will show that there is hardly a word or action of the main protagonists (and especially of Margaret), or of the author's accompanying commentary, that does not contribute to the gradual development of character in response to changing circumstances. The truth of the matter is that Mrs Gaskell's manner is so gentle and unobtrusive that the reader is often unaware of the underlying subtlety and the steady creative pressure.

North and South is not a novel to be easily slotted into one particular compartment. It is undoubtedly a social condition-of-England novel; but it is also a regional novel, a novel of sensibility, and a psychological novel. It may not equal the fictional creations of Charlotte and Emily Brontë in power and originality, or those of George Eliot in scope and profundity, but it undoubtedly deserves to be rescued from the category of minor Victorian fiction to which it is too often relegated.

Barchester Towers

Anthony Trollope

Anthony Trollope was born in 1815, the year of Waterloo, and died in 1882, and although he was in many ways the most conventional of the Victorian novelists, he is today among the most widely read of all of them. Yet, towards the end of his life, he was considered by the critics as the least likely of all his prominent contemporaries to survive, and for a number of years after his death his reputation was in almost total eclipse. But then came one Trollope revival after another, and his popularity shows no sign of waning.

The basic reason for the appeal of Trollope's novels was perhaps best summed up by his contemporary, the American Nathaniel Hawthorne:

> They precisely suit my taste, solid and substantial, written on the strength of beef and through the inspiration of ale, and just as real as if some giant had hewn a great lump of earth, and put it under a glass dome, with all its inhabitants going about their daily business, and not suspecting that they were being made a show of.

There is a solid Englishness, an inspired ordinariness and normality about Trollope's work that was bound, in spite of fluctuations of fashion, to have an enduring effect.

It was with the first of his large fictional canvases, a

group of novels dealing with the imaginary English county of Barsetshire (centred on its cathedral city of Barchester) that Trollope came into his own and achieved some of his finest work.

By then he was already forty years old, and still very much under the shadow of his mother Frances (or Fanny) Trollope's own tremendous literary success, though most of her novels have long since been forgotten. She had been forced to write in order to support her improvident husband, a failed barrister and intellectual, and their large family. Anthony Trollope's childhood had been made wretched by the family's comparative poverty and his father's outbursts of half-insane rage. Anthony was educated at Harrow and Winchester, but his poverty-stricken appearance, clumsiness, untidiness, extreme shyness and dismal scholastic attainments made him an object of scorn both at school and at home. In 1827 (when he was twelve) his mother took most of the family to America, leaving him behind, virtually alone and grossly neglected, for nearly three years. On her return, Mrs Trollope published her best-selling book, *Domestic Manners of the Americans*, thereby saving the family from further financial disasters. By now Anthony's elder brother was showing marked promise as a writer himself, but the best that could be done for Anthony, the dunce of the family, was to get him a poorly paid job in the Post Office. Tall, gawky, with a raucous voice and a touchy temper, he was at first in continuous danger of dismissal. But his life was transformed when in 1841 he was transferred to Ireland. There his nature expanded under the influence of Irish charm and kindliness. He took up hunting, which became a lifelong passion, and made a happy marriage. He also began to rise in the service of the Post Office, first in Ireland, and then in England, and was subsequently sent to various parts of the world on important Post Office business. While in Ireland he had started writing, and published two novels dealing with the terrible distress suffered in Ireland during the 'hungry forties'. Both were unsuccessful, as was a subsequent book. Discouraged, he wrote no more for several years, but then on a visit to Salisbury in the course of his Post Office duties, he happened to take an evening stroll round the cathedral close; the atmosphere put him in mind of his schooldays at Winchester, and suddenly he remembered a controversy he had heard while he was there concerning the administration of an almshouse. He began work on a novel called *The Warden*, which was published in 1855.

Its hero, Dr Septimus Harding, a gentle and unworldly clergyman, is the devoted Warden of Hiram's Hospital, an almshouse for old men. When an energetic young reformer named John Bold attacks the generous stipend attached to the Wardenship as an unjustified sinecure, Dr Harding, feeling that there may be some substance to the charge, resigns in spite of the efforts of his worldly-wise son-in-law, Archdeacon Theophilus Grantly, to dissuade him, and the refusal of the Bishop (Archdeacon Grantly's father) to appoint anyone else in his place. The situation is complicated by the fact that Dr Harding's second daughter, Eleanor, is in love with John Bold and eventually marries him.

When Trollope published *The Warden*, he had no thought of starting a series, but he found that his fictional cathedral town and the characters who inhabited it continued to occupy his imagination, and so he went on to write the much longer *Barchester Towers*, published in 1857.

As he had not planned it beforehand it did not carry on easily from the former novel, and in order to introduce new characters and situations Trollope had to deal rather summarily with some of the old ones. Thus, both Bishop Grantly and John Bold are killed off. The appearance of a new bishop, Dr Proudie, also meant the appearance of the domineering Mrs Proudie, one of the outstanding comic figures of English fiction, while the disappearance of Eleanor's first husband opened the way for one of its most natural and charming love stories.

Summary

At the beginning of the novel Archdeacon Grantly, as he sits beside his dying father, is entertaining hopes of succeeding him as Bishop, but the government appoints Dr Proudie, a stranger to Barchester. It does not take Archdeacon Grantly long to realize that the real reins of power are going to be held by the Bishop's wife and by her crony, the self-seeking and hypocritical Obadiah Slope, the Bishop's chaplain. It is Mr Slope who preaches the first sermon of the new regime in Barchester Cathedral, a deliberately provocative one criticizing the High-Church ritual traditional to Barchester. The issue on which battle is joined, though, is the appointment to the still vacant Wardenship of Hiram's Hospital. It is assumed that the new Bishop will, in view of the honourable and unselfish circumstances in which Dr Harding had resigned (as recounted in *The Warden*), have no hesitation in reappointing him.

A memorable reception now takes place at the Bishop's palace. One of the reforms introduced by the new Bishop, at the suggestion of his wife and his chaplain, has been the insistence that absentee clergymen should return to the diocese. This in particular affects Dr Vesey Stanhope, a prebendary at the cathedral and holder of two livings, which he has for the past twelve years left in charge of curates while he and his family live a life of dilettante ease in Italy. The arrival of the bizarre Stanhope family at the reception creates a sensation, particularly the exotically beautiful and mysteriously crippled Signora Madeline Vesey Neroni (the second Stanhope daughter, separated from her Italian husband) who, after being carried into the reception by four attendants, reclines on a sofa, and soon has most of the men paying court to her. Among them is the awestruck and dazzled Mr Slope, whose attentions to the Signora infuriate Mrs Proudie.

Mr Slope now offers Dr Harding the Wardenship on the Bishop's behalf, but with so many conditions attached that Dr Harding has no choice but to reject the offer. This was exactly what Mr Slope had intended, for Mrs Proudie is determined that the Wardenship shall go to her own protegé, Mr Quiverful, the desperately poor incumbent of a small country living, who has a wife and fourteen children. The Bishop, when he hears of Dr Harding's refusal, agrees with his wife's choice. When, however, Mr Slope learns that Dr Harding's widowed daughter, Eleanor, has a tidy fortune of her own, he determines to marry her, and sets out, therefore, to obtain a reversal of the decision over the Wardenship in favour of her father. Eleanor, anxious only for her father's welfare, encourages the repulsive Mr Slope's visits, completely unaware of their ulterior motive, though both her father and her brother-in-law, Archdeacon Grantly, believe that she has fallen in love with him. The situation is further complicated by the fact that Madeline Neroni and her spinster sister, Charlotte, have decided that the only way their scapegrace brother Bertie can pay off his debts is by marrying Eleanor.

Meanwhile, Archdeacon Grantly has persuaded his old friend, the Reverend Francis Arabin, a gentle and sensitive character, and a poet, but also a doughty champion of the High Church cause (he has already crossed swords with Mr Slope in a number of polemical pamphlets) to leave his Oxford fellowship and accept the living of St Ewold, a short distance from Barchester.

As the next step in his plan of campaign, Mr Slope calls on the honest and naïve Mr Quiverful. By suggesting to him that Dr Harding has a moral right to the Wardenship, and by dangling before him the prospect of a more lucrative living, Mr Slope obtains from Mr Quiverful a renunciation of his claim. But Mrs Quiverful, desperate at finding the promise of a less poverty-stricken existence snatched away, obtains an interview with Mrs Proudie and tells her what has happened.

Mrs Proudie is furious at the treachery of her former ally, and the battle between wife and chaplain for control of the Bishop is joined. At first Mr Slope prevails, but he has his Achilles heel. Though persisting in his wooing of Eleanor (to which she is still blind) he has fallen head over heels in love with the captivating Signora Neroni.

Eleanor and her father are now staying for a while at Plumstead Episcopi, the home of Archdeacon Grantly and his wife. Also in the party is Mr Arabin, who has been gradually falling in love with Eleanor, though utterly bewildered by a phenomenon so unfamiliar to him. It is at this point that Eleanor receives a letter from Mr Slope telling her of Mr Quiverful's decision not to contest the Wardenship. Everyone assumes the letter contains a proposal of marriage.

Mr Slope's ambitions are soon engaged in another direction as well. The old Dean, Dr Trefoil, falls seriously ill, and Mr Slope envisages himself stepping into his shoes. He writes to powerful allies in the government and press to solicit their support.

Matters come to a head at a garden party given by Wilfred Thorne, the squire of Ullathorne (a friend of Archdeacon Grantly) and his formidable spinster sister, Monica. There, Eleanor sets her father's mind at rest as to her feelings for Mr Slope. There, too, the Signora Neroni again steals the show as far as the men are concerned. She even sets her cap at the grave Mr Arabin, worming out of him the fact that he is in love with Eleanor and that he believes she is going to marry Mr Slope. And Mr Slope does indeed manage to get Eleanor alone, proposes to her and attempts to embrace her – receiving a box on the ears for his pains. Just after this, news arrives at Ullathorne Park that Dean Trefoil has died and Mr Slope hurries back to Barchester. Before the party breaks up Eleanor receives another proposal of marriage from Bertie Stanhope, who blandly admits, however, that he has been egged on to do so by his sister Charlotte. Needless to say, Eleanor rejects him too.

Back in Barchester, Mrs Proudie launches her counter-attack. By now she has the Bishop thoroughly under her thumb again, and she persuades him to appoint Mr Quiverful to the Wardenship of Hiram's Hospital. But Mr Slope still hopes to carry the day as far as the Deanery is concerned when a local newspaper comes out strongly in his support.

Meanwhile, Bertie Stanhope has been packed off to Italy by his father, and after he has gone, Madeline Neroni asks Eleanor to visit her. In a moment of generosity she tells Eleanor that Mr Arabin is in love with her, but warns her that he is the kind of man who will find it almost impossible to say so. The conversation has the effect of making Eleanor realize the nature of her own feelings for Mr Arabin. The following day Mr Slope, too, calls on the Signora, to find himself one of a train of admirers. The Signora makes a fool of Mr Slope in front of them all, taunting him not only with his ambitions of becoming Dean, but also with his discomfiture at Eleanor's hands. It is hardly surprising that Mr Slope is cured of his infatuation with the Signora. This is not the end of his humiliations, however. It is not he who is offered the Deanery but Dr Harding. But to Archdeacon Grantly's horror, his father-in-law is reluctant to take the job, believing that it should go to a younger man.

Meanwhile, Miss Thorne has decided to act as a match-maker. She has Eleanor and her small son to stay with her at Ullathorne, and then invites Mr Arabin as well. Miss Thorne sees to it that the two are left alone. But Mr Arabin cannot bring himself to say what is in his heart, and Eleanor, knowing that this is the crisis of their lives, gently leads him on to make his proposal.

Dr Harding is overjoyed by the news of the engagement between Eleanor and Mr Arabin, and, with the help of Archdeacon Grantly and Dr Gwynne, manages to per-suade the ecclesiastical authorities to offer the Deanery not to himself but to Mr Arabin. It is typical of Dr Harding's character, too, that he should make a point of accompanying Mr Quiverful, arm in arm, on the latter's first introduction to the inmates of Hiram's Hospital, thus securing their loyal support of the new Warden.

As for Mr Slope, he is dismissed, at Mrs Proudie's insistence, from his chaplaincy and departs to London where, soon after, he marries a wealthy widow, finds a London living and becomes a notable Low Church preacher. With his departure, the Bishop relaxes his rule about absentee clergymen, and the Stanhope *ménage* return to Italy. After their marriage, Eleanor and Mr Arabin insist that Dr Harding comes to live with them in the Deanery.

Critical commentary

On the face of it, a novel about the doings of a group of clergymen in a quiet English cathedral town would seem to be a case of chronicling the smallest of small beer. So, in essence, it is; and yet the reader finds himself hanging on to each small twist and turn in the plot, each small manoeuvre and counter manoeuvre, and at the end of it he has the sensation of having experienced something far more momentous than the setting and the events in themselves would warrant. For the very isolation of the characters from the wider world, both geographically and by their vocation, has provided the perfect laboratory conditions for the study of human behaviour and social patterns. In some of the later Barsetshire novels (they were not written in a block, and many other novels appeared in the intervals between them) the scene and subject-matter are somewhat broader. *Doctor Thorne*, for example, the third of them (published in 1858) centres upon a medical practitioner instead of a clergyman and upon Mary Thorne, one of the most delightful of English heroines, and sketches in the social and political background of the country as a whole. Both *Framley Parsonage* (1861) and *The Small House at Allington* (1864) – two of the favourites among Trollope fans – though closer in atmosphere to the first two novels of the series, include representatives both of the great aristocratic political families and of government officialdom. Even the concluding novel of the sequence, *The Last Chronicle of Barset* (1866–1867) which is about an austere clergyman unjustly accused of stealing a cheque (and in which the redoubtable Mrs Proudie dies) is rather wider in its ambience than *Barchester Towers*. Nevertheless, all of them deliberately concentrate on a restricted society in order to observe its members the more closely. At the same time, *Barchester Towers* is the purest example of the technique and the one that most convinces the reader that he is watching a microcosm of human behaviour. It was a prototype of all those later novels which make use of the closed society – such as, in our own time, C. P. Snow's *The Masters*, set in the equally small world of a Cambridge college – which nevertheless reflects the strivings for power which agitate the greater world beyond.

The fascination of *Barchester Towers* derives, however, from the special nature of Trollope's realism. In his *Autobiography* (which appeared in 1883, a year after his death) Trollope insisted that he was only interested in 'men and women such as we see ourselves'. Many critics have commented on this approach. The early twentieth-century literary historian, Sir Walter Raleigh, for example, pointed out that Trollope 'starts off with ordinary people that bore you in life and books and makes an epic of them.' And Henry James, who is the most percipient of all Trollope's critics, declared that 'his great, his inestimable merit' was 'a complete appreciation of the usual ... He felt all daily and immediate things.' To find a comparable naturalness and immediacy of realism in the presentation of daily living one would probably have to go back to Jane Austen or Daniel Defoe.

This means, it is true, that Trollope lacks the kind of imaginative daring and depth which enabled such contemporaries as Dickens, Thackeray, Charlotte and Emily Brontë and George Eliot at their best to impose upon their fictional material the unifying force of great poetic drama. On the other hand, it also means that Trollope is very rarely guilty of exaggeration or distortion. He never spreads his pathos too thick, or allows his dramatic situations to degenerate into the grosser forms of melo-drama – as both Dickens and Thackeray tended to do at times. Unlike them, too, he never allows his characters to be all good or all bad. Even the worst of them – as in real life – are shown to have their saving graces. In *Barchester Towers* Mrs Proudie, for instance, is genuinely moved by Mrs Quiverful's anxiety over the future of her large and impoverished family, and Trollope even insists that Mr Slope, though admitting that he thoroughly dis-likes him, has some good qualities 'according to his lights'. Similarly, the good characters are shown to have human weaknesses. In reading Trollope one can always be con-fident that his characterization is the product of a sane and steady observation of ordinary, everyday life. It is for this reason, above all, that – to quote David Cecil:

> the fabric of his work is as uniformly fresh as on the day it was made. The modern reader never has to adjust his mind to a Victorian angle in order to enjoy it. He can sit back and take the book just as it comes to him.

Part of this effect derives from what Joseph Conrad called 'his gift of intimate communion with the reader'. It is an approach on which Trollope himself was most insistent, and in *Barchester Towers* he states:

> Our doctrine is, that the author and the reader should move along together in full confidence with each other.

So determined was he to practise this doctrine that at times, to quote Henry James, he 'took a suicidal satis-faction in reminding the reader that the story he was telling was only, after all, a make-believe.' A typical in-stance occurs in *Barchester Towers* when Trollope points out that Eleanor and Mr Arabin could have avoided the misunderstanding over Mr Slope that is keeping them apart if only they could have shown a little more insight

– and whimsically adds: 'But then where would have been my novel?'

Unusual though such an attitude on the part of a novelist may be, it really *does* establish a bond of complicity with the reader, making him confident that neither his good sense nor his feelings are going to be taken advantage of, and Trollope's unemphatic, rather gruff, and not particularly subtle style, and his avoidance of anything approaching the kind of rhetoric in which both Dickens and Thackeray indulged on occasions, assists in the process.

His defiantly no-nonsense approach extended to (or perhaps derived from) his methods of composition. After the publication of *Barchester Towers* secured his success, his output was phenomenal. In the period between 1861 and 1867 alone he published ten novels, three volumes of short stories, and four works of non-fiction. In all he produced forty-seven novels, many of them of considerable bulk and containing well over 2,000 characters, in addition to volumes of short stories, lengthy travel books and many other works. A considerable proportion of these, moreover, were written while he was still working extremely hard for the Post Office, from which he did not resign until 1867, and which entailed travelling many thousands of miles. In addition he hunted twice a week until the last few years of his life, edited a magazine, engaged in all kinds of other activities and travelled to South Africa and Australia.

In his *Autobiography* he revealed how it was done. He rose every morning at 5.30. He trained himself to write exactly 250 words every quarter of an hour. He kept worktables showing the exact number of words he must produce day by day, week by week and month by month. He prided himself on having never failed to meet an editor's or a publisher's deadline. His journeys by coach, train, or even ship were not allowed to interfere with his programme.

Trollope was absolutely frank about his motives, stating in his *Autobiography* – after he has announced that his earnings from his writings amounted to about £70,000 –

> I am a writer, and I am paid for my work. I get all that I can. I enjoy telling you how much I did get. Every author wants money, and it is arrant humbug when he says that he doesn't.

He had no patience with an artistic or aesthetic approach to literature, and defending his rigid work-schedule he wrote:

> There are those who would be ashamed to subject themselves to such a task-master, and who think that the man who works with his imagination should allow himself to wait till inspiration moves. When I have heard such doctrine preached I have hardly been able to repress my scorn. To me it would not be more absurd if the shoemaker were to wait for inspiration.

It was these revelations that were largely responsible, after the posthumous publication of the *Autobiography* in 1863, for the rapid decline of Trollope's reputation in a period which was wedded to romantic ideas of inspiration and art for art's sake. Undoubtedly there was some justification for the criticisms. There are some obvious pot-boilers among Trollope's novels, and some of the best of them contain passages which bear the marks of fatigue and overwork.

On the other hand, it does not always do to take the Trollope of the *Autobiography* at his face value. In spite of his protestations of being a mere journeyman of fiction, he had that obsessive interest in his characters and their dilemmas that is symptomatic of the born novelist. It is by no means true, either, that Trollope habitually manipulates his characters and situations in order to indulge his reader's propensities to daydreaming and wishful thinking. There may be a good deal of the idyll about

Barsetshire, and *Barchester Towers* may have the obligatory happy ending, but on the whole Trollope maintains his objective control and remains faithful to his own particular form of realism. His characters may not be analysed in any depth, because it is his chief concern rather to show them in everyday action. They do not rise to tragic heights, and in his comedy it was not his way to create figures who expand into an imaginative world of their own. But it would be difficult to find a single one of them who does not ring true. No-one who reads *Barchester Towers* is ever likely to forget the imperious Mrs Proudie, the scheming Mr Slope, the worldly but likeable Archdeacon Grantly, the gentle Dr Harding, and the delightful Eleanor. All these characters are treated with justice and sympathy. Trollope believed in the essential goodness of human nature. He was one of the few novelists who could depict virtue without making it appear unnatural, and it should be added that no one could create a character so convincingly good as Dr Harding without knowing himself what true goodness was. The values that permeate Trollope's work, in spite of his own prickliness of temperament, are fundamentally civilized and humane. It is perhaps Henry James who best summed him up when he wrote that, though he might not be distinguished by his eloquence, Trollope '... will remain the most trustworthy ... of the writers who have helped the heart of man to know itself.'

The Mill on the Floss

George Eliot

'George Eliot' was born Mary Ann Evans in 1819, in a Warwickshire farmhouse attached to a large estate of which her father was manager. Her family belonged to that section of the rural middle classes which unquestioningly accepted the traditions of the old pre-industrial, semi-feudal caste system. It was one of the basic axioms in the *mores* of this class that a woman's place was in the home. As a child and young woman, Mary Ann struggled to subscribe to this axiom, and the concept of a woman's duty remained with her all her life, and runs through all her work.

As a child, Mary Ann used to accompany her father as he drove round inspecting the scattered properties belonging to his employer, and thus she gained an intimate knowledge of the Warwickshire countryside round Coventry (or Middlemarch, as it became in the novel of that name). This, combined with the more direct experience gained during her long country rambles with her elder brother Isaac, also constituted a life long influence. She was separated from her brother, for whom she had an almost obsessive love, when they were both sent away to school. From the headmistress of the school she attended at Coventry between the ages of thirteen and sixteen, she imbibed the strenuously moral principles of Evangelical Christianity. The conflicting pressures of an already powerful intellect, a passionate nature, the consciousness of her plainness, a yearning for someone to cling to, and high moral purpose, made her an unusually intense, rather awkward young woman.

When her mother died in 1836 and her elder sister married a year later, she took sole charge of her father's household. She devoted herself to her woman's duties of cooking, sewing and supervising the dairy, again with her customary stern conscientiousness. Her father, though, was by no means unaware of her unusual abilities, and masters were brought from Coventry to teach her German and Italian in both of which she achieved fluency, and also music. She wrote poetry and read voraciously – though for a time she wondered whether, on moral grounds, she ought to give up reading novels. At the same time, she could not help feeling hemmed in and intellectually frustrated.

In 1841, Isaac married and took over the farmhouse from his father, who retired with Mary Ann to Coventry. There, she became friendly with the gifted and highly intellectual circle that frequented the home of Charles Bray, a Coventry manufacturer who was also a scholar and philosopher. It was an exciting and unsettling experience for Mary Ann and before long, under the influence of the advanced liberal theories about human personality and the Christian religion of her new friends, she announced the loss of her faith and refused to attend church. This led to a serious quarrel with her father, and the breach was only healed when she consented to resume churchgoing. But she did not give up her new rationalist opinions. She took over from Mrs Hennell (Charles Bray's sister) the task of translating the immense and scientifically documented *Life of Jesus* by David Friedrich Strauss, the best-known of the contemporary German scholars who were subjecting Christianity to a strictly rationalist analysis. This was published, without her name, in 1846. Her father was greatly distressed by his daughter's free thinking, but they remained close to each other and Mary Ann nursed him with great devotion through his last illness. On his death in 1849 the Brays took her to the Continent with them. When she returned to England she decided to go to London and earn her living as a professional writer. She obtained the post of sub-editor of the highbrow *Westminster Review*, applying herself with tremendous industry to reviewing and translating for the periodical. Among the books she translated during this period was *The Essence of Christianity* by Ludwig Feuerbach – another German rationalist, anti-mystical interpreter of Christianity. This book was in fact her first to be published, and the only one to bear her real name.

At that date it was a remarkably courageous step for a spinster of thirty-two to break away from a sheltered family life in order to undertake an independent career in a profession which was highly suspect among the middle classes. Even more remarkable perhaps, was the fact that she was accepted on an equal footing by the foremost thinkers of the period, among them Thomas Carlyle and Herbert Spencer. She was strongly influenced by Spencer's evolutionary theories, and it was through him that she met George Henry Lewes, and the two fell in love. Lewes was a brilliant and versatile thinker and writer. He was a disciple of the contemporary philosopher, Auguste Comte, the chief exponent of the positivist philosophy, which excludes metaphysics and revealed religion, and substitutes a 'religion of humanity'. It was this philosophy that largely filled the void left in Mary Ann's life by the loss of her orthodox Christian faith – though it is important to note that she brought to it the full force of her passionate, imaginative but high-principled nature, so that it assumed both the lofty moral tone and the poetic, sacramental overtones of the more mystical type of religion.

Now came the second great crisis of her life. Lewes's wife had left him and their three children. Divorce was out of the question because, in the eyes of the law, Lewes had condoned his wife's conduct. After much heart-searching, Marian Evans (as she now called herself) decided to accompany Lewes when, in 1854, he went to Germany to research for his *Life of Goethe*. On their return, the couple lived openly together as man and wife and Marian became a devoted mother to Lewes's three boys. To Marian's great distress her brother Isaac broke off relations with her, but none of their worthwhile friends abandoned them and their home became a cultural centre for writers, artists and musicians. When Lewes died in 1878, George Eliot gave up her own writing and devoted herself to preparing Lewes's unfinished work for the press. In this she was helped by an old friend, J. W. Cross. When she married Cross in 1880, she received a letter of forgiveness and reconciliation from her brother, but she herself died at the end of the same year.

It was Lewes who first urged Marian to turn to fiction, and in 1857 a long short story 'The Sad Fortunes of the Reverend Amos Barton' was published, the first of three tales that appeared in book form as *Scenes from Clerical Life* in 1858. With their publication, the thirty-eight year old Marian Evans was transformed into George Eliot. She chose the name, she explained, because 'George was Mr Lewes's Christian name, and Eliot was a good, mouth-filling, easily pronounced word.' There were plenty of precedents for the choice of a male pseudonym for a woman seeking to compete in a man's world, and hardly anyone detected that the author of the highly-praised *Scenes from Clerical Life* was a woman, with the notable exception of Dickens.

George Eliot's first full-scale novel, *Adam Bede*, was published in 1859. It is the story of an honest and high-principled young countryman, Adam; an evangelical woman preacher, Dinah Morris, whom he eventually marries; and the beautiful but frivolous country girl, Hetty Sorrel, with whom Adam is in love. Hetty is seduced by a young squire, Arthur Donnithorne, and is eventually convicted and transported for murdering her illegitimate child by him. *Adam Bede* displayed the imaginative vision, the deep poetic sensibility, the brilliant handling of country humours, and also the intellectual power and strong moral outlook that were characteristic of all her mature work. The novel was tremendously successful and was translated into many languages. Then, in 1860, came *The Mill on the Floss*, which has perhaps been George Eliot's most popular novel.

Summary

The Tulliver family, who live at Dorlcote Mill on the river Floss (a fictional name for the river Severn), are closely modelled on George Eliot's own. In particular, the vividly beautiful evocation of the childhood of Maggie Tulliver and her older brother Tom, recaptures George Eliot's most cherished memories of her own childhood intimacy with her beloved brother Isaac. There are, however, dark shadows in the relationship as far as Maggie is concerned. Tom, a fair, solid, and unimaginative boy, is fond of his vivid, precocious sister, but he is not above playing a cat and mouse game with her sensitive affections, finding a cruel if unconscious pleasure in punishing her by a feigned withdrawal of love if she displeases him in any way. Maggie suffers under this torture, but burns too with a sense of its injustice, and from time to time breaks out into fierce rebellion.

The suppressed passion in the child Maggie's nature, and the gathering pressure of an almost intolerable sense of frustration, are conveyed with George Eliot's characteristic insight and dramatic concreteness in her description of the way Maggie treats her old doll 'by alternately grinding and beating the wooden head against the rough brick of the great chimney ... with a passion that expelled every other form of consciousness – even the memory of the grievance that had caused it.'

There is another reason, though, for Maggie's sense of injustice in her relationship with Tom. Mr Tulliver decides that his son, who has little use for books, shall receive a proper education. But it is accepted as a fact of life that Maggie's superior intelligence and passion for reading should receive no encouragement. Even her father's loving pride in her quick-wittedness and spirit is tempered by fears for her future, because 'a woman's no business wi' being so clever; it'll turn to trouble, I doubt.'

In the Victorian world, male supremacy was still unchallenged. George Eliot knew from personal experience the unsatisfied intellectual hunger from which Maggie suffered, and she knew, too, that deprivation of this kind could endow learning with an almost mystical significance, and with a reach of wisdom it does not necessarily possess.

In the meantime, Mr Tulliver's affairs have been going badly. His formidable sister-in-law, Mrs Glegg, disapproves of his spending money on Tom's education, and when he hotly tells her to mind her own business, she reminds him sharply of a loan she made to him some years before. Another side of George Eliot's genius is seen in these domestic scenes. In spite of the seriousness of her themes, and her anxiety at times in *The Mill on the Floss* to demonstrate her learning (like Maggie) by all kinds of erudite references and quotations in various languages, George Eliot in her handling of the various Tulliver relations shows that she had a strong sense of comedy, combined with a remarkable ability to place it solidly in a specific social context.

In fact, Mrs Glegg thinks better of demanding the return of her money. It is not the sort of thing one does with one's own 'kin' – a word much on her lips, and the corner-stone of her philosophy. Mr Tulliver, however, who is headstrong and touchy, proudly insists on repaying her, even though it means borrowing the money through Mr Wakem, the lawyer whom Mr Tulliver regards as his enemy, chiefly because he represents the other side in a long-standing dispute over water rights on the Floss.

Lawyer Wakem's hunchbacked son, Philip, is sent to

Mr Stelling's parsonage where Tom is already a boarder-pupil, and when Maggie visits, she and the gentle, scholarly Philip find that they have a good deal in common and become great friends. Shortly after this, Maggie herself is sent away to school in company with her pretty cousin, Lucy Deane. But when Maggie is thirteen (and Tom sixteen) disaster strikes her family. Her father loses his lawsuit over the disputed water rights, and as a result of legal costs, faces ruin and the loss of the Mill. Then, after a fall from his horse, he is stricken by some form of paralysis. Tom, brought home from his studies, obtains a job with Lucy's father, Mr Deane, the most prosperous of his uncles, in the firm of Guest & Company, of which Mr Deane is one of the partners. But for Maggie the future at home seems bleak.

The hated Wakem buys Dorlcote Mill and offers to instal Tulliver (who has recovered) as manager. Tulliver is revolted by the idea of being beholden to his enemy, but he agrees, partly out of pity for his wife, partly because he himself could not bear the thought of abandoning the place where his forefathers had lived for generations.

But though Tulliver is determined to serve Wakem honestly, his hatred does not abate one iota, and he forces Tom to join him in writing an oath of continuing enmity in the Family Bible. Life for father and son becomes a grim struggle with one end in view – to pay off the debts and redeem the Mill for themselves. Meanwhile Maggie, after reading *The Imitation of Christ* by the mediaeval monk Thomas à Kempis, seeks consolation in a kind of religious exaltation. The unreal, self-deceiving element in Maggie's new ideal is clearly recognized by Philip Wakem, whom she continues to meet in secret. When Philip makes a passionate declaration of his love, Maggie eventually acknowledges her own, though she feels there is some element missing in her response.

Their love, in any case, soon runs into obstacles. Tom has been doing well at Guest & Company and he begins to see prospects of freeing the Mill from the clutches of Wakem. When he accidentally discovers the relationship between Philip and Maggie he is furious, and threatens to tell Maggie's father unless she swears on the Bible that she will never see or communicate with Philip again. For her father's sake, Maggie agrees, though she turns on her once adored brother with vehement accusations of meanness, hypocrisy and cruelty.

Eventually, Tom is in a position to announce proudly to his father that they can now pay off all their outstanding debts. In great jubilation, Tom and his father inform their assembled creditors and then the old man, in a highly excited frame of mind, rides back to the Mill. Wakem is just leaving as he enters the yard. The lawyer makes a criticism of Tulliver's management of one of the fields and in the ensuing quarrel Tulliver charges at Wakem with his horse, knocks him down and starts beating him wildly with his riding-crop. Maggie intervenes, and Wakem rides away vowing vengeance. Tulliver has a seizure, and, after begging Tom to try and get the Mill back from Wakem, dies. Tom and Maggie are reunited in their sorrow.

Two years pass. Mrs Tulliver, following the death of her sister Mrs Deane, has gone to keep house for the widower and his daughter Lucy, who is now unofficially engaged to the rather dandified Stephen Guest, son of the senior partner of Guest & Company. Tom is in lodgings, pushing ahead with his business enterprises. Maggie, determined to be independent, has been away, teaching at a school. But now she is staying with the Deanes on holiday.

Maggie, who has developed into a striking and vivacious young woman, makes an impression in the lively social circle that gathers round Lucy and Stephen. One of the members of this circle is Philip Wakem and Maggie dutifully obtains her brother's consent to attend gatherings at which Philip will be present. It is evident to Lucy that Philip is still very much in love with Maggie, and she is determined to see them marry. Tom now suggests to Mr Deane that Guest & Company buy Dorlcote Mill from Wakem, instal Tom himself to run it as a business venture for the company, but allow him gradually to buy it back, thereby keeping his promise to his dead father. Urged by Lucy, Philip intercedes with Wakem – and also confesses to his father that he wants to marry Maggie. Mr Wakem is at first furious, but eventually he comes round. In Lucy's eyes all is now set fair for a marriage between Maggie and Philip. But Tom, now back at the Mill, warns Maggie that if she ever marries Philip he will break with her for ever – and she decides to go back to teaching for a time in order to think things over.

But there is another reason, even if she cannot as yet admit it openly to herself, for Maggie's decision. From their first meeting, she and Stephen Guest have been conscious, to their own consternation, of a strong mutual attraction. Its fundamentally instinctive and sensual nature is most subtly and convincingly conveyed – far more convincingly indeed than in the majority of even the most permissive modern novels where all the sexual implications can be explored without restraint. If Lucy happens to leave Maggie and Stephen alone, for instance, they seldom speak to each other but each is 'oppressively conscious of the other's presence, even to the finger-ends.' The looks they exchange, or struggle not to exchange, are fraught with the same physical intensity. When there is a grand party at the Guests' house, they find themselves automatically gravitating towards each other 'like some action in a dream'; and when they find themselves, again almost automatically, leaving the dance-floor together 'they walked unsteadily on, without feeling anything but that long, grave mutual gaze which has the solemnity belonging to all deep passion.' When the scene culminates in Stephen, on a sudden and irresistible impulse, showering kisses on Maggie's bare arms, the sensation of physical excitement is almost unbearable – for the reader as well as for Stephen and Maggie. These effects, so absolutely true to life, could only have been achieved by a woman who understood passion herself. Much of George Eliot's greatness lies in the depth and scope of her understanding of human nature and human flesh.

But it also lies in her firm grasp of the ramifications that attend all human actions, including the purely instinctive ones, and of the fact that passion – sadly, and sometimes tragically – inevitably operates within a social and ultimately a moral context. When Stephen at last pours out his feelings to Maggie, and, though deeply moved, she reminds him that they have both given their pledge to others, he advances the time-worn plea: 'The pledge *can't* be fulfilled ... It is unnatural: we can only pretend to give ourselves to anyone else ...' But Maggie replies that although love is indeed 'natural', 'surely pity and faithfulness and memory are natural too?' These are the words of a woman who has suddenly, under the stress of experience, achieved maturity. The 'morality' they contain is not that of routine and convention, but the independent product of a truly profound nature.

But although Maggie and Stephen have agreed to renounce each other, they cannot avoid meeting in Lucy's home. Philip, his senses made acute by his own love for Maggie, catches the speechless undercurrent between her and Stephen. When, in Lucy's absence, he has planned to take Maggie on the river, he deliberately backs out so that Stephen can do so instead. Maggie and Stephen do not have the strength to cling to their resolution. Lost in their wordless, sensual dream, they glide along the river, hour after hour, completely forgetting the time, until they suddenly realize that it is growing dark and that they have gone too far to get back that night. According to the conventions of the day, Maggie is now irretrievably compromised. Stephen urges her to accept the situation and to elope with him. With this aim, they board a passing cargo boat bound for a nearby town where they can hire a chaise to take them to Scotland to be married. At first Maggie, temporarily lost to everything except her emotions, drifts along with Stephen's plan. But when they land, she forces herself, with a tremendous effort, to come out of her dream, and tells Stephen that she cannot marry him.

When she returns to Dorlcote Mill, the rigidly respectable Tom refuses to let her in. Maggie's mother, however, bravely accompanies her daughter to St Ogg's, where they take lodgings together. Maggie is cruelly ostracized by conventional society which regards her as little better than a 'fallen woman'. She is not universally condemned, however. The clergyman, Dr Ken, believes in her innocence and respects her decision not to marry Stephen Guest. Maggie, stricken by remorse, is overwhelmed to find that she is not condemned by Philip either; he writes her a tender and forgiving love letter. To Maggie's surprise, her aunt Glegg also rallies to her defence and gives Tom a verbal trouncing for breaking the unwritten law that one must stick by one's own kin. Eventually, too, Lucy secretly calls on Maggie to tell her that she understands and forgives her. Nevertheless, Maggie cannot forgive herself and her life is wretched, especially when she has to endure the further temptation of a despairing letter from Stephen begging her to come to him.

But now fate intervenes again. The river Floss suddenly rises, floodwaters surround the house where Maggie is lodging and she is accidentally swept out alone in one of the rescue boats. However, she manages to get it into the mainstream so that the current can carry her towards Dorlcote Mill to rescue her brother. The Mill is nearly engulfed when she reaches it but Tom manages to scramble into the boat. There is a moment of blissful reunion in which Maggie and Tom recapture the intimacy of their lost childhood and then a mass of wreckage bears down on them, hurling them from the boat to their deaths.

Tom and Maggie are buried side by side. Philip, who remains single, and Stephen and Lucy (who eventually marry) often visit the grave with its inscription (which is also inserted on the novel's title page): 'In their death they were not divided.'

Critical commentary

The descent into sentimentality in connection with Maggie and Tom at the end of the book points to one of its main defects: the relationship between them is too close and too intense for comfort. In a sense it is Tom who is responsible for Maggie's tragedy in that it was his attitude towards Philip in the first instance that had left her vulnerable to Stephen's appeal. It is difficult not to see an element of jealousy in Tom's behaviour – for example his violent reaction to Maggie's misadventure on the river with Stephen Guest. An abnormally intense brother-sister relationship is, of course, a perfectly legitimate theme for a novel. The real weakness, in this case, lies in the fact that in writing *The Mill on the Floss* George Eliot called up too much of her own highly-charged emotional relationship with her own brother and then failed to subjugate it completely to her artistic purposes. The sentimentality is the evidence of insufficient assimilation, and the mature, critical intelligence which George Eliot displays in most of her comments on the action is temporarily in abeyance.

There is a similar lack of control, F. R. Leavis has suggested, in her handling of Maggie's spirituality, or soul-hunger. In it he sees 'a discordance, a discrepancy, a failure to reduce things to a due relevance', that arises from an identification between Maggie and her creator both too close and too over-idealized, so that her commentary on Maggie's immaturity is itself not fully mature. The emotional quality that emerges when George Eliot is describing these exaltations of Maggie's, 'represents . . . a need or hunger in George Eliot, that shows itself to be insidious company for her intelligence – apt to supplant and take command.'

Not always, of course; there are plenty of instances in

The Mill on the Floss when George Eliot draws attention, compassionately but ironically, and even sharply, to Maggie's mistakes and self-deceptions; and, in spite of everything, Maggie is one of the most memorable and humanly moving portraits in fiction of the growth and development of a young woman. Given the kind of person she is and the kind of circumstances in which she is placed, hers is a genuine tragedy.

There have also been many criticisms of Stephen Guest. The Victorian Leslie Stephen, for example, described him as 'a mere hair-dresser's block', and others have regarded him as an utterly unworthy foil to Maggie. It is true that his first appearance in the novel, with his 'diamond ring, attar of roses, and an air of nonchalant leisure' is hardly promising. There are times when he seems more like a schoolgirl's daydream than a flesh-and-blood man – and perhaps for the still immature Maggie he *does* to some extent fulfil that function. On the other hand, he is real enough within the role he is called upon to play in Maggie's destiny – when he is protesting his love, urging her to elope with him and writing his last despairing letter; or if it comes to that, when he is feverishly kissing her bare arm. In a sense, too, it is artistically right that he should be a little wooden, not quite realized, because the kind of soundless, wordless sensuality he represents for Maggie *is* largely a depersonalized quality. For the rest, all the characters of *The Mill on the Floss*, not only those mentioned in the summary but all the minor ones as well, are vividly alive.

By date *The Mill on the Floss* is a mid-Victorian novel. In many respects it is a typical one. There is nothing at all revolutionary in its technique. It is long, leisurely and discursive in treatment, with frequent and lengthy comments by the author. It is solidly set in the old English world of squire, church, rural continuities and strict moral and social observances. The world it depicts is presented with the usual Victorian careful attention to external detail.

Yet George Eliot's novels are closer to the present day than any that had gone before. This is not because she abandoned the old tradition of English fiction, but because her own character, personal problems and interests forced her to adapt it in such a way that its fundamental character was altered. Her younger contemporary, Henry James, who saw her as standing alone and setting 'a limit ... to the old-fashioned English novel', perhaps put his finger on the basic reason when he described her as 'really philosophic'. By that he meant not only that she was profoundly interested in philosophy as such, but also that her main concern in approaching her story was a comprehensive one that involved a detailed analysis of all the factors and a considered judgement on them. For her, theme was more important than story. The theme came first, usually in the form of some central moral dilemma, and the characters and situations were then designed to give it life and substance. Character, in consequence, is important in a George Eliot novel in a way that was, by and large, new. For one thing her natural *métier*, as the modern critic, Barbara Hardy, has said, was 'the drama of intellect and sensibility in strong and unusual characters'. In showing how such characters reacted to the moral challenges with which they were confronted, the old conventions of plot – such as heroes and heroines who are expected to be both young and handsome, and marriage as the rounding off of the tale – had to be abandoned. If the logic of a certain theme in relation to a certain character demanded failure, tragedy or death, then that logic had to be faithfully observed.

A George Eliot novel, therefore, is open-ended in the sense that the moral or philosophical issues it embodies have an abstract and generalized significance, moving outwards from the particular instance to ultimate issues – and on the whole it was along these lines that the serious novel developed up to about the 1930s. But the final word as far as *The Mill on the Floss* is concerned must be that whatever criticisms may be directed against it they cannot detract from the wisdom, compassion, tolerance and love, or from the profundity of imaginative vision, that inform the novel as a whole.

The Woman in White

Wilkie Collins

William Wilkie Collins was born in London in 1824, the
son of a despotic father who was determined that he
should enter a thoroughly safe and respectable profession,
in spite of the fact that he himself was an artist and a
Bohemian. When he was twelve, Wilkie's family moved
to Italy and lived there for the next three years. On their
return to London, Wilkie was respectably apprenticed
to a tea-broker. The work was monotonous and he found
relief in writing an unpublished erotic novel about life
in Tahiti. In 1848 he was entered at Lincoln's Inn and
was called to the Bar three years later. But after the death
of his father he joyously abandoned the legal profession
and set out to make his living as a writer. After publishing several novels, he met Charles Dickens, became his
close friend, and in 1855 began contributing to Dickens's
periodical *Household Words* in which a number of his
later novels (including, in 1860, *The Woman in White*)
were serialized. He collaborated with Dickens in a number of stories, and Dickens's last, unfinished novel, *The
Mystery of Edwin Drood* (1870) was conceived under his
influence.

One night in 1855, when he was walking in a quiet
London suburb with his brother and John Millais the
painter, a young woman rushed, screaming, out of one
of the houses. Wilkie went to her aid and found that she

was escaping from a brutal husband. He subsequently found lodgings for her and her baby daughter and for the next fourteen years she was his unofficial wife. When she eventually left him (to marry a plumber), he installed a younger woman in her place by whom he had three illegitimate children. He combated a painful illness by taking large doses of laudanum and later took to opium smoking. He died in 1889.

Wilkie Collins believed that 'the Novel and the Play are twin-sisters in the family of Fiction ... the one is a drama narrated, as the other is a drama acted' – and defiantly asserted that 'I have always held the old-fashioned opinion that the primary object of a work of fiction should be to tell a story.' That objective was certainly achieved in *The Woman in White*. Its plot, moreover, was of a new and special kind, as he explained in a preface to the original edition:

> An experiment is attempted in this novel, which has not (so far as I know) been hitherto tried in fiction. The story of the book is told throughout by the characters of the book. They are all placed in different positions along the chain of events; and they all take the chain up in turn, and carry it on to the end.

Summary

The first link in that chain as far as *The Woman in White* is concerned was that strange real-life encounter with a distraught woman, arriving suddenly out of the darkness, which Collins had himself experienced. It is reproduced in the novel when Walter Hartright, an artist who is about to take up an appointment as a teacher of drawing to the two nieces of Mr Frederick Fairlie of Limmeridge House in Cumberland, is suddenly confronted, while walking at night on Hampstead Heath, by 'a solitary woman, dressed from head to foot in white garments'. She tells him that she has been cruelly wronged, and begs his help. When Walter tells her about his new appointment, the strange woman in white announces that she knows Limmeridge House, and mentions the name of Mrs Fairlie. Walter helps her find a cab to take her into London. Soon afterwards, a carriage stops near Walter. He overhears the driver asking a policeman if he has seen a woman in white, explaining that she has escaped from a private lunatic asylum.

Arriving at Limmeridge House, Walter is received on behalf of his invalid employer by a plain, but intelligent and lively young woman named Marian Halcombe, who explains that she is the daughter of the late Mrs Fairlie by her first husband, and that it is she and her half-sister Laura whom Walter is to instruct. Walter tells her about his adventure on Hampstead Heath, and Marian asks him not to mention it to anyone else. When Walter meets the beautiful Laura, he is startled by her resemblance to the woman in white. Marian finds some old letters of her mother's which seem to suggest that the mysterious woman might be Anne Catherick, whom Mrs Fairlie had befriended when the former was a child apparently suffering from some mild form of mental affliction – and who bore a strange resemblance to Laura.

Walter and Laura fall in love, but Laura has promised her father to marry his old friend, Sir Percival Glyde of Blackwater Park, a man many years older than herself. Walter, in despair, resolves to leave. But before he goes, Marian tells him that Laura has received an anonymous letter warning her against Sir Percival. A rumour that the ghost of Mrs Fairlie has been seen at her tomb leads Walter to keep a midnight vigil in the churchyard – and there, at Mrs Fairlie's grave, he meets the woman in white again, in the company of her friend, Mrs Clements. The woman in white is indeed Anne Catherick. It was Sir Percival Glyde who had caused her to be confined in the asylum and it was she who had sent Laura the anonymous letter. But the mention of Sir Percival's name has terrorized Anne Catherick, and Walter can get no further information from her. When he and Marian go to the nearby farmhouse where Anne Catherick and Mrs Clements have been staying, they find that they have gone. Marian and the honest old family solicitor, Mr Vincent Gilmore, assure Walter before he leaves that the charges contained in the anonymous letter will be thoroughly investigated before the marriage between Laura and Sir Percival takes place.

It is Mr Gilmore who now takes up the links in the 'chain'. He relates how Sir Percival has explained to him and Marian Halcombe that Anne Catherick had been mentally deranged since birth, and that, as she was the daughter of an old servant of his, he had paid for her to be confined in a private asylum. The anonymous letter, therefore, he claims, is the product of delusions. Mr Gilmore is convinced by his explanations, especially when Marian, who, on Sir Percival's insistence, had written to Anne's mother Mrs Catherick, receives a letter fully confirming Sir Percival's account.

Mr Gilmore now goes into the complicated question of Laura's financial position when she reaches the age of twenty-one, a few months after the projected marriage to Sir Percival; and Wilkie Collins, who had himself been called to the Bar and who consulted several impeccable legal authorities before writing his novel, was proud of the accuracy and expertise with which he presented it. The main points are that part of Laura's inheritance, in the event of her death, would go to her aunt Eleanor who is married to the Italian Count Fosco. The great bulk of her fortune, however, would be at Laura's own disposal. Mr Gilmore accordingly draws up a marriage settlement whereby, in the event of Laura pre-deceasing her husband, he would enjoy only the interest on this part of her fortune, so that when he died the principal would go to whatever legatees Laura might designate in her will. To Mr Gilmore's consternation, Sir Percival's solicitors insist that if Laura died, the whole principal should go to Sir Percival. Mr Gilmore pleads with Mr Fairlie, as Laura's guardian, to reject this clause – but, plaintively protesting that his nerves cannot stand the strain, the despicable Fairlie refuses, and Gilmore has perforce to consent.

Marian Halcombe's diary now takes up the story. Laura has confessed to Sir Percival that she loves someone else, and begs to be released from her engagement. He refuses, protesting his own devotion in the most plausible terms. Marian receives a letter from Walter telling her that he has been followed by Sir Percival's agents who are searching for the woman in white and who suspect that he is harbouring her. Through the influence of friends, Marian obtains for him a post as draughtsman to an archaeological expedition to Central America, and Walter sorrowfully departs.

After the marriage, the couple settle at Blackwater Park, Sir Percival's country house in Hampshire, accompanied by Laura's long-estranged aunt Eleanor and the latter's husband, Count Fosco. Marian is invited to make her home there too. She is intrigued by the baffling personality of the grossly fat and dandified Count Fosco who is witty, intelligent, and cultured, but who fills her with revulsion. Marian suspects that he is a political exile of some kind, and it is also soon apparent that he has considerable influence over Sir Percival. It is he, for example, who dissuades him from trying to force Laura to sign a document without reading it. But this is only after Marian has discovered, by writing secretly to Mr Kyrle, Mr Gilmore's partner (Gilmore himself is away convalescing from an illness), that the document in question was an attempt to make Laura surrender her fortune straight away, and Marian is convinced that Count Fosco had intercepted and read her letter to the solicitor before deciding to come to Laura's support.

Anne Catherick now arrives in the neighbourhood and manages to see Laura alone, telling her that she is dying and informing her that she is in possession of a damaging secret about Sir Percival which she promises to reveal at their next meeting. Sir Percival, however, comes across

Laura with the letter, forces her to hand it over and, convinced that she knows the whereabouts of Anne Catherick, locks her in her room and dismisses her maid, Fanny.

Before Fanny leaves, Marian manages to give her a letter to Mr Kyrle informing him of Sir Percival's conduct towards his wife, and another to Mr Fairlie, begging him to allow herself and Laura to return to Limmeridge House. At great personal risk, Marian also manages to hide herself on a verandah overlooking the garden, where she overhears a conversation between Count Fosco and Sir Percival. She learns that the Count knows of the letters she has just written ... that the letter from Mrs Catherick exonerating Sir Percival from blame in the matter of her daughter's confinement had been dictated by Sir Percival who has a hold over Mrs Catherick, and that Sir Percival is desperate for money. She also notes Count Fosco's excitement when Sir Percival tells him that Anne Catherick bears a remarkable resemblance to his wife, Laura.

But Marian has caught a chill as the result of her vigil and falls seriously ill. The postscript to her diary, expressing admiration for her courage and resource, and commiserations on her failure to protect her sister is written by none other than Count Fosco.

Equally surprising is the narrator of the next part of the story: it is Mr Fairlie. He describes the arrival of Laura's maid, Fanny. She explains to him that before she had left the inn where she had been staying the night after her dismissal, Countess Fosco had visited her and drugged her tea, though on her recovery she had found that the letters entrusted to her by Marian were still in her possession. In fact Countess Fosco had substituted a blank sheet for Marian's letter to the solicitor. Marian's letter to her uncle, requesting refuge for herself and Laura, has not been tampered with however, and Mr Fairlie writes to Marian asking her to come and explain matters to him. Count Fosco arrives at Limmeridge House with the news of Marian's illness. Nevertheless, he urges Fairlie to allow Laura to return to him and, in order to ease her journey, offers to accommodate her *en route* at his own house in London. Mr Fairlie gives him a letter for Laura inviting her to Limmeridge House.

The next piece of narrative is in the form of a statement from Eliza Michelson, housekeeper at Blackwater Park. She describes how Sir Percival had ordered her to dismiss most of the servants, explaining that he would be shortly closing Blackwater Park and taking his wife and her sister abroad. Sir Percival then persuades Laura to go to London to the house of Count Fosco by telling her that Marian (who has begun to recover from her illness) has already been taken there, and that this is merely a stopping-place on their way to Limmeridge House. After Laura has gone, Mrs Michelson discovers that Marian is still in the house, transferred to another wing while Mrs Michelson had been away on an errand contrived by Sir Percival and Count Fosco. Mrs Michelson, distressed by the deception practised on Laura, gives in her notice, but stays on to nurse Marian after Sir Percival has left.

Then come several short statements: from a cook at Count Fosco's London house who describes the arrival of (as she supposes) Lady Glyde and her subsequent collapse; from the nurse who attended her – and from the doctor who signed her death certificate from heart failure. The inscription on 'Lady Glyde's' tomb follows, and then a brief, startling narrative by Walter Hartright, now back in England, describing his visit to Laura's grave to be confronted there by Marian Halcombe, and beside her another woman who raises her veil – to reveal the features of Laura herself.

Walter Hartright continues the narrative. He is now living secretly in London under an assumed name, with Marian and Laura posing as his sisters. For it was not Laura who had died, but poor Anne Catherick, recaptured – already close to death – by Count Fosco. Laura had been incarcerated in Anne's place in the private lunatic asylum, the authorities of which had no reason to doubt that she was indeed Anne Catherick, in view of the remarkable resemblance between Laura and the dead woman – who had, of course, been buried as Lady Glyde. But Marian, suspicious of the accounts of her sister's death, had visited the asylum, recognized Laura, and succeeded in effecting her escape. Marian had then taken her sister to Limmeridge House, but Laura's appearance had been sadly changed by her sufferings and her memory of her incarceration (under the influence of a drug administered by Count Fosco) is confused – so Mr Fairlie had insisted that he did not recognize her as his niece.

Walter devotes himself to the task of establishing Laura's identity. He obtains the statements of Mrs Michelson and the others. Armed with these, he goes to Mr Kyrle who tells him that they do not constitute sufficient legal evidence and that Walter's only hope is to prove a discrepancy between the date of the doctor's certificate of the supposed Lady Glyde's death, and that of Laura's journey to Count Fosco's house in London – but unfortunately none of those concerned can provide such proof. Mr Kyrle informs Walter that Sir Percival is back in London and also hands him a letter addressed to Marian Halcombe. On leaving the solicitor's office, Walter discovers that he is being followed. He returns home by a circuitous route and gives Marian the letter. It is a warning from Count Fosco not to cross his or Sir Percival's path, but reiterates his admiration for her.

Finding his inquiries at Blackwater Park blocked by Sir Percival's agents, Walter decides that he must go over to the offensive and eventually discovers Sir Percival's secret, which is that his parents were unmarried so he has no right to his title. In a race to collect the evidence, in the form of a forged entry of marriage in a church register, Walter is set upon by thugs hired by Sir Percival, but manages to escape – only to find Sir Percival already in the church vestry tampering with the register. Sir Percival, however, accidentally sets fire to the vestry and is trapped inside. He perishes in the flames – and so does the register with its crucial forged entry.

In the course of these proceedings it has transpired that Anne Catherick was really Laura's illegitimate sister, hence the likeness between them. On returning to London, Walter finds that Marian and Laura have been obliged to make a hasty removal because Count Fosco has discovered their whereabouts. Laura has by now recovered her health and looks and she and Walter marry. Walter, still hoping that an inconsistency in the crucial dates can be discovered, now resolves to find a way of forcing the facts from Count Fosco. Eventually he obtains the leverage he wants from his Italian friend, Professor Pesca. Count Fosco is a traitor to the cause of an Italian secret society to which he had once belonged and as such is a marked man. Walter confronts Count Fosco and extracts from him, as the price of his escape from England and from the vengeance of the secret society, the information, backed by the necessary proof, that Laura was in fact still at Blackwater Park on the day the doctor signed the death certificate of the woman he had been told was Lady Glyde.

Walter also exacts a full confession of the plot concocted by Count Fosco and Sir Percival which forms the next narrative section. It is redolent of the Count's wit, learning, and contradictory personality – he boasts that nothing could have defeated him had it not been for his 'fatal admiration' for Marian and claims for himself the immunity from ordinary moral standards that belongs to him as a superior being. Not long afterwards, Count Fosco is killed by a member of the secret society he has betrayed.

Laura's identity is at last established. Her fortune has gone, but she and Walter, their baby son and Marian, live contentedly together on Walter's earnings as an engraver, until, on the death of Mr Fairlie, Laura inherits his property and Limmeridge House becomes their permanent home.

Critical commentary

The Woman in White certainly lives up to Wilkie Collins's claim that his primary aim was to tell a good story, and it marked a considerable advance as far as control and ingenuity were concerned. The plot is, however, a very complicated one, and to some critics this has been a cause for complaint. Collins's contemporary, Anthony Trollope, for example, wrote of his work: 'The construction is most minute and wonderful. But I can never lose the taste of the construction.'

This points to a fictional method which was new in Trollope's day, but one with which the modern public is thoroughly familiar, for Wilkie Collins was a pioneer of the detective story. With *The Woman in White*, most of its ingredients have made their appearance – except one. There is the careful laying of clues; the meticulous placing of small details and episodes which all have their part to play in the final picture; the exactitude of place, time and date; the painstaking collection of evidence and the use of statements by witnesses; and the final denouement in which the whole mystery is explained. In addition, there is a memorable villain in the person of Count Fosco, the prototype of many of the later sinister fat men of detective fiction, film, and television.

The missing element is the absence of an actual detective, though Walter Hartright makes a very satisfactory substitute – and in any case this element was to be introduced into *The Moonstone* (1868), generally regarded as Wilkie Collins's best novel after *The Woman in White*, with the appearance of a police investigator named Sergeant Cuff. It was in fact, Charles Dickens who, much influenced by his friend, invented the first English fictional detective fifteen years before, in *Bleak House* (1852–1853). But it was Sergeant Cuff with his cool, logical deductions who was the real prototype of the modern detective. *The Woman in White*, however, is not only a story of mystery and detection. For one thing, elements of the old Gothic horror novel still survive in it. All kinds of assaults are made on the reader's nerves: the main characters are frequently subject to premonitions; people moan and shriek in their sleep; a spaniel is brutally shot for no satisfactory reason on the day Marian arrives at Blackwater Park; another dog cringes in terror when Sir Percival tries to pet it, and both landscapes and houses are described in phrases that suggest evil or foreboding. Yet, at the same time, part of the strength of *The Woman in White* lies in the fact that it is solidly rooted in social realities.

It would be wrong, though, to regard *The Woman in White* as no more than a sensational novel of mystery and detection. Even the most melodramatic of the characters and situations had their actual counterparts in Victorian life. Like Dickens in his crime novels, Wilkie Collins was seeking to combine the excitements of the old Gothic romance with the more recent type of novel, and on the whole *The Woman in White* is a triumphant vindication of the attempt. For one thing, its characters are far superior to the cardboard figures of most modern thrillers. Marian Halcombe in particular, with her plain face and beautiful body, her wit, intelligence, courage, and passionate loyalty, is a truly memorable fictional creation. Count Fosco, too, is a much more complex villain than most.

It is difficult for a modern reader to credit the bland assumption that women are by nature inferior and subservient beings with no brains or wills of their own, which lies behind Sir Percival Glyde's bullying of his wife and his attempt to make her sign the document which will hand over her fortune to him. Nevertheless, such things *did* happen, and wives *were* shut away in lunatic asylums so that their husbands could get at their money. At the time Wilkie Collins was writing, the law still allowed little protection in practice to married women and their property. As a modern critic, Sheila Smith, has said, he 'evokes a solid, commercial society and discloses the pressures and horrors behind the façade.'

It was his awareness of these issues, indeed, that turned Wilkie Collins in his final phase to propaganda novels – beginning with an attack on contemporary English marriage law in *Man and Wife* in 1870, and then going on to novels dealing with the problems of prostitution and other issues of the day. He continued to be a skilful storyteller and to employ all kinds of sensational incident, but the general effect of these later novels was neatly summed up by the nineteenth-century poet Algernon Charles Swinburne in this couplet:

What brought good Wilkie's genius nigh perdition?
Some demon whispered. 'Wilkie! Have a mission!'

But there is no question of the genius displayed in *The Woman in White*, which will continue to be remembered and read, both for the new resources it introduced into English fiction, and for its own sake.

Great Expectations

Charles Dickens

The publication in 1837 of *The Pickwick Papers* marked the beginning of Dickens's career as the greatest and most prolific of British story-tellers. Practically every novel that flowed from his pen was a masterpiece, but there is a good deal to be said for choosing *Great Expectations* (published 1860–1861) as a follow-up to *Pickwick*. Although quite late in date, it can be regarded as a kind of watershed in his literary career. For one thing, it is probably the most highly organized of all his novels, and perhaps the richest in poetic symbolism. It contains both the 'dark Dickens' (a term applied by modern critics to the more embittered, socially penetrating novels) and the 'sunny Dickens', which is more in evidence in *Pickwick* and *David Copperfield* (1849–1850); while, like the latter novel, it is written in the first person and has many autobiographical elements in it.

The importance of Dickens's childhood experiences has already been discussed in the chapter on *Pickwick*, and much of his life can be seen as a frantic search for a way of making good his early feelings of deprivation. Sometimes he sought it in spells of phenomenal hard work; at other times in outbursts of animal spirits.

He sought it, too, in his relationships with women. In its early years his marriage with Catherine Hogarth was a happy one, but perhaps it was impossible for any woman to satisfy Dickens's hunger for love, or his yearning for an all-loving, all-understanding Madonna-figure. To begin with, this need was partially met by Catherine's sixteen-year-old sister Mary, and when she died Dickens was heartbroken. Her place was to some extent filled by another of his young sisters-in-law, Georgina, who took his part when the deterioration of his relationship with his wife led, in 1858, to a separation. But the immediate cause of the separation was probably a young actress named Ellen Ternan, by whom Dickens may have had a child, but who was no more able than anyone else to live up to his expectations.

In spite of the conviviality and exuberance he often displayed in company, Dickens was in many ways, therefore, a deeply frustrated and lonely man. One of the ways in which he tried to fill the void in his emotional life was by cultivating a peculiarly close relationship with his public. In the magazines he edited he was continually addressing his readers in terms of the most confidential intimacy. The public readings from his works which he began in 1858 served the same need, and the physical and emotional strain imposed by them was largely responsible for his premature death in 1870. There is little doubt, too, that Dickens's craving for reparation of his own deep-seated sense of childhood hurt lay behind his passionate reforming campaigns. As he knew in his bones what it was like to be an outcast he felt a burning sympathy for all other outcasts: the poor, the mad, the eccentric, the child and the criminal. It has been suggested, in fact, that there is a natural bond in Dickens's work between the child and the criminal.

Nowhere, perhaps, can the interaction between the forces that shaped Dickens's life and his creative vision be seen more powerfully at work than in *Great Expectations*.

Summary

The young hero, Pip (a childhood contraction of his surname Pirip), is yet another of the many orphans in Dickens's novels. He has been brought up by his fierce and unloving sister and her husband, Joe Gargery the blacksmith, very much in awe of his wife but Pip's warm friend and champion. The first chapter is one of the most dramatic in the whole of Dickens. It is one, moreover, that immediately brings orphan child and criminal into contact. On a cold afternoon in the local churchyard, with the wind blowing across the marshes from the sea, Pip is suddenly confronted by a convict named Abel Magwitch who has escaped from a prison-hulk moored off the nearby coast. Terrorized by the convict's threats, Pip brings him food and drink and a file to remove his leg-iron. In delivering these, Pip comes across another escaped convict who disappears into the mist.

The following day, with the convict Magwitch still shivering out on the marshes and Pip shivering for fear of what will happen when his sister discovers that the pork pie he has taken to the convict is missing, is Christmas Day – a deliberately ironic touch in view of the fact that for Dickens Christmas was always charged with a special emotional intensity as a symbol of family warmth and unity. Pip is saved from exposure over the pork pie by the arrival of a squad of soldiers detailed to search for the escaped convicts. They want Joe, who as a blacksmith can help them to rivet on fetters, to come with them, and Pip goes too. Magwitch is found, locked in deadly combat with the other escaped convict, but before he is taken back on board he saves Pip from any further trouble over the pork pie by pretending that he had burgled the Gargery home himself.

Another variation of the theme of lovelessness now begins. The rich and eccentric Miss Havisham of Satis House invites Pip to become the playmate of her young ward, Estella. Miss Havisham is perhaps the weirdest and poetically the most powerful of all Dickens's half-crazed characters. When Pip is first presented to her, she is sitting in an armchair dressed in the wedding finery which she has worn every day since, as a young woman, she was jilted at the altar. After stopping all the clocks in the house, she had insisted that everything be left exactly as it was on her wedding day, even the decaying remains of the wedding-feast. For Pip, though, the vital element in this house of the dead is the beautiful Estella. But she is cold, distant, unattainable – as her name, meaning a star, implies. This is what Miss Havisham has trained her to be; for, in her crazed mind, Estella is destined to become an instrument of vengeance against the whole tribe of men.

After Pip has been working for some time as an apprentice to Joe at the smithy, a London lawyer named Jaggers arrives with the astounding news that an unknown benefactor wishes Pip to be brought up as a gentleman (so that he is now 'a young fellow of great expectations'). Pip jumps to the conclusion that he has Miss Havisham to thank, especially as he knows that Mr Jaggers is her lawyer. Miss Havisham says nothing to disabuse him, and later encourages him in his devotion to Estella, though Estella herself warns Pip that she has no heart – 'no softness there, no – sympathy – sentiment – nonsense'.

In London, Pip grows into a fine young gentleman. He becomes a close friend of Herbert Pocket, a relative of Miss Havisham's (with whom he had had a fight at Satis House when they were boys), but falls foul of a surly and unprincipled young aristocrat named Bentley Drummle. He visits Mr Jaggers and meets his housekeeper Molly, one of the many criminals whom Jaggers has successfully defended. When Pip's sister dies, he attends her funeral, but is ashamed to find that he now looks down on the rough and illiterate Joe. He is, however, not so besotted with his grand way of life as to be incapable of generosity for, when on his twenty-first birthday he receives a large cheque from his unknown benefactor, he sets his friend Herbert up in business, though without his knowledge. In the meantime, Pip is paying court to Estella, but she shows no sign of any softening towards him, and to add to his despair, encourages the attentions of his enemy, Bentley Drummle.

Then one night Pip receives a visit from an elderly man, coarse in speech and appearance, whom he recognizes as Magwitch. Transported to Australia, Magwitch has prospered there, devoting his wealth, through his lawyer Jaggers, to making a gentleman out of Pip – the one human creature from whom he had received some warmth and kindness. Now, under the assumed name of Provis, he has come to England to see Pip, at great peril to himself because as a convict transported for life he will be hanged if discovered in England.

At first Magwitch fills Pip with nothing but repulsion. He has built the edifice of his 'great expectations' on the fantasy foundation of Miss Havisham's bounty. Now he realizes that they were laid by a criminal and were, for all he knows, the proceeds of crime. What is more, it follows that his belief that part of Miss Havisham's plans for him was that he should marry Estella, is also a fantasy. It is as if all these years he has been caught up in the dead, unreal atmosphere of Satis House, a partaker of Miss Havisham's own delusions.

After a sharp struggle with his conscience, Pip realizes that it is his duty to do everything in his power to help Magwitch, whose old enemy Compeyson (the convict Pip had seen him fighting with on the marshes years before) is already on his track. It emerges, too, that Compeyson was the man who had jilted Miss Havisham after extracting a considerable sum of money from her.

After Estella has married Bentley Drummle, who treats her with great brutality, Pip pays another visit to Satis House. Miss Havisham's mouldering wedding dress catches fire, and though Pip beats out the flames, badly burning himself in the process, Miss Havisham dies.

Back in London, Pip learns another startling piece of news. Estella's mother was Jaggers's housekeeper – and her father was Magwitch himself, though the latter thinks that his daughter had died in infancy. Pip also discovers that Magwitch is now in great danger and decides to take him to the continent. They are about to board the steamer from their row-boat when a police launch, with Compeyson on board, catches up with them. Magwitch and Compeyson close with each other and fall into the water. Compeyson is drowned, but Magwitch, badly injured against the hull of the steamer, is rescued and placed in a prison hospital.

Pip devotes himself to the dying man. He keeps from him the knowledge that his property will be forfeit to the State (so that his efforts to secure Pip's future have been in vain) and tells him that the daughter he thought to be dead – 'is living now. She is a lady and very beautiful. And I love her.'

After Magwitch's death, Pip falls seriously ill – and the first face he sees, as he emerges from his delirium, is that of Joe who has hurried to London to nurse him. When Pip is on the road to recovery, Joe, fearing that too great a social gap has grown up between them, secretly departs. But Pip has learned his lesson. As soon as he is well enough, he hurries down to his childhood home to tell Joe what is in his heart, and departs to face his future, secure in the knowledge of Joe's love and forgiveness.

Pip takes on a job as a humble clerk in Herbert Pocket's firm, accompanies him to a branch he has opened in the Far East, and eventually works his way into a partnership. When, eleven years later, he returns to England, he visits the site of the now demolished Satis House – and meets Estella there. On the face of it this is one of those gross coincidences so beloved by writers of romance. In fact Estella's presence has the poetic rightness of the sudden appearance of a character in a fairy tale, and the impression is heightened by the mysterious background of night, moon, and stars, so that Estella seems almost like an emanation of the 'cold, silvery mist'.

Estella's brutal husband has died after squandering most of the fortune left her by Miss Havisham. Now she realizes that all that had happened to her was the inevitable consequence of excluding love from her heart. 'I have been bent and broken,' she tells Pip, 'but – I hope – into a better shape.'

There is evidence that Dickens meant to end the novel there. In the event he could not bring himself to do so, but he resists the temptations of a conventionally happy and over-sentimental ending and leaves the question of an eventual marriage between Pip and Estella an open one.

Critical commentary

Great Expectations marks one of the peaks of Dickens's achievement in his handling of plot, comedy, character- ization, theme and, above all perhaps (though these ele- ments cannot really be separated), of imagery and symbol. In view of what has been said about Dickens's own early ex- periences and the special feelings he had, in consequence, about childhood, it is hardly surprising that much of the imagery – in situation as well as in language – derives from them. To take one of the less distressing aspects first, it is significant that his favourite childhood reading was *The Arabian Nights Entertainments*. Next to the New Testament and the plays of Shakespeare, it is the book he quotes from or alludes to most frequently in his novels. The influence of this primitive, oriental pattern of story- telling with its continuous postponements and renewals, was probably one of the reasons why Dickens made such brilliant use of the similar pattern of serialization. What is certain is that even the most complex and sophisticated of his novels retain something of the compulsive quality to be found in the ancient story-tellers, combined with the passionate make-believe of a lonely childhood. In- corporated into them all is the child's-eye view, the quality that belongs to myth and folk-tale and which is one of the reasons for their universal appeal.

Frequently, however, a nightmare element enters into this child's-eye view. An obvious example is in the des- cription of Pip's first horrifying meeting with Magwitch.

But often it breaks into the comic scenes as well. The Christmas dinner at the Gargerys', attended by such unforgettable characters as Mr Wopsle, the ham actor, Mr Hubble, the wheelwright, and Joe's Uncle Pumblechook, is rightly regarded as one of the highlights of Dickensian comedy. But there are some distinctly bizarre elements about it. For example, there is the way in which the adults ingeniously turn their own greedy devouring of roast pork into an occasion for delivering homilies to Pip (except for Joe who is surreptitiously helping him to gravy, and who is still at heart a child himself):

> 'Swine,' pursued Mr Wopsle, in his deepest voice, and pointing his fork at my blushes, as if he were mentioning my Christian name; 'Swine were the companions of the prodigal. The gluttony of Swine is put before us, as an example to the young ...'

All this is undoubtedly very funny, but it also has about it what the novelist George Gissing, in a very perceptive study of Dickens which was published in 1898, aptly called 'the inextricable blending of horrors and jocosity'. Many of the comic characters and scenes in Dickens have a grotesque, fantastic element, a tendency suddenly to swell out like gigantic shadows thrown on to a wall – the kind of comedy, in fact, which would make a child uncertain whether to laugh hysterically or scream with terror.

Other animals figure in this scene too. Mrs Joe Gargery calls Pip 'a little monkey' and Pip envisages his situation as that of 'an unfortunate little bull' goaded in the arena. The effect of this animal imagery is to emphasize the status of the child as an outcast from adult society. In addition, Pip in the same scene is treated almost as if he were a criminal; Mr Hubble for instance, declares that the young are 'naturally wicious' at which all the other adults (except Joe) murmur 'True!' – and gaze at Pip in a particularly unpleasant and personal manner. And Pip, of course, *has* just been associating with criminals, and also feels himself a criminal because of the file and provisions he has stolen on Magwitch's behalf.

A little later, the animal imagery is applied to actual criminals. The soldiers arresting Magwitch and Compeyson 'growled' at them 'as if to dogs' – and to Pip's imagination the prison-ship lying beyond the mud of the foreshore 'looked like a wicked Noah's ark'. It should be noted, too, that in the churchyard Magwitch had called Pip 'a young dog', said he would like to eat him, and smacked his lips over his plump cheeks.

The animal imagery 'shared' between Pip and Magwitch in effect expresses the kinship between them as fellow outcasts from love. Other similar clusters of imagery can be noted in *Great Expectations*, and their presence is indicative of a very important point that must be made about Dickens – that his approach was fundamentally that of a prose poet. F. R. Leavis wrote in 1950, in a reassessment of Dickens:

> The final stress may fall on Dickens's command of word, phrase, rhythm and image; in ease and range there is surely no greater writer of English except Shakespeare.

The theme of the outcast from love runs right through the book. Miss Havisham, of course, is an extreme example. She exemplifies the terrible results of a capacity for love turned into a purely negative hatred, and she is also a profound study of the effects of a refusal to come to terms with grief and loss. She is like a figure in the mediaeval *danse macabre* (or dance of death) – an embodiment almost of death-in-life. Her setting emphasizes this: the mouldering splendour and the disintegrating wedding-cake covered with cobwebs and with spiders crawling out of it. The whole picture has the kind of horrifying clarity with which, all senses on the alert, certain unpleasant scenes are witnessed in childhood – and remembered with a shudder ever after. The Latin word 'satis', incidentally, means 'enough' – finished, that is, or ended, and Satis House is in effect a house of the dead.

As for Estella, at one level the whole business of her parentage is pure melodrama, but at the poetic level it is justified, because it, too, reinforces the underlying theme of lovelessness. For fundamentally, Estella and Pip are in exactly the same situation. Estella has been brought up as a fine lady and Pip as a poor boy, but the 'great expectations' of both in effect derive from the same criminal source, and Magwitch is in a sense father to both of them. In addition, both have paid the same price for failing to reconcile the child and the criminal within them, that of lovelessness – Estella by allowing Miss Havisham to turn her into an instrument of vengeance and hatred, and Pip by turning his back on Joe Gargery.

Yet reconciliation *can* be achieved, Dickens is saying, but only by the very means that has been rejected – that of love itself. This is the main significance of the deathbed scenes in the prison hospital. For Pip brings to Magwitch the reassurance of a love stripped clean of all 'great expectations', utterly free from the taint of material obligations of any kind.

In opening his heart to Magwitch, moreover, Pip has also opened the way back to Joe Gargery and all he stands for in the way of simple human values. Dickens was just as prone to sentimentality as he was to melodrama, and there are some tear-jerking moments in the reunion at Pip's sick-bed between the two. But fundamentally it rings clear and true, because it is in essence a return to Pip's better self, and when he exclaims: 'O God bless him! O God bless this gentle Christian man!' he means precisely what he says.

It is significant that in order to achieve his 'redemption' he has in effect to revert to childhood. 'I fancied I was little Pip again', he says, and then just afterwards: 'the tenderness of Joe was so beautifully proportioned to my need, that I was like a child in his hands.' It is a further illustration of the fact that having loved Magwitch the criminal, Pip can also love the outcast child and so achieve a healing synthesis of the two. It may also be indicative of

Dickens's need to bring together the idealized loving father of infancy and the feckless, improvident father of his later childhood who had landed in a debtor's gaol, filling the abandoned boy with terror and a sense (as he himself admitted) of 'a prison taint'. But it is also in the spirit of the New Testament pronouncement: 'Except ye … become as little children, ye shall not enter the kingdom of heaven.'

Perhaps the greatest achievement of the novel is in its profoundly imaginative demonstration of the transfiguring power of human love. G. K. Chesterton was not exaggerating when he wrote of 'that great furnace, the heart of Dickens'.

Our Mutual Friend

Charles Dickens

The first words of *Our Mutual Friend* are: 'In these times of ours ...' It is the only novel of Dickens's which is devoted to society as it was in the mid-Victorian world. His previous plots, while containing much that was of urgent contemporary relevance, were usually set some years back (and farther back still, of course, in his two historical novels). *Our Mutual Friend* (1864–1865) was also the novel which, next to *Barnaby Rudge* (1841), took Dickens longest to write. In part, this was owing to the interruptions caused by his public readings, and in part to his failing health. But almost certainly it was also because the contemplation of the world in which he was living filled him with so much alarm and despondency.

Summary

The opening chapter of the novel introduces 'Gaffer' Hexam, engaged in his daily business of fishing corpses out of the Thames, while his daughter Lizzie reluctantly rows his boat. The scene then switches to the *nouveaux riches* Veneerings:

> Mr and Mrs Veneering were bran-new people in a bran-new house in a bran-new quarter of London. Everything about the Veneerings was spick and span new ...

At their dinner-table are assembled, among other guests, the worthless Lammle and the fatuously ponderous Mr Podsnap. Their conversation turns to the impending return of John Harmon to inherit the fortune of his estranged father. His inheritance is dependent, however, on his marrying a girl named Bella Wilfer; failing this it will go to his father's foreman, Mr Boffin. Old Harmon, nicknamed 'the Golden Dustman', had made his fortune out of 'coal-dust, vegetable-dust, rough dust – all manner of dust.' This chapter ends with one of the Veneerings' guests opening a newspaper which contains the announcemen of John Harmon's death – by drowning.

Two guests, Mortimer Lightwood, a solicitor professionally concerned with such cases, and his friend Eugene Wrayburn, a languidly aristocratic young barrister, help in the inquiries on the body Hexham and his daughter have found in the river. The papers on the corpse confirm that it is John Harmon. Also present at the identification is an agitated stranger who gives his name as Julius Handford, and then disappears. During these proceedings Wrayburn is much taken by the beauty of Lizzie Hexam.

The scene shifts to the shabby home of the soft-hearted Wilfer (a clerk in Mr Veneering's business house), his imperious wife, and their beautiful but haughty and headstrong daughter, Bella. The mysterious Julius Handford arrives and takes lodgings with the Wilfers, under the name of John Rokesmith.

The genial Nicodemus (or Noddy) Boffin and his equally good-natured wife are full of plans for spending their newly inherited wealth. Boffin takes on an old scoundrel with a wooden leg named Silas Wegg who poses as a literary man, to help him with his education, and appoints the mysterious John Rokesmith to be his private secretary. The Boffins then call on the Wilfers and suggest that, as Bella has been disappointed in her expectations, she should come to live with them. In the course of their call they refer to John Rokesmith, the Wilfers' lodger, as 'our mutual friend'.

A ruffian known as 'Rogue' Riderhood, meanwhile, is spreading rumours, much to Lizzie's distress, that Gaffer Hexham was responsible for the murder of John Harmon. Her brother, Charley, is befriended by a grimly dedicated schoolmaster named Bradley Headstone through whom Dickens vents his distrust of contemporary educational methods – already fiercely expressed in *Hard Times* (1854) – which in his view encouraged materialistic, insensitive attitudes.

Rogue Riderhood now denounces Gaffer Hexam as the murderer of John Harmon, in the hope of receiving the reward that Boffin has offered. But before Hexam can be questioned, his body, too, is found in the river. Eugene Wrayburn goes to Lizzie to comfort her, and continues to call on her after she has gone to live with Jenny Wren, the diminutive, crippled dolls' dressmaker, one of Dickens's weirdest but most engaging child grotesques. Lizzie's brother also brings his schoolmaster to meet his sister, and Bradley Headstone falls violently in love with her, and into just as violent a jealousy of Wrayburn.

The Boffins call on an old woman named Betty Higden, who scrapes a living as a 'child-minder' and looks after a nameless orphan known as 'Sloppy'. The ruling passion of old Betty's life is a determination never to enter a workhouse – one of the main targets of Dickens's social indignation ever since the publication of *Oliver Twist* (1837–1838) – and when the Boffins adopt Sloppy, old Betty, in order not to stand in his way, takes to the road with a basket of goods provided by the Boffins.

Mr and Mrs Lammle, hoping to make money on the transaction, now plan a match between poor little Georgiana Podsnap and Fledgeby, a young man who has been nicknamed 'Fascination' because of his callow ineptitude in the presence of the opposite sex – but who operates a moneylending business behind the reluctant cover of an old Jew, named Mr Riah, whose near-saintly character and unfailing good manners are in the strongest possible contrast to those of his young master and the whole Veneering world.

At this point, the mystery of 'John Rokesmith' (alias Julius Handford) is revealed to the reader. He is none other than John Harmon. On his voyage back to England to collect his inheritance he had confided in Radwood, the third mate of the ship who bore a remarkable resemblance to him, his plan of concealing his own identity for a time so that he could form some judgement beforehand of Bella, the girl allotted to him in his father's will. Radwood (intending to masquerade as John Harmon) had, with the help of Rogue Riderhood, drugged Harmon, removed his papers, and then thrown him into the river. Harmon had, however, managed to struggle ashore, while the mate had himself been murdered – and it was the mate's body, with John Harmon's papers on it, which Gaffer Hexam had retrieved. But the real John Harmon has decided not to reveal himself because he does not want to take the inheritance away from the Boffins who are doing good with it, and because, now deeply in love with Bella, he is determined that if he can win her it must be for himself alone. By now, however, Bella has made up her mind to make a grand marriage, and when John Harmon proposes she coldly rejects him.

Meanwhile, John Harmon (in yet another disguise) has extracted a written confession from Rogue Riderhood that his accusation of murder against the late 'Gaffer' Hexam was false, and he sends a copy to Lizzie who is greatly relieved. Pestered by both Bradley Headstone and Eugene Wrayburn, Lizzie eventually turns to Mr Riah for protection. He finds her lodgings outside London, and she gets work in a paper mill nearby.

Something very strange now happens to Mr Boffin. He appears to lose all his former amiability, becomes mean and avaricious – and, above all, treats his secretary 'John Rokesmith' with great severity. One night, Wegg and his friend Venus (who runs a macabre business selling various

anatomical specimens to the teaching hospitals) watch Mr
Boffin dig an old bottle out of one of the mounds of dust.
In one of the other mounds Wegg himself discovers a box
containing a will leaving Harmon's money not to Boffin,
but to the Crown. Wegg and Venus conspire to blackmail
Mr Boffin.

While these events are taking place, old Betty Higden
creeps into a meadow to die. Lizzie Hexham discovers her
and reassures her that she will not send her to the workhouse or allow her to have a pauper's burial. 'John Rokesmith' and Bella make arrangements for the old woman's
funeral and Bella takes the opportunity of being alone
with John to beg his forgiveness for her previous mercen-
ary behaviour, and to express her indignation at the way
Mr Boffin is treating him. Bella is further chastened by
her friendly contact with Lizzie Hexam and by Lizzie's
purity of motive in running away from the temptation
represented by Eugene Wrayburn. Shortly afterwards,
however, he discovers Lizzie's whereabouts, and Bradley
Headstone also tracks her down and sees her with him.

By now, the Lammles are being pressed for payment on
a bill acquired by Mr Riah – as they think, for the real
purchaser is Fascination Fledgeby. The Lammles hope to
get out of their predicament by informing the Boffins that
Rokesmith has been pestering their ward, Bella, in the
hope that this will lead to Rokesmith's being dismissed,
and the appointment of Mr Lammle in his place. Mr
Boffin does in fact dismiss Rokesmith, but Bella, full of
indignation on his behalf, announces that she is leaving
too. This time, when 'John Rokesmith' proposes, she
joyously accepts him and not long afterwards they marry,
settle down contentedly and in due course have a baby.
In the meantime, the Lammles' plan of ingratiating themselves with the Boffins has misfired and they are forced to
live cheaply abroad. Mr Riah, unable to demean himself
any longer with such a scoundrel as Fledgeby, gives up his
job with him.

After being again rejected by Lizzie, Eugene Wrayburn

is struck down by a man dressed to look like Rogue Rider-hood (it is in fact Bradley Headstone) and thrown into the river. But Lizzie hears the splash and rescues him. When he recovers sufficiently, Lizzie agrees to what is assumed to be a death-bed marriage. Meanwhile, Head-stone gets into a fight with the real Rogue Riderhood at the edge of a deep lock and deliberately takes him over with him, and both men are drowned.

Bella now learns the true identity of her husband, and that Mr Boffin's change of character had been a plan to open her eyes to the corrupting power of money and to show her where her true feelings lay.

Silas Wegg's plot is thwarted, with the help of Mr Venus, who has repented of his part in it. It was, in fact, the bottle that Wegg had seen Mr Boffin removing from the mound, and not the box which he himself had found, which had contained the real last will and testament of old Harmon. This had left the whole fortune to Mr Boffin, but he had hidden it in the hope that young John Harmon would one day turn up, and he now insists on waiving his own legal right to it.

In the general tidying-up that follows, Jenny Wren is helped in her dolls' dressmaking and strikes up a roman-tic friendship with Sloppy; Mr Riah is rewarded for his help in undoing Fascination Fledgeby, and Bella's father becomes secretary to his son-in-law. Eugene Wrayburn recovers and is a changed man, profoundly grateful to have married Lizzie. The Wrayburns and Harmons become close friends.

Critical commentary

There are evident flaws in *Our Mutual Friend*: for ex-ample, the contrivances of the plot, involving a missing heir, a number of disguises, and no less than three wills; the melodramatic elements in Bradley Headstone's char-acter; the rather wooden figure of the good Jew Riah; the impossibly stilted form of speech attributed to Lizzie and

Charley Hexam; various passages of gross sentimentality, and the unbearably coy descriptions of the wedded bliss of Bella and John Harmon.

All these features, however, are present in Dickens's earlier novels: he was always an uneven writer, and lapses of style or taste were the price that had to be paid for his incredible fluency and fertility. A more serious flaw, perhaps, is his tendency in *Our Mutual Friend* to protest rather than to demonstrate. Not that he had hesitated to give vent to his personal opinions and prejudices in his earlier novels – what is new in *Our Mutual Friend* is an occasional note of stridency and shrillness. It arises from the fact that at this stage in Dickens's life a certain self-defeating, negative element had entered into his thinking. There is, for example, his onslaught on organized charity in any form as a sapping of individual effort and integrity, and a corruption both of the giver and the receiver. Whereas, too, Dickens had earlier been an ardent advocate of universal education, in *Our Mutual Friend* he has turned against the whole concept, seeing in it nothing but a breeder of pedantry and a means of perpetuating a corrupt and worthless society.

There is no doubt that these are symptoms of the increasing disgust with which Dickens had come to regard the society in which he lived. There are times in *Our Mutual Friend* when this disgust seems to extend to himself, so that he writes as if he were contemptuously parodying his own earlier methods by exaggerating the grotesqueness of the comedy, the baroque nature of the backgrounds, and the violent and macabre elements in the melodrama. At the same time, the exaggerations themselves result in the release of new effects of language, imagery, and imaginative insight.

There are some startling ones: for example, in the description of the dinner party at the Veneerings. Twemlow, much in demand by the Veneerings because he is the cousin of a lord, is compared to a dining-room table: 'Mr and Mrs Veneering ... arranging a dinner, habitually started with Twemlow, and then put leaves in him or added guests to him ...' Mrs Podsnap, another of the guests, is described as 'quantity of bone, neck and nostrils like a rocking horse', and Lady Tippins 'with an immense obtuse drab oblong face, like a face in a tablespoon', is also introduced in non-human terms. The hard, brittle epithets and images which Dickens employs here, often spat out without the connective articles (there is no 'a', for example, before Mrs Podsnap's 'quantity of bone'), mark a change from his earlier exuberantly ironic style, as though, to quote Angus Wilson, he had 'devised a new and brilliant shorthand to level his fierce attack at a rotten society.'

Mr Podsnap (one of Dickens's major comic creations) is also described as, 'a too, too smiling large man, with a fatal freshness on him' – that odd phrase 'fatal freshness' is more suggestive of a joint of beef in a butcher's shop than of a living human being. The inhabitants of the Veneering world, indeed, are often presented as zombies or living corpses – not so very different, in fact, from the corpses which are fished out of the river, or from the anatomical specimens Mr Venus keeps in his shop. This is all part of Dickens's sustained onslaught on the corrupting and de-humanizing effects of a society which was (in his view) devoted to purely materialistic values. In this connection there are all kinds of telling correspondences: there is an obvious similarity, for example, between the way in which Gaffer Hexam makes his living from the flotsam and jetsam of the river, and the way old Harmon has made his fortune from the flotsam and jetsam of the dry land – and those mounds of dirt and rubbish symbolically dominate the whole book.

There is a good deal of pessimism and disillusionment in all this, and there are moments when Dickens comes close to the universal disgust of Jonathan Swift. On the other hand, the old faith in the essential goodness of the human heart, which had been so pronounced a feature of *Pickwick* and the Christmas books, does occasionally break through. Money does not corrupt either the Boffins, John Harmon, or, in the long run, Bella Wilfer, for example. At the same time, the thorough and merciless hatred directed against the whole world of the Veneerings is far more positive in its effects than negative, resulting in a sustained brilliance of satire and a variety of ironic resources expressed in the most vigorous and original language and imagery, which perhaps only Swift himself has ever equalled.

There is, too, one notable advance, already evident in *Great Expectations*, and that is in the characterization of the heroine. For Bella Wilfer, like Estella in the earlier novel, is in marked contrast to the doll-like heroines that had gone before, truly convincing as a woman, with a woman's body as well as a woman's mind. Most critics are agreed that it was Ellen Ternan, the young mistress of Dickens's later years, who was responsible for this advance. It was she, too, who was probably responsible for the remarkable power and understanding of Dickens's study of sexual jealousy in the character of Bradley Headstone.

This, however, is only one part of Headstone's make-up. He is also a study in criminal psychology. In one of his childhood reminiscences of the notorious criminal area of London known as Seven Dials, Dickens had exclaimed: 'Good Heaven! what wild visions of prodigies of wickedness, want, and beggary arose in my mind out of that place!' These 'wild visions' had always haunted Dickens, and now he gave them full rein in his portrait of Bradley Headstone. Perhaps Dickens's own feelings of guilt in the knowledge that he, like so many other outwardly respectable Victorian men, was leading a double life, with a mistress tucked away in a secret love-nest, had made these 'wild visions' more accessible to him. The language applied to Headstone is full of horror and violence. When the passions that lurk beneath the respectable exterior are aroused, for instance, his lips quiver uncontrollably, his face turns 'from burning red to white, and from white back to burning red.' At one point, he punches a stone wall until his knuckles are raw and bleeding, and at another (while he is planning his attack on Eugene Wrayburn) blood suddenly gushes from his nose. All this, of course, is undoubtedly melodramatic. But it is the melodrama of the Elizabethan playwrights rather than that of the Gothic thriller. Bradley Headstone would not have seemed at all overdone to an audience accustomed to the ravings of, say, the mad Hieronymo in Thomas Kyd's *The Spanish Tragedy* (1592).

This is not the only way in which *Our Mutual Friend* is reminiscent of Elizabethan drama. A good deal of the action has the same kind of poetic symbolism. An outstanding instance is in the frequent use of disguise. John Harmon assumes three separate identities; Bradley Headstone, too, uses a disguise in his attack on Eugene Wrayburn. In addition, the principle of disguise is employed by Boffin when he pretends to have changed his character.

Water is also used throughout the novel in a way that recalls both Elizabethan drama and folk-tale. The novel begins with Gaffer Hexam retrieving from the river the falsely identified corpse on which the whole plot hinges. Later Gaffer Hexam himself is drowned; Rogue Riderhood is nearly drowned when he is run down by a steamer, and actually so when he and Bradley Headstone plunge to their deaths together. The Thames is often depicted as a kind of polluted 'river of life'. On the other hand, John Harmon, the hero of the novel, emerges from the river a changed man with a new identity – and Eugene Wrayburn – as Alan Shelston, a recent writer on Dickens has pointed out, endures what is in effect 'a ritualistic immersion' whereby he is born anew, his old dilettante boredom and selfishness washed away. Again, Wrayburn's conversion is as unbelievable realistically as that of Orlando's wicked brother Oliver in Shakespeare's *As You Like It* – but perfectly convincing in terms of poetic convention.

Some consideration of these symbolic elements is inescapable in discussing *Our Mutual Friend*. The final emphasis, though, must fall on the more important fact that in this his last completed novel Dickens revealed fresh resources of linguistic energy and imagery. 'It is my infirmity', he wrote, 'to fancy or perceive relations in things which are not apparent generally.' One only has to turn to some of the similes used in the second chapter of the novel to describe the Veneerings and their guests to realize how true this is – and the 'infirmity' to which Dickens referred is, of course, one that is absolutely essential to the true poet. It is the poet in Dickens above all that enabled him to turn *Our Mutual Friend*, in spite of all its weaknesses, exaggerations and improbabilities, into what Lionel Stevenson has called 'a terrifying epic of a doomed society'.

Through the Looking-glass, and What Alice Found There

Lewis Carroll

Lewis Carroll's real name was Charles Lutwidge Dodgson. He was born in 1832 in the village of Daresbury in Cheshire, the son of the vicar. He was educated at Rugby and then at Christ Church, Oxford. He gained a first-class degree in Mathematics in 1854, and was appointed lecturer in mathematics at Christ Church, a post which he held until 1881. His first publications were mathematical text-books and he continued at intervals to publish books and papers on both mathematics and logic, of which the most valuable is *Euclid and his Modern Rivals* (1879). It was in 1865 that he first used the pseudonym of Lewis Carroll, when he published the first of his two Alice classics, *Alice's Adventures in Wonderland*. The other children's books in the 'Lewis Carroll' series were: *Phantasmagoria* (1869); *Through the Looking-glass* (1871); *The Hunting of the Snark* (1876); *Rhyme and Reason* (1883); *A Tangled Tale* (1885); and *Sylvie and Bruno* (in two parts, 1889 and 1893).

Although he was ordained, he never occupied a living and, owing to a stammer, seldom preached or conducted a service. He was completely orthodox in his Church of England views and completely Tory in politics.

Basically then, his life was the sheltered, uneventful and highly conventional one of the typical bachelor don. In his hobbies, though, he was rather more colourful. From childhood he was interested in puppetry and sleight-of-hand, and throughout his life enjoyed performing tricks, especially for children. He took up photography when it was still in its infancy, and became highly proficient in it. He was devoted to such games as croquet, backgammon, billiards – and chess. He invented many mathematical and word puzzles, games, ciphers and aids to memory. He was fond of opera and the theatre at a time when such interests were frowned upon by the Church authorities, and the famous actress Ellen Terry was one of his lifelong friends.

But his greatest joy was entertaining little girls. In his diary he adopted the Roman symbol of a white stone to denote a particularly lucky day, and nearly always when he wrote 'I mark this day with a white stone' he was referring either to a meeting with one of his established small girl-friends, or to his encounter with a new one. Far and away his favourite among them was Alice Liddell, the daughter of the Dean of Christ Church, who was ten years old when, in 1862, Lewis Carroll and another clergyman took her and her two sisters on a rowing trip up the Thames – and entertained them with the story which later became *Alice in Wonderland* (illustrated, like its successor, with the wonderful drawings of John Tenniel). There is no indication that Lewis Carroll was conscious of anything but the purest intentions in his relations with his small girl-friends and there is not a single hint of any impropriety in the affectionate reminiscences written by many of them in later life.

On the other hand, there are aspects which, in the light of modern knowledge of the workings of the subconscious mind, obviously indicate some ambivalence of motive. He thought the naked bodies of little girls extremely beautiful. He enjoyed sketching or taking photographs of them in the nude – though only with their mother's permission, and only if the children concerned were completely at ease about it. He left instructions that, in case these pictures should cause embarrassment, they should, after his death, either be destroyed or returned to the sitters or their parents.

It would be ludicrous, therefore, to suggest that Lewis Carroll was in love with Alice Liddell in the usual sense. In her later married life, she looked back with affection and gratitude to her childhood friendship with him. But the evidence is that his feelings towards her were much like those of a man in love, and that he felt for her all that he was capable of feeling.

Summary

There must be a distinctly 'Wonderland' element in any attempt at a precise summary of *Through the Looking-glass*, but the book does have its dream-like shape and progression, largely because of the game of chess. According to Alice Liddell, the starting-point of the book was the chess tales that Carroll used to tell the Liddell girls when they were learning how to play the game.

This motif is introduced early on in the first chapter when Alice, indoors on a winter's afternoon with the snow falling outside and 'sitting curled up in a corner of the great armchair', asks her black kitten if it can play chess. Shortly afterwards, Alice says to the kitten: 'Let's pretend that you're the Red Queen, Kitty!' and when it fails to imitate the actual chess piece placed in front of it, Alice holds the kitten to the mirror, and threatens it with expulsion to 'Looking-Glass House'. A moment later, Alice herself is on the other side of the mirror among little animated chess pieces scattered in the hearth. After she has set the White Queen on the table, so that she can attend to her screaming baby (a white pawn) and then placed the White King beside her, she looks into the King's memorandum-book and sees a poem which can only be read when she holds it up to the mirror.

The next chapter takes Alice into the garden of talking flowers, where she catches sight of a hill which recedes when she approaches it. On the advice of the flowers, she walks in the opposite direction and, as this is looking-glass land, is soon facing it. It is now that Alice realizes that all the surrounding country is marked out as a giant chess-board by means of little green hedges and brooks. 'It's a great huge game of chess that's being played – all over the world...' Alice exclaims – one of the remarks which made some commentators think that *Through The Looking-glass* was an allegory of the political situation that eventually led to the First World War. Then the Red Queen, having met Alice in the garden and made her the White Queen's pawn, takes her hand and rushes her along at break-neck speed. Her comment: 'Now *here*, you see, it takes all the running *you* can do, to keep in the same *place*' has also been frequently quoted as denoting a rapidly changing political situation. The Red Queen now zooms away on one of her sweeps across the board leaving Alice to contemplate her next move. In a preface to a later edition of the book, Lewis Carroll claims that the game 'is correctly worked out, so far as the *moves* are concerned', and that the eventual checkmate of the Red King is 'strictly in accordance with the laws of the game' – and he added a diagram to support his contentions. Chess experts agree that the game is more or less plausible, though some of the moves are careless to say the least – hardly surprising in view of the characters attributed to the pieces. The details of the game are interwoven with the fantasy with remarkable skill. Alice never speaks to a piece that is not on the square neighbouring her own, for instance; and the two Queens rush about busily while their husbands for the most part remain fixed and inactive – as in an actual chess-game; while the eccentricities of the Knights, including their tendency to fall off their horses, are in perfect accord with the zig-zag leaps they perform on a chess-board.

So Alice sets off on her first move, and having traversed three squares, gets into a waiting train. After some puzzling exchanges with the Guard and her fellow-passengers, who include a goat, a gnat, and an old gentleman dressed in white paper (this is intended to be a political joke, and Tenniel's illustration is almost certainly a cartoon of Disraeli), the train gives a leap into the air, and deposits Alice on the fourth square. She finds herself in a wood 'where things have no names', and where she promptly forgets her own name.

Alice now meets Tweedledum and Tweedledee – who are mirror-image forms of each other, as Carroll indicates by having Tweedledee constantly exclaim 'Contrariwise' – and as Tenniel was careful to make plain in his illustrations (he collaborated closely with Carroll in getting all the left-right details correct). It is Tweedledee who sings that marvellous nonsense-song 'The Walrus and the Carpenter' – the characters of which the modern novelist, J. B. Priestley has interpreted as archetypes of two kinds of politician.

Tweedledum and Tweedledee quarrel over a broken rattle and prepare to fight, but it grows dark as 'the monstrous crow' flies overhead, and in the hurricane it produces a shawl is blown into Alice's hands. Then, the White Queen comes running wildly on one of her pre-cipitate chess moves. There is another famous discussion, between Alice and the White Queen, in which the latter explains, 'The rule is, jam tomorrow and jam yesterday – but never jam *today*,' and adds: 'That's the effect of living backwards.' This is followed by a superbly fanciful illus-tration of the White Queen's 'logic' in which she puts a sticking-plaster on her finger and then starts screaming – before she actually pricks her finger.

In one of the most effective dream sequences in the book, the White Queen now changes into an old sheep, knitting behind the counter of a shop stocked with strange goods that disappear from the shelves whenever Alice focuses her eyes upon them. The shop then merges into a boat, with Alice at the oars – and as the boat glides along and she gathers sweet-scented water-rushes there are some poignant evocations of the real Alice as Carroll remem-bered her long ago on the Thames. Then the boat merges

into the shop again, with the Sheep, alias the White
Queen, walking to the far end in order to set an egg
upright on a shelf – and also to make her next move in
the chess game.

The shop merges into the countryside, and the egg
swells into Humpty Dumpty, sitting on his wall. There
are various cryptic exchanges, a typically reverse reference to 'un-birthday presents', and a discussion on the use
of names which veils some complex points in semantics
(which Carroll also dealt with in his learned book, *Symbolic Logic*). As Humpty Dumpty is the philologist of
the book, Alice recites the 'Jabberwocky' poem to him,
and he explains the difficult words for her – 'Brillig', for
instance, 'means four o'clock in the afternoon – the time
when you begin *broiling* things for dinner.' At the end
of the scene, of course, the conceited Humpty Dumpty
has his 'great fall', and all the King's soldiers, continually
stumbling over each other, and all the King's men, continually tumbling off their horses, rush on in a scene of
great confusion (beautifully illustrated by Tenniel). Alice
finds the White King himself nearby 'busily writing in
his memorandum-book'. In his account of the Messengers'
approach, Carroll was poking fun at the very earnest
Anglo-Saxon scholarship practised at Oxford in his day –
and both his and Tenniel's renderings of the Messengers'
costume and 'attitudes' were almost certainly taken from
one of the Anglo-Saxon manuscripts in Oxford's Bodleian
Library. (Also, many of the words in the 'Jabberwocky'
poem are related to Anglo-Saxon ones). Angus Wilson
quoted part of this passage on the title-page of his novel
Anglo-Saxon Attitudes (1956) – an instance of the way
Carroll's work has entered into the mythology and literary provenance of adult writers.

After the White King has eaten his ham sandwich and
munched his hay, he, his Messengers, and Alice hurry
off to see the Lion and the Unicorn, 'fighting for the
crown'. While they are watching, Alice sees the White
Queen 'running across the country' (frightened of the

Red Knight, though Carroll's diagram chess-board shows that she was in no danger from him and could have taken him herself, but, true to her general carelessness and stupidity, she fails to notice the fact). Various turns of phrase, combined with Tenniel's illustration, show that the Unicorn is Disraeli (who Carroll, as a Tory, supported) and the Lion his great Whig (or Liberal) rival, Gladstone. When in accordance with the last line of the ancient poem about the Lion and the Unicorn – the deafening noise of the drums causes Alice to jump across another brook, and so into another square, she is hailed by the Red Knight with a cry of 'Check!', but is rescued by the White Knight, after a ding-dong fight, according to 'the Rules of Battle'. It is generally agreed that the White Knight is a comic self-portrait. When he has removed his helmet, he reveals 'shaggy hair', a 'gentle face and large mild eyes', like Carroll's own. The White Knight's fondness for bizarre gadgets (such as the upside-down box; the mouse-trap, in case mice infest his horse's back; and the recipe for a pudding made of blotting-paper, gunpowder and sealing-wax) is a comic reminder of Carroll's own interest in such things – though some of *his* inventions, which included a pocket chess-set for travellers, were not all quite so crazy. Alice's reflections, just before the White Knight sings his long song, touch a melancholy note which probably reflects Carroll's hope that Alice Liddell, too, would remember their friendship.

When the White Knight has finished his song and Alice has helped him back into his saddle after another of his numerous falls, she runs down a hill and jumps over the last brook into 'The Eighth Square', where she finds that a golden crown has appeared on her head. In chess terms, the white pawn has reached the last row at the opposite end of the board, where it is converted into a queen. Perhaps, too, there is the feeling in Carroll's mind that Alice Liddell had run down the hill and jumped over the last brook into womanhood.

Alice finds the fat and stupid White Queen on one side

of her, and the sour-faced, sharp-tongued Red Queen on the other (the White King is placed in check by this move, but neither side notices it). The two Queens subject Alice to an odd examination and prove to her that she is not really fit to be a Queen (there are all sorts of further paradoxes and upside-downnesses during this conversation), invite her to a royal feast, fall asleep, and then vanish.

Eventually, Alice finds herself at the banquet seated at the head of the table between the White and the Red Queen. It is a decidedly surrealist affair, with the leg of mutton standing up and bowing on its dish, the plum-pudding protesting 'in a thick, suety sort of voice' after Alice has cut a slice from it, and the behaviour of the Queens growing increasingly rowdy and threatening.

Then Alice seizes hold of the Red Queen – thus achieving a perfectly legitimate check-mate of the Red King who has been asleep throughout the whole of the game. But the Red Queen grows smaller and smaller in Alice's grip – until she finds that it is the black kitten she is shaking. The book ends with one of Carroll's most moving poems, an acrostic in which the first letters of each line spell 'Alice Liddell', and which contains the line – 'Still she haunts me, phantomwise.' The poem (like the prefatory verses) evokes the boating trip 'In an evening of July' when Carroll first told the Liddell girls the story of Alice, and expresses the hope, attended by reflections on the fleetingness of human life, that other children will hear and enjoy the tale.

This concluding emphasis on life as a dream is a fitting one. It is a reminder that the book itself has been a dream (perhaps a dream within a dream). It is a reminder, too, that in spite of all the fascinating intellectual games it contains, it really does express Lewis Carroll's personal vision of life.

Critical commentary

In spite of their stern moral and religious principles, the rigidity of their social attitudes, and their overwhelming concern with respectability, the Victorians had a great capacity for comedy and humour. Some foreign commentators, though, have been puzzled by their predilection for nonsense, puns, and linguistic juggling which are such notable features not only in the work of Lewis Carroll but also in the nonsense verses of his contemporary, Edward Lear (the first volume of which appeared as early as 1846), in the two volumes of *Bab Ballads* (1869 and 1873) by W. S. Gilbert, the librettist of the famous Gilbert and Sullivan operas, and in many other publications both in verse and prose. To a large extent, however, at a time when so many people were deeply disturbed by the breakdown of many of the old intellectual, philosophical, and religious certitudes in the face of the assaults of Darwinian scientific discoveries and speculations, the appeal of nonsense lay precisely in its non-sense, which afforded a blessed relief from too much painful thought. At the same time, a delight in juggling with words and language has been common from the beginning of civilized human history, and the very oppressiveness of their moral and social environment heightened that delight as far as the Victorians were concerned. Nonsense represents the subconscious, irrational impulses of the mind, and one of the reasons why the Alice stories have been so successful, among adults as well as among children, is that they incorporated this element.

That *Through the Looking-glass* is no simple children's book will have been evident from the synopsis. During the past fifty years or so there has been a tremendous amount of very adult comment on the inner meanings of Lewis Carroll's work. So much so that G. K. Chesterton, writing in 1932 (a hundred years after Carroll's birth) expressed his 'dreadful fear' that Alice's story had already passed into the clutches of the scholars, so that it was becoming 'cold and monumental like a classic tomb'.

The possible implications that lie behind the title, for example, have attracted a great deal of attention. A looking-glass, of course, reflects things the other way round, and this idea dominates the whole book. This wrong-way-round kind of game was a favourite of Lewis Carroll's. He wrote letters in mirror-writing, for instance; he drew pictures which changed into different ones when held upside-down; he liked to play his collection of musical boxes backwards, and so on.

At one level this is merely fun of the kind that naturally fascinates the mind of a child. Many of the adult commentaries based on it do seem unnecessarily pompous and erudite, but the fact that they have been made cannot be overlooked. To the psychologists, his obsession with reversals is evidence of disguises, concealments, and evasions. To the mathematician, they simply point to Carroll's mathematical preoccupations. In particular, they have intrigued philosophers and scientists who are interested in the whole complex question of left and right handedness, symmetry and asymmetry – and even, more recently, in matter and anti-matter. There can be little doubt that *Through the Looking-glass* influenced the early science-fiction writers who explored the possibilities of left-right reversal – H. G. Wells's *The Plattner Story* is the classic example. The novelist Compton Mackenzie went so far as to declare that Lewis Carroll's reverse-image world 'prepared the mind of the average man to accept the truth of relativity, the stellar arithmetic of Sir James Jeans' as well as 'the swirling phantasmagoria of psycho-analysis'.

It is interesting, too, to note that Arthur Stanley Eddington (like Sir James Jeans, a famous astronomer) was much intrigued by 'Jabberwocky', the poem which Alice eventually manages to read in the mirror. He refers to it on a number of occasions in his scientific writings. For example, he compares the abstract, syntactical structure of the poem to the branch of mathematics known as 'group theory'. He also suggests in his book *The Nature of the Physical World* that the physicist's description of an elementary particle is really a kind of Jabberwocky – words, that is, applied to 'something unknown' that is 'doing we don't know what ...' The first two lines of the poem read:

> Twas brillig and the slithy toves
> Did gyre and gimble in the wabe

and Eddington applies these fascinating word-coinages to the more baffling aspects of the behaviour of oxygen and nitrogen electrons in the structure of the relevant atoms. This is by way of being a tribute to the scientific, philosophical and linguistic implications of Carroll's work in *Through the Looking-glass*.

As far as children are concerned, the natural response to this poem is Alice's own: 'It seems very pretty ... but it's rather hard to understand!' But the vast amount of adult attention devoted to the poem is an indication of the importance the word-coinages and the other verbal jugglings in *Through the Looking-glass* assumed. For one thing, they appealed to many writers who were interested in breaking up the formal structures of words and sentences (just as some painters, for example Picasso, did those of line and form). Thus, the American critic Edmund Wilson has argued that James Joyce, in his novel *Finnegans Wake* (1939), in seeking to express states of mind 'which do not usually in reality make use of words at all' does so by adopting something that is more like 'the looking-glass language of "Jabberwocky" than ... anything resembling ordinary speech.' That Lewis Carroll's book was in Joyce's mind is evident from the fact that he makes Humpty Dumpty one of the central symbols of *Finnegans Wake* – the great cosmic egg, whose fall, like that of the drunken Finnegan, reflects, in the texture of Joyce's fable, the Fall of Lucifer and the Fall of Man.

Some literary critics have also seen the influence of

Carroll's book in the work of Franz Kafka, the great twentieth-century Austrian novelist of frustration, disorientation and persecution, particularly the game of chess, in which the pieces are engaged in moves they cannot properly comprehend and at the mercy of other hands and wills which are neither reliable nor consistent, and which may themselves only have the remotest idea how the game is to end – a most appropriate metaphor, it has been suggested, for the condition of modern man, lost and rootless in a vast and baffling universe.

Many of the more baffling conversations in *Through the Looking Glass*, though at one level they are simply there for the fun of it, pose all kinds of complex philosophical questions. An outstanding example is the occasion when Tweedledee asks Alice what she thinks the Red King, fast asleep near by, is dreaming about, and Alice protests that it is impossible to tell.

> 'Why, about *you*!' Tweedledee exclaimed, clapping his hands triumphantly. 'And if he left off dreaming about you, where do you suppose you'd be?'
> 'Where I am now, of course,' said Alice.
> 'Not you!' Tweedledee retorted contemptuously. 'You'd be nowhere. Why, you're only a sort of thing in his dream!'
> 'If that there King was to wake,' added Tweedledum, 'you'd go out – bang! – just like a candle!'

The attitudes Carroll has in mind here are those of the eighteenth-century philosopher, Bishop Berkeley, who argued that all material objects, including human beings, are only 'sorts of things' in the mind of God; and of Dr Johnson, who believed that he had refuted Berkeley by kicking a large stone. Bertrand Russell, the mathematician and philosopher commented on the Red King's dream in a BBC radio programme: 'A very instructive discussion from a philosophical point of view ...' Carroll comes back to this fascinating speculation at the end of the book, when Alice wonders 'who it was that dreamed it all ... it *must* have been either me or the Red King. He was part of my dream, of course – but then I was part of his dream too!'

But it must be remembered that *Through the Looking-glass, and What Alice Found There* was written to entertain children, and that it is still enjoyed by children who have not the slightest inkling (except perhaps at some instinctive level) of all the clever theories the adults, including the author himself, bring to it. The greatest triumph of the book, perhaps, is that it operates so successfully on two distinct planes.

Middlemarch

George Eliot

It has often been said that *Middlemarch* (published 1871–1872) is the nearest equivalent in English fiction to Tolstoy's *War and Peace*, if for no other reason than the sheer size of the canvas that it covers. Its genesis helps to explain its scope. George Eliot first referred to 'A novel called *Middlemarch*' in her journal at the beginning of 1869. But at this stage it was to be about a brilliant young doctor named Lydgate who settles in Middlemarch (that is, Coventry) and whose scientific aspirations are hampered by lack of funds and by marriage to the worldly Rosamond Vincy. George Eliot began work on the novel in the August of the same year, and added a sub-plot about Rosamond's brother, Fred. Then, over a year later, in December 1870, she reported in her journal: 'I am experimenting in a story "Miss Brooke", which I began without any serious intention of carrying it out lengthily ...' It was not until some time later that she realized that the stories of Lydgate and of Dorothea Brooke were in many respects complementary – and decided to merge the two with Dorothea as the central character. By now, however, each story had expanded in various directions, and in its final form the novel contained in addition two other quite considerable story-lines: that of Mary Garth, and that of the hypocritical evangelical banker Nicholas Bulstrode – as well as a number of subsidiary narrative threads.

Summary

The novel begins with the orphaned Dorothea and her sister Celia living at Tipton Grange with their uncle, Mr Brooke. The two sisters are strongly contrasted. Whereas Celia, the younger, is pretty, practical and content to abide by the conventions of society, the handsome, passionate, highly intelligent and deeply religious Dorothea is dissatisfied with the role of Lady Bountiful – the only one society allows her – and longs for some wider sphere of activity. She is wooed by her neighbour, the limited but good-natured young Sir James Chettam. But it is another neighbour, a physically unattractive bachelor clergyman thirty years her senior named Edward Casaubon, who fascinates Dorothea because for years he has been engaged on a mammoth research project, and, in a typically exalted mood, she imagines that to sit at his feet and perhaps even be allowed to help would provide her with the opportunities for devotion to higher things for which her nature craves. Casaubon's own energies, such as they are, are mainly concentrated on his studies, and although he can hardly help being attracted by Dorothea's devotion, he is impatient for the courtship to end so that he can get back to them. The auspices could hardly be worse – but the pair are duly married and set out for their honeymoon in Rome – while Sir James Chettam transfers his affections to Celia and eventually marries her.

Although the story of Dorothea and Casaubon has so far occupied the forefront of the novel, all the other main characters have been skilfully introduced, among them Tertius Lydgate, the well-connected and dedicated young doctor who has recently taken up a medical practice in the area.

Lydgate is attracted to Rosamond Vincy, the beautiful but self-willed daughter of the Mayor of Middlemarch. He has no intention of marrying, however, until he has 'trodden out a good clear path for himself' in his beloved medical researches and plans for medical reforms. Rosamond, with her fair skin, the 'delicate undulations' of her slim figure, her hair of 'infantine fairness', and her eyes 'of heavenly blue, deep enough to hold the most exquisite meanings an ingenuous beholder could put into them' was the type of woman, as the tart tone of these comments indicates, whom George Eliot most disliked. But on the whole her analysis of Rosamond preserves a remarkable artistic objectivity, and she emerges as perhaps the most memorable study in fiction of a certain type of feminine egoism.

The reality and concreteness of her presentation in these early scenes owe a good deal to the contrasting but just as fully realized presence of Mary Garth, who is short, plain and 'brown' but in her own sturdy but generous-hearted way, every bit as feminine as the beautiful Rosamond. Mary is companion-housekeeper at a large farmhouse called Stone Court (in the nearby village of Lowick) to her crotchety and tyrannical uncle, Peter Featherstone. Rosamond is also a niece of Mr Featherstone's, through his second marriage. Rosamond's good-natured but pleasure-loving and extravagant brother Fred hopes to inherit his uncle Featherstone's land and money when he dies. Fred and Mary are in love, but she refuses to accept him unless he changes his careless ways and works for his living.

The story now switches to Dorothea and Casaubon in Rome – and to the profound and moving anatomy of an unhappy marriage. Casaubon is finding his young wife's youthful enthusiasm for his researches irritating rather than helpful – because in his heart of hearts he suspects that they are futile and that the 'Key to all Mythologies' will never be written.

Also in Rome is Will Ladislaw, a young half-Polish relative of Casaubon whose education he had paid for. Will's conversations with Dorothea throw into relief the narrowness and Puritanism of her education, cultural ideas and responses to the beauties of Rome, and give her a first glimpse of the existence of wider horizons. With his youthful good looks and bright golden hair he affords, too, the greatest possible contrast to Casaubon. By the time Dorothea and Casaubon leave Rome, Will – in the most romantically adoring and honourable way imaginable – has fallen in love with Dorothea.

Back at Middlemarch, Mary Garth's upright and kind-hearted father, Caleb, has put his signature to one of Fred Vincy's bills. When Fred cannot raise the money (he already has unpaid bills at college where he had been unsuccessfully studying to be a clergyman) Caleb, his wife and Mary have to put their savings together in order to meet it, much to Mary's anger. Not long after, Fred falls seriously ill. Lydgate is called to attend him and this throws him into close contact with Rosamond. He tries to stick to his resolution against marriage, but the sight of the tears in Rosamond's blue eyes when he speaks coldly to her is too much for him.

At Lowick Manor, her new home, Dorothea is beginning to face the dreary reality of marriage to Casaubon. After a minor disagreement he has a slight heart attack and Lydgate attends him, privately warning Dorothea that he must avoid mental agitation or excessive application to his studies. Old Mr Featherstone also falls seriously ill. On the night of his death, he tries to get Mary Garth to burn the most recent of his two wills. She refuses, in the absence of a lawyer or witnesses, to be involved in such an action. In fact, the later will disinherits Fred Vincy, leaving the bulk of the property and money to an unknown and unattractive illegitimate son of Featherstone's named Joshua Rigg, who soon moves into Stone Court. To the Garth family's great joy, Sir James Chettam asks Caleb to become agent both of his own estate of Freshitt and of Tipton Grange.

Mr Brooke, affected by the excitement attending the attempts of the Whigs to carry the Parliamentary Reform Bill, decides to go into politics himself. He buys *The Pioneer*, a local newspaper, and asks Will Ladislaw (who is staying with him) to run it and to write his political speeches. Will accepts, glad of the chance to live near Dorothea. Casaubon, however, wrongly suspecting that Dorothea engineered Will's invitation to Tipton Grange, writes to tell Will he is not welcome at Lowick Manor, ostensibly because he is shocked by Will's inflammatory articles in *The Pioneer* – but secretly because he is jealous of him.

Casaubon, anxious to press on with his researches, demands from Lydgate the truth of his condition – and is told that he might die suddenly at any time. Shaken, Casaubon at first coldly rejects Dorothea's mute sympathy, withdrawing alone to his study. Dorothea is deeply hurt and at first bitterly resentful until her compassion reasserts itself and husband and wife achieve a moment of genuine tenderness and communion.

Lydgate, now married to Rosamond, finds his wife has little sympathy with his ideals and aspirations, while her determination to cut a dash in Middlemarch society is landing them in debt. Among the frequent visitors to their elegant house is Will Ladislaw, whose radical views Lydgate shares, and with whom Rosamond enjoys flirting. One of Lydgate's companions, little though he likes him, is the local banker, Nicholas Bulstrode, chief instigator of plans for a new Fever Hospital – who offers Lydgate a free hand in its running, though without salary. Bulstrode is disliked in Middlemarch, largely because of his canting evangelicism, and Lydgate increasingly shares his unpopularity besides incurring the hostility of the older-established doctors because of his reforming zeal and up-to-date methods of treatment.

An atmosphere more reminiscent of Dickensian melodrama than a George Eliot novel is gathering round Bulstrode. Joshua Rigg has to turn his drunken, sponging step-father, John Raffles, out of Stone Court. Raffles accidentally picks up and takes with him a piece of paper – with the name Bulstrode on it (to whom Joshua has sold Stone Court). Later Raffles, having found the piece of paper, reappears apparently in possession of some mysterious secret about Bulstrode's past, in which Will Ladislaw too is somehow implicated.

To Dorothea's dismay, her husband asks her to promise, in the event of his death, to go on with his work herself. Mercifully, Casaubon dies before she can commit herself. In his will he leaves all his money and property to Dorothea – but with a codicil whereby she forfeits them if she ever marries Will Ladislaw. Neither the idea of Will as a potential lover nor the suspicion that Casaubon regarded him in that light had ever entered Dorothea's head. She experiences 'as if it had been a sin ... a violent shock of repulsion from her departed husband.' To her dismay it is followed by 'a sudden strange yearning of heart towards Will Ladislaw.' Mr Brooke, after a disastrous nomination speech, withdraws his candidature and tells Will he is going to sell *The Pioneer* and (prompted by Sir James Chettam, who dislikes Will) advises him to leave Middlemarch. Will, ignorant of Casaubon's codicil, is too proud to court Dorothea for fear of appearing a fortune-hunter, but obstinately stays in Middlemarch.

Dorothea is now alone and in control of Lowick Manor. On Lydgate's recommendation, she appoints a kindly, middle-aged clergyman, Camden Farebrother, to the living on her estate. Farebrother is a link with another of the story-lines for he is in love with Mary Garth. Despite this, when Fred Vincy (having at last obtained his degree) asks him to plead his cause with Mary, Farebrother generously does so. Fred Vincy rescues Caleb and a party of railway surveyors from an attack by angry farmhands who are frightened that the coming of the new railroad will harm their way of life. Caleb, convinced that there is good in Fred, now takes him into his office to teach him estate management.

Rosamond has a miscarriage as a result of going riding – against her husband's express wishes – with one of Lydgate's grand cousins; and, largely as a result of her fecklessness and extravagance, Lydgate has to mortgage their furniture to keep creditors at bay.

Raffles now appears once more, and the secret of the hold he has over Bulstrode is revealed. As a young man, Bulstrode had married an older woman, Mrs Dunkirk, the wealthy widow of the man with whom he had worked in a not always honest pawnbroking business. Before marrying him, Mrs Dunkirk had wanted to find her runaway daughter Sarah and her son. Bulstrode, with an eye on the Dunkirk fortune, had bribed Raffles – the only other person to know Sarah's whereabouts – to keep silent. When Mrs Dunkirk died, Bulstrode as her husband had safely inherited all her money. Moving to Middlemarch, he had later married Harriet Vincy and become a wealthy and apparently respectable banker.

Learning from Raffles that Sarah Dunkirk's son is in fact Will Ladislaw, Bulstrode offers Will part of the inherited Dunkirk fortune. Will contemptuously rejects Bulstrode's attempt to salve his conscience and save his reputation by means of tainted money. But the episode decides Will to leave Middlemarch and he calls on Dorothea to say goodbye. He now knows about the codicil to Casaubon's will, but his poverty and pride still stand in the way of his love. Their parting is full of agonizing silences and frustrations.

By now the Lydgates' financial situation is desperate. Against her husband's wishes again, Rosamond writes for help to Lydgate's rich and aristocratic uncle, Sir Godwin, and is snubbed for her pains. Swallowing his pride, Lydgate asks Bulstrode for a loan, which he refuses. However, Raffles is now found at Stone Court, seriously ill, and Bulstrode summons Lydgate to attend him. Anxious to secure Lydgate's goodwill in case Raffles in his delirium should blurt out his secret to him, Bulstrode now advances Lydgate the thousand pounds he needs. Lydgate leaves express instructions not to give Raffles any alcohol, but when the housekeeper innocently asks Bulstrode if she can give the patient brandy, Bulstrode (after a terrible struggle with his conscience) allows her to do so – and Raffles dies. Lydgate is puzzled by his death but stifles his uneasiness, while Bulstrode now feels that he is safe. Raffles had, however, previously told his story to a horse-dealer at a fair, and the rumours begin to gather. They affect Lydgate as well as Bulstrode when it emerges that he had attended Raffles and has also been suddenly freed of his financial embarrassments. At a public meeting in the Town Hall to discuss various local health matters Bulstrode is denounced and both he and Lydgate are forced to quit the meeting.

Lydgate confides his problems to the sympathetic Dorothea, but when the next day she calls on Rosamond (bringing with her a cheque which will free Lydgate from his indebtedness to Bulstrode) it is to find her with her hands clasped in Will Ladislaw's. Dorothea leaves the letter she brought for Lydgate and hurries away. When she has gone, Will turns on Rosamond in a fury, making it crushingly clear that she means nothing to him. In the solitude of her home, meanwhile, Dorothea – for the first time fully admitting to herself the force of her love for Will – abandons herself to a storm of grief and jealousy. The following day, however, she goes to see Rosamond, who, her illusions shattered and expecting nothing but scorn from Dorothea, is shaken out of her self-centredness by her visitor's warmth and kindness. Acting with genuine unselfishness for once, she assures Dorothea that she herself means nothing to Will, and that Dorothea is the only woman he cares for. She follows this up later by letting Will know what she has done.

Rosamond and her husband are now reconciled while Will calls on Dorothea at Lowick Manor and reiterates the impossibility of their marrying because of his poverty. Dorothea assures him that it means nothing to her to give up Casaubon's fortune (she has money of her own anyway), and finally emotion overcomes them both and sweeps aside all doubts and objections.

The various story-lines are now expertly rounded off. Mrs Bulstrode persuades Caleb to let Fred Vincy manage Stone Court. Fred and Mary marry, prosper and have three sons. The Lydgates move to London and he becomes a successful society doctor, much to his wife's delight and his own chagrin when he remembers his earlier dreams. Dorothea and Will have a son, and Will is elected to Parliament and does well in his political career.

Critical commentary

On the whole, *Middlemarch* is an astonishing feat of synthesis. It is one, moreover, that takes in a wide range of social as well as personal relationships, and it is not by accident that George Eliot subtitled the novel 'A Study of Provincial Life'. The period is that of the struggle over the passing of the Parliamentary Reform Bill of 1832 (George Eliot took great pains with her historical and social facts), and the characters between them represent the main strands of the provincial class system of the period. The Brooke family belong to the country gentry; the Vincys are typical representatives of the newly prosperous bourgeoisie, at a point when the younger generation were beginning to acquire social pretensions and indulgences of their own, and the Garths belong to the solid yeoman class from which George Eliot herself derived. Just as important are the outsiders, characteristic of the social mobility that was beginning to affect provincial as well as urban society: Lydgate, bringing with him the aura of wider intellectual horizons; Bulstrode, with his mysterious London past and dubious fortune, and Dorothea's lover, the half-Polish bohemian Will Ladislaw. In the view of Lionel Stevenson, *Middlemarch* 'Can almost be regarded as an attempt to reveal the whole Barsetshire panorama within the limits of a single work.' An earlier novelist than Trollope, though, must also be mentioned. The work of the 'miniaturist' Jane Austen may seem at the opposite pole to a vast novel like *Middlemarch*, but there are similarities between, say, the Highbury of Austen's *Emma* and the Tipton of *Middlemarch*, while in both cases marriage, with all its personal and social implications, provides the major unifying principle.

The brief Prelude to *Middlemarch*, though, is as far removed from the cool and ironic Jane Austen as it is possible to imagine. It begins with a typically Victorian sentimental picture of the infant St Theresa and her brother as they 'toddled from rugged Avila, wide-eyed and helpless-looking as two fawns.' It goes on to speak of St Theresa's 'flame ... fed from within' which 'soared after some illimitable satisfaction, some object which would never justify weariness, which would reconcile self-despair with the rapturous consciousness of life beyond self' – and which in her case found its outlet in 'the reform of a religious order'. But there have been many latter-day Theresas who 'have found for themselves no epic life wherein there was a constant unfolding of far-resonant action; perhaps only a life of mistakes, the offspring of a certain spiritual grandeur ill-matched with the meanness of opportunity...'

What is the point of this strange preamble? It is true that it bears on the case of Dorothea, but there is little real artistic justification for thus stealing the thunder of the story that is to follow. The point would not be worth dwelling on except that the general tone of the Prelude and the recurrence of words like 'rapturous' and 'ardour' are indicative of that element of emotional exaltation not properly brought under artistic control which was noted in connection with *The Mill on the Floss*. As F. R. Leavis says: 'It is a dangerous theme for George Eliot, and we recognize a far from reassuring accent.'

There are other lapses of a similar kind in the characterization of Dorothea. The tone falters badly, for example, in the scene where Lydgate calls on Dorothea to tell her about his troubles. It is in this scene that the dangers inherent in the Prelude particularly manifest themselves in George Eliot's anxiety to bring out the exalted, saintly attributes of her heroine. There is no question of Dorothea's real generosity or of Lydgate's very understandable gratitude as she assures him of her faith in him, promises to stand by him, to increase her contribution to the New Hospital and – after he has confided his difficulties with Rosamond – to go and talk to her. But there are too many phrases like 'noble nature', 'sweet trustful gravity' and so on applied to Dorothea. By the time Lydgate exclaims 'God bless you, Mrs Casaubon!' and rides away saying to himself 'This young creature has a heart large enough for the Virgin Mary', a decidedly theatrical, almost ludicrous note has crept in. At moments such as these, Dorothea, to quote F. R. Leavis again, is 'a product of George Eliot's own "soul hunger" – another day-dream ideal self.'

The self-sacrificial mood in which Dorothea pays her second visit to Rosamond is also perhaps too good to be true, and one cannot help wondering whether rage and jealousy, if uglier, would not have been more humanly convincing. The final two paragraphs of the book, moreover, take up again the idea of Dorothea as a latter-day St Theresa. It is done in a more restrained manner than before, but there is no doubt that George Eliot's preoccupation with this element constitutes the main weakness of the novel.

On the other hand, there can be no doubt that Dorothea is also a very real and warm-blooded presence. As Arnold Kettle has commented, it is Dorothea who 'of all the characters in the novel, most deeply captures our imagination. It is her aspiration to a life nobler than the Middlemarch way of life that is the great positive force.'

Will Ladislaw (who, it has been suggested, is based on George Henry Lewes) has often been criticized on the grounds that, like Stephen Guest in *The Mill on the Floss*, he never really comes to life, and that he is fundamentally a romantic, wish-fulfilling product of the immature side of George Eliot's imagination.

On the other hand, the relationship between Dorothea and Casaubon (who may be based on Herbert Spencer, the evolutionary philosopher who had once snubbed the youthful and hero-worshipping Mary Ann Evans – before she became 'George Eliot') is handled with the profoundest insight, understanding and compassion. The various levels of mutual disillusionment are most subtly explored, in a way that makes the 'frank' discussions of incompatibility in so many modern novels seem superficial by comparison. The physical element is there, expressed in what are fundamentally the only real terms – those of a longing for or a withholding of tenderness. Thus Dorothea's instinctive caresses are accepted at the intellectual level only, as 'of the most affectionate and truly feminine nature' – but at the same time Casaubon shows 'by politely reaching a chair for her' that he regards 'these manifestations as rather crude and startling'. Similarly, when Dorothea puts her hand on her husband's he lays his other hand on hers 'in a conscientious acceptance of her caress, but with a glance which he could not hinder from being uneasy.' The word 'conscientious' in itself speaks volumes.

The relationship between Lydgate and Rosamond, resulting in Lydgate's abandonment of his earlier high ideals about his work (which in some ways echo those of Dorothea) is almost as effective, and there are dozens of instances of the most subtle and delicate psychological penetration and insight in the depiction of many of the other characters, including some of the minor ones. There is, for example, the way in which Mrs Bulstrode reacts to the shock of her husband's disgrace. She loves him and knows she will forgive him, but first she shuts herself in her bedroom, because 'she needed to sob out her farewell to all the gladness and pride of her life.' Then, before she goes down to her husband to assure him of her continuing love, she instinctively performs a kind of symbolic preparation for the changed way of life that is before her by discarding her ornaments and putting on her plainest clothes. This scene in itself, with its deep human understanding, is sufficient to establish George Eliot as a great novelist.

It is here, rather than in matters of scope or scale, that a comparison between *Middlemarch* and Tolstoy's masterpiece is justified. Whole areas of experience, imaginative, psychological and spiritual, which Tolstoy explores in *War and Peace* are absent in Middlemarch. But no other English novel conveys so profoundly and so compassionately the strivings and relationships of individual men and women within the whole complex pattern of a specific and richly realized society.

The Way We Live Now

Anthony Trollope

The Way We Live Now explores a world very different from that of the Barsetshire novels. There, too, there was plenty of human frailty, dishonesty and jockeying for position. But there was also the sense of a stable social order centred on a rural way of life, and something of the golden glow of a retrospective idyll. From the mid-1860s onwards, Trollope's novels, as their centre of gravity tends increasingly to move from the country to London, display a mounting disquiet about the social, political, and moral well-being of the nation. This is present in most of the political novels, especially those of the Palliser series. Thus, the idealism of Phineas Finn in the novel of that name (1869) and its sequel *Phineas Redux* (1873) has a hard time combating the corruptions of the political life. The world of *The Prime Minister* (1875) and of *The Duke's Children* (1880) is one of frequent moral compromise, and both Phineas Finn and Plantagenet Palliser face the central question, asked by Phineas: 'Could a man be honest in Parliament, and yet abandon all idea of independence?' It is in *The Way We Live Now* (1874–1875), however, that this disquiet is most powerfully concentrated and savagely expressed. It is a very long novel, containing a huge cast and at least five major story-lines, all of them most skilfully dovetailed.

Summary

The novel hinges on the story of the Carbury family, and the widowed Lady Carbury is probably the pivotal character. She is in effect the representative of ordinary fallible human nature within the world Trollope is depicting. But, if she is an adroit practitioner of the values of her world, she is also their victim. The child of a broken marriage, herself married off at eighteen to a forty-four year old baronet who had treated her abominably, she has been forced since childhood to perfect the arts of deceit in order to survive. She is seen exercising them when she is first introduced, composing three letters, each couched in exactly the right terms of flattery and cajolement, to three very different editors of three very different periodicals, soliciting reviews of her bright but superficial book, 'Criminal Queens', which is about to be published. It is a subtle narrative device to start in this way, on the fringes of the society Trollope is about to depict, because by showing the cynicism, mutual back-biting and backscratching of the literary world Trollope demonstrates straight away how far the stain of corruption has spread.

For Lady Carbury, her literary labours are entirely subordinate to the ruling passion of her life: her beautiful but vicious and heartless young son, Sir Felix, who has already run through his own inheritance and is now demanding subsidies from the much smaller amounts left to his mother and his sister Henrietta (or Hetta). Though she has beauty, spirit and intelligence, Hetta has been brought up from infancy to believe that she is of no account beside Felix, and that 'men in that rank of life in which she had been born always did eat up everything.'

The head of the family is Roger Carbury, forty years old, still unmarried, and living at Carbury Hall, the small ancestral property in Suffolk. Roger is rooted in the countryside and is the one character in the book who refuses to compromise in any way with the prevailing scramble for riches. He is, in fact, the mouthpiece of the traditional values of the old English squirearchy in which Trollope himself most passionately believed.

Roger is deeply in love with his cousin Hetta, but has a rival in his close friend and distant relative, Paul Montague. Paul, basically honest and decent, typifies the rapidly increasing tie-up between English and American commercial enterprise in the 1870s, for he has business connections in America. While living there, he has formed an attachment to an American lady, Mrs Hurtle, one of Trollope's most remarkable creations. Beautiful, intelligent, cultured, and above all determined to fight for and preserve her independence, she may be seen as a representative of 'the New Woman', a term becoming current at the time.

It is taken for granted that Sir Felix Carbury must marry money. By far the richest potential candidate for the doubtful honour is Marie Melmotte, whose father's fortune is believed to be 'fathomless, bottomless, endless'. Augustus Melmotte himself is another remarkable creation: a portent of the great multi-millionaires of doubtful antecedents and principles soon to dominate the financial scene both in Europe and America. Rising from some anonymous continental gutter, he has gained his vast wealth by the most questionable means. Nevertheless, when he holds a ball at his great house in Grosvenor Square, the whole of London society flocks to it – all of them after what they can get. The ball, in fact, is a kind of microcosm of Trollope's main theme – that every section of society, not only the new rich but the old aristocracy as well, are willing to prostitute themselves to the new Mammon.

Typical of the latter category is Lord Alfred Grendall, who virtually sells himself to Melmotte as his paid sponsor in high society, while Miles Grendall, one of Lord Alfred's sons, becomes Melmotte's private secretary. Needless to say, Lady Carbury has seen to it that Sir Felix, too, shall be at the ball, and he and Marie Melmotte see a good deal of each other. Hetta is also there and spends much of her time with Paul Montague. They realize that they are in love with each other, though Paul is still entangled with Mrs Hurtle.

Paul's American partner, Fisker, now arrives in London. He is looking for capital to finance the building of a railway line from Salt Lake City in Utah to Vera Cruz in Mexico. Paul introduces Fisker to Melmotte who agrees to become the London chairman of the newly formed railway company. Most of Melmotte's hangers-on become shareholders or sleeping directors, among them Lord Alfred, his son Miles, and Sir Felix.

The situation is not dissimilar to that which Trollope describes in the literary world – the paperwork, whether in the form of shares or reviews, matters more than the real substance.

Lady Carbury now invites Melmotte's wife and Marie to one of her Tuesday evening literary gatherings – and Felix reluctantly agrees to be present. Marie Melmotte has had a wretched life, dragged from one country to another, sometimes in great poverty, and now utterly bewildered by her father's sudden rise to wealth. Since her arrival in London, she has been ruthlessly thrown on the marriage market by her father who wants an aristocratic title in the family. But Marie is not without spirit and, beginning to entertain the possibility of choosing a husband for herself, sees no reason why it should not be the beautiful Felix.

Felix himself is quite indifferent to Marie, content to go on sponging on his mother and sister in order to continue his dissipations and his wild gambling at the appropriately named Beargarden, a club frequented by his extravagant aristocratic cronies such as Miles Grendall and 'Dolly' (short for Adolphus) Longestaffe. Lady Carbury, though, determined that Felix shall follow up his advantage with Marie, takes him and Hetta on a visit to Roger at Carbury Hall – because she knows that the Melmottes will be staying nearby with the Longestaffes. The Longestaffes are in financial difficulties and hope that Melmotte will help them out. Mr Longestaffe has promised his wife and daughters that, as a reward for lowering themselves by entertaining the Melmottes, he will take them to London for the season – and, when later he breaks his promise, his high-spirited younger daughter Georgiana accepts an invitation to stay with the Melmottes in their London house.

Felix, urged on by his mother, reluctantly visits the Longestaffe house in order to see Marie – though on his way back to Carbury Manor he also goes to see Ruby Ruggles, the grand-daughter of one of Roger's tenant-farmers, with whom he has been heartlessly dallying. Before the Carburys return to London, Roger proposes yet again to Hetta who – ashamed of her mother's manoeuvres – reacts more gently to his proposal than she has done on previous occasions. Roger, in consequence, is now more hopeful, especially when Mrs Hurtle arrives in London. Meanwhile, Paul confesses to her that he now loves another woman; but Mrs Hurtle is not inclined to give him up without a struggle.

Eventually, Lady Carbury succeeds in getting her son to ask Melmotte for Marie's hand in marriage. Felix is haughtily incensed when Melmotte – 'This surfeited sponge of speculation, this crammed commercial cormorant' – dares to suggest that a handsome high-bred English gentleman like Sir Felix Carbury should also be able to provide for a wife such as Marie.

Nevertheless, Felix sets out to raise enough money to impress Melmotte. He makes an attempt to collect gambling debts owed him by Miles Grendall (in the course of which he discovers Miles cheating at cards) and 'Dolly' Longestaffe, who promises to settle with Felix out of the cash payment he will get from the sale of one of his family's country houses to Melmotte. Melmotte has already taken possession of the property, and, in order to get hold of the title-deeds before paying the Longestaffes any money, has forged 'Dolly's' signature on a letter.

Lady Carbury now puts into Felix's head the idea of

eloping with Marie, on the supposition that Melmotte would eventually be won round afterwards. By now, however, Melmotte has told his daughter that he has negotiated her marriage to young Lord Nidderdale. He tells Lady Carbury that if Felix marries Marie he will cut her off without a penny; but if Felix will agree in writing to give up his suit, Melmotte will see to it that he makes money in the City. Lady Carbury consults her editor friend, Mr Broune, and he advises her not to trust any of Melmotte's promises. Mr Broune also makes Lady Carbury a proposal of marriage. She refuses him, largely because of Felix, but gradually she and Broune draw closer together.

Back in Suffolk, Ruby Ruggles tells her grandfather that she won't marry John Crumb, the ponderous but honest miller to whom she is engaged – because she is in love with Sir Felix. After old Ruggles, in a drunken fury, has beaten her, Ruby runs away to London and John Crumb vows vengeance on the 'baronite'. Trollope handles the dialect exchanges skilfully and his rustic characters are more convincingly and sympathetically presented than in many other novels of the period. For Trollope, the peasantry are an essential part of the old hierarchical order in which he believed so deeply. Thus, it is presented as in the natural order of things that old Ruggles and John Crumb should appeal to the squire, Roger Carbury, who himself goes to London to search for Ruby. While he is there, he sees a good deal of Paul Montague, who at last steels himself to break with Mrs Hurtle. By a somewhat glib coincidence, Ruby Ruggles has found refuge with an aunt in whose boarding-house Mrs Hurtle is lodging; it is perhaps the only really noticeable join in the dovetailing of the plots. Ruby has been seeing a good deal of her 'baronite' in London, even though Felix has definitely committed himself to running away with Marie, who has stolen and cashed a cheque of her father's in order to provide Felix with ready money for the journey. When Felix blithely tells Ruby that the thought of marrying *her* has never crossed his mind, she is heartbroken, though when Roger tries to persuade her to return to the country and marry John Crumb, she defiantly refuses.

In the meantime, Melmotte's career has been soaring. He is accepted as Conservative candidate for Westminster and entrusted with the task of entertaining the Emperor of China, arriving on a state and trade visit – Trollope gives a grimly ironic account of the competition for invitations. In the City, too, Melmotte carries all before him, and at the board meetings of the Railway Company he does exactly what he wants because most of the directors are in his pocket, with the exception of Paul Montague who is increasingly rebellious. When the electoral campaign begins – savagely satirized by Trollope as an ignoble and dishonest farce – Melmotte is opposed by a Liberal candidate whose newspaper publishes scandalous stories about Melmotte's financial dealings, but that does not stop him being elected.

Marie now sets off for Liverpool to meet Felix and board a ship for America. Felix, with the proceeds of the cheque Marie had sent him, goes to the Beargarden, drinks and gambles the whole of the money away and misses his train to Liverpool. Marie is brought back home by Melmotte's agents.

Lady Carbury again confides in Mr Broune who tells her some much needed home truths about her over-indulgent treatment of Felix but, in order to save him from prosecution over the stolen cheque, Broune himself pays back the money to Melmotte. Marie still refuses to marry Nidderdale, and though she cannot help realizing that Felix has behaved despicably, she is still determined to become his wife.

Things now begin to go badly wrong for Melmotte. 'Dolly' Longestaffe is desperate for his rake-off from the sale of the family's country house and, in trying to force the money from Melmotte, discovers the existence of the forged letter authorizing the transfer of deeds to Melmotte. Rumours begin to spread that Melmotte has crookedly raised apparently much needed money on the Longestaffe property. Following this, the value of the shares in the railway drops, and the City begins to get nervous about Melmotte. The result is that when the grand banquet for the Emperor of China takes place, a number of the more prudent and influential guests, including the Lord Mayor of London, stay away.

Some of the other story-lines now demand attention. Georgiana Longestaffe announces that she is going to marry a successful fifty-year-old Jewish banker named Brehgert. Georgiana's father is horrified, openly insults Brehgert because he is a Jew, and insists that his daughter return at once to the country. Brehgert takes the insults of her family with dignity and forbearance. But when he explains that, as a result of his dealings with Melmotte, he faces considerable financial loss and will not immediately be able to provide her with the London house on which she had set her heart, she expresses her disappointment in a superior and high-handed manner – and is shocked and mortified when Brehgert breaks off their engagement.

Paul Montague at last declares himself to Hetta and she accepts him, to the bitter disappointment both of her mother and of Roger Carbury. Felix, however, angry when his sister reproaches him for his heartless behaviour to Marie Melmotte, lets out the story of Paul's attachment to Mrs Hurtle. Hetta breaks with Paul, telling him that it is his duty to marry Mrs Hurtle. As for Felix, he takes up with Ruby Ruggles again; but John Crumb comes up to London and gives Felix such a thorough thrashing that his looks are permanently spoiled and his spirit broken. In due course, John and Ruby are married.

Playing desperately for time, Melmotte now promises 'Dolly' and his father a settlement within the next few days. He has invested a considerable sum of money abroad in his daughter's name as an insurance for himself. When he tells Marie to sign over this money, so that he can pay off the Longestaffes, she refuses (still hoping to buy Felix), even after her father has savagely beaten her. Melmotte then forges her signature, and that of his clerk as witness, in order to raise money in the City. Unfortunately for Melmotte, the clerk discovers the forgery, so Melmotte orders his wife and daughter to pack up their jewels and prepare for flight. Marie makes one last play for Felix by going to Lady Carbury and telling her of the money in her own name. But Felix, still bandaged to the eyebrows after his battering from Crumb, refuses even to see her.

Melmotte makes his final appearance in the House of Commons. There is a certain grandeur about him now, and it is difficult not to reflect that he is in many ways more of a man than the effete and vicious aristocrats who had fawned and sponged on him in the days of his glory, and who have now deserted him. He dines in the House of Commons dining-room, though no one will sit at the same table with him, and savours to the full his cigar and his bottle of champagne. 'It was thus,' Trollope says, 'that Augustus Melmotte wrapped his toga about him before his death.' For on his return home, Melmotte takes prussic acid and is discovered dead the next morning.

Brehgert is entrusted with the task of disentangling the complicated affairs of Melmotte's financial empire – an ironic touch because the Longestaffes, eager to save their own money from the crash, must see a good deal of him. As for Georgiana, she eventually runs away with a curate. He is penniless but at least he is a gentleman, and ultimately the Longestaffes buy him a decent living.

In the meantime, Paul and Hetta are eating their hearts out for each other. Eventually Hetta goes to Mrs Hurtle who, with much generosity, reassures her that Paul really had broken with her and that their later meetings were entirely innocent. Lady Carbury is reconciled to her daughter marrying Paul, and Roger announces that their first child shall be his heir.

Melmotte's widow and daughter go to California with Fisker, and Mrs Hurtle accompanies them. Much later, Marie consents to be Fisker's wife. By an ingenious piece of craftsmanship, Lady Carbury again comes into the

centre of the picture as the novel draws to its conclusion.
With the help of Mr Broune, Felix has been packed off
to Germany in the charge of a clergyman. With Hetta
married, Lady Carbury is alone. She is even stripped of
her dreams of authorship, for though she has managed to
write a novel, Mr Broune has made her face the fact that
fiction is not her *métier*. She is about to sell her house and
go into lodgings when Mr Broune proposes again. She has
so poor an opinion of herself that she is genuinely astonished, but Mr Broune persists, and finally she agrees to
marry him. She does not have to give up her house 'and
Mrs Broune's Tuesday evenings were much more regarded
by the literary world than had been those of Lady Carbury.' The last chapter sees the whole family (with the
exception of Felix) reconciled and reunited at Carbury
Hall, in the heart of the English countryside, which to
Trollope represents all that is sane and healthy in English
culture.

Critical commentary

It will have been obvious from the synopsis of *The Way
We Live Now* that it is fundamentally an indictment of
the corrupting power of money, and in this respect it has
been compared to the novels of the French realist Balzac
and to the Dickens of *Our Mutual Friend*. The indictment
takes in, moreover, most of the economic forces that were
coming to the fore in the later stages of Victorian capitalism, among them share-pushing and jobbery, unprincipled
speculation on the Stock Exchange, the advent of American commercial methods, and the rise of a new and sinister
type of international financier. This corrupting influence
is shown to extend to practically every aspect of the
national life, including culture, personal relationships,
and the time-hallowed standards of private and public
integrity. No wonder that some critics have called *The
Way We Live Now* 'Trollope's *Vanity Fair*' – and in fact
contemporary critics of the novel levelled against him
much the same charges of cynicism and misanthropy as

had been earlier directed against Thackeray.

Although Trollope stood as a Liberal when he himself made an attempt to get into Parliament, his own description of himself as 'an advanced conservative liberal' was nearer the mark. The 'gentleman' remained his unquestioning standard of reference and the targets of his savage attacks in the novel are the deviations from that norm. In spite of the passionate indignation behind his exposure of corruption and chicanery, no radical solutions are proposed, and the one positive political principle that Trollope can offer, through the character of Roger Carbury, is the concept of a rural community based on a proper relationship between squire and peasantry – already lost, if it ever really existed, in an idyllic past. Although the analysis of contemporary financial and commercial methods is searching and devastating in its implications, as European and American capitalism began to enter into the phase of international consortia and imperialist expansion, other forces, such as the advance of the lower-middle classes and the growth of the trade-union movement, are ignored.

Certain limitations of the imagination are also apparent. For example, there is nothing to compare with the psychological penetration and profundity displayed in the novels of George Eliot and none of the tragic interplay between character, circumstance, and environment that is so notable a feature in the fiction of Thomas Hardy. The vibrations of poetic vision, language, and imagery which distinguish Dickens's *Our Mutual Friend*, which is also a novel which grew out of the spirit of the times, are almost entirely absent. Trollope was basically a practical, factual, down-to-earth realist, and did not pretend to be otherwise. At the same time, there is a great deal of wit, wisdom, truth, and compassion in *The Way We Live Now*, and the novel must survive as a powerful indictment of any society that wholly surrenders itself to purely materialistic values – an indictment not only of what life was like then, but also of the way we live now.

The Egoist

George Meredith

All Meredith's novels are, with varying degrees of completeness, based upon a single and unifying critical theory. This theory was given its fullest expression in a famous lecture which he delivered in 1877 entitled *On the Idea of Comedy and of the Uses of the Comic Spirit*. Strongly influenced by contemporary writers on evolution, Meredith's argument, in its bare essentials, is as follows: although, with the emergence of consciousness, the operations of natural selection had come to an end as far as Man was concerned, so that he himself had become the agent of his own creation, the older biological factors of evolution remained active; the predatory element, above all, was still apparent in Man's powerful drive to assert his own selfish desires irrespective of the rights or personalities of others – in other words, in 'egoism'. It follows, according to Meredith, that each man's task in life (if he is to contribute to the forward movement of humanity), is to struggle to keep in check this primitive egoism. In doing so, he has a notable ally in the Comic Spirit. Its operations in attempting to control the varied manifestations of egoism form the basic motif of all Meredith's novels – and in particular of *The Egoist* (published 1879), which is generally acknowledged to be his masterpiece.

Meredith himself (as he was ruefully aware) was guilty of a typical piece of egoism when he took pains to conceal the fact that his father, like his grandfather before him, was a naval tailor and outfitter at Portsmouth, where he was born in 1828. After attending a day school in Portsmouth, he was sent, in 1842, to a school at Neuwied on the Rhine, run by the Moravians (a Protestant sect), whose teachings on the brotherhood of man had a profound influence on him. In 1842, too, the political ferment in Europe that eventually exploded in the revolutions of 1848, was already active – and Meredith imbibed its principles and never abandoned them.

After leaving Neuwied he was articled to a solicitor in London; but he soon began writing essays and poems. In 1849 he married a widowed daughter of Thomas Love Peacock, seven years his senior. In 1858 (after the birth of a son, Arthur) Meredith's wife ran away with Henry Wallis, one of the Pre-Raphaelite painters. Her death, three years later, deserted and alone, revived in Meredith bitter-sweet memories of the past, which resulted in *Modern Love*, a sequence of sixteen-line sonnets in which he analysed, often with painful intensity and a frankness unusual for the times, the course of an unhappy marriage culminating in tragedy. In 1864 he made a second and eminently happy marriage to Marie Vulliamy, the daughter of a neighbour. His second wife died in 1885 but Meredith went on writing both novels and poetry right up to his own death in 1909.

His first novel, *The Shaving of Shagpat: an Arabian Entertainment*, was published in 1856. It was closely modelled on *The Arabian Nights* – and its hero has to overcome the selfishness and conceit in his own nature before he can enter into full manhood and achieve the power to defeat the tyrant Shagpat, who symbolizes the illusions of worldly pretension. Among the novels that followed, two must be singled out. The first of these is *The Ordeal of Richard Feverel* (1859) in which the father of the hero, Sir Austen Feverel, has brought up his son in ignorance of sexual love, and is Meredith's first considerable portrait of obsessional egoism. The second is *Evan*

Harrington (1861) which introduces a naval tailor, named 'the Great Mel' (like Meredith's own grandfather) who was a legendary figure because of his grand manner and dashing ways. Basically the story is about the struggles of the Great Mel's son to break away from the world of illusion – and egoism – represented by his father.

There are many other notable novels, too, that explored this basic theme (some of them in a political and revolutionary context) but there is no doubt that *The Egoist* marks the culmination of the process, and that its hero, Sir Willoughby Patterne, is the quintessence of the type.

His name itself is significant. Sir Willoughby is placed at the centre of the story, with the other characters grouped around him in a deliberately formal pattern – and there are various indications that the design Meredith had in mind was that of the Willow Pattern Plate. The formal element is heightened by the fact that the novel is subtitled 'A Comedy in Narrative' and that it is organized to some extent along the lines of a play, with an unusual number of scenes in dialogue.

Summary

There is a *Prelude* to the novel which refers to an imaginary 'Book of Egoism' (quotations from which occur from time to time throughout), and to a tribe of sardonic imps, whose task is to persecute any human being whose conduct becomes irrational. But the basic plot of the novel is simple enough. Young Sir Willoughby Patterne of Patterne Hall is handsome, rich, distinguished, brought up by a doting mother and two doting aunts, and the cynosure of the whole county. But another side of his nature is shown when Lieutenant Crossjay Patterne of the Royal Marines, a poor relation who has distinguished himself for bravery, calls at Patterne Hall to seek help in the education of his son. However, because he turns out to be not a romantically youthful hero, but a 'thick-set stumpy man' of middle age and not at all presentable, Crossjay is told that Sir Willoughby is 'not at home'. The 'ring of imps' takes note – and so does Constantia Durham, the beautiful but rather flighty young heiress to whom Sir Willoughby is engaged.

The engagement has been a bitter blow to Laetitia Dale, the clever and beautiful daughter of a poor neighbour. Laetitia has adored Sir Willoughby from childhood. He has graciously accepted her adoration, but is far too proud to think of allying himself to someone who has neither wealth nor rank. When, however, Constantia elopes with a Captain of Hussars, Laetitia becomes a frequent visitor to Patterne Hall, until suddenly Sir Willoughby goes off for three years on a world tour in company with his cousin, the scholarly and likeable Vernon Whitford.

On his return, Sir Willoughby tells Laetitia that he will be calling on her father – but when he does so it is not to ask for her hand but to discuss the renewal of the Dales' lease. Laetitia finds some small solace for yet another disappointment in the company of the twelve-year-old Crossjay Patterne, son of the Lieutenant of Marines whom Sir Willoughby had earlier insulted. Vernon Whitford, though a comparatively poor man, has paid for young Crossjay to lodge with the Dales while he coaches him, free of charge, for his entrance to the Royal Navy.

Sir Willoughby now proposes to Clara Middleton, the daughter of a wealthy doctor of divinity of somewhat epicurean tastes. But Laetitia is still a constant visitor. For one thing, she is much in demand by Sir Willoughby's mother, who is ill; and in any case Sir Willoughby, as a man 'who lived backwards almost as intensely as in the present', likes to keep his trophies close at hand.

Sir Willoughby is a little disturbed when his witty neighbour, Mrs Mountstuart, calls Clara 'the dainty rogue in porcelain' in recognition not only of her beauty, but also of her liveliness of disposition. Sir Willoughby cannot tolerate anything approaching independence of spirit in a woman, and after he has tried to exact from Clara an oath that if he were to die before her she would never re-marry – would still be his 'beyond death' – she begins to feel uneasy at the voracious nature of her lover's demands.

She finds her spirits rising, however, whenever she can romp with young Crossjay, who has conceived a schoolboy passion for her. From him she learns of Sir Willoughby's insult to his father, and that it is Vernon and not Sir Willoughby to whom the boy is indebted. She finds herself admiring Vernon, especially when he expresses a tolerant, warm-hearted view of mankind, in marked contrast to that of Sir Willoughby. Vernon tells Clara that he will shortly be going to London to set up as a full-time writer, and asks her to intercede with Sir Willoughby so that Crossjay's tuition can be continued. Sir Willoughby grandly informs her that he has 'never abandoned a dependent' – but makes it clear that he does not agree with the idea of putting the boy into the Navy; he will make a gentleman of him, but only if his destiny is completely surrendered to *him*. He also objects to Vernon's wish to leave Patterne Hall, because he cannot tolerate the passing of any familiar face from his own ambience. He announces, therefore, that he will only pay for Crossjay's education if Vernon stays on.

As time goes by, Clara increasingly thinks of marriage to Sir Willoughby 'as that of a woman tied not to a man of heart, but to an obelisk lettered all over with hieroglyphics, and everlastingly hearing him expound them.' Eventually she suggests to Sir Willoughby that Laetitia is much better suited to him. Sir Willoughby immediately assumes that Clara is jealous of Laetitia. He therefore gives Laetitia a strong hint that it would suit him very well if she were to marry Vernon – provided, that is, her own devotion to him were unaffected.

Clara now consults Vernon, and he advises her to confront both her fiancé and her father with the exact truth of her feelings and doubts. To the modern reader, of course, this seems obvious enough; but at the period at which Meredith was writing, an engagement was regarded as almost as binding as marriage itself – and unless this is appreciated the rest of the novel, which is concerned with Clara's protracted struggle to escape, loses its point.

The outcome is forecast by one of Meredith's typical symbols. On her way back from confiding in Laetitia Dale, Clara is nearly run down by a railway trap containing Colonel De Craye, who has agreed to be Sir Willoughby's best man. In the carriage, too, is the Colonel's wedding present, a fine Chinese porcelain vase, which is broken into fragments in the accident, inevitably recalling Mrs Mountstuart's earlier description of Clara as a 'dainty rogue in porcelain'.

Clara makes her father promise to take her away from Patterne Hall for a while. On the eve of their intended departure, Sir Willoughby circumvents their move by means of the port in his cellar, 'an aged and a great wine'. On the following morning, Dr Middleton is in no fit state to travel. Accordingly, Clara writes to her old friend, Lucy Darleton, asking if she may come and stay with her. As she does not wish Sir Willoughby to know she has written, she gives the letter to young Crossjay to post, and Colonel De Craye, who has already realized that all is not well between the engaged couple, accidentally learns of it. He is greatly attracted to Clara himself, and begins to hope that he may eventually step into Sir Willoughby's shoes.

Clara secretly sets out to walk to the nearby railway station, determined to travel alone to Lucy Darleton's home. Vernon, however, learns of this, and when it comes on to rain he follows Clara to the station and takes her into the railway inn to dry her clothes. De Craye, who has guessed the reason for her absence, also turns up, and offers to accompany her on her journey. Mrs Mountstuart sees them together and, in order to avoid a scandal, Clara returns to Patterne Hall.

Sir Willoughby, however, has been terrified by the realization that yet another woman has contemplated running away from him. He seeks out Laetitia, appeals to her for sympathy, and hints that he may release Clara from her engagement. Once again Laetitia's hopes are raised, but Sir Willoughby has only been seeking an insurance policy for his self-esteem through Laetitia, and refuses to believe that Clara really wishes to end their engagement.

He now learns that De Craye had been with Clara at the station, and his terror at being made a fool of is greater than ever. When he informs Clara that Vernon as a student had, in a moment of mistaken chivalry, married a woman of low class and character who had later died, he realizes from Clara's startled reaction that she is attracted to Vernon.

Crossjay now accidentally overhears Sir Willoughby, desperate about being utterly abandoned, make Laetitia a formal proposal of marriage. To Sir Willoughby's consternation and astonishment, Laetitia, broken by the continuous cat-and-mouse game, refuses him. He is now more determined than ever to hold Clara to her promise, while her father sternly informs her that he, too, will insist on her keeping it unless she can show him solid reasons against doing so.

It is young Crossjay who is finally responsible for her salvation. He reveals what he has overheard. At first, Sir Willoughby tries to brazen it out by pretending that he had been proposing to Laetitia on behalf of Vernon. But when Laetitia's father arrives at Patterne Hall, the cat is out of the bag, and Dr Middleton is converted to his daughter's cause. Sir Willoughby struggles to salve his pride by posing as Vernon's advocate for Clara's hand. He is further discomfited by the promptitude with which Clara agrees, but at least he has the solace both of seeing his friend De Craye equally discomfited, and of eventually receiving Laetitia's reluctant and still coldly unenthusiastic consent to his marriage proposal. The title of the final chapter, 'Upon which the Curtain Falls', reasserts the dramatic structure of the novel and leaves Sir Willoughby restored 'to something of the splendid glow' he had formerly enjoyed in the eyes of the county as elaborate preparations are made for his wedding day; while Clara, on holiday in the Alps with her father, is joined by her new *fiancé* – and 'sitting beside them the Comic Muse is grave and sisterly. But taking a glance at the others of her late company of actors, she compresses her lips.'

Critical commentary

No major nineteenth-century English novelist has suffered so complete an eclipse in recent years as George Meredith. From about the date of the publication of *The Egoist* until, roughly, some ten years after his death in 1909, his reputation – as poet as well as novelist – stood tremendously high. Meredith was the idol of the young intelligentsia of the period, who felt that he was the English writer who, more than any other, had conferred upon the novel a high intellectual and stylistic distinction as well as being thoroughly 'modern'. His contemporary Oscar Wilde, for example, declared that to this 'incomparable novelist ... belongs philosophy in fiction. His people not merely live, but they live in thought.' Yet in the 1920s Virginia Woolf was complaining of Meredith the stylist: 'now he twists himself into iron knots, now he lies flat as a pancake'; the critic F. R. Leavis was describing him as 'the flashy product of unusual but vulgar cleverness', and the American poet, Ezra Pound, was pronouncing an even more succinct verdict – 'Meredith is chiefly a stink.'

There is no doubt, though, that this reaction was too extreme. There is certainly plenty of substance beneath all the stylistic decorations of *The Egoist*. The characters are by no means shadowy presences: each of them is firmly individualized, with characteristic habits, gestures, and turns of speech – including Crossjay, who is one of the most lively, convincing and unsentimentalized twelve-year-olds in fiction. The women are particularly successful, far more flesh-and-blood than in the majority of the novels of the period. The gradual change that comes over Laetitia's feelings is the product of a genuine and deep human understanding. The bewilderment of the inexperienced Clara Middleton in face of her lover's exorbitant demands, her gradual enlightenment as to the emotional truth of the situation, and her struggles to escape, are subtly and movingly conveyed. As for Sir Willoughby himself, he is a monster of the same proportions as the self-centred and hypocritical Tartuffe in the play of that title by the great seventeenth-century French dramatist, Molière, and in many ways just as universal a figure. In spite of the machinery of Meredith's theory of comedy that surrounds him, Sir Willoughby is a remarkable study in the pathology of monomania – and it is interesting to note that Sigmund Freud regarded Meredith as probably the most penetrating psychologist of all the English novelists.

Meredith's concept of egoism, moreover, must not be dismissed as a mere adventitious or disabling theory. His later novels were not all as closely concerned with it as *The Egoist*. For example, *Diana of the Crossways* (1885), regarded by many critics as his next best novel, concentrated on the theme of a married woman estranged from her husband. After the death, in 1891, of his son Arthur who had turned against him, Meredith seems to have reverted to his old pains and guilts, for his last three novels all deal with broken marriage vows. But the idea of egoism had not disappeared. As the modern critic Patrick Yarker has said, in these novels 'the target of his attack was less personal than social, for each shows that modern society fosters egoism.'

There was a good deal more to Meredith's egoism than a whimsical play of fancy, and his style, over-ornate though it is to modern tastes, should not be dismissed as entirely worthless. It helped to inaugurate a new, more impressionistic approach to the writing of fiction which is seen, at varying levels of intensity, in the work of such writers of our own century as Virginia Woolf, James Joyce, and D. H. Lawrence. For all these reasons, *The Egoist* will, whatever the vicissitudes of fashion, continue to occupy an important place in the history of English fiction.

The Portrait of a Lady

Henry James

It could be argued that Henry James ought to be treated in the context of the American rather than the English novel. He was born in New York in 1843, the son of a well-to-do writer on philosophical and theological subjects; he studied at the Harvard Law School, and did not take out British citizenship until 1915, the year before his death. But from 1868 he lived mainly in England, and by 1875 he had come to the conclusion that Europe was his spiritual home. In addition, he was the advocate and practitioner of artistic theories and values which had a profound influence on English novelists for at least half a century.

Before the advent of Henry James it did not occur to the majority of novelists that the novel might be shaped and moulded according to the same principles as those that applied to poetry, music, painting, or sculpture. This does not mean, of course, that the looser, more compendious kind of novel did not often equal or surpass those composed on the more consciously artistic principles advocated by Henry James and his followers, but his principles were particularly important at a time when standards were increasingly threatened and debased by modern best-seller techniques and mass-audience formulae.

Henry James described the great French novelist

Gustave Flaubert (1821–1880) as a man who was 'born a novelist, grew up, lived, died a novelist, breathing, feeling, thinking, speaking, performing every action of his life, only as that votary.' The words are just as applicable to James himself. So much so that there is not a great deal to be said of his life except in terms of the pursuit of his art. He was a notably good friend – kind, generous, and tolerant – but the majority of his circle were fellow-writers. He moved about a good deal in American, European and English society, but mostly as a compassionate but fundamentally detached observer. He never married, and increasingly towards the end of his life (and especially after his removal in 1898 from London to Rye in Sussex) he proclaimed that loneliness must be the inevitable lot of the truly dedicated artist

His father had insisted on a varied schooling for Henry and his older brother William (who became a distinguished philosopher and psychologist) – and, above all, on an early introduction to the artistic and cultural treasures of Europe. Before he entered Harvard, therefore, Henry James had attended schools at Albany, New York, London, Paris, Geneva, Boulogne and Bonn, so that from an early age, as Walter Allen has put it, 'rootlessness was thrust upon him; he was conditioned to the role of the spectator.'

These early experiences provided him with one of the major themes of his fiction, what he called the 'international subject' – the reactions, that is, of expatriate Americans to the impact of the older and more sophisticated civilizations of Europe. After publishing, from about 1865, a number of sketches, reviews, short stories, and *nouvelles* (short novels) in periodicals, this theme was firmly established in his first major novel, *Roderick Hudson*, which was published in volume-form in 1876, and is about a young American sculptor whose character and native genius are alike corrupted when a well-meaning patron takes him to live and work in Italy.

There followed one of the most remarkable explorations

or pilgrimages in literary history, recorded in James's letters, prefaces, notebooks, and other critical writings, as he resolutely sought for the forms and approaches that would best suit his own genius. In Paris the French realists were for a time his idols, but he gradually came to the conclusion that their concern for the 'picturesque' in realism usually meant the 'unclean' and that this had 'somehow killed the spiritual sense'.

He admired the novels of George Eliot, in which he found strong delineation of character combined with an equally strong moral sense. Her only fault in his view was that she was lacking in artistic form and in 'full aesthetic life'. Closer to his ideal was the Russian, Turgenev, because he displayed that synthesis of characterization firmly based on a central moral issue, and artistic structure and shapeliness after which James himself aspired.

It was after James finally settled in England in 1876 that the fruits of his arduous artistic exploration fully ripened. A deepening of his 'international subject' took place when he began to make his central expatriate American characters women instead of men and developed his other major, closely related theme – that of the corruption of innocence. These twin motifs were first brought together in a woman protagonist and with full effectiveness in *Daisy Miller* (1878), the story of an American girl bewildered and exploited by the tortuous sophistications of Europeans. This novel brought James his first popular success. But he achieved an altogether new richness and profundity with the publication in 1881 of *The Portrait of a Lady*. For many critics, this novel, distinguished by a subtlety and concreteness of style in the service of a profound analysis both of character and of social and cultural values, is James's masterpiece.

Summary

The 'individual centre of consciousness' (a more accurate term than 'character', James believed) is Isabel Archer, the attractive, independent and highly intelligent niece of Mrs Touchett, who has brought her over from America (following the death of her father) to stay at Gardencourt, the house on the Thames not far from London where Mrs Touchett has been living for many years with her husband Daniel and her son Ralph.

In his later novels (after a period of some years when he wrote, not very successfully, for the theatre) James aimed at what he called 'the divine principle of the scenario' – at eliminating, that is, virtually all authorial comments so that his characters would reveal themselves as far as possible by what they themselves said or did, or by what others said about them. There are approaches to this technique in *The Portrait of a Lady*. Isabel's independence of spirit, her wide-eyed eagerness for new experiences, the originality of her mind and her latent powers of imagination, are conveyed early on by means of the conversation and comments of other characters. Thus, when Mrs Touchett asks her son if he considers his cousin pretty, he replies:

> 'Very pretty indeed; but I don't insist upon that. It's her general air of being some one in particular that strikes me...'

Similarly, Isabel's ignorance of the world, in conjunction with an independence which suddenly strikes one as vulnerable, is demonstrated when her aunt has to explain to her that in England it is not 'done' for a young girl to sit up late talking to a young man – as Isabel had wished to do with Lord Warburton, a friend of the Touchetts and a frequent visitor at their house.

Old Mr Touchett, who is a semi-invalid, and Ralph, who is consumptive, are both captivated by Isabel's ingenuous charm and intelligence. Ralph hides his deeper feelings, from himself as well as others, under a mask of flippancy and wit. Lord Warburton, however, proposes to Isabel. She genuinely likes the charming, good-natured and politically radical peer; she is flattered and momentarily tempted. But she decides against the offer because somehow she feels she has been reserved for some more difficult choice. 'I can't escape unhappiness,' she tells Lord Warburton. 'In marrying you I shall be trying to.'

In part, her decision has been caused by the news that Caspar Goodwood, a young, tough, determined American who had wooed her unsuccessfully in America, has arrived in London. The news is brought by Isabel's friend Henrietta Stackpole, a newspaper reporter, and the two women, escorted by Ralph, go to London on a visit. Casper renews his suit with his usual pertinacity. Isabel tells him that she does not wish to marry at the moment, and exacts from him a promise to leave her alone for two years.

Ralph and Isabel are summoned back to Gardencourt when old Mr Touchett falls seriously ill. Also visiting the house is an old acquaintance of Mr Touchett, a widow named Madame Merle. An American by birth and now a thorough cosmopolitan, she impresses Isabel by her culture and social poise.

On his deathbed, Mr Touchett confides to Ralph that he would like him to marry Isabel, but Ralph explains that he does not feel it right, in view of his health, to contemplate matrimony. However, he longs to see how Isabel would develop her moral and imaginative capacities if she were truly free and independent – and so he begs his father to add a codicil to his will whereby he leaves half his fortune to Isabel. 'Spread your wings; rise above the ground,' Ralph tells Isabel when, after his father's death, she suddenly and unexpectedly finds herself a rich woman.

Mrs Touchett and Ralph now take Isabel to the Continent and eventually they arrive in Florence, where Madame Merle joins them and loses no time in calling on her old friend Gilbert Osmond to tell him of Isabel's presence in Florence – and the fact that she has recently inherited a fortune. Gilbert Osmond is a forty-year-old American expatriate who has lived in Florence for many years. He is handsome, with 'a fine, narrow extremely

modelled and composed face, of which the only fault was just this effect of running a trifle too much to points ...'
In his youth, Osmond had dreamed of distinguishing himself; 'but as the years went on the conditions attached to any marked proof of rarity had affected him more and more as gross and detestable. He had, therefore, done nothing apart from achieving a style,' which his private income is insufficient to sustain as elegantly as he would wish. He has a daughter named Pansy, who has just finished her schooling in a convent.

Much as he dislikes effort of any kind, Osmond, egged on by Madame Merle, stirs himself to woo Isabel. Lord Warburton also turns up in Florence and repeats his proposal. But Isabel has fallen in love with Osmond and accepts him. Caspar Goodwood hurries across the Atlantic and sternly rebukes her for not having waited the two years which she had, in his view, practically promised him.

Mrs Touchett and Ralph also disapprove of the match with Osmond, and Ralph, admitting at last that he loves Isabel himself, cries out: '... you were meant for something better than to keep guard over the sensibilities of a sterile dilettante!' Indignantly, Isabel protests that her lover is 'simply a very lonely, a very cultivated and a very honest man.'

For a time Isabel is happy. Then 'the shadows had begun to gather; it was as if Osmond deliberately, almost malignantly had put the lights out one by one.' Isabel's offence in his eyes is that she has too much of an imaginative life of her own: he has come to hate her simply for being herself. As for Isabel, her husband's mind, which she had once thought so spacious and beautiful, now reveals itself as narrow, airless and egotistical.

Pansy, now nineteen, has fallen in love with a young American named Edward Rosier, but Osmond turns him away because he is not rich enough. Lord Warburton, he decides, would be a more acceptable suitor, despite the discrepancy in age, and, to her great distress, he orders Isabel to take advantage of her old influence on Lord

Warburton to persuade him to propose to Pansy. Madame Merle is also in Osmond's confidence in the matter, and Isabel comes upon the two of them conferring in an atmosphere of great familiarity. To Ralph, however, who has accompanied Lord Warburton to Rome, and whose health is rapidly deteriorating, Isabel tries to put on a brave show, though he is much too sensitive and intelligent not to see through it.

When Pansy confides in Isabel that she is still in love with Rosier, Isabel does her best to persuade her that, to please her father, she must try and encourage Lord Warburton, though she hates herself for her hypocrisy in playing a part contrary to her nature. Eventually, Warburton returns to England without making a proposal – and Osmond accuses Isabel of having deliberately wrecked his plans for Pansy out of jealousy of her own stepdaughter. Isabel's own pain is accompanied by a profound feeling of pity for Pansy.

Caspar Goodwood also arrives in Rome. In his usual blunt manner he criticizes Osmond, and reiterates his own love. Partly in order to get rid of him, Isabel asks him to accompany Ralph, who wants to die at home, back to England. Meanwhile, Pansy still shows signs of clinging to Edward Rosier, and Osmond sends her back to the convent to be disciplined into obedience to his wishes, and (as Isabel realizes) to remove Pansy from her influence.

Isabel receives a telegram from Mrs Touchett announcing that Ralph would like to see her before he dies. Osmond forbids Isabel to go, and in his usual suave, roundabout way, threatens her with even greater unhappiness if she defies him. But Osmond's sister, the flighty and disreputable Countess Gemini, tells Isabel the truth about the mysterious Madame Merle – that she had once been Osmond's mistress and that Pansy is their daughter. Osmond had not married Madame Merle because she had no money, and they had parted some time before, but with the understanding that they would help each other whenever the opportunity arose. Isabel has to face the humiliating knowledge that her marriage to Osmond had been engineered by Madame Merle.

These revelations decide Isabel to disobey her husband and to go to England. Before she leaves Rome, she calls on Pansy at her convent. The girl is crushed, ready to do exactly as her father wishes. But she tells Isabel that she can only face the future with her support and begs her not to abandon her.

Madame Merle has also been visiting Pansy, and she and Isabel confront each other in the convent. Madame Merle guesses from Isabel's expression that she has discovered her secret. She is momentarily discomfited, then rallies to provide Isabel with her final illumination – that she owes her fortune to Ralph.

When Isabel reaches Ralph, she realizes instinctively that he needs her now so that they can face the truth together, and in doing so they reach a deep sense of loving communion.

After Ralph's funeral, Lord Warburton tells Isabel that he is about to marry an English lady. The thought of Osmond's reception of this news and of the whole way of life he represents makes Isabel react with 'a kind of spiritual shudder'. Then her hour of temptation arrives when Caspar Goodwood makes a last desperate bid for her. He urges her not to return to Osmond, and she comes near yielding. But believing it is her moral duty to stick to her marriage and do what she can to help Pansy, she returns to Rome, and to whatever life lies ahead.

Critical commentary

It will be seen that *The Portrait of a Lady* is at one level very much a fable of the 'international subject'. Isabel is in many ways the prototype of the independent and spirited, but inexperienced, American girl abroad. Caspar epitomizes the stiff, unyielding but absolutely honest American, whose values are instinctively in opposition to

European standards. The Touchetts are expatriates whose true selves have not been adversely affected by exile. Madame Merle and Gilbert Osmond, on the other hand, represent those Americans who have, in various complex ways, been distorted and corrupted by the European experience until they have become cosmopolitans in the worst sense of the term. And Lord Warburton represents British aristocractic values at their best.

It is not, however, such a simple pattern as this balancing of types would suggest. As F. R. Leavis had said:

> What we have ... is a characteristic, critical, and constructive interplay done in dramatic terms, between different cultural traditions; an interplay in which discriminations for and against are made in respect of both sides, American and European, and from which emerges the suggestion of an ideal positive that is neither.

The importance of James's 'international subject' is not confined to the nineteenth century. As Bernard Bergonzi has pointed out:

> Strange though they seem, James's immensely rich and cultivated Americans, moving in a world without fixed points of connection or sense of community, anticipate the rootlessness and alienation that typify so much present-day existence ...

The 'international subject' is rendered through a series of scenes and incidents of the greatest vividness and concreteness, and the characters are presented in all their idiosyncratic individuality of appearance, habit, and speech. Though Isabel is very much the 'central consciousness', we see her through *their* consciousnesses as well – and *The Portrait of a Lady* is the first major demonstration of the technique of 'the point of view' (or, rather, the grouping of varying points of view) which many critics have regarded as one of James's most notable contributions to the art of fiction. It is clear, too, that James's concept of a moral dilemma as the testing-ground of character is built into the very core of the novel.

James wrote many more novels, revealing him both as a chronicler of the social and cultural crises of the times and as 'the historian of fine consciences', to quote his friend and fellow-novelist Joseph Conrad. Most of these contained further technical innovations. The influence of painting increasingly accompanied that of drama – a novel must be 'composed' with carefully arranged masses of light and shade, with a unifying element – 'the Commanding Centre' he called it – drawing the whole together. An outstanding example of a novel embodying these principles is *What Maisie Knew* (1897), where the central consciousness is that of the child Maisie, caught between her equally immoral and irresponsible divorced parents, yet successfully maintaining her own incorruptibility. James was increasingly concerned with what he felt was the rapidly spreading decadence of western society, describing it as 'a mad panorama, phantasmagoria, and dime museum'. This drove him into an even more ardent assertion of the importance of art and the dedicated artist, and many critics would agree with Walter Allen that the novels of his final period – *The Wings of the Dove* (1902), *The Ambassadors* (1903), and *The Golden Bowl* (1904) – represent 'The final splendid flowering of James's genius ... novels of a classical perfection never before achieved in English, in which practice and theory are consummately matched.'

But there are many other critics who think the later novels show an attenuation of James's genius, in theme, treatment, and language. F. R. Leavis believes that in them 'James paid the penalty of living too much as a novelist, and not richly enough as a man.' James's striving for artistic perfection certainly resulted in all kinds of stylistic complexities – Bernard Bergonzi complains of an 'almost unfathomable subtlety' and James's brother William demanded 'What the dickens could they mean?'

On the other hand, the modern American critic, R. P. Blackmur, has argued that 'James made the theme of the artist a focus for the ultimate theme of human integrity.'

In addition, it must be remembered that these late novels, with their impressionistic techniques, symbolism, psychological complexity and subtle stylistic effects in many respects paved the way for such twentieth-century novelists as Virginia Woolf and James Joyce; while James's increasing preoccupation with the theme of the corruption of innocence was a particularly timely one for a materialistic and acquisitive society, and one that has an enduring validity.

What is certain is that there are very few critics who would dispute that *The Portrait of a Lady* demonstrates at their finest most of the qualities that make Henry James a great novelist who has made invaluable contributions to the English fictional tradition.

Allan Quatermain

H. Rider Haggard

Henry Rider Haggard was born at Bradenham Hall, Norfolk, in 1856, educated at Ipswich Grammar School, and at the age of nineteen obtained an administrative post in South Africa, first in Natal and then in the Transvaal. He returned to England in 1879, settled down to writing and to marriage, farming on his Norfolk estate, and becoming a specialist on various rural and agricultural questions. But he also maintained a keen interest in colonial matters, was knighted in 1912, made a Knight Commander of the British Empire in 1919, and served on the Dominions Royal Commission. He died in 1925.

The four years Rider Haggard spent in South Africa entered deeply into his imaginative life – and provided his most lucrative stock-in-trade as a popular novelist. Three novels in particular, closely linked in theme and atmosphere and by the presence of the same main characters, achieved a spectacular success in their day, and still command a considerable public. The first of them was *King Solomon's Mines* (1885). Inspired by Robert Louis Stevenson's famous adventure story *Treasure Island* (1883), it employed the perennial appeal of a lost treasure, located not on a desert island but in the mysterious ancient ruined city of Zimbabwe, which had recently been discovered in East Africa. It was followed by *She* (1887), about a beautiful white sorceress who rules over a savage black empire. The central character in both these novels is the brave, sagacious and modest hunter and explorer Allan Quatermain – and it is his name that provides the title of the third novel in the trilogy which was also published in 1887.

Summary

The story begins when Allan Quatermain, who after forty years spent in Africa has been living in England for some time, is mourning the death of his only son. In his grief, he begins to yearn for the life of the African wilds. His old friends (and companions of the adventures related in the two preceding books), Sir Henry Curtis and Captain John Good RN, feel much the same. When, therefore, Quatermain tells them of the legends he had heard while he was in Africa of a mysterious white race, and suggests that they search for it, the others enthusiastically agree, and they set out on their expedition.

To his great joy, Quatermain meets again the giant Zulu, Umslopogaas, the courageous comrade of his earlier exploits, still armed with the great axe he calls Inkosi-kaas; and Quatermain puts him in command of their bearers.

They reach a mission-station where the missionary shows them a curious sword, inlaid with gold, which is said to have come from the fabled country of the white men. Quatermain appends a footnote about the workmanship. There are other footnotes throughout the narrative, some by Quatermain, others ascribed to the editor of his papers. This is one of the devices Rider Haggard uses to give his fanciful story an air of authenticity: he had grasped the most important fact that, in order to be convincing, fantasy must evolve round a certain number of concrete points, that it must always contain an admixture of realism.

The Quatermain party set out 'into the unknown', eventually reach a great unknown lake, and embark in a

canoe. A tremendous current seizes them and sucks them
into a long underground tunnel. After various other adventures they emerge into a broad lake. They are approached by various craft – and see that the people in them are
white! Unfortunately, in order to demonstrate their fire-
power, Quatermain's party shoot one of the hippopotami
swimming nearby, not knowing that they are sacred animals. Nevertheless, they have their first awe-struck sight of
Milosis, capital of the strange country of Zu-Vendis, and
are taken into the great hall of the palace where the
court is assembled. The soldiers are armed with swords
identical in pattern to that which the missionary had
acquired. In the centre of the hall is a solid mass of black
marble, to which is attached a prophecy that 'when it was
shattered into fragments a king of alien race should rule
over the land.' They are presented to the joint Queens of
Zu-Vendis who are both startlingly beautiful. Nyleptha is
fair and frank looking, while her sister, Sorais, is black-
haired and reserved. Nyleptha and the tall, strikingly
handsome Sir Henry are immediately attracted to each
other, and the susceptible Good is much taken with Sorais.
It is obvious that their fate is being hotly debated and that
Agon, the aged high-priest, is hostile to them because of
their killing of the sacred hippopotamus. It is also evident
that Nyleptha's interest in Sir Henry has roused the
enmity of a powerful lord named Nasta.

The religion of the country is based on sun-worship,
and the priesthood is powerful – as Quatermain and his
companions discover to their cost the following morning
when they are summoned to the sumptuous Temple of the
Sun. They are placed on a brazen floor, but Queen Nyleptha manages to give them a signal which causes them to
leap back just as the floor opens to disclose a roaring
furnace beneath. Eventually the two queens persuade
Agon to give up his attempt to sacrifice the strangers.

By the time Allan Quatermain and his friends have
learned the language of Zu-Vendis, they have become such
great favourites with the queens that they are, for the

moment, safe. Sir Henry has a secret audience with Queen Nyleptha, and they declare their love for each other. But when Agon urges Nyleptha to marry Nasta and she refuses, Nasta leaves the palace in anger. What is even more ominous is that Queen Sorais has also fallen in love with Sir Henry. After Sorais has attempted to murder Nyleptha, and tried to persuade the still adoring Good to accompany her, she escapes from the palace and sets out with her followers for Nasta's stronghold. Queen Nyleptha marries Sir Henry in a grand public ceremony (as a sop to Victorian propriety, Quatermain also reads the Christian wedding service over them), and she puts him in command of her armies. Sir Henry decides to meet the superior forces of Nasta and Queen Sorais at a pass some distance from Milosis.

The Battle of the Pass is a tremendous piece of bravura writing, one of the most exciting accounts of a battle in English fiction. In the course of it many deeds of valour are performed but Quatermain is badly wounded in saving Good's life. While the outcome of the battle is still undecided, news reaches Quatermain that back in Milosis the priests, in league with Sorais, have plotted to kill Nyleptha at the next dawn.

Quatermain and Umslopogaas set off on a desperate ride to circumvent the plot. They reach the palace just before dawn, and manage to get the Queen and her waiting-maids to the head of the great staircase before Agon strikes. But they find the bronze doors, which they could have closed behind them, have been taken off their hinges and hurled to the ground far beneath. Fortunately, further building operations have been planned and blocks of granite are lying about. The Queen's serving women set to heaving these into the doorway, while the badly wounded Quatermain sits against a pillar directing operations – and Umslopogaas stands on the other side of the slowly rising wall to hold off the attackers, led by Nasta (who has also managed to reach Milosis) and Agon.

Umslopogaas, though wounded in a dozen places, fights

like a demon. He cuts down Agon, and then, surrounded by enemies, grapples with Nasta and throws him over the balustrade to his death – just as Nyleptha's supporters in Milosis come storming in to the rescue. Umslopogaas staggers into the great hall, stops near the sacred block of black marble, and splinters it with a last blow of his great axe before dropping down dead. And so the ancient prophecy is fulfilled and Nyleptha diplomatically seizes the opportunity to point out to the multitude that a stranger-king does indeed now rule in Zu-Vendis in the person of her husband, Sir Henry.

Not long afterwards, Sir Henry and Good arrive. They have won the Battle of the Pass and Sorais is their prisoner. Good, still in love with her, offers to marry her, but the proud Queen of the Night (as Quatermain calls her) stabs herself and dies. Sir Henry is crowned King-Consort and peace returns to Zu-Vendis. The embalmed body of Umslopogaas is entombed in a space hollowed out of the masonry at the top of the stairway he has defended, facing – according to his last wish – in the direction of Zululand.

As for Allan Quatermain, he retires to a house in the country not far from Milosis, to write his story and prepare for death.

Critical commentary

In some ways, the most important point to be made about *Allan Quatermain* as far as the history of the English novel is concerned, is that it raises the whole question of what the word 'success' really means when applied to late nineteenth-century fiction. Before, say, 1870, it was a fairly simple question to answer. By and large, success and literary quality were conterminous. The most popular writers of the day – Charlotte Brontë, Thackeray, Dickens, and so on – were also the greatest; but now, for a variety of reasons connected with the advance of elementary education and an increasingly commercial approach, attended by the new advertising techniques, the popularity-equals-greatness equation no longer applied.

Rider Haggard himself was well aware of the situation. In one of his review-articles he wrote:

> A weary public calls continually for books, new books to make them forget, to refresh them, to occupy minds jaded with the toil and emptiness ... and vexation of our competitive existence.

In other words, as conditions rapidly began to approximate to those of our own time, books were called upon to perform the role now filled by television. The demand, then as now, was increasingly for distraction rather than for creative enjoyment. As far as the novel was concerned, this meant that there were fewer readers prepared to make any really serious imaginative or intellectual effort.

The situation was further complicated by the advent of a number of very competent novelists whose main objective was to achieve a mass appeal but who, once their imaginations started working, found themselves activated by quite other motives. It is these novelists who are often the most difficult to judge fairly.

Rider Haggard is in many ways typical of this category. Ifor Evans's view that he 'misses only by a little the opportunity of being something more than a writer of successful romances' is a representative one. *Allan Quatermain* obviously relies on many of the most facile bestseller techniques, including plenty of vicarious blood-and-thunder. There are times when the narrative has the same mechanical, eye-on-the-box-office approach so evident in modern novels that have been deliberately written for film adaptation. The pairing off of the fair and good Nyleptha and the dark and wicked Sorais is a particularly glib example.

To the modern reader, too, some elements in *Allan Quatermain* are difficult to take. The love scenes between Sir Henry Curtis and Nyleptha, for example, are quite ludicrous, and Sir Henry's behaviour both as a lover and husband almost unbelievably fatuous. To present-day tastes, too, the calm assumption of the superiority of the

English gentleman and of his inalienable right to Empire is both absurd and repellent. On the other hand, *Allan Quatermain* is far less jingoistic in tone than the vast majority of contemporary novels with a 'red on the map' element. There is no patronage, for example, of the black characters, whether friends or foes. They may be described as barbarians or savages, but they are never treated with less than respect, while Umslopogaas is one of the great heroes of the book. This respect, moreover, is accompanied by an acknowledgement that what is generally called 'savagery' is in many respects superior to western civilization. Rider Haggard may endow Umslopogaas and other Africans with some of the romanticized qualities of Rousseau's 'noble savage', but there can be no doubt of the genuineness of his strictures on many aspects of contemporary commercial 'civilization', including the white man's greed and exploitation. These opinions, often expressed in *Allan Quatermain*, come from the author himself and have nothing to do with the quest for mass sales. Fundamentally, the values of *Allan Quatermain* are sound and humane.

Above all, Rider Haggard's African novels (he was far less convincing in those with an English setting) have qualities of imagination far above the best seller level of the day, as a number of his modern defenders, Graham Greene among them, have pointed out. Although he was not adverse to exploiting the patriotic emotions attached to the British Empire in its expansionist and adventurous phase, *Allan Quatermain* is also a fantasy in which the Dark Continent, still mysterious and incompletely explored, played much the same part that the unknown expanses of Time and Space do in modern science fiction. And when a dramatic situation grips Rider Haggard's imagination – for example the defence of the stairway and the heroic death of Umslopogaas – he has few rivals for sheer narrative skill, while the blend of fantasy and concrete detail in his descriptions of the imaginary Milosis at times approaches the vividness and intensity of poetry.

The Master of Ballantrae

Robert Louis Stevenson

In the changed conditions attending the relationship between the writer of fiction and his public, touched on in
the chapter on *Allen Quatermain*, there was an increasing
concern among the more serious novelists about the
aesthetic premises on which their work was based. The
main debate centred on the issue of realism. On the one
side were those who argued that the novel, as the product
of eighteenth-century rationalism and empiricism, was by
its very nature 'realistic', and that the way forward lay in
a bold and uncompromising extension of it. On the other
side were those who, feeling that realistic fiction had
become too over-charged with fact, believed that the salvation of the novel as an art form lay in a greater emphasis
on the elements of romance, fantasy, adventure, and
reverie.

These opposing viewpoints were best represented by
two writers who were close personal friends, who admired
each other's work, and who brought to the problems of
their craft the highest possible artistic ideals. One of these
was Henry James, who, in an article entitled 'The Art of
Fiction' (1884), insisted that 'solidity of specification' or
'the air of reality' was essential to a novel. The other was
Robert Louis Stevenson, who addressed 'A Humble
Remonstrance' to his older friend James in which he
declared that, on the contrary, what should distinguish a

novel were its 'immeasurable differences from life'. In this and other essays, and through practising what he preached, Stevenson was responsible for a notable revival of the novel of adventure.

The facts of Stevenson's own life-story are so strange and romantic that they have tended, perhaps, to deflect attention from the value of his fiction. Born 1850 in Edinburgh, he was the son of a distinguished lighthouse engineer. Because of a weak chest, young Stevenson was forced to spend much of his early life in bed. As a result he read avidly, especially in the old legends of Scotland and the novels of Sir Walter Scott, and was, as he says, 'from a child, an ardent and uncomfortable dreamer'. He was educated at Edinburgh Academy and then at Edinburgh University, where he studied engineering and visited lighthouses in many remote parts of Scotland which, as David Daiches, one of his recent biographers has said 'fed his appetite for the kind of scenery that calls out for appropriate action.' But in 1871 Stevenson refused to continue his engineering studies, though he agreed to read law, and was eventually called to the Scottish Bar. He distressed his devout parents even more when reports reached them of carousals in the shady quarters of Edinburgh, and when he announced that he had become an atheist. However, he made a number of important literary friends both in Edinburgh and London, among them the poet, writer and influential editor W. E. Henley, with whom he later collaborated on several plays. He trained himself as a writer by 'playing the sedulous ape', as he put it, to famous authors of the past, and he began to achieve a reputation as a careful and elaborate stylist. In spite of his continuing ill-health, he yearned for a life of action and his first books were *An Inland Voyage* (1878), an account of a canoe-trip with a friend through Belgium and Northern France, and *Travels with a Donkey in the Cévennes* (1879).

He was spending an increasing amount of time on the Continent, largely for the sake of his health, and it was at

Grez, in the valley of the Loing, that he met a remarkable woman, several years his senior, named Mrs Fanny Van de Grift Osbourne. When she returned with her son and daughter to California, Stevenson followed. After a nightmare journey by emigrant ship and train he reached her in San Francisco, and, when she had obtained her divorce, they married. Following a long honeymoon spent in an abandoned miner's shack in the mountains (which produced *The Silverado Squatters*, published in 1883), the Stevensons returned to Scotland where they were reconciled to Louis's parents. Stevenson made several collections of his carefully chiselled essays and short stories. While in Scotland, to please his stepson Lloyd Osbourne, he wrote his famous boys' adventure story *Treasure Island*, which was published in volume form in 1883. The Stevensons settled for a time in Bournemouth where, in addition to many of the poems contained in *A Child's Garden of Verses* (1885) and other works, Stevenson wrote two of his most important novels. The first of these was *Kidnapped* (1886), which is one of the most exciting pursuit-and-escape novels in English fiction. The second was *The Strange Case of Dr Jekyll and Mr Hyde* (also published in 1886), which is probably Stevenson's best-known novel, and which embodies his lifelong preoccupation with the co-existence of good and evil in the human personality.

Then in 1887, after the death of Louis's father, the Stevensons left England never to return. To begin with they lived in America, near Lake Saranac in the Adirondack Mountains, where Stevenson began *The Master of Ballantrae*. In 1888 the family – including Fanny's children and Stevenson's mother – set out on a long voyage in the South Seas, and it was during this period that Stevenson completed *The Master of Ballantrae*, which was published in 1889. Eventually, they all settled in Samoa where Stevenson bought an estate called Vailima. There his health improved and he became a legend both in Samoa, where he involved himself in local politics and was much loved for his great charm of personality, and in faraway England. These last five years of his life also saw a remarkable new creative flowering. In addition to several exciting novels of adventure written in collaboration with his stepson Lloyd Osbourne, he wrote a brilliantly evocative long short story set in the South Seas, called *The Beach at Falesá* and his unfinished novel set in the Scotland of the eighteenth century, *Weir of Hermiston* (1896), which most critics think would have been his masterpiece had it been completed.

He died suddenly towards the end of 1894. His Samoan friends, who knew that he wanted to be buried on a near-by mountain, showed their love for him by working in relays to hack a pathway with knives and axes.

Summary

The story is told by the dour, stolid Mackellar, steward in the household of Lord Durrisdeer of Ballantrae. Mackellar is both a fully realized character playing an important part in the action, and a most effective 'chorus', commenting on events as they unfold. The foundations of the tragedy, he relates, had been laid in 1745, when Bonnie Prince Charlie landed in Scotland to lead the last full-scale rebellion on behalf of the deposed Stuarts against the Hanoverian monarchy. According to a common practice among noble Scottish families at the time, it had been decided that one son should offer his sword to the Stuart prince (so that in the case of his victory the family might expect to be rewarded), while the other son affirmed his loyalty to King George (so that in the event of *his* victory the family estates would not be confiscated). The two sons are James, the Master (the title used in Scotland for the eldest son), who has a dubious reputation but a magnetic personality, and his younger brother Henry, 'who was an honest solid sort of lad'. Although old Lord Durrisdeer, who has always favoured his elder son, and his orphan ward Alison Graeme (heiress to a large fortune and engaged to the Master) and Henry himself are all of the opinion that the elder son should stay at home, the Master has set off with a small band of retainers to join Prince Charles.

The rebels are disastrously defeated at the Battle of Culloden and the Master is believed to have been killed. Alison, for the sake of the family fortunes, eventually agrees to marry Henry and she has a daughter, Katherine, by him – though continuing, in company with her father-in-law, to dote on the memory of the Master. Then one day Colonel Burke, one of the exiled Prince's Irish officers, arrives with the news that the Master is alive and in Paris, high in the favour of the Prince. After the Battle of Culloden, he had been captured by a ferocious pirate named Teach and had secured an extraordinary domination over him. He had then escaped with a considerable treasure and made his way to America. After further wanderings and adventures in the American wilds, the Master had been forced to bury his treasure, though careful to make a map of the location, and had eventually turned up in Paris.

Colonel Burke has a letter for Alison, which Henry generously hands to his wife unopened, and there are letters, too, for Henry and his father – demanding a large sum of money. These exactions continue regularly during the next seven years and Henry feels honour bound to meet them, though they are a heavy drain on the estate. Then the Master turns up in person at Durrisdeer. Made much of by his father, he settles in comfortably, pays marked attentions to Alison, exerts his charm to win over little Katherine, and while treating Henry politely in public, seizes every opportunity to insult and persecute him in private. The characterization of the Master is the most powerful instance in the whole of Stevenson's work of his preoccupation with moral ambiguities, with the energy and attractiveness of evil, and with the concept of the Devil – a very typical preoccupation of Scottish Calvinism and part of Stevenson's religious background.

When it turns out that the Master has for some time been a spy in the service of the Hanoverian government he loses something of his heroic glow in Alison's eyes, though the old Lord manages to find excuses for him. One of the purposes of the Master's visit is to wring even more money out of the estate to finance some project he has in mind in India, and part of the estate has to be sold. Matters eventually come to a head when the Master taunts his brother with Alison's preference for himself, and Henry strikes him. The brothers fight a duel. It provides an excellent example of Stevenson's handling of scenes of action, reminiscent in some ways of his fellow-countryman Sir Walter Scott, but with a lighter touch that recalls rather the Frenchman Alexandre Dumas (1803–1870), whose novels of adventure (such as *The Three Musketeers*) Stevenson much admired.

Although the Master tries to beat Henry by a foul, it is Henry who eventually wins the duel and the Master falls to the ground. But when Lord Durrisdeer and Alison reach the scene, it is to find that the Master has been carried off by the smugglers who haunt the area – though no one knows whether he is alive or dead. Henry has a mental breakdown during which his wife nurses him devotedly. But he is possessed with morbid forebodings of his brother's return and, in the opinion of Mackellar, his sanity has been permanently affected.

Nevertheless, several years pass peaceably, in the course of which the old Lord dies, Henry inherits the title and property, and an heir, named Alexander, is born. But the Master is not dead and eventually returns from India to Durrisdeer, accompanied by his Indian servant, Secundra Dass, and obviously once more impoverished. He settles himself in as if by right and shows signs of aiming to exercise his spell on young Alexander. Mackellar, too, feels his fascination: 'He had all the gravity and something of the splendour of Satan in the "Paradise Lost". I could not help but see the man with admiration,' he reflects. But he fears that the strain will prove too much for his employer, and Lady Durrisdeer agrees with him. Plans are secretly made for the family to go to an estate they own in New York, while Mackellar is legally placed in charge of Durrisdeer with instructions to allow the Master to live there with a small allowance.

It does not take the Master long, however, to discover his brother's whereabouts with the help of his servant Secundra Dass, who, unknown to Mackellar, understands English and has been eavesdropping on his conversation with the servants. When the Master and Secundra Dass set out for America, Mackellar accompanies them in order to protect the interests of his employer. On the voyage he is inevitably thrown much into the company of the Master and is again intrigued by his contradictory personality. But this does not prevent him trying to push the Master overboard during a tempest. Paradoxically, the attempt raises him in the Master's estimate because, he tells him, he values loyalty. When they reach New York, Henry receives the reappearance of his brother with a mixture of morbid fatalism and a brooding resolution. The Master lives in great poverty, but eventually plans an expedition to search for the pirate treasure which he had buried years before. In the meantime, a pamphlet has arrived from England incorrectly reporting that the Master is about to be restored to his sequestrated title and estates, and this has a highly inflammatory effect on Henry who fears that his son will be cheated of his inheritance.

When the Master sets out in search of his treasure, he is accompanied by a number of ruffians who are in Henry's pay; and shortly afterwards Henry, attended by Mackellar, joins an expedition organized by the Governor which is going into the same area. One day John Mountain, one of the Master's party, staggers into the Governor's camp. He has a terrible story to tell. It had been some time before the Master had learned that he was in the hands of conspirators in the pay of his brother. He and Secundra Dass had tried to escape, but had been circumvented by the conspirators, who wanted the Master to lead them to his treasure before they disposed of him. The Master had kept his head, exerting the force of his personality to try and divide his enemies and using every possible trick and stratagem. Then he had, apparently, fallen sick in his tent and died, and Secundra Dass had dug a grave and buried him. At the same time, marauding Indians had infiltrated into the area and silent night-time scalpings went on until only Mountain and Secundra Dass were left. When the two of them had at last stumbled on the Governor's large and well-armed expedition, Secundra Dass had turned back in the direction from which they had come.

In order to humour Henry, half mad with hatred, the Governor and his party go in search of Secundra Dass. They find him, ankle-deep in his master's grave, frantically digging. Eventually he disinters the Master's body and sets about trying to revive it. After a while, the Master's eyes open and, Mackellar relates, 'the week-old corpse looked me for a moment in the face ...' Henry falls dead at the sight – and at almost the same moment the Master, too, finally dies. Secundra Dass explains that if it had not been so cold, the Oriental techniques of feigning death and surviving in a state of semi-hibernation that he had taught the Master would have undoubtedly succeeded. The brothers are placed in the same grave and Mackellar has a stone erected over it which pays tribute to both.

Critical commentary

Stevenson composed *The Master of Ballantrae* partly in America and partly in the South Seas. Its origins, though, go much further back. It was in 1876, when he was a young man of twenty-five tramping through south-west Scotland that he had passed through Ballantrae (in Ayrshire) and the name stuck in his imagination. Over five years later, when travelling through Perthshire, the rough idea of the story was (he said) 'conceived in the Highland rain, the blend of the smell of heather and bog-plants.'

In the opinion of some critics, *The Master of Ballantrae* is nothing like as successful when the main centre of interest shifts from Scotland. It is true that Stevenson's imagination, as in the case of Sir Walter Scott (and of most other writers) was always most powerfully engaged when he was dealing with the backgrounds and atmosphere he knew intimately from the impressionable years of his childhood. On the other hand, it can be argued that it was as a wanderer and an exile that he was most fully in command of his Scottish material. Stevenson himself had strong misgivings about the later part of the novel, writing to Henry James, in the course of composing it: '... steep, sir. It is even very steep, and I fear it shames the honest stuff so far ...'

But on the whole the later sections are imaginatively in keeping with the theme as a whole. The fact that Lord Durrisdeer and his family have to uproot themselves from their native land and seek refuge abroad is in itself a powerful illustration of the diabolical force of the 'incubus' (as Stevenson calls the Master in his letter to Henry James) which pursues them. It is in keeping, too, that the Master, possessed as he is by some evil force he cannot control, should restlessly wander about the world. As for the episode of the burial and disinterment, it may be 'steep' from a realistic point of view, but atmospherically it is tremendously effective, and as a poetic symbol of a kind of horrifying vitality that seems almost supernatural in its refusal to be scotched, it is fully justified.

Although the two brothers are inevitably the main protagonists and the other characters play subordinate roles, there is nothing of the cardboard cut-out about the old Lord Durrisdeer, Secundra Dass, or even the assortment of villains who make brief appearances during the Master's last ill-fated expedition. Alison Graeme is rather a different matter – though she was the most convincing woman character he had drawn to date. The unsatisfactory nature (or complete absence) of women and the almost total lack of the sexual relationship in Stevenson's earlier novels had already been noted by Henry James who commented: 'the idea of making believe appeals to him much more than the idea of making love.' It was, perhaps, only when he came to his last unfinished novel, *Weir of Hermiston*, that Stevenson created fully satisfactory women.

Nevertheless, when Stevenson, in his letter to Henry James, claimed that 'five parts' of *The Master of Ballantrae* were 'sound, human tragedy', he was not only speaking the truth, but probably being over-modest; for to many readers the tragedy is fully sustained throughout.

The Picture of Dorian Gray

Oscar Wilde

Towards the end of the nineteenth century, a reaction began to develop against Victorianism in all its aspects; this was attended by a growing confusion in values, and a frantic search for entirely new attitudes towards life and art. Among the manifestations of this search was the aesthetic doctrine of 'art for art's sake' – the belief that art and morality were entirely separate, and that the former must be regarded as wholly autonomous. The idea of 'decadence' was often closely related to it – the interest in corruption and evil as possible repositories of beauty, and therefore legitimate areas for the artist's exploration. These attitudes had their roots in the Pre-Raphaelite movement and, further back, in certain aspects of Romanticism, but the end-of-the-century mood, and all the political, social and economic developments that had brought it about, threw them into special prominence.

It is in this context that Oscar Wilde pre-eminently belongs. *The Picture of Dorian Gray* was his only novel, but it is important both because it is so representative of that context and because it embodies more of its author's strange personality, perhaps, than any other of his writings.

His full name was Oscar Fingal O'Flahertie Wills Wilde, and he was born in Dublin in 1854. His father was a celebrated oculist, whose notorious love affairs even-

tually brought him into the law courts; and his mother
was a writer who in her youth had been an ardent Irish
nationalist. Wilde read Classics at Trinity College, Dublin, and then won a classical scholarship to Magdalen
College, Oxford. At Oxford he sat at the feet of the philosopher and art historian Walter Pater, author of *Studies
in the History of the Renaissance* (1873), whose advocacy
of a hedonist cultivation of the senses in the service of
art and life exercised a tremendous influence on the young
aesthetes of the day. Wilde had a brilliant academic career
at Oxford and won the Newdigate Prize for poetry. He
also gained a reputation as an outrageous dandy and
poseur, and as a dazzling wit and conversationalist.

In London he produced a volume of poems and promoted sales by parading the streets dressed in knee-
breeches, silk stockings, a flowing tie, a strange wide-
brimmed hat, and a velveteen jacket with sprays of flowers
in the buttonhole. This was good publicity, but did not
solve his financial problems. So he went on a lecture tour
to America, uttering one of his famous witticisms on
landing in New York: 'I have nothing to declare except
my genius.'

Then, in 1884, Oscar Wilde married the daughter of a
well-known barrister. He and his wife set up house in Tite
Street, Chelsea, where two sons were born to them. But
in 1886 (at the age of thirty-two) Wilde was seduced into
homosexual practices by his friend Robert Ross. During
the next three or four years he wrote book reviews and
articles on the theatre – and talked. His talk was now so
famous that he was invited everywhere and his sayings
were delightedly handed round and repeated in the newspapers. He also wrote short stories, fairy tales (such as
The Happy Prince and *A House of Pomegranates*, which
are still children's favourites) and essays.

The Picture of Dorian Gray first appeared in the
American *Lippincott's Magazine* in 1891, and was issued
in volume form the following year with some additional
chapters and a preface. The novel was attacked for im-

morality and Wilde defended it vigorously and wittily in a number of letters to the press. After hearing his fellow-countryman, George Bernard Shaw, speaking on Socialism, Wilde wrote his long essay *The Soul of Man Under Socialism*, which reveals his intelligence and fundamental humanity at their best. He spent much of 1891 in Paris, writing in French his remarkable play *Salomé*. Though banned in England (until 1931) it was produced in Paris by Sarah Bernhardt and it became an outstanding success on the Continent.

The effect of the English ban of *Salomé* was to turn Wilde to comedy. His first theatrical success in England came with *Lady Windermere's Fan*, which was first produced in London, to great acclaim, in 1892. It was followed by two other notable successes, but the most famous of all Wilde's comedies was *The Importance of Being Earnest*, which was first produced in 1895 and has been popular ever since.

Fame and financial success, however, seemed to have a coarsening effect on Wilde, increasing his taste for luxury and his conceit. By this time rumours were rife about the relationship between Wilde and a young nobleman Lord Alfred Douglas, many of them put about by the latter's father, the Marquis of Queensberry, with whom Lord Alfred had a long-standing feud. In 1895, Wilde was persuaded to bring a quite unnecessary suit for libel against the Marquis. At first, Wilde treated his court appearances as an opportunity to display his witticisms. But as Bernard Shaw commented, he had utterly 'miscalculated the force of the social vengeance he was unloosing on himself.' Queensberry turned the tables and Wilde was soon on trial for offences which were at that time criminal. There was a tremendous public outcry against him and he was sentenced to two years hard labour.

While in prison, he composed a long letter to a friend describing his conversion to Christianity which was published in 1905 under the title of *De Profundis*. On his release, however, and after an abortive attempt to enter a Roman Catholic retreat, Wilde reverted to his former paganism. Broken in health, he went to live in France and took the defiantly flamboyant pseudonym of Sebastian Melmoth. There he wrote the stark and moving *Ballad of Reading Gaol*, published in 1898 and regarded by some critics as one of the outstanding poems of the period. After that his vitality and talent alike seem to have deserted him, and his financial problems increased. Shortly before his death in 1900 he declared 'I am dying beyond my means' – his wit at least had remained with him to the end.

Summary

The Picture of Dorian Gray opens in Basil Hallward's studio. He is working on the portrait of a singularly beautiful and wealthy young man, and it is obvious to Lord Henry Wotton, who is visiting the studio, that this portrait is going to be its creator's masterpiece.

Shortly afterwards, the sitter himself arrives – his name is Dorian Gray. While Basil paints, Lord Henry urges Dorian to 'live out his life fully and completely', to 'always be searching for new sensations' – and delivers the typical Wildean witticism: 'The only way to get rid of a temptation is to yield to it.'

Lord Henry's harangue immediately has its effect on Dorian Gray, bringing into his face and eyes the heightened expression which enables Basil to put the finishing and masterly touches to his portrait. Then, when Lord Henry goes on to impress upon Dorian that even his beauty will fade, Dorian stands in front of the finished picture, and exclaims:

> If it were I who was to be always young, and the picture that was to grow old! ... I would give my soul for that!

This is in effect an oath, similar to that whereby Faust sold his soul to the devil. The subconscious realization of this nearly causes Basil to destroy the canvas before the scene ends. In the event, though, he has it framed and sent to Dorian's house.

Fired now by Lord Henry's advocacy of experience, Dorian falls romantically in love with a youthful and innocent actress named Sybil Vane, and announces that he is going to marry her. He takes Lord Henry and Basil to the sordid little theatre where she is employed. Sybil gives a bad performance, explaining to Dorian in the green-room afterwards that now she has experienced real love she cannot bear to mimic it, and so never wants to be an actress again. Dorian promptly discards her, telling her: 'Without your art you are nothing.' When he returns home he happens to glance at Basil Hallward's portrait of him: it seems to him that the expression has changed slightly, that there is 'a touch of cruelty in the mouth'.

Shaken by this discovery, Dorian begins a letter to Sybil begging her forgiveness, but before he has finished it Lord Henry brings him the news that she has committed suicide. Dorian is genuinely shocked, until Lord Henry consoles him with the reflection that by dying still young and in love Sybil had performed a beautiful action, and that it has, after all, been a new experience for Dorian, and a prelude to many that will follow.

Basil Hallward asks permission to exhibit the portrait in a show he is giving in Paris. Dorian fobs him off with various excuses, and eventually Basil agrees that he is right – and pours out the confession that in painting the portrait he had been giving expression to his adoration of the sitter. After Basil has gone, Dorian has the picture carried to his old schoolroom at the top of the house, covers it with a curtain, and locks the door.

He is now further influenced by a 'yellow book' which Lord Henry has given him and which, it is generally agreed, was meant to be *A Rebours* (which roughly means 'backwards' or 'in reverse'), a novel by Joris-Karl Huysmans which was published in 1884 and exercised a great influence on the aesthetes of the period.

For the next few years Dorian models himself on the hero of this 'yellow book' by trying to recapture all the sensations that had belonged to the historical past – in other words, 'living backwards'. He attends Roman Catholic services in order to savour their ritual; he studies oriental perfumes, jewels, embroideries, ancient music and musical instruments, ecclesiastical vestments, mediaeval poisons, and all the curious lore attached to them. At the same time he finds himself possessed by 'mad hungers that grew more ravenous as he fed them', and there are whispers of unmentionable debaucheries in the dens of London's East End. After these, he visits the locked room at the top of his house to stand, with a mirror in his hand, in front of the portrait, 'looking now at the evil and ageing face on the canvas, and now at the fair young face that laughed back at him from the polished glass.'

There is now an abrupt leap forward of thirteen years. Dorian is thirty-eight – but still completely unchanged in appearance. Basil Hallward has called on him to plead with him to reform his way of life. Dorian takes him to the secret room and shows him 'the hideous face on the canvas'. When Basil realizes what has happened to the beautiful youth he has worshipped and idealized for so long, he tries to make Dorian kneel with him in prayer. Dorian snatches up a knife and stabs him and a blood-red blotch appears on the hand in the portrait. Dorian covers it up again and sends for Alan Campbell, a biologist and one of the many young men he has corrupted. Dorian blackmails him into using his expert knowledge to destroy every vestige of Basil's body. Later Alan, horrified at having condoned murder, commits suicide.

While visiting one of his sordid haunts, Dorian is confronted by an ageing prostitute – an innocent girl until she met Dorian – who jeeringly addresses him as 'Prince Charming'. A sailor overhears her. He catches up with Dorian in a dark alley and reveals himself as James, Sybil Vane's sailor brother, who has remembered that 'Prince

Charming' was the name his sister had applied to Dorian. Dorian moves under a lighted lamp so that he can see his face – beautiful with 'the bloom of boyhood, all the unstained purity of youth'. James, convinced that he had made a mistake, lets Dorian go. But when the prostitute tells him that Dorian has not changed an iota in the eighteen years since he seduced her, James tracks Dorian down again at his country estate, where he is holding a shooting party, and lies in wait for him. He is, however, accidentally shot by one of the guests. In his relief at his narrow escape, Dorian resolves to turn over a new leaf, and makes a start by sparing a village girl he had been about to seduce.

Glowing with self-righteousness, on his return to his London house he hurries to the portrait to see if it has begun to register the moral improvement. But all that has happened is that the mouth now shows 'the curved wrinkle of the hypocrite'. His renunciation of the country girl and his new resolutions had alike been the products of mere curiosity, and the desire for a new sensation. He looks at the portrait again and sees that the red stain 'seemed to have crept like a horrible disease over the wrinkled fingers. There was blood on the painted feet, as though the thing had dripped.'

Suddenly, revolted beyond endurance, Dorian picks up the knife with which he had killed Basil and plunges it into the canvas. There is a horrible cry and a crash. When the servants break into the room, they find on the wall a portrait of their master in the full bloom of his youthful beauty – and on the floor a dead man with a knife in his heart, 'withered, wrinkled, and loathsome of visage'.

Critical commentary

The ending of *The Picture of Dorian Gray* has the sort of shock we associate with an Alfred Hitchcock film, and, to a certain extent, the novel belongs to the straightforward 'horror' genre. But it can also claim to be a genuine variation both of the Faust theme (with Lord Henry Wotton as a very suave and witty Mephistopheles) and the split-personality theme – in this latter respect it may owe something to Stevenson's *The Strange Case of Dr Jekyll and Mr Hyde* (which was published in 1886).

It is as a document of the aesthetic movement of the late nineteenth century, however, that Wilde's novel has its historical importance. It is full of echoes, for example, of Walter Pater. This is particularly the case with Lord Henry's hedonistic sermon to Dorian at their first meeting in Basil Hallward's studio. The echoes, though, have been subtly distorted. Whereas Pater had appealed for a search for new 'impressions', Wilde has substituted the obviously more sensual word 'sensations' – and in fact Pater wrote a review of Wilde's novel in which he was at pains to distinguish between Lord Henry's philosophy and his own. Wilde must have been well aware of the changes of emphasis he had introduced, but there is no doubt that these corresponded to the interpretation of Pater's writings that was current among the avant-garde artists and writers of the time.

The Preface to the novel, too, is by way of being a manifesto on behalf of these daring new ideas, containing such characteristic pronouncements as these:

> There is no such thing as a moral or an immoral book.

> Vice and virtue are to the artist material for an art ...
> All art is at once surface and symbol.

> All art is quite useless.

These ideas, or variations of them, animated most of the literary and artistic experiments taking place throughout Europe at the time, and for many years after. The violence of the obloquy directed at Wilde's name by the public at large from the moment of his arrest, and for many years afterwards, were to a large extent symptomatic of the fear and uneasiness inspired by the challenge to the old and still largely accepted Victorian standards and conventions represented by the literary and artistic movements with which he had come to be so closely identified.

Yet, paradoxical though it may seem, *The Picture of Dorian Gray*, is in essence a moral fable. There could, after all, hardly be a more lurid condemnation of a life devoted exclusively to the search for sensation. As Hesketh Pearson, one of Wilde's twentieth-century biographers, has put it: 'the moral is driven home with a crude pulpit-punch that should satisfy a Salvationist.'

What, then, are we to make of Lord Henry's 'philosophy'? It is into this that the best of Wilde's brilliance, eloquence and wit are poured. It is this that was meant to shock – and undoubtedly did shock. But in view of the moral that Wilde drew from it, it is basically a matter of words. The inescapable conclusions are that morally Wilde wanted both to have his cake and eat it, and that, in spite of everything, he was at heart a Victorian himself.

The treatment of Dorian's wickedness bears this out. There are awful hints of unmentionable crimes, but apart from a few melodramatic and stagey glimpses of Limehouse there is no attempt to realize them imaginatively or to render them realistically. *The Picture of Dorian Gray* is, in this respect, pallid and prim beside Huysman's *A Rebours* and many other contemporary European novels, and there is no advance of realism in the presentation of evil.

Wilde is essentially a writer who produced brilliant and highly polished surfaces. There is plenty of wit and intelligence, and even some genuine wisdom in *The Picture of Dorian Gray*, but none of the depth, psychological, philosophical or imaginative, of the truly great novels of the nineteenth century. There is certainly no better way, though, of understanding the various moral and artistic attitudes that dominated the intelligentsia of this country towards the end of the nineteenth century, and of deriving much stimulus and entertainment at the same time, than by reading *The Picture of Dorian Gray*.

Tess of the D'Urbervilles

Thomas Hardy

Thomas Hardy began and ended his creative life as a poet. Although he lived until 1928 (his eighty-eighth year) his last novel was published in 1896. In general manner, approach, structure, and technique his novels were typical of their period and Hardy has been described as 'the last of the Victorians'. But, because of the ideas in his novels, he has also been called 'the first of the moderns'. Nowhere are these divergent elements more apparent than in *Tess of the D'Urbervilles*.

Thomas Hardy was born in 1840 in Higher Bockhampton, a small village near Dorchester in Dorset. He was educated at local schools and apprenticed at sixteen to a Dorchester architect who specialized in ecclesiastical works. It was at this time that he began writing verse. In 1862 (when he was twenty-two) he was appointed assistant to one of the leading London architects, and in the following year he won two architectural prizes. In London he continued to write poems and essays, and spent much time studying the paintings in the National Gallery – at one stage he thought of becoming an art critic. It was during this period, too, that his reading of the evolutionary scientists and philosophers turned him into an agnostic.

But he never felt at home in London, and in 1867 he returned to Dorset, resumed his work on church restoration with the same firm of ecclesiastical architects – and wrote his first novel. It was rejected by the publisher's reader, George Meredith, who advised him to write something with a stronger plot. The result was *Desperate Remedies* (1871), a sensational story, rather in the Wilkie Collins manner. It attracted hostile reviews on the grounds of immorality (because it had in it a wealthy unmarried lady with an illegitimate son). In order to counteract this he wrote his charming romantic comedy *Under the Greenwood Tree* (1872), which was subtitled 'A rural painting of the Dutch school'.

By now Hardy was courting Emma Lavinia Gifford, sister-in-law of the rector of a church in Cornwall which Hardy was engaged in restoring, and it was she who was to some extent the prototype of Elfride, the heroine of his next novel, *A Pair of Blue Eyes* (1873).

About this time, Sir Leslie Stephen invited Hardy to write a serial for *The Cornhill Magazine*, and *Far From the Madding Crowd*, one of Hardy's most successful novels, appeared in it during 1874. Like his three previous books it was published anonymously and many readers thought it was by George Eliot. But it appeared under Hardy's own name in volume form, and his fame was established. He was now able to abandon architecture, to marry Emma, and set up in London as a full-time writer.

It is significant, though, that *Far From the Madding Crowd* had been written in his childhood home and derived its strength from the rural backgrounds and values he understood so well. When he attempted a comedy of high society, *The Hand of Ethelberta* (1876), it was a comparative failure and he went back to Dorset to write *The Return of the Native* (1878), the first of the four tragic novels which in the view of some critics raised his work to a level comparable to that of the tragedies of Ancient Greece and of the greatest of the nineteenth-century writers. The other three tragic novels were: *The Mayor of Casterbridge* (1886); *Tess of the D'Urbervilles* (1891), and *Jude the Obscure* (1896).

In 1883, Hardy and his wife finally left London, and Hardy carried out his last work in architecture by designing his own house, Max Gate, near Dorchester, from which he seldom stirred during the rest of his long life. Apart from the years in London and a few visits to the Continent, therefore, Hardy spent the greater part of his life in the county of his birth, and he wrote nearly all his best poetry and prose in it. His marriage was not a very happy one, but in 1914, two years after his first wife died, he married his secretary-companion, Florence Dugdale. He was awarded the rare distinction of the Order of Merit in 1910, and when he died his ashes were interred in Westminster Abbey – but his heart was buried in his parish churchyard in Dorset.

Summary

Tess of the D'Urbervilles begins with Parson Tringham, an antiquary, informing the tranter (or carter) Jack Durbeyfield, Tess's father, that he is really 'Sir John' the descendant ('a little debased') of an ancient aristocratic family named d'Urberville. As a result, Durbeyfield hires a carriage to take him back to his own village of Marlott where Tess and the other girls are waiting for the May Day dance to begin. Tess is thus placed in her 'natural' setting, a participant in age-old village customs and rituals. Watching these proceedings is Angel Clare, a stranger from a higher social class. He and Tess become aware of a mutual attraction.

Durbeyfield meanwhile is at the inn, celebrating the discovery of his ancient lineage. He is not sober enough the next morning to take a consignment of beehives to the nearby town of Casterbridge (Dorchester). So Tess goes instead, but falls asleep over the reins. The horse wanders over to the wrong side of the road and the shaft of a mail-cart going in the opposite direction pierces its chest and kills it.

Anxious to make up to her parents for the loss of the

main source of their livelihood, Tess reluctantly agrees to call on the wealthy Stoke D'Urberville, to whom her father assumes he must be related, in the hope that they might help him and perhaps adopt Tess and make a grand lady of her. Ironically enough, this family has no connection at all with the original d'Urbervilles, having merely annexed the name when they settled in the county.

Tess is received by Alex D'Urberville, the son of the house, and his mother gives Tess the job of looking after her poultry farm. Tess and her family think this is a mark of favour, but in fact Alec has told his mother (who is blind) nothing of Tess's story and has engineered the situation for his own nefarious ends. After repulsing his advances for several months, Tess, returning late after an expedition to the nearby town, accepts a lift from Alec. He takes her to an ancient wood where she falls asleep – and where her seduction, or near-rape, takes place.

Tess becomes pregnant, but not long after the birth of her child it dies. Tess is heartbroken, but gradually she recovers and once more feels 'the pulse of hopeful life still warm within her.' Her experience has matured both her beauty and her character. 'Almost at a leap', Hardy tells us, 'Tess ... changed from simple girl to complex woman.'

She obtains work as a dairymaid on a farm called Talbothays. There she meets Angel Clare, who had briefly crossed her path at the beginning of the story, and who is now studying to become a gentleman farmer. They fall in love, but when Angel asks Tess to marry him she at first refuses because according to the merciless social ethic of the day her past has made her unfit to be his wife. Eventually, though, she agrees. On the night before the wedding-day, when they are staying at the same inn, she writes an account of her seduction and pushes it under the door of Angel's room. It goes under the edge of the carpet, so that Angel does not find it – an episode picked on by many critics as a typical example of the way Hardy frequently wrenches at the normal flow of events by means of bizarre accidents and coincidences, though Hardy himself called such devices 'intensifications', and they can be seen as a means of jolting the reader on to another level of meaning.

The whole atmosphere surrounding the marriage is one of foreboding. Tess is upset because she feels she has seen their wedding-carriage in a dream, and Angel suggests that she may have heard the old legend of the D'Urberville coach in which a 'dreadful crime' had been committed. An 'afternoon cock' crows – an ill omen among the country folk; and one of the dairymaids, who is in love with Angel, tries to drown herself. Then, on their wedding night, Angel confesses to a debauchery he had committed in his youth. This emboldens Tess to pour out her own confession, confident that Angel will forgive her as freely as she does him. The result is the reverse of what she expected. Angel cannot stomach the truth. For him Tess is 'a visionary essence of woman'. They spend a few miserable days together while Angel tries to struggle with the situation and Tess piteously pleads for his understanding and compassion. But Angel is cold and unyielding. It is Alec D'Urberville, he tells her, who is her 'husband in nature, not I.' His conflict expresses itself in one of Hardy's weird, grotesque episodes, which have often been called 'Gothic'. In his sleep, Angel takes Tess in his arms and carries her to a nearby ruined abbey where he lays her in an empty stone coffin. Ludicrous though the episode is in many ways, as so often happens with Hardy, in its context it has an odd, grim effectiveness.

After a few days, Angel leaves Tess and emigrates to Brazil. Tess hands over to her feckless parents half the money Angel had given her before parting. She is soon forced to look for work and joins Marian, one of the dairymaids from Talbothays, on a farm in another part of the county called Flintcomb-Ash.

The contrast between Flintcomb-Ash farm and Talbothays is as sharp as that between Tess's former flowering-time of love and hope and her present state of abandonment and desolation. Marian describes Flintcomb-Ash as 'a starve-acre place', and the backbreaking and badly paid work of swede-hacking in bitter cold weather, under the tyrannical supervision of a farmer who has conceived a grudge against her, comes close to breaking Tess's spirit. She decides to appeal to Angel's parents, but as she is approaching old Mr Clare's vicarage she overhears Angel's brothers discussing his 'unfortunate marriage'. She is too proud to reveal herself and walks the long way back to the grim, inhospitable realities of Flintcomb-Ash. Hardy is at pains throughout the novel to make it clear that Tess really is a D'Urberville and that she has inherited their pride of race. This, indeed, is one of the prerequisites for her tragic status.

When Tess gets back to Flintcomb-Ash, an itinerant hell-fire preacher is holding forth in the great barn. It is, of all people, Alec D'Urberville. It is difficult to understand what exactly Hardy had in mind here. Alec's is admittedly a typical case of the lecher's conversion – as Tess recognizes. Perhaps Hardy was thinking of old legends to the effect that the Devil often adopts the disguise of his 'adversary': diabolical imagery often attends Alec – as when some time later, during the burning of couch-grass, he appears to Tess through the flames carrying a pitchfork. What is certain is that Alec's conversion, and rapid re-conversion after he has met Tess again, does somehow serve to set their relationship in a lurid, ominous light. For Tess, the good and natural bond is that with Angel – and he has wantonly broken it. But she realizes that a bond of sorts *does* exist between herself and Alec, bad and fraught with disaster though she knows it to be. In despair she writes to Angel begging him to return to her.

Fate, though, is once more against Tess. Her father dies, the lease on their cottage is not renewed and the whole family (including Tess) load their goods on a cart and go to Kingsbere – chosen by Mrs Durbeyfield as their new home because her husband's D'Urberville ancestors are buried there.

When Tess and her family reach Kingsbere, their lodgings are already occupied and they are forced to unload their goods and spend the night in the churchyard – among the tombs of Tess's grand ancestors. But Alec (the false D'Urberville) is also at hand. He has been haunting Tess, urging her to accept his 'protection' for herself and her family, and impressing upon her the idea that her husband has utterly abandoned her, until she reaches a point at which she begins to feel 'that in a physical sense this man alone was her husband.'

In fact, Angel (after a serious illness) is on his way home, full of love and repentance. Unaware of Tess's situation, he arrives at the house where she is lodging with Alec – only to discover the terrible truth. Angel leaves, and half-crazed with grief and despair, Tess stabs Alec and hurries away after Angel. They break into an empty house and spend a few poignantly blissful days together. Discovered, they set out northwards, in pursuance of Angel's plan of escaping overseas. When they reach Salisbury Plain, among the brooding monoliths of Stonehenge, Tess, utterly exhausted, lies down on the altar stone to sleep. As she sleeps her pursuers close in, and she hands herself over to them, calm now in the knowledge that she has been reunited in love with Angel. And so poor Tess is taken away, tried, condemned to death, and hanged.

Critical commentary

The first point that should be made in any discussion of *Tess of the D'Urbervilles* is that, like all Hardy's best work, it grew out of his own past and out of the Dorset countryside to which he belonged. From an early age he was steeped in the natural history of the area, and in the sense of an ageless past that invested every acre with reminders of prehistoric inhabitants, Ancient Britons, and

Roman and Anglo-Saxon invaders. Dorset is part of the old Anglo-Saxon kingdom of Wessex – and Hardy called the books set in the county of his boyhood and youth 'the Wessex Novels'. He was a keen reader of local pamphlets, ballads, and the files of old newspapers – and he found the germs of many of his plots in them. At sixteen, he himself witnessed the last public execution in Dorchester, that of a woman who had killed her husband out of jealousy – and remembered it many years later when he came to write *Tess of the D'Urbervilles*.

All of these early interests played their part in the formation of Hardy's later art and philosophy. So, too, did his own origins and background. His father and grandfather were master stonemasons and small builders, and his mother came from a long line of yeoman farmers. There were legends in the Hardy family to the effect that they, like Tess's family, had once occupied a much grander social station. These facts frequently recur in Hardy's poems and novels, and the recreation of the factual and emotional texture of the past played a tremendously important part in his work.

Hardy's deep understanding of nature and the life of the countryside had very little sentimental romanticism about it. There was, for one thing, a strongly marked social element in it. The move which Tess and her family are forced to make is a case in point. There were many such migrations among the agricultural community in Hardy's time, and they were symptomatic of profound changes taking place as traditional methods of farming gradually gave way to modern ones. Part of Hardy's purpose, indeed, in contrasting Talbothays and Flintcomb-Ash had been to make this point. At the former, Tess and her fellow-workers were natural components of an organic agricultural community, whereas at the latter they had been mere wage-slaves to an impersonal system. Hardy's attitude has a good deal of feudal nostalgia about it; on the other hand, the continual references to the economic and social changes taking place in nineteenth-century agriculture show that Arnold Kettle, in his argument that *Tess of the D'Urbervilles* 'has the quality of a social document ... the thesis is that in the course of the nineteenth century the disintegration of the peasantry ... had reached its final and tragic stage ...' is pointing to an element in the novel that must not be overlooked.

There is also something 'natural' about the story of Tess, in a realistic folk sense, as opposed to a romantic one. Hardy divided the novel into a number of 'phases' – and the first of these are entitled: 'Phase the First. The Maiden', and 'Phase the Second. Maiden No More'. At first sight this seems almost comically banal, and at odds with the powerful tragedy that emerges. But it has its justification. As Penelope Vigar, a recent writer on Hardy, has said, from one point of view Tess's story 'in its very ordinariness, is simply that of the traditional "ruined maid" in ballad and folk legend.' Throughout the novel, Hardy is at pains to relate Tess to a traditional way of rustic life – by showing her taking part in village dances for example, such as the one at which she and Angel first catch sight of each other. These elements help to relate Tess to an immemorial past when people lived closer to Nature (in a very real way) and before industrialization had broken up the old patterns and what Hardy called 'the ache of modernity' had deeply affected them. At the same time, a contributing element in Tess's tragedy is the fact that, because of her superior schooling which enables her to consort with people like Angel and Alec, she is herself to some extent affected by this 'ache of modernity'. If she had been a simple peasant girl like her mother, she might not have been cursed with imagination and sensitivity, and in all probability her illegitimate baby would have been the kind of disgrace that, although condemned, is also in a sense accepted within the context of a village community, and would not have had the same tragic consequences.

But Hardy sees Tess as 'natural' in a deeper sense than this. He defiantly subtitled his novel 'A Pure Woman', and in view of the fact that the heroine not only has an illegitimate baby but also murders her seducer, this raised a howl of protest at the time of its publication But the whole concept of the novel was in fact provocative in the sense that Hardy is deliberately contrasting the laws of society, which sees Tess as impure, and the laws of Nature (including those of her own nature) which, because she does not betray them, make her in Hardy's view essentially pure.

Tess is frequently shown against contrasting natural backgrounds. The time of her greatest happiness takes place at Talbothays, and not only because of the presence of Angel. It is at Talbothays that she comes to her full bloom, and her kinship with Nature, in its most beneficent aspects, is most fully illustrated. Her beauty is set against the lushness of the land and the contentment of its animal and human inhabitants alike. The passages in which Hardy describes this are among the finest in his work. They have much the same tone and atmosphere, the same sense of a deep organic relationship between human beings and the soil, that is to be found in D. H. Lawrence's evocations of the Erewash Valley and the Brangwen farm in his novel *The Rainbow*, and help to explain why he was attracted to Hardy's work.

The harshness of the landscape, the farm and its people at Flintcomb-Ash (the name itself, of course, is descriptive) could hardly be greater, and they reflect the hardness and bitterness of Tess's own lot as the victim, not of Nature, but of man-made laws.

Another aspect of Hardy's evocation of Nature appears in the seduction scene. This takes place in an ancient wood (its age is deliberately stressed) and in an atmosphere that is almost dreamlike, as if it were an emanation both of the natural background and of all the human past associated with it. Hardy's reticence in describing the seduction was not due to modesty but to his desire to place it in a timeless, natural context, which is reinforced by his comment that the reaction of the country folk to such an event was to say 'in their fatalistic way: "It was to be".'

Another point about the seduction scene is its 'impressionistic' technique. Frank O'Connor, the Irish story-teller, has pointed out that a 'pictorial imagination of almost unnatural sensitiveness' informs Hardy's work. Hardy was undoubtedly influenced by the French Impressionists, but also by Pre-Raphaelite moralistic pictures such as Holman Hunt's 'Awakening Conscience', which depicts a young 'kept woman' registering pain and distaste in the presence of her seducer. Some of the later scenes of the novel show Tess in a similar situation, and naturalistic set-pieces alternate with the impressionistic ones throughout. The individual aspect of Tess's age-old predicament is, however, stressed when, during the disgrace of her pregnancy, she reflects 'the familiar surroundings had not darkened because of her grief, nor sickened because of her pain.'

Tess's kinship with all growing things and wild creatures – especially birds, which attend her at all her great crises – is continually stressed. If she could have remained at this level, the implication is that she would not have suffered. But human consciousness – and therefore the various social laws and taboos that proceed from it – is also the product of blind evolutionary forces.

Hardy's attitude towards Nature, in other words, was an ambivalent one – and this leads us to his famous 'fatalistic' philosophy. A great deal has been written about this, but it is important to note that practically the last words that he wrote, in the preface to his final volume of poems, were:

(... no harmonious philosophy is attempted in these
pages – or in bygone pages, for that matter.

The word Hardy preferred was 'seemings' – the conclusions, that is, that *appear* to be implicit in the human condition and in the scientific and philosophical discoveries and theories of the period in which Hardy was living, and which 'seemed' to him to contain more of the truth than the traditional religion in which he had been brought up (though he always retained a kind of primitive mysticism, believing in emanations and hauntings, particularly in association with ancient places).

These conclusions derived from Darwin's *The Origin of Species* – Hardy was nineteen when this epoch-making book was published in 1859 – and from the various evolutionary and deterministic theories based on it, especially Herbert Spencer's *First Principles* (1862), and also from his later reading of continental pessimistic philosophers such as Schopenhauer and von Hartmann. From his reading Hardy drew the inference that the universe was ruled by blind chance rather than by any conscious power or plan, either benevolent or malign. It seemed to him that although mankind had, by the purely accidental processes of evolution, achieved some instances of what he called 'a higher consciousness', Nature itself had not kept pace with these finer potentialities and therefore provides no opportunities for their fulfilment ... 'this planet' he wrote 'does not supply the materials for happiness to higher existencies.' To be an unusual human being, it followed, was inevitably to invite tragedy.

This is the fundamental theme of all Hardy's four great tragic novels – but it must be emphasized that in all of them the imaginative vision on the whole transcends the more intellectualized, dogmatic statements of Hardy's pessimistic beliefs, and that their faults occur precisely in those parts where it fails to do so – and particularly in the use of coincidence, sometimes grotesque in its improbability, and the over-reliance on a rather heavy-handed irony. These faults are, it should be added, made worse by the clumsiness with which they are often expressed, and Hardy's prose is always the reverse of elegant. At the same time, when his imagination is really at grips with a situation, the defects of style do not detract from the tragic effect.

There is one sentence in *Tess of the D'Urbervilles*

which has aroused especially adverse comment as far as Hardy's philosophy is concerned. It occurs in the final chapter, when Angel and Tess's younger sister stand on a hill overlooking the prison where Tess lies after being sentenced to death – and see the black flag hoisted to signify that the execution has taken place:

'Justice' was done, and the President of the Immortals, in Aeschylean phrase, had ended his sport with Tess.

In that last bitter reference to 'the President of the Immortals' many critics have seen an unwarranted intrusion of Hardy's pessimistic doctrine of a cruelly indifferent fate controlling the destinies of men. As his contemporary, the critic Edmund Gosse, ironically demanded:

What has Providence done to Mr Hardy that he should rise up in the arable land of Wessex and shake his fist at his Creator?

And E. M. Forster has complained that Hardy's characters are involved in so many 'snares' that 'they are finally bound hand and foot'.

There is, in fact, something of a paradox here. Tess's tragedy *is* to a considerable extent the product of Hardy's philosophy. She is a tragic figure, not because she possesses some fatal flaw in her character, but because her sensitivity, integrity and essential 'purity' cannot possibly stand up against the blind operations of the universe. Without these operations, working through the various accidents and coincidences (the letter that stuck under the carpet; Angel's illness that prevented him returning to England earlier, and so on) her story would have been different. On the other hand, Hardy's philosophy, in a sense, does no more than provide the conditions – one might even say the conventions – for the tragedy. When once the conditions, no matter how irritating, are accepted, the tragedy is there in its own right. Tess is also a victim of the stupidity and cruelty of the moral code of the day, and the economic and social elements play their part as well. When Hardy, in his often odd and lumbering way, gets to grips with her situation, the tragedy becomes not one of theory but of a suffering human being – a human being who, moreover, as a child of Nature solidly placed on the earth, embodies a health- and life-giving principle which is the reverse of pessimistic. It is perhaps D. H. Lawrence who has best understood this, and best summed up Hardy's fundamental achievement:

It is not as a metaphysician that we must consider Hardy. He makes a poor showing there ... His feeling, his instinct, his sensuous understanding is, however, apart from his metaphysics, very great and deep, deeper than that, perhaps of any other English novelist.

New Grub Street

George Gissing

In the eighteenth century, London's Grub Street was inhabited mostly by hack-writers struggling to eke out an existence by miscellaneous journalism, and George Gissing's novel is about struggling writers in the London of his day.

George Gissing was born in Wakefield, Yorkshire, in 1857, the eldest son of a pharmaceutical chemist, who died when George was thirteen. After attending a Quaker school in Cheshire, he was given a scholarship at Owen's College, Manchester. There he achieved brilliant distinction in the Classics. Then he met a seventeen-year-old prostitute and quixotically decided to reclaim her, selling all his available possessions to give her money, unaware that most of it went on gin. Eventually, in order to provide her with further funds, he rifled the Common Room at College, was caught, expelled, and sentenced to a month's imprisonment.

When he left prison, Gissing emigrated to America, tried unsuccessfully to establish himself as a writer and teacher, and came close to starvation and suicide. In 1877 (now aged twenty) he returned to England, married the young prostitute and struggled to make his living as a writer. The marriage was a miserable one because of his wife's alcoholism, and eventually she left him and reverted to her former profession, though Gissing continued to send her money out of his own meagre earnings. Not surprisingly, perhaps, his first novel, *Workers of the Dawn*, was about an idealistic young man patiently and vainly trying to educate an ignorant and resentful wife and to cure her of drinking. Gissing had to pay for its publication himself (in 1880) with a small legacy he had received. His second novel, *The Unclassed* (1884) introduced both a young prostitute who is redeemed by her pure love for an extreme radical schoolmaster, and a depraved girl who ruins the life of her idealistic cousin by playing on his generosity in order to trap him into marriage. It was no more successful than his first. Two other novels followed, dealing with a higher social milieu, but in *Demos* (1886) he returned to slum life – with a difference. Whereas in his earlier novels Gissing had adopted an extreme radical stance, in this novel he presented the working classes as too downtrodden by generations of drudgery, deprivation, and squalor to be capable of political responsibility. As this coincided with an outbreak of socialist agitation, the novel had a topical appeal and sold reasonably well. Although Gissing never achieved a wide public, he was now rescued from actual want.

In 1888 Gissing's estranged wife died of drink. The experience of seeing her lying in a squalid room powerfully affected Gissing and his next novel *The Nether World* (1889) is the most sordid and pessimistic of all his works, a savage indictment both of the slums and of the society that brought them into being. After this novel, Gissing visited Greece and Italy, and *The Emancipated* (1890), is set partly in Italy. Thereafter, most of his novels were about middle-class life, and the impact of contemporary conditions on sensitive individuals struggling to win free from circumstances and conventions.

In 1891, with a kind of fatalistic masochism, Gissing married another uneducated girl whom he casually met, and who continually reviled him and beat their children. Gissing hung on for their children's sake, but in 1897 there was a separation and his wife eventually went insane. His novel *In the Year of Jubilee* (1894) indirectly reflects the miseries of his second marriage. Other novels, such as *The Odd Women* (1893), dealt with aspects of women's aspirations to education and independence. While he was in Italy again, he also wrote his *Charles Dickens: A Critical Study* (1898) – still one of the finest existing studies of Dickens's work – and a charming travel book, *By the Ionian Sea*, which appeared in 1901.

New Grub Street (his ninth novel, published in 1891) was, however, the only one of his works to achieve anything approaching a popular reputation. In reasonably comfortable circumstances for the first time in his life, his last years were his happiest. He met a cultured French-woman named Gabrielle Fleury. Although unable to marry her because his second wife was still alive, for the last five years of his life Gissing lived with Gabrielle and her mother in France. There, among other works, he wrote *The Private Papers of Henry Ryecroft* (1903) – the imaginary (and largely autobiographical) journal of a scholarly recluse who finds contented release from poverty and worry in books, memories, and reflections. It mirrored one aspect of Gissing's own aspirations and, next to *New Grub Street*, it has been his most popular work. In the same year, still only forty-six, he died of consumption.

Summary

New Grub Street, it has been his most popular work. In London. Jasper Milvain, an ambitious young man trying to make his way as a writer, is visiting his mother and two sisters, Maud and Dora. The contrast which constitutes the main theme is quickly set when Jasper hears from his friend Edward Reardon who has published two moderately successful novels of genuine quality (but who is now suffering from 'writer's block') and who is 'the old type of impractical artist' who cannot and will not 'make concessions'.

Also living in Wattleborough is Amy Reardon's uncle, John Yule, a wealthy retired business man. He is visited by his brother Alfred, a poor and grimly dedicated scholar who has achieved a modest reputation for his learned articles. Alfred is accompanied by his daughter Marian, his indispensable research assistant in the British Museum. Marian becomes friendly with Maud and Dora Milvain, and Jasper finds himself attracted to her – much to his distress, because he is convinced that a writer who is determined to be successful must only marry where there is money.

When Jasper calls on the Reardons in London, Amy contrasts his attitude with that of her husband – and urges Reardon to try and follow in his friend's footsteps. Alfred Yule, meanwhile, learns that he is being considered for the editorship of a periodical. His first reaction is savage glee at the thought of the opportunities an editorship would give him to flay his literary enemies. Alfred visits much of his resentment upon his wife, an uneducated woman whom he despises. Thus, Alfred Yule's solution of the marriage problem is contrasted with Reardon's, whose wife *is* an educated and genteel girl. Alfred's temper is not improved when the hoped for editorship goes to somebody else.

When Mrs Milvain dies, Jasper brings his sisters up to London and sets them to work on writing pot-boilers for the expanding market for children's books. Jasper, still reluctantly attracted by Marian Yule, seeks her out again. Marian is well aware of Jasper's faults – but, lonely, hemmed in by narrow circumstances and bullied by her father, Marian's 'womanhood went eagerly to meet' the first man 'who had approached her with display of feeling and energy and youthful self-confidence ...' She knows, too, that Jasper is moved in spite of himself.

In an attempt to be more practical (and more like Jasper) Reardon decides to write a sensational novel. But he is exhausted in body and spirit and makes up his mind that he must live cheaply in the country for a time, while Amy and their small son Willie stay with her mother. Amy loves her husband after a fashion, but her ambition had been to see him famous so that she could 'shine with reflected light before an admiring assembly.' When, therefore, Reardon's novel is rejected and he takes a humble clerkship at a hospital, she is horrified. Reardon knows that this is the crisis in their relationship and asks Amy to follow him to whatever life he can offer her, no matter how humble, but she is not moved by his request and leaves him. Her mother, Mrs Yule, receives her kindly, but her brother John insultingly asks Reardon what he intends to do about supporting his wife and child. Reardon half-starves himself so that he can send Amy half of the weekly pittance he earns as a clerk.

Marian's life at home has been becoming increasingly wretched. Her father's treatment of her mother is more tyrannical than ever, and he takes every opportunity of expressing his hostility towards Jasper Milvain. Then John Yule, Alfred's brother, suddenly dies. Alfred hurries down to Wattleborough for the funeral, confidently expecting that his brother will have left him well provided for. But it is Marian who receives a legacy of £5,000 and Amy who receives double that amount. Alfred tries to persuade Marian to invest her money in his projected periodical. But she has another use for her legacy, and when Jasper hears of it he proposes and she joyously accepts him.

The feelings of Marian (one of the most likeable characters in the book) are beautifully and delicately handled by Gissing, in spite of the fact that his style possesses little fluency or poetry.

In the meantime, Reardon, by a superhuman effort, has finished another novel, though agonizingly aware that it is much inferior to his previous ones. His friend, the gentle and quixotic Harold Biffen, is also working painstakingly on a novel – an experiment, he explains, in 'absolute realism in the sphere of the ignobly decent'. Biffen lives on the verge of starvation, making a few shillings by coaching. He has no hope of ever being able to afford to marry, though he humbly adores Amy from afar.

Reardon's novel is accepted, but on terms that make it only too evident that the publisher has no confidence in it, and which merely suffice to pay off his debts and to postpone the impending crisis in his affairs. The gentle Biffen tries to argue him into a more optimistic frame of mind, but when Reardon secures a much better job as secretary to a home for destitute boys at Croydon, he takes the news to Amy in a haughty and unforgiving spirit, and though she offers to go with him, she is unable to give him the assurance of love he secretly craves, and the fact of her inheritance makes him even more touchy. The rift between them seems irreparable, and at the same time Reardon's health is getting progressively worse.

Alfred Yule tells Marian that if she marries Jasper he will have nothing further to do with her, and she resolves to leave home. Then come two terrible blows. Marian learns that her inheritance will only come to £1,500 after all (owing to the bankruptcy of the firm in which it had been invested). It also turns out that her father is going blind, and that his eyes will have to be operated on. Marian tells Jasper that she must use her money to help her parents and he breaks off the engagement.

By now Biffen has finished his novel, though he is nearly killed rescuing the manuscript from a fire in his lodgings. Reardon is also in a very bad way, with congestion of the lungs, but, as his son is ill, insists on catching a train to Brighton. When he arrives, husband and wife fall into each other's arms. Willie dies, and Reardon himself has to retire to bed. Amy nurses him tenderly and Biffen hurries down to Brighton to help her; but Reardon, too, dies – happy in the thought that he has regained Amy's love. Six months later, Biffen's novel is published and Jasper generously writes a glowing review of it. In spite of its merits and originality, however, it is commercially a failure, and he receives the grand total of fifteen pounds for it. Biffen reacts in his usual philosophical way. 'The work was done – the best he was capable of – and this satisfied him.' But the realization of the utter hopelessness of his love for Amy eventually decides him, without fuss or self-pity, to commit suicide.

There are other casualties of the battle for survival in *New Grub Street*. Alfred Yule's operation is a failure and he becomes completely blind. Marian takes him and her mother with her to a provincial town where she has obtained a job as an assistant librarian, and her father dies there not long afterwards. As for Jasper Milvain, he writes a study of Reardon's work and secures the reissue of his two best novels. This means that he sees a good deal of Amy, and before long they are married. Amy uses her fortune to help Jasper conduct the campaign of lavish entertaining and all the other social activities so necessary, in Jasper's view, for success in the literary world. As a result, he achieves his main objective, appointment to the editorship of an influential periodical.

Critical commentary

In spite of this happy ending for Jasper and Amy, it is obvious that *New Grub Street* is on the whole a pessimistic novel – George Orwell described Gissing as 'the chronicler of vulgarity, squalor and failure'. It is evident that *New Grub Street* embodied many of Gissing's own experiences as well as his generally sombre, low-key attitude to life. Its gloom is perhaps of a rather narrow and specialized kind, mainly concerned with a small professional group, but there are important social and cultural implications. Gissing was writing about a period in which the modern communications industry was just coming into being. For writers merely out to make money, there were unparalleled opportunities to cater for a massive new semi-literate public. But for writers without private incomes who genuinely loved literature, who had intellectual interests, or who sought to maintain their artistic integrity, the difficulties of staying afloat, unless they possessed genius (and not always then) were immense. No other novel of the period presented this situation more comprehensively, profoundly, and compassionately than Gissing's *New Grub Street*.

In the 'grey exactitude' – as V. S. Pritchett has called it – of Gissing's description of the average author's life of his day it is the petty, ignoble aspects which are emphasized. He makes no concessions to romantic notions of the glamour of genius and the bohemian life, except in the case of Biffen, who is closest to the popular idea of the purely dedicated artist.

New Grub Street was a genuinely popular book, and one which has held its own ever since it was published. One of the reasons for this lies in the unemphatic, unspectacular nature of Gissing's realism. In his book on Dickens, Gissing insisted that:

> ... truth, for the artist, is the impression produced on him and ... to convey this impression with entire sincerity is his sole reason for existing.

On the whole he abided faithfully by this doctrine. He rejected the 'naturalism' of Zola and his followers in France because it imitated the experimental method of the laboratory. His sympathies were closer to the contemporary Russian realists, and from the point of view of literary history, Gissing's work is important as an early instance of their influence in English fiction. In a most telling phrase, he underlined Dostoyevsky's power to portray 'minds maddened by hunger' – a phrase which could be applied most aptly to *New Grub Street*.

Like Dostoyevsky, Gissing penetrated the lower reaches of urban life, populated by the drab, anonymous crowds, the outcasts and misfits of society. It was in this respect and not in form or method (which remained predominantly Victorian) that Gissing's originality lay. No English novelist, except Dickens, has so fully captured the feel and the smell of the more dreary aspects of London life. As the American critic Irving Howe has said, the setting of Gissing's drama in *New Grub Street* 'is the modern city, that jungle of loneliness and strife.'

Consequently, in a modern industrialized society, characters like Reardon, Biffen, Marian and Alfred Yule, have a symbolic, universal value; their sorrows and their resentments are those of countless thousands who know that they are not being allowed to fulfil their capacities for a fully human life. *New Grub Street* is above all the novel of the lonely, the uprooted, the rejected, and the exiled.

Arnold Bennett, a novelist of the early twentieth century who owed a good deal to Gissing, summed up his achievements when he wrote:

> to take the common gray things which people know and
> despise and without tampering to disclose their epic
> significance and grandeur – that is realism, as distinguished
> from idealism or romanticism.

At the same time, *New Grub Street* does contain lively and positive qualities. The descriptions of London, for instance, reveal an occasional subdued poetry – as when Biffen walks to Putney Heath to commit suicide. None of the men in the novel are cardboard figures, and Amy and Marian are two of the most convincing women in nineteenth-century fiction. 'Gissing is unusual among English male novelists,' V. S. Pritchett has pointed out, 'in discerning the mental life of his women.'

Lying behind the cultural standards that Gissing so passionately defends in *New Grub Street* there is, in spite of all the acerbities of his nature, genuine compassion and humanity, and it is impossible to read the novel without being aware of these qualities.

Esther Waters

George Moore

George Moore and his novel *Esther Waters* throw into special prominence the controversy over realism in fiction which agitated the last two decades of the nineteenth century. The fact that Moore was to some extent outside the normal English literary tradition may have helped in this process. For one thing he was an Irishman, born in 1852 at Moore Hall in County Mayo, son of a country squire. Although Moore's parents were Protestants he was sent to a Jesuit school, but soon rebelled against both religion and learning. He arrived in London in 1870, with a vague idea of becoming an artist. As soon as he came of age he went to Paris to study painting and spent nearly seven years in France. He decided that he had no talent for painting, but he got to know Manet, Degas and other leading Impressionists and their influence, combined with that of his artistic training, was later to affect his attitude towards style and composition in his writing, especially in his own later 'impressionistic' phase.

Moore also met Mallarmé and the French Symbolist poets of the day, at a time when they were barely known in England. But these interests were soon superseded by an enthusiasm for the contemporary French realistic novelists, and above all for Emile Zola, 'the father of French Naturalism', as he has been called. Zola believed that just as the scientist lays out his materials in the laboratory in order to see what happens to them under certain conditions, so the novelist should assemble characters of a certain type and hereditary constitution, place them in a certain environment, and see what logically resulted in terms of behaviour. Implicit in this method was a painstaking research of all the documentary details. Moore was tremendously impressed by the Naturalistic theories and determined to put them into practice himself.

When, therefore, he returned to London, he was culturally more French than English, and at a time when French fiction was, in English minds, synonymous with indecency, he shocked contemporary opinion by defending Zola in an article of 1882 – 'the first eulogy', he proudly wrote to inform Zola himself, to be published in England. Moore followed this up with a novel, *A Modern Lover* (1883) which told, in unusually frank detail for that time, the story of an egotistical painter and the three women in his life. Its success was largely one of notoriety, for the novel was banned by the circulating libraries, the unofficial censors and guardians of public morals of the period. Moore promptly wrote a pamphlet 'Literature at Nurse', which scathingly attacked both the libraries and the general timidity of the English public, and reasserted his Naturalistic doctrines.

Moore's next novel, *A Mummer's Wife* (1884) is about a young woman who rebels against a narrow, pious background and a nagging husband by eloping with an actor and, after a short-lived success on the stage, drinks herself to death. Obviously it owes a great deal to Zola's *L'Assomoir* (1878) which was also about drunkenness (the title means a low drinking den or tavern). Moore had also faithfully followed Zola's precepts by thoroughly researching his subject. He wanted to portray a drab industrial town, and when he was told that Hanley in the Potteries was the ugliest town in England, he went there, notebook in hand, to compile an extensive dossier. As the story was largely concerned with shabby theatrical life in provincial towns, he also spent several weeks travelling round with a light-opera troupe. *A Mummer's Wife* was, in fact, a genuinely new departure in English fiction, abandoning the old traditions of a romantic plot with a happy ending in order to pursue, with grim objectivity, the consequences which would, he believed, naturally follow the initial circumstances he had posited.

Moore's next novel, *A Drama in Muslin* (1886), which he called 'a study of the life of a group of girl friends', was so frank and outspoken about their sexual frustrations and problems that one of the periodicals declared that 'a more repulsive tale' had never been written. Several rather inferior novels followed – and then in 1894 came George Moore's masterpiece, *Esther Waters*. Two other novels, *Evelyn Innes* (1898) and *Sister Teresa* (1901) followed, and these three are sometimes regarded as the books of Moore's prime. From 1901 to 1910 he lived in Ireland, publishing volumes of short stories and memoirs. In 1921, having returned to London, Moore published his last novel, *Héloïse and Abélard*, and died in 1933.

Summary

One of the outstanding features of *Esther Waters* is that nearly all the main characters are working class – which was not usual at the time Moore was writing, and is not that common now. Esther Waters herself is a poor girl, brought up as a member of the very devout Plymouth Brethren. She has been working as a servant in London for some time, and, when the story opens, is taking her first situation in the country, as a kitchen-maid at a big house on the South Downs with extensive racing stables, owned by a family named Barfield. On her arrival, Esther is befriended by William Latch, one of the servants. At first she falls foul of William's mother, the sharp-tongued cook, and is afraid of being dismissed. But Mrs Barfield is herself a Plymouth Sister and takes Esther under her wing. Mrs Barfield and Esther both disapprove of racing on religious grounds, but before long Esther finds herself affected by the racing atmosphere and she buys a ticket in a sweepstake organized by William Latch. By now, Esther is in Mrs Latch's good graces but incurs the enmity of another servant, Sarah, because she had drawn the winning horse in the lottery and also because William has transferred his favours from her to Esther.

A servant's ball is held to celebrate the various successes of the racing stables. Esther is hailed as the belle of the ball, and William makes much of her. Before long they become lovers, in a scene which seems mild enough today, but was specific enough at the time to seem incredibly daring. Not long afterwards, William elopes with one of the Barfield daughters and Esther finds herself pregnant. Mrs Barfield, however, treats her kindly, giving her a small sum of money, and writing a 'character' for her – that indispensable document for a servant girl in Victorian times, the absence of which meant that many girls in Esther's position had no recourse but to go on the streets.

Esther returns home. Her mother, ill and pregnant herself, receives her lovingly. Her stepfather wants to turn her out, but relents when he learns that she can pay her way. When from time to time, however, he starts beating his wife in order to extract money from her for his drinking, Esther buys him off, and her tiny savings rapidly dwindle.

The descriptions of Esther's experiences in the maternity hospital and of her actual birth-pangs shocked contemporary readers even more than Moore's daring in the seduction scene. It was in such passages that Moore seemed most Zola-like – and in which he was also at his best. There is nothing morbid or sensational in the writing, and the tone is exactly right. It is right, too, when Moore describes Esther's feelings when the new born baby – 'a pulp of red flesh rolled up in flannel' – is laid beside her. It is, in fact, strangely tender and moving, coming from a rather pompous and affected man who avoided lasting attachments with women and who never married.

While she is in hospital, Esther's mother dies, and the rest of the family emigrate to Australia. Esther, left alone with her baby, is reduced to her last few shillings and is about to apply for admittance to a workhouse when she gets a job as a wet-nurse. This means that she has to put her child, Jackie, in a baby-farm run by a rascally couple named Spires. As a wet-nurse Esther is pampered and well fed so that she will have plenty of milk for her employer's baby, but is practically kept a prisoner. 'By what right, by what law,' she wonders, 'was she separated from her child? ... it seemed to this ignorant girl that she was the victim of a far-reaching conspiracy; she experienced the sensation of the captured animal ...'

Eventually, when she is told that her baby is ill, she goes to him, and with him in her arms, wanders to the river where she contemplates suicide. For the sake of her child she seeks refuge instead in the workhouse. The workhouse authorities find her a job in the household of a shopkeeper and she succeeds in placing the baby Jackie with a kindly widow named Mrs Lewis. But forced to work seventeen hours a day, and fearful of what will happen to Jackie if her health breaks down, Esther leaves the job. She gets another one, but is dismissed when it is discovered that she has an illegitimate child. Realizing that this is a fact she must conceal, she obtains a good post with kindly people, but when the teenage son falls in love with her and asks her to marry him, she feels she must leave. Her employers pay her a month's wages and give her a good reference and she lives with Mrs Lewis and Jackie while looking for another job. Eventually she is engaged by a gentle spinster in Kensington, named Miss Rice, who earns a living as a novelist. Mistress and servant grow fond of each other, and Esther's life is easier. Then, when Esther is twenty-five (and Jackie six) she meets a young man named Fred Parsons who is a Plymouth

Brother. He reintroduces her to her old faith and asks her to marry him. She is fond of him and agrees, but soon afterwards runs into William Latch. His marriage has proved a disaster and he is now seeking a divorce. He persuades Esther to take him to see his son, and the two take a great liking to each other. Esther is at first jealous, bitter and resentful, but after a time her old love for William revives. She breaks off her engagement with Fred and marries William who is now the landlord of 'The King's Head', and also runs a bookmaking business. The pub is a great centre for betting men, among them Barfield's son, now a gentleman-rider. The Barfields have fallen on evil days, however, and the old riding stables are closed. Sarah, the servant with whom William had once flirted at Woodview and who is now in service in London, also comes into their life again.

William takes Esther and Sarah to Epsom on Derby Day, described in some of George Moore's most vivid prose and with a visual command which shows that his early training as a painter had stood him in good stead.

On the ground, Esther meets Fred Parsons again and Sarah takes up with a scoundrel named Bill Evans. William catches a chill from frequenting racecourses in bad weather and transfers his betting business to 'The King's Head', though this is against the law. Fred Parsons, who has now joined the Salvation Army and is engaged in a campaign to stamp out gambling in the area, warns them that they are in danger of prosecution. But, without the betting, the pub would do little business, and William is forced to carry on as before. Then Bill Evans persuades Sarah to steal her mistress's silver and pawn it in order to provide money for his gambling. When Esther pleads with William, he generously offers to redeem the pawned silver, but Bill Evans has disappeared with the pawn ticket and Sarah is arrested at 'The King's Head', and sent to prison. This attracts the attention of the police to the pub, and eventually they raid the premises. William is fined and forced to conduct his bookmaking on the race-tracks again, while Esther tries hard to expand the normal business of the pub. But a renewal of their licence is refused, and a little later William falls seriously ill and dies.

Esther and Jackie, penniless once more, are about to enter the workhouse when, as a last desperate resort, Esther (who is still illiterate) gets Jackie to write for her to Mrs Barfield. She receives a reply offering her employment and enclosing the money for her fare. So once again Esther sets out for Woodview. She finds it in a semi-derelict condition. Mrs Barfield, now a widow, is living alone in reduced circumstances in a portion of the house. The two women keep their distance as mistress and maid, finding it more 'comfortable' that way, but they attend meetings of the Plymouth Brethren together and there is a close communion between them. The picture of their life together is in some respects similar to that of the two sisters in Arnold Bennett's *The Old Wives' Tale* (1908), and it is clear that *Esther Waters* is one of the influences behind that famous novel.

Esther is able to support Jackie out of her wages and eventually he becomes a soldier. The novel ends with his visiting his mother on one of his leaves.

Critical commentary

The soberly happy ending may be seen as an example of the 'modified realism' which George Moore achieved in *Esther Waters*. Not long after the publication of *A Drama in Muslin* he had begun to experience a reaction against Zola and Naturalism, partly influenced by the Russian novelists, whose realism was always attended by compassion and a deep concern for moral and spiritual values. Nevertheless, *Esther Waters* is very much a novel in the realistic mode and the French influence is still strong. It owes a good deal, for example, to *Germinie Lacerteux* (1865), a story about an illiterate servant-girl by the brothers de Goncourt. In addition, Moore made detailed 'documentary' observations of the servant-girl in his own lodgings. He still despised all contemporary English efforts at realism. In particular he was scornful of Hardy's *Tess of the D'Urbervilles*, declaring that its scenes of so-called passion were unforgivably timid and evasive. And it was partly as a riposte to Hardy's novel that Moore deliberately chose what is the same basic theme of seduction and betrayal.

There is another novel which must also be mentioned. This is Gustave Flaubert's *Madame Bovary*, which was published in 1856 and is perhaps the most famous of all the nineteenth-century realistic novels. Although its theme of adultery outraged Victorian susceptibilities, the artistic dedication with which the author approached it and his almost obsessive attention to exactitude of style and perfection of form, made it a tremendous influence among those English writers who wanted to produce novels which not only provided entertainment, but were also works of art. Among these was George Moore, who claimed that *Esther Waters* was 'pure Flaubert'.

Flaubert's influence is evident in *Esther Waters* mainly in technical matters. The beginning of the chapter describing the heroine's first arrival at Woodview is, for example, almost duplicated by the beginning of the chapter in which Esther, after so many years and sufferings, returns there. This device may be seen as an attempt to follow in Flaubert's footsteps in the achievement of balance, symmetry and form. In these passages, too, there is the same careful choice and placing of detail, colour, and epithet, and the same tone of controlled, solid, and rather flat objectivity that are to be found in Flaubert's novel.

Esther Waters – written at exactly that point in Moore's career when literary apprenticeship, extreme realistic theory, modifications in approach brought about by experience and temperament, and inborn talent, all naturally fused – undoubtedly constitutes his masterpiece.

Jude the Obscure

Thomas Hardy

Although Hardy lived until 1928, *Jude the Obscure* was his last novel and he devoted the rest of his long life after its publication almost exclusively to his poetry. It would not be possible, however, to arrive at a complete understanding of Hardy's life and work without reading his last novel, which can be seen as the culmination of his explorations in the fictional mode.

In his Preface to the first edition (1896) Hardy stated that his main purposes were:

> to tell, without a mincing of words, of a deadly war waged
> between flesh and spirit; and to point to the tragedy
> of unfulfilled aims.

Summary

For the boy Jude, living in the village of Marygreen, 'spirit' (and as it turns out 'unfulfilled aims' as well) is represented by nearby Christminster, the ancient university city (modelled on Oxford), to which he dreams of going one day as a student. The local schoolmaster, Richard Phillotson, has taken a kindly interest in him, and after he himself has gone to Christminster in the hope of getting ordained as a clergyman, he sends Jude books from which the boy tries to teach himself Latin and Greek. Jude also apprentices himself to a local stonemason with a view to working in Christminster and in the hope that, once there, he will soon be 'knocking at the doors of those strongholds of learning'.

But 'spirit' is about to come into violent conflict with 'flesh'. On his way home from work, day-dreaming about his future academic triumphs, Jude is struck on the cheek by a 'pizzle' (the penis of a boar) thrown at him by Arabella Donn, daughter of a small pig-farmer. Jude is the complete innocent and Arabella, 'a complete and substantial female animal – no more, no less', has no difficulty in sweeping him off his feet. When Jude tells her that he is leaving shortly for Christminster, she employs the age-old expedient of implying that she is pregnant, and Jude immediately marries her. Before long, Jude discovers that Arabella's pregnancy was a false alarm and that his marriage is a throughly unhappy one. However, when Arabella decides to emigrate with her parents to Australia, Jude is free once more, and at last he sets out, tools on back, for Christminster, where he wanders in a romantic dream round the ancient colleges.

Soon he is entertaining romantic notions of another sort as well, in connection with his cousin Sue Bridehead, who is also living in Christminster. Sue herself is introduced in a curious and symbolic little episode. She buys a pair of plaster statuettes of Venus and Apollo and it strikes her that they are 'so very large ... and so very naked' that she wraps them up before taking them back to her lodgings. She stands the statuettes on her chest of drawers, underneath a print of the Crucifixion which is hanging on the wall. The juxtaposition of the pagan statues and the Cross effectively symbolizes the duality in her nature. There is in Sue's action, at the same time, something of the studentish determination to prove a point, and the naughtily defiant element is reinforced by her fear that her prim landlady will see the naked figures. In other words, she is in the same state of immaturity as Jude, and the title Hardy originally intended for the novel – 'The Innocents' – is as apt for her as it is for him.

After Sue's landlady discovers the statuettes and smashes them to pieces in disgust, Sue decides to leave Christminster. She goes with Jude to call on Phillotson, now a schoolmaster once more (his plans for a Christminster degree and ordination having come to nothing). Phillotson has a vacancy for a pupil-teacher, gives the job to Sue, and is soon hopelessly in love with her. Meanwhile, Jude writes to the heads of a number of colleges. He receives only one long-delayed reply pointedly addressed to 'Mr J. Fawley, stone-mason' and advising him to stick to his trade.

He now decides to study for the Church, and goes to Melchester in order to apply for a place in the theological college there. Sue is also in Melchester, at the teachers' training college – and by now engaged to Phillotson. Despite this, on a day off from college, Sue accompanies Jude on a long country ramble. In the course of it she prattles, in her charming and captivating way, about her brave new ideas and unconsciously points to the reality behind her talk of 'freedom' when she says: 'I crave to get back to the life of my infancy and its freedom.' When they find they have walked too far, they have to spend a night in a cottage – though respectably separated. For this Sue is severely reprimanded by her college authorities and sentenced to a week's solitary confinement in her room. She escapes by climbing through the window and then wading across a river, reaching Jude's lodgings soaked to the skin. While her clothes are drying, she wears Jude's Sunday suit – a somewhat sledgehammer symbol of the fact that despite her advanced ideas and her undoubted attractiveness, her sexual nature is quite unformed. After she has been expelled from the training college, Sue (knowing now that Jude already has a wife) marries Phillotson.

Arabella herself now turns up in Christminster, and after he has been drinking, Jude spends a night with her. He is disgusted with himself, especially when Arabella tells him that she has made a bigamous marriage in Australia. The episode has demonstrated that the snares

of the flesh are still as real for Jude as the more complicated ones represented by Sue. In some respects there
could hardly be a greater contrast than that between the
two women. Yet there are similarities between them, if
only in the fact that both of them, in their very different
ways, exploit Jude's weaknesses, simplicities, and confu-
sions – though only because he is open to exploitation.

This is borne out by the next encounter between Jude
and Sue, when Sue admits the truth about her marriage
to Phillotson and Hardy allows her to reveal the physical
incompatibility between them with a frankness very rare
at the time. When Sue and Jude part this time, it is with
a long and passionate kiss. Its import is so obvious that
Jude realizes he cannot go on training for a church which
regards sexual love 'as at its best a frailty, and at its worst
damnation', and he burns all his theological books.

As for Sue, 'that ethereal, fine nerved, sensitive girl
quite unfitted by temperament and instinct to fulfil the
conditions of the matrimonial relation with Phillotson,
possibly with scarce any man', begs her husband to give
her her freedom. Characteristically, she bases her appeal
on the intellect, quoting from John Stuart Mill's famous
essay 'Liberty' – and hardly surprisingly poor Phillotson,
who loves her devotedly, moans 'What do I care about
J. S. Mill!' Eventually though, he agrees to let her go,
impressed by the affinity he senses between her and Jude.
The essential unawareness of Sue's sexual nature, however, is quickly demonstrated when she announces to
Jude her high-souled determination not to sully their
relationship by going to bed with him.

Phillotson suffers even more than Jude. Not only is he
desolate and alone, but the committee of his school
demand his resignation on the grounds that he has condoned his wife's adultery. When he refuses to resign, a
public meeting is called at which his accusers and his
supporters come to blows. This sudden excursion into
comedy is Dickensian in manner and tone. It is a rare
and, on the face of it, incongruous one in so tragic a

novel. On the other hand, it is significant that Phillotson's accusers are the representatives of the oppressive forces of society, while his main supporters are the rebels – the travelling salesmen and the fairground people. The latter, in this case, stand for vitality and spontaneity – just as the circus folk in Dickens's *Hard Times* (1854) had done. Phillotson is therefore seen here as a focus of healthier and ultimately more realistic values, though the immediate outcome for him is that he falls ill and is dismissed from his school.

Eventually, he divorces Sue, and Jude also divorces Arabella so that she can marry her Australian lover. There is a temporary hitch in Arabella's plans, however, and she appeals to Jude for help. This has the effect of provoking Sue's jealousy, and at last she abandons her ideal of a Platonic union. She and Jude decide to get married, but on the way to the parish clerk to make the arrangements Sue has doubts about the institution of marriage. 'Don't you think it is destructive to a passion whose essence is its gratuitousness?' she says – and Jude, happy now in the possession of the passion, agrees.

While they are still, characteristically, debating the question, a letter arrives from Arabella announcing the imminent arrival of a son she had borne to Jude while she was in Australia, but whom she says she cannot afford to keep herself. This child is undoubtedly one of the weirdest in fiction. For one thing he has the unlikely nickname of 'Little Father Time' – because, he explains, 'I look so aged.' A child introduced in such portentous terms is hardly likely to be a very real one. He is, in fact, a grotesque intrusion from a more symbolic or allegorical type of fiction – rather like the Spirit of Times Past which Dickens conjures up for Scrooge's dream in *A Christmas Carol* (1843). For the sake of the boy, Jude and Sue make another attempt to get married but this time they are put off by the sordid atmosphere of the Registry Office and creep away 'stealthily and guiltily, as if they had committed a misdemeanour.'

A happier time, nevertheless, follows for them both, though they fail to make 'Little Father Time' cheerful or childlike, and he remains a shadow over their lives. Then gossip drives them from their home, and for the next few years they lead a semi-nomadic life, staying in various lodgings. Two children of their own are born during this period, but Hardy makes little attempt to render concretely the more normal, sensual aspects of their lives together, almost as if he is impatient to return to the relentlessly tragic implications of their situation. Meanwhile, Arabella, now widowed, turns up again, with the intention of getting Jude back for herself.

Jude insists on returning to Christminster with Sue and the three children – because 'I love the place', he explains. When they arrive, a procession of university dignitaries is taking place and Jude impractically insists on watching before setting off to search for lodgings. They are turned away from several houses because of the presence of the children and Sue's pregnancy – to the growing distress of Little Father Time. Eventually, a landlady takes in Sue and the children but cannot accommodate Jude who goes off to spend the night at an inn. Sue now gives a typical demonstration of *her* impracticality. Impulsively she confides in the landlady that she is not married and is told that she must leave in the morning. What is worse, she is totally insensitive to what is passing through Little Father Time's mind, and upsets him further by telling him that another baby is on the way. Next day, Sue and Jude find that Little Father Time has hanged himself and the other children, leaving the laconic note *'Done because we are too menny.'*

What Hardy is trying to do is to use this appalling episode as he has used Little Father Time himself, to achieve a Choric, distancing effect, and to transfer the temporal and personal story of Jude and Sue to the timeless plane of pure tragedy. Thus, Hardy says of Little Father Time and his terrible action:

On that little shape had converged all the inauspiciousness
and shadow which had darkened the first union of Jude,
and all the accidents, mistakes, fears, errors of the last.
He was their nodal point, their focus, their expression in
a single term.

Although nearly all the critics are agreed that his 'slaughter of the innocents' is too violently melodramatic to be
successful artistically, Hardy was using it to illustrate
another aspect of his overall social and philosophical
scheme. For when Sue, weak and ill after a miscarriage,
accuses herself of being responsible for Little Father
Time's action, Jude tells her:

> 'No ... It was his nature to do it. The doctor says there
> are such boys springing up amongst us – boys of a sort
> unknown to the last generation – the outcome of new
> views of life. They seem to see all of its terrors before they
> are old enough to have staying power to resist them.
> He says it is the beginning of the coming universal wish
> not to live.'

The intrusion of a purely intellectual argument – bor-
rowed from the pessimistic philosopher Schopenhauer –
so incongruous at such a moment of tragedy, points to a
change that now comes over the novel as theory increasingly takes over and the conversation and behaviour of
Jude and Sue frequently veer towards the stilted and the
melodramatic.

Sue decides that the children's deaths are a divine
punishment for the irregular union in which she and
Jude have been living. Jude tries to argue her out of this
frame of mind, protesting 'Do not do an immoral thing
for moral reasons!' But Sue is fixed in her purpose and
when Phillotson, prompted by Arabella, asks Sue to re-
marry him, she agrees. In a characteristically melodramatic gesture she announces her decision to Jude at the
graveside of their children. Jude, clear-sighted as to the
unrealistic nature of Sue's mood of self-abnegation, pro-

tests that it will be no more than 'a frantic prostitution', but she cannot be shaken.

The perversity of Sue's course of action is soon made apparent. When she sees the marriage licence on Phillotson's desk she starts back and 'Her look was that of the condemned criminal who catches sight of his coffin.' Again, when the widow Edlin is setting out a pretty nightdress for Sue to wear, Sue savagely rips it to pieces and insists on wearing instead a coarse unbleached calico one – her substitute, perhaps, for a hair-shirt. And when the marriage takes place, Sue insists once more on a sexless union.

As for Jude, Arabella gets him drunk and marries him again. They lead a cat-and-dog life, but by now Jude has become little more than an automaton, dazed by illness and grief. He has one last meeting with Sue at which she tells him that her marriage to Phillotson is only 'nominal', and then flings herself into his arms. Jude makes a final appeal, but Sue's self-inflicted martyrdom is too strong for her. She goes back to Phillotson, and in spite of the aversion she still feels for him, announces that she will now share his bed. A neighbour gives Jude the news of Sue's final surrender as he lies dying. He calls it the 'ultimate horror' declaring that for him and Sue 'the time was not ripe ... Our ideas were fifty years too soon to be any good to us.'

Jude's deathbed is attended by all kinds of ironies, with Arabella out enjoying herself with a new lover while Jude lies alone and half-delirious reciting from the Book of Job, the cheers from the Remembrance Day games and celebrations of the university he had yearned to enter reaching him through the open window.

Critical commentary

'Jude the Obscene' was what one contemporary wit called Hardy's last novel, and Mrs Oliphant (herself a novelist) declared in a review of it:

> There may be books more disgusting, more impious as
> regards human nature, more foul in detail, in those dark
> corners where the amateurs of filth find garbage to their
> taste; but not ... from any Master's hand.

The Bishop of Wakefield, horrified by the book's 'insolence and indecency' threw it in the fire. The shock-waves reached New York, where one of the reviewers declared:

> It is simply one of the most objectionable books that we
> have ever read in any language whatsoever.

In a 'Postscript' which Hardy wrote in 1912, he spoke of the outcry as 'completely curing me of further interest in novel-writing.' It is true that after *Jude the Obscure* he returned to his first love, poetry. But it is doubtful whether a writer of his integrity would have given up writing fiction simply because of hostile reviewers. It is more likely that he knew instinctively, as an artist, that he had come to the end of the kind of exploration he had been conducting in the Wessex novels and that his imaginative vision henceforth had to seek an entirely different mode.

There are signs in *Jude the Obscure* of the kind of strain that inevitably results when a writer is grappling with a vision of society that has become almost intolerable. For example, Hardy uses a new kind of language – barer, more factual and with little of the sensuous richness of his earlier novels. Often he employs his characteristic devices of dramatic irony and coincidence in an almost take-it-or-leave-it manner that make them in one way even more obtrusive than usual, but in another oddly powerful, as if with the tension of an angry impatience. At times he even adopts a savagely jocular, mocking tone very close to that of the later Dickens. The strain in *Jude the Obscure* is evident, too, in Hardy's effort to widen the scope of his tragedy in order to take in his own extended vision of the world of the late 1890s. His condemnation of society had been forthright enough in *Tess of the D'Urbervilles*; but in Hardy's last novel it is much more detailed. In addition, with *Jude the Obscure* – as Douglas Brown, one of his modern critics, has pointed out – Hardy 'enters the lists alongside George Eliot and Henry James with a tragic psychological fiction.'

The most striking manifestation of Hardy's break with his earlier approach is his almost complete abandonment of Nature and the countryside as an integral setting for his characters. There is very little that could be compared with the richly poetic evocations of the natural scene in nearly all his earlier novels. The six parts of *Jude the Obscure* are named after places, but none of these conveys any real sense of attachment or stability. The feeling of immemorial continuities, of a way of life rooted in the soil has gone – and so, apart from a few stray echoes, has the comic rustic 'chorus'. The main characters are, like the modern world to which they belong, fundamentally rootless, and their inner restlessness is reflected in continuous changes of location, journeyings, boarding of trains, sojourns at inns or temporary lodgings. To Ian Gregor, for example, 'the world of the novel seems to be less in Wessex than at the nerves' end.' Wessex, indeed, instead of being the solid, concrete presence it was in the earlier novels, has practically vanished before the inroads of the new economic and industrial forces already hinted at in *Tess of the D'Urbervilles*.

Jude's situation 'At Marygreen' (the title of the first part of the novel) is symptomatic. He does not really belong, in the way that Tess belongs, by ties of ancient blood, to her native place. Jude had been brought to Marygreen as a child and dumped on Drusilla Fawley, his great-aunt and only surviving relative. But Jude's own rootlessness is matched by that of the village itself. It is, in the words of Terry Eagleton, 'a depressed and ugly enclave ... a plundered landscape, denuded of its historical tradition.'

Jude the Obscure comes very close to being a great tragic novel. Where it fails is in Hardy's anxiety to give complete expression to the modern ideas he had been painfully evolving over the years. These ideas are perfectly valid material for a novelist, but it cannot be said that Hardy had found the tone, technique, or form to integrate them successfully.

All the same, the novel comes very close to achieving a major breakthrough in fiction. There is a good deal of truth in Kathleen Batchelor's suggestion that:

> The tragedy of *Jude the Obscure* is not, in its essence,
> one of the times in which Jude and Sue lived. It is a
> tragedy of two people who could not get close enough to
> the reality of their deepest feelings to be able to act on
> them and stay with them.

These deeper levels in the relationship between men and women were new territory for the 1890s. It is doubtful whether the existing forms of fiction could have contained them, and in addition Hardy himself was hampered by Victorian hesitancies and prejudices, particularly in his tendency to exalt spirituality and to shrink from the physicality of sex (as Sue herself does). Nevertheless, his exploration of the complex pattern of the relationship between Sue and Jude, with its struggles, gropings, bewilderments, rationalizations and nuances of feeling, was a considerable achievement for its time. Again it becomes apparent why D. H. Lawrence was so deeply interested in Hardy. There are, at this deep level of psychic exploration, a number of similarities between Sue and the Miriam of Lawrence's *Sons and Lovers* (1913), and between Sue and Jude and the characters of *The Rainbow* (1929). In order to break into this new territory, D. H. Lawrence knew that he had to reject what he called 'the skin-and-grief form' of the old traditional novel. But it was Hardy who had pointed the way.

The Nigger of the Narcissus:
A Tale of the Sea

Joseph Conrad

The Nigger of the Narcissus has an unfortunate title, but
it must be borne in mind that the term 'nigger' was not
such an emotive one at the time Conrad was writing, and
that he was using it descriptively and symbolically, and
not insultingly. If that obstacle can be surmounted, the
novel can be seen not only as an exciting tale of the sea,
but also as a significant new portent in the history of
English fiction, and as crucial in Conrad's own development.

Joseph Conrad was born Teodor Josef Konrad Nalecz
Korzeniowski, in 1857, at Berdiczew in south-eastern
Poland – the most landlocked region in the whole of
Europe. His parents belonged to the Polish landowning
aristocracy, but when Jósef was three years old his father
was arrested for conspiring against the Russian authorities (who at that time ruled Poland), and the family were
exiled to a remote town in Northern Russia. His mother
died there in 1865, and though his father was released
two years later, his health was affected and he died in
Cracow in 1869, leaving the orphaned Jósef in the care of
an uncle. After attending school in Cracow, he astonished
his guardian by announcing his determination to go to
sea, fired by the novels of Captain Marryat which he had
read in translation. Like most Poles of his class he spoke
fluent French, so in 1874, when he was nearly seventeen,

he went to Marseilles, where he saw the sea for the first time in his life and joined the crew of a French sailing vessel. After several voyages, mostly in the Carribbean, he and three other young men formed a syndicate, purchased a small sailing vessel and engaged in gun-running to the Carlist rebels in Spain.

The collapse of the gun-running enterprise, which left him badly in debt, decided Conrad to join the crew of a British merchantman lying in Marseilles, though he still, at the age of twenty, knew no more than a few words of English. The ship eventually took him to Lowestoft where he set foot on English soil for the first time and began teaching himself English by studying a local newspaper. He progressed so well that two years later, after several coastal trips and a voyage in a wool-clipper sailing to Australia, he passed the first of the officers' examinations of the British Merchant Service.

During the next six years he made a number of voyages as third, and later second, mate, mostly to the China Seas, the Indian Ocean and the Malay Archipelago. On one of these there was a negro member of the crew named James Wait – the name of the central character of *The Nigger of the Narcissus* – while the ship in which, in 1884, Conrad sailed as second mate from Bombay to Dunkirk, was actually named the *Narcissus*.

In 1886, Conrad became a naturalized British subject, and in the same year he obtained his Master's ticket. From then on he held a number of commands, one of them of a river steamer in the Belgian Congo. He picked up a tropical fever there which permanently affected his health, but which also seems to have had the effect of turning him to writing. During the next five years he worked during his off-duty hours on his first novel, *Almayer's Folly*, which is about a feckless Dutch planter in Indonesia who marries a native girl and whose grandiose visions end in opium addiction and eventual death. Conrad's last voyage, in 1893, was as captain of the *Torrens*, a famous sailing vessel of the day. John Galsworthy, later author of *The Forsyte Saga*, was a passenger for part of the voyage and reported that Conrad still spoke 'with a strong foreign accent'. But when *Almayer's Folly* was eventually published in 1895 it was clear that this man, who had not even begun to learn English till he was twenty-three, might one day become a master of English prose.

Unable to go to sea again because of his health, Conrad married an Englishwoman and settled down to earn his living as a writer. His second novel, *An Outcast of the Islands* which, like its predecessor, is about the degeneration of a white man in the tropics (this time Borneo), was published in 1896. With the publication of *The Nigger of the Narcissus* in 1897, Conrad's apprenticeship was over and he was firmly set on the path which would lead to *Nostromo* (1904) which some critics regard as the greatest novel of the twentieth century.

As F. R. Leavis has said, Conrad's genius 'was a unique and happy union of seaman and writer', and one of the reasons for the leap forward in *The Nigger of the Narcissus* was that it was the first of Conrad's novels to deal with the world he knew so well from the inside – the small, enclosed world of a ship at sea.

Summary

The plot itself (which is narrated in the first person) is of the slightest. The crew of the sailing ship *Narcissus*, berthed in Bombay, come aboard. Many of them are based on the crew members of the ship of the same name on which Conrad had sailed. The chief mate, Mr Baker, musters the hands. At the last moment, the negro seaman James Wait comes aboard, announcing that he had been taken on by the captain that morning. He is 'calm, cool, towering, superb'; but he has a cough 'metallic and explosive, like a gong', and not long after the *Narcissus* has put to sea, he declares that he is dying – and proceeds to exploit to the full the awe and pity that his announcement arouses. He is excused duty and the crew wait on him: 'with rage and humility, as though we had been the base courtiers of a hated prince; and he rewarded us by his unconciliating criticism.' He tyrannizes over the crew to such an extent that the Chief Mate reports to the Captain that he is a threat to discipline, but the Captain, himself coming under the strange spell of James Wait's ominous 'accomplice' (that is, Death) orders the construction of a sick-bay for him in the deck-house.

Two members of the crew alone are exempt from James Wait's capricious tyranny: the squalid Donkin, who accuses him of malingering, alternately insulting and scrounging from him, and yet paradoxically winning his favour; and old Singleton, who 'with venerable mildness', tells him: '... get on with your dying ... don't raise a blamed fuss with us over that job. We can't help you.'

Off the Cape of Good Hope the *Narcissus* is struck by a gale. She is hurled on to her side and in imminent danger of turning turtle. At great risk to themselves, a number of the crew manage to rescue James Wait, who as usual rewards them with complaints. Eventually, the ship rights herself, and Singleton, after thirty hours at the wheel, collapses and for the first time faces the truth that he is growing old. Gradually, the horrors of the tempest recede into the background and Wait's dying again becomes the dominating preoccupation. As he feels himself growing weaker, and terrified by the hellfire sermonizing of the cook, who is subject to spells of religious fervour, Wait insists that Donkin was right in his accusation of malingering and announces that he is going to get up and return to duty. When the Captain orders him to remain in his cabin, there is nearly a mutiny, led by the troublemaker Donkin.

The unrest among the crew is heightened by the fact that the ship is now held up by contrary head-winds. According to Singleton, who believes implicitly in the old seamen's superstition that 'mortally sick men ... linger till the first sight of land', these are caused by James Wait.

When the ship is at last in sight of the island of Flores (in the Azores) Wait does indeed die and Donkin ransacks his belongings. Although the crew have been expecting his death, it comes as a shock: 'A common bond was gone; the strong, effective and respectable bond of a sentimental lie.' But as soon as Wait's body has been consigned to the deeps, a favourable wind springs up, much to the satisfaction of old Singleton who feels the old superstitions have been thoroughly vindicated. A week later the *Narcissus* is in the English Channel, and before long she has docked in London and the crew have dispersed.

Critical commentary

An instructive approach to *The Nigger of the Narcissus* is by way of a contrast. In his Preface, Conrad makes a number of pronouncements like this:

> Fiction ... must be, like painting, like music, like all art,
> the appeal of one temperament to all the other
> innumerable temperaments, whose subtle and resistless
> power endows passing events with their true meaning,
> and creates the moral, the emotional atmosphere of the
> place and time.

This lofty profession of aim is a reminder that Conrad was a close friend of Henry James and his most considerable follower in the practice of the 'art of fiction'. Yet nothing could sound less like Henry James's world of subtle and refined characters moving in their refined ambience than, say, the exciting and action-packed description of the gale encountered by the *Narcissus* on her way home from Bombay. On this reckoning, the only thing James and Conrad would seem to have had in common is that they were both exiles from their native lands.

At one time, it was a critical commonplace to refer to Conrad as 'the Kipling of the seas'. Misled by this description, many readers were disappointed when they found that, in spite of the promise of the exciting and exotic settings, Conrad's novels were not anything like as full of incident as, for instance, Rudyard Kipling's *Plain Tales from the Hills* and *Soldiers Three*, which were published in 1888. The actual plot of *The Nigger of the Narcissus* could indeed be contained within the limits of the normal short story.

Although he made use of action, Conrad was not primarily an action-writer. He really was the disciple of Henry James in that he was a most careful stylist. A large section of *The Nigger of the Narcissus* is given over to the superb description of the storm, but there are equally vivid evocations of the sea in very different moods. However, Conrad's preoccupation with style in his descriptive passages led to faults as well as virtues, and particularly to what F. R. Leavis has called the 'disconcerting weakness or vice' of an over-elaboration of style and an 'adjectival insistence upon inexpressible and incomprehensible mystery', a weakness which marred several of Conrad's later novels, causing one wit to comment – after reading Conrad's novel, *The Rover* (1923) – that he had 'just been listening to a performance on the Conrad'.

It was this tendency towards portentousness that led E. M. Forster to complain of some of Conrad's later work that he always seemed to be 'promising to make some general philosophic statement about the universe, and then refraining with a gruff disclaimer' so that 'the secret casket of his genius contains a vapour rather than a jewel ... No creed, in fact. Only opinions ... held under the semblance of eternity, girt with the sea, crowned with stars, and therefore easily mistaken for a creed.'

One of the great merits of *The Nigger of the Narcissus*, however, is that it is on the whole free from purple passages and the mistiness attending them, and that Conrad's basic message emerges clearly and, for the most part, unambiguously. The finest passages of the novel are nearly always those in which the backgrounds are described not for their own sakes, but in connection with the human beings who belong to them. He is particularly vivid and concrete, moreover, when he is dealing with the day to day life of the ship.

The focus of Conrad's interest is not so much the sea as the men who sail upon it. In advising a young would-be novelist he said: 'Try and make it a novel of *analysis* on the basis of some strong situation,' and Conrad is as much a 'novelist of fine consciences', a term he applied to Henry James, as James was himself. As John Holloway has pointed out:

> Conrad has, as his strongest link with James, his sense of
> life as a sustained struggle in moral terms; an issue
> between good and evil in the fullest sense of these words,
> which individual men find they cannot evade.

The most subtle and serious of the moral challenges faced by the crew of the *Narcissus* is, of course, that represented by the dying negro. As his disease advances, he becomes not so much a human being as an embodiment of death and corruption – so that his blackness is in effect a symbol of the ultimate darkness. The rough kindliness of James Wait's fellow-seamen, in consequence, gradually loses its positive and humane quality:

> Through him we were becoming highly humanized,
> tender, complex, excessively decadent: we understood
> the subtlety of his fear, sympathized with all his repul-
> sions, shrinkings, evasions, delusions – as though we had
> been overcivilized, and rotten, and without any knowledge
> of the meaning of life.

This sense of an unknown horror or evil residing in the human psyche was to become one of the outstanding features of Conrad's later work.

As a corollary to the creeping demoralization represented by the dying negro, is the subversive influence of the waster Donkin, whose 'picturesque and filthy loqua-city flowed like a troubled stream from a poisoned source.' Whereas James Wait represents the corruption of death,

Donkin represents the danger of corruptions within society, and it is significant that they are grudgingly attracted to each other. But the crew have another challenge to face – that of the storm – and as C. B. Cox has said, during that ordeal 'the ship becomes an archetype for human society on its journey through an inexplicable universe ...' It is a universe as hostile and indifferent to man as that of Thomas Hardy.

In overcoming this challenge, the crew of the *Narcissus* achieve an heroic status which temporarily raises them above the corrupting influence of James Wait and Donkin. It is, however, a precarious triumph. Just as we are always aware that the ship has only its planks to oppose to the powerful forces outside, so we feel that it is only the simple virtues possessed by the men who are her crew that stand between humanity and the horror and darkness beyond. The attraction for Conrad of the subject of a ship at sea with its enclosed, specialized society is that inevitably it strips away all inessentials. In *A Personal Record*, a book of reminiscences published in 1912, Conrad made this significant statement:

> Those who read me know my conviction that the world,
> the temporal world, rests on a few very simple ideas:
> so simple that they must be as old as the hills. It rests,
> notably, among others, on the idea of Fidelity.

For Conrad 'Fidelity' is embodied above all in the courage, endurance, and sense of discipline that belong to the crew of a ship. *The Nigger of the Narcissus* is fundamentally a novel about fidelity, and the attempts of the elements, the dying negro, and Donkin to overthrow it. The real hero of the book is old Singleton, not only because of his incredible thirty hours at the wheel during the tempest, but also because he is the one man completely immune to the blandishments of James Wait and Donkin. And yet Singleton is a man, Conrad says, who 'in the last forty-five years had lived ... no more than forty months ashore', and for most of that time he was so drunk that he was seldom 'in a condition to distinguish daylight'. In other words, he is the least complicated of all the crew, essentially a grown-up child who can only function within the little world of a ship at sea. The more sensitive men succumb to the insidious temptations of the negro's long drawn-out dying: only Singleton rejects him.

As in Hardy's world, it is only the least sensitive characters who can be immune from tragedy. In this vision there is something which comes close to despair, for if humanity is sustained by men like Singleton (fine and heroic though he is) then the human civilization of centuries is fragile indeed. In addition, the fact that the small knot of discipline represented by the crew of the *Narcissus* can be undone by a James Wait or a Donkin, raises the possibility that that, too, is an illusion to which men cling in order to hide from an ultimately meaningless universe. It is this terrifying possibility which Conrad first raised in *The Nigger of the Narcissus* and which he was to explore with increasing honesty and tragic intensity in the great novels which followed.

The War of the Worlds

H. G. Wells

Herbert George Wells was born in 1866 at Bromley, in Kent. Both his parents had been in domestic service, but at the time of his birth his father was running a seedy little crockery shop, and also earning a few pounds as a professional cricketer until an injury forced him to give up the game. The Wells family began drifting towards bankruptcy, so Wells's mother returned to her old mistress at Uppark in Sussex as housekeeper, while Wells was sent, at the age of fourteen, to work at a draper's shop. Then, for a time he was apprenticed to a pharmacist in nearby Midhurst, and, as he needed Latin for this, he went to the local grammar school which he much enjoyed. But his mother decided to send him to another drapery store as an articled apprentice, which he disliked so much that after two years he ran away. Fortunately his old headmaster employed him as a pupil-teacher and encouraged him to sit for a scholarship to the Normal School of Science (later renamed the Imperial College of Science and Technology) at South Kensington in London. He was successful, and found himself sitting at the feet of the biologist Thomas Henry Huxley and other famous scientists. But he had great difficulty in making ends meet, became involved in social and political activities, was converted to socialism, and fell in love with his cousin Isabel. The result of all these distractions was that he failed his final examinations (though he later gained his Bachelor of Science degree with high honours as an external student).

After marrying Isabel in 1891, he earned a bare living in London as a teacher, journalist and writer of science textbooks. It was not until 1893 that he achieved any real success and found himself in demand as a story-writer, essayist and reviewer. His early short stories were published in 1895 in a still widely read collection under the title of *The Stolen Bacillus and Other Incidents*. In the same year he also published his first full-length novel, *The Time Machine*. It was an instant success and, before the year was ended, he had published yet another novel, *The Wonderful Visit*, a fantasy about an angel descending in England to be appalled by the narrowness and monotony of men's lives.

After 1895, Wells never looked back, and for the next half century books poured from him, so that when he died he had published over a hundred volumes, the majority of them great popular successes, not only in his own country but throughout the civilized world.

It was science-fiction that predominated in Wells's literary output up to the end of the nineteenth century. In 1896 came *The Island of Dr Moreau*, a remarkable novel about a scientist who turns animals into half-men – whereby, in almost Swiftian vein, Wells depicts the bestial elements that still survive in mankind. In 1897 *The Invisible Man* was published – one of his most popular books – and also the tales collected in *The Plattner Story and Others*. *The War of the Worlds* (1898) was followed a year later by both *When the Sleeper Awakes: A Story of Years to Come* and *Tales of Space and Time*.

These 'scientific romances' (as Wells called them) continued into the present century with such brilliant examples as *The First Men in the Moon* (1901); *In the Days of the Comet* (1906); *The World Set Free* (1913) – which envisaged the invention of the nuclear bomb – and *The Shape of Things To Come* (1933).

But starting in 1900 with *Love and Mr Lewisham*, Wells also launched into a series of realistic social comedies, Dickensian in the brilliance of their humour and characterization, and drawing on his own youthful experiences as a draper's assistant, struggling young student and writer, and prematurely married man (his marriage had come to grief in 1895, though he soon married again). The finest of these were *Kipps: The Story of a Simple Soul* (1905); *Tono-Bungay* (1909), and *The History of Mr Polly* (1910). In addition, there was a third major category in Wells's fiction – his novels of ideas – and from the publication in 1911 of *The New Machiavelli* he increasingly inclined towards this type. When Henry James wrote to chide him with neglecting his art, Wells replied: 'I had rather be called a journalist than an artist.'

Wells was a man of remarkable energies and very varied interests. He waged campaigns for innumerable good causes. In 1903 he became one of the leading members of the Fabian Society, resigning five years later because he was impatient with their doctrine of 'gradualness' in the implementation of socialism. He believed that the Fabian Society should become a training-ground for an intellectual élite (whom he called the 'Samurai') who would devote themselves to the achievement, with the help of science and technology, of an ideal commonwealth, and eventually of a new world order. He was an ardent supporter of the League of Nations after the First World War, and set himself the task of re-educating world opinion in a better appreciation of the ideals behind it. Single-handed he wrote a vast popular history, entitled *The Outline of History* (1920). Ten years later, in collaboration with two biologists; his elder son G. P. Wells and Dr Julian Huxley, he wrote *The Science of Life*, an equally vast biological manual for the general reader. Again single-handed, he wrote a voluminous exposition of everyday economics, *The Work, Wealth and Happiness of Mankind* (1932).

Up to the outbreak of the Second World War Wells

was probably one of the most influential thinkers in the world. *The Outline of History* was translated into practically every language, and by 1939 had sold well over two million copies in English alone. He was a force to be reckoned with in world affairs, as exemplified by his visits in 1934, first to Franklin D. Roosevelt in America and then to Josef Stalin in Russia. In spite of his undoubted influence and success, in his later years Wells became increasingly pessimistic about the future of mankind. He died in London in 1946.

Summary

The War of the Worlds is about an invasion of Earth by the Martians, whose own planet is dying. The first 'cylinder' lands on a common in Surrey. Excited crowds gather round, and the narrator gets his first sight of a Martian: 'A big, greyish, rounded bulk, the size perhaps of a bear', glistening 'like wet leather', with 'two large, dark-coloured eyes', and a 'lank tentacular appendage' gripping the edge of the cylinder as it heaves itself out, with another swaying in the air.

A deputation from the crowd approaches in the hope of establishing friendly relations – only to be destroyed by a terrible heat ray. There is a panic-stricken flight from the common. Those outside the area at first refuse to believe in the seriousness of the threat, until a second cylinder arrives. The narrator (after having taken his wife to relatives) watches the first of the towering Martian fighting-machines go into action, spreading death and destruction. He gives shelter to an artilleryman, the sole survivor of a battery which had been attacked by the Martians, who, however, leaves him the next morning to search for the remnants of his battalion. The narrator sets off to rejoin his wife and passes through terrible scenes of devastation and panic.

There is now a shift in the 'point of view' as the narrator reports the experiences of his brother, a medical student in London. By this device he is able to describe how the initial mood of confidence in the capital was succeeded by shocked disbelief at the news that guns and high explosives had been quite ineffectual in stopping the advance of the Martians. As the further news arrives that in addition to their heat-ray the Martians are now using a deadly black smoke, panic mounts and a headlong mass exodus from London begins. Scenes such as these are now historical fact, after the experience of two world wars, but for Wells to envisage them so convincingly back in 1898 was in itself a remarkable feat of the imagination. The narrator's brother, himself caught up in the fleeing crowds, manages to reach the Essex coast and embarks in a steamer under the protection of the Royal Navy. In an exciting passage, one of the British ironclads charges at the Martian fighting-machines, which have waded out on their long, stilt-like legs in pursuit of the escaping steamers. The ironclad runs down two of them, although she is ablaze from the Martian heat-rays and soon afterwards explodes.

The story now reverts to the first-person narrator. He and a clergyman he has run into take refuge in an abandoned house – and another of the cylinders arriving from Mars lands practically on top of it, half burying it under earth and rubble. Unable to escape, the two men are able to study the Martians at close quarters, unseen by them. They watch their 'handling machines' building various pieces of apparatus. In describing the Martians themselves, Wells's imagination provides some fascinating additional details. The Martians, we are told, do not need sleep and they have no reproductive organs – their young being 'budded off, just as young lily bulbs bud off, or the young animals in the fresh-water polyp.' They are able to exchange thoughts by telepathy, but they also communicate by means of various hooting and whistling sounds. These are particularly in evidence when they are seeking their nourishment: and the shocked watchers discover that the Martians 'did not eat, much less digest', but 'took the fresh living blood of other creatures, and injected it into their own veins.' In horrified fascination, the narrator and his companion witness this process put into operation upon a well-dressed, middle-aged man who has been captured by the invaders. Soon afterwards, the clergyman meets the same fate and the narrator himself only just manages to escape. He is, however, still holed up in the destroyed house. Eventually, though, their sinister-looking preparations complete, the Martians move off to link up with other groups.

Pushing on towards the centre of London, the narrator comes across the artilleryman to whom he had earlier given shelter. The man tells him that the Martians have now moved into north London, and that there are rumours that they are about to deploy another devastating weapon and that they have also built a flying machine. In the artilleryman's view, human civilization as at present constituted is doomed. All the 'tame' people, he predicts, will eventually allow themselves to be caught and fattened up in cages for the Martians to feed on. But the few really 'strong' individuals like himself will learn how to survive and, in the long run, how to defeat the Martians.

Leaving the artilleryman still expounding his ideas, the narrator cautiously ventures closer into London. Near South Kensington, he suddenly hears a strange wailing sound. Then there is silence. He reaches Primrose Hill, where the Martians have their main encampment – and finds them lying dead – 'slain by the putrefactive and disease bacteria against which their systems were unprepared ... slain, after all man's devices had failed, by the humblest things that God, in His wisdom, has put upon this earth.'

The remainder of the novel tells of the rejoicing among the human survivors, and the gradual return to normality. An *Epilogue*, supposedly added by the narrator some years later, raises the possibility of the Martians attempting another invasion and condemns the complacency of the vast majority of people in refusing to entertain the possibility, or to take steps to circumvent it.

Critical commentary

One of the ways in which *The War of the Worlds* is superior to the majority of science fiction stories is that it contains so much of its creator's thought, feeling, and personality. At the very beginning of the novel, for example, a somewhat sermonizing note is struck when he describes how, on the eve of the Martian invasion of Earth, men went about their daily affairs 'with infinite complacency ... serene in their assurance of their empire over matter.' It would not be right, he adds, to judge the Martians too harshly: for when – when, not if – our own planet reaches the same condition as Mars and we are forced to abandon it, can we be sure that *we* will be any less ruthless than the Martians?

It is hardly an optimistic view – either of the human race or of the planet earth itself. In part this meant that Wells was following the gloomy prognostications of the contemporary scientists who had most influenced him: for example T. H. Huxley, who believed that from the evolutionary point of view, the future of the human species was by no means assured; and W. Thompson (Lord Kelvin) who argued that the law of entropy would eventually lead to the cooling of the sun and the reduction of the planets to a system of dead matter whirling in the nothingness of space. In addition, there was probably a deep personal pessimism at work.

None of Wells's scientific romances comes to a definite conclusion about the eventual fate of the human race. In a depressed mood he tended to subscribe to the theory of total extinction of all living things. Then, when he found this thought unbearable, he would go back to the idea that mankind, by a proper harnessing of intellectual and moral resources (and by listening to him) could find ways of rising above the laws of evolution, becoming their

master instead of their victim. These two moods sometimes co-existed in the same work, and *The War of the
Worlds* is one of the outstanding examples.

There are times, though, when a decidedly misanthropic element enters the novel, as in the scene where the
narrator and the clergyman come to blows over their
rapidly dwindling store of provisions. There is an almost
Swiftian disgust in some of Wells's accounts of human
behaviour in crisis, and even when this is not present
there is often a strong satirical element.

A somewhat ambivalent attitude is revealed in the
description of the artilleryman's behaviour. On the one
hand, he is revealed as a wind-bag, who in spite of his
grand talk about a new race of men and women who will
rescue the world, does nothing practical, and on the other,
Wells shows a sneaking sympathy with his ideas. Wells
himself was later on to think (for a time at any rate) in
terms of a special élite (directed by himself, of course),
who were not so very different from the 'supermen' of
the nineteenth-century German philosopher Nietzsche,
who had a considerable influence on many of the intelligentsia of Wells's day. Eventually, as we have seen, Wells's
ideas were to take precedence over the promptings of his
creative imagination and, ultimately, to swamp them. In
The War of the Worlds, however, they were on the whole
held in a proper artistic balance.

It is also significant that in the passage already referred
to, about man's complacency on this supposedly safe
globe, Wells writes of intelligences 'across the gulf of
space' which 'are to our minds, as ours are to the beasts
that perish.' That phrase 'the beasts that perish' is not
one we would normally associate with either science or
science fiction. It provides a clue, in fact, to one of the
most pervasive influences, both on Wells's style and indirectly on his thinking – that of the Bible – and when
the famous journalist, W. T. Stead, reviewed *The War
of the Worlds* on its first appearance, he described it as
'The Latest Apocalypse of the End of the World'.

Norman and Jeanne Mackenzie, Wells's most recent biographers, are doubtless right in relating this apocalyptic element both to the anxiety and insecurity Wells experienced in childhood, and to the Evangelical Christianity he imbibed from his mother. What he eventually did, they believe, was:

> to equate man's animal inheritance with original sin ...
> salvation now meant saving the human species from
> the evolutionary process which, unchecked, damned it as
> surely as the Fall.

In *The War of the Worlds* these elements produce a fruitful underlying tension and a sense of profounder dimensions.

The patriotic note that is struck on several occasions in the novel, and notably in the description of the brave little British ironclad engaging the Martians in their war machines, may seem surprising for a man who was a socialist and an internationalist. It is one that, in the heyday of Britain's imperial glory, somehow crept into the utterances of many other radicals. There is in fact a relationship, whether intentional or subconscious on Wells's part, between *The War of the Worlds* and the flood of books that appeared during the last decade of the nineteenth century full of dire warnings, somewhat in the mood of Rudyard Kipling's famous poem *Recessional*, with its refrain of 'Lest we forget!' The fear of decline, accompanied by a mood of despair and foreboding, pervaded the whole of Europe during this period leading up to the First World War, and to some extent it is this mood that lies behind the pessimistic findings of contemporary science.

Plenty of faults can be found with *The War of the Worlds*. The switch from the narrator's eye-witness account to that of his brother is clumsily handled. The narrator himself, although he becomes human (and very much like Wells) when he admits his weaknesses, is for the most part a shadowy figure. The other characters are even more so. Their exterior appearances and habits are excellently caught, but there is very little inner exploration. This is indeed the common weakness of science-fiction as a literary genre: the externals of plot assume an excessive and often exclusive importance, and in consequence it seldom does more than entertain. Any novel that is going to be read must do that, of course, but if it is to survive it must stir more than the mere topsoil of the imagination. There is no doubt that *The War of the Worlds* succeeds in doing so, though there is also evidence that sometimes this is in spite of the theorizing Wells. In many ways he misunderstood his own genius – and Henry James was right in urging him to be an artist rather than a propagandist for his own ideas. Although he did not always realize it, these were essentially the products of his imagination, craving to be transformed into concrete artistic terms, and not into sermonizing. There was, in consequence, a dichotomy in his work. As Anthony West (Wells's son by the novelist Rebecca West) has put it, much of Wells's later work 'represents an attempt to straddle irreconcilable positions' so that he was frequently 'engaged in shouting down his better judgement.'

All the same, it is better judgement that predominates in *The War of the Worlds*. A good example of the way in which Wells the imaginative novelist continually insists on breaking through is the description of the 'stout, ruddy, middle-aged man,' with his 'staring eyes' and 'the gleams of light on his studs and watch-chain', whom the Martians capture for their larder. These vivid, factual, almost Dickensian details pinpoint another of the main reasons for the superiority of Wells's science-fiction – his ability to bring together two quite different narrative modes. It was this gift that caused Wells's friend and fellow-novelist Joseph Conrad to call him 'Realist of the Fantastic'.

In discussing Wells's science fiction it is inevitable that

another great contemporary practitioner of the genre should come to mind – the Frenchman Jules Verne, whose novels, such as *Journey to the Centre of the Earth* (1864) and *Twenty Thousand Leagues Under the Sea* (1869), were tremendously popular throughout Europe and America in Wells's day, and, like Wells's own, continue to be widely read.

Nevertheless, there is a crucial difference between the work of the two writers. Jules Verne himself acknowledged it when in 1903 he said of Wells:

> I do not see the possibility of comparison between his work and mine ... his stories do not repose on very scientific bases ... I make use of physics. He invents.

'He invents' – that is the significant phrase – and Wells himself made much the same point in 1933. When he wrote of novels like *The War of the Worlds*:

> As a matter of fact there is no literary resemblance whatever between the anticipatory inventions of the great Frenchman and these fantasies. His work always dealt with the actual possibilities of invention and discovery, and he made some remarkable forecasts. The interest he evoked was a practical one ...

Wells, too, made some 'remarkable forecasts' (aeroplanes, tanks, and nuclear fission among them) but his attitude towards science was prophetic in a wider, more poetic sense. E. M. Forster has insisted that 'mystery is essential to plot' if it is to be more than a string of incidents, and that 'to appreciate a mystery, part of the mind must be left behind, brooding, while the other part goes marching on.' This is precisely what happens in *The War of the Worlds*. Wells knew that this sense of mystery is absolutely vital to the scientific attitude if it is to be a positive and fruitful force in the development of the mind of man.

In *The War of the Worlds*, and other stories like it, Wells the creative writer, as distinct from Wells the scientist and popularizer of science, was making use of the scientific data of his day as a form of metaphor. Fundamentally, he was a mythologist of science, and just as the inner content of the myths, fables and fairy-tales of ancient times is still potent and meaningful today, so Wells in *The War of the Worlds* reveals some of the inner and enduring truths about science and about the nature of the human condition itself.

Bibliography

Thomas Nashe

The Unfortunate Traveller, or the Life of Jacke Wilton edited, with
an introduction, by H. F. B. Brett-Smith (Oxford, 1920)
Thomas Nashe. A Critical Introduction G. R. Hibbard
(London 1962)
Two Elizabethan Writers of Fiction R. G. Howarth
(Cape Town, 1956)
The English Novel in the Time of Shakespeare J. J. Jusserand
(London, 1890)

John Bunyan

John Bunyan: His Life, Times and Work John Brown, revised by
F. M. Harrison (London 1928)
Journey into Self M. E. Harding (New York, 1956)
Bunyan, Maker of Myths Jack Lindsay (London, 1937)
John Bunyan R. Sharrock (London, 1954)

Daniel Defoe

Studies in the Narrative Method of Daniel Defoe A. W. Secord
(Urbana, Illinois, 1924)
Daniel Defoe J. R. Sutherland (London, 1950)
Daniel Defoe: How to Know Him W. P. Trent (Indianapolis, 1916)
Daniel Defoe F. Watson (London, 1952)

Jonathan Swift

The Satire of Jonathan Swift H. Davis (New York, 1947)

'Gulliver's Travels': A Critical Study W. A. Eddy
(Princeton, New Jersey, 1923)
The Masks of Swift W. B. Ewald (Oxford, 1954)
Swift: A Critical Biography J. Middleton Murry (London, 1954)
The Mind and Art of Jonathan Swift R. Quintana (London, 1953)
Swift: An Introduction R. Quintana (London, 1955)

Samuel Richardson

Samuel Richardson Austin Dobson (London, 1902)
Samuel Richardson B. W. Downs (London, 1928)
'Richardson, Fielding, Sterne' Arnold Kettle, in *An Introduction to the English Novel* (London, 1951)
Samuel Richardson, Printer and Novelist A. D. McKillop
(Chapel Hill, 1936)
'Clarissa' V. S. Pritchett, in *The Living Novel* (London, 1949)
Samuel Richardson, Master Printer W. M. Sale (Ithaca, New York, 1950)
The Epistolary Novel G. F. Singer (Philadelphia, 1933)
Samuel Richardson C. L. Thomas (London, 1900)
The Rise of the Novel: Studies in Defoe, Richardson and Fielding Ian Watt (London, 1957)

Henry Fielding

Fielding and the Nature of the Novel Robert Alter
(Harvard University Press, 1968)
Fielding the Novelist F. T. Blanchard
(New Haven, Connecticut, 1926)
The Novels of Fielding A. Digeon (London, 1925)
Fielding: his Life, Work and Times F. H. Dudden, two volumes
(Oxford, 1952)
Fielding: A Collection of Critical Essays edited by Ronald Paulson
(Prentice-Hall, 1962)
Henry Fielding: A Critical Anthology edited by Claude Rawson
(London, 1973)
Henry Fielding: Profiles in Literature Claude Rawson (London, 1968)
Henry Fielding and the Augustan Ideal under Stress Claude Rawson
(London, 1972)
Henry Fielding's Theory of the Comic Prose Epic E. M. Thornbury
(Madison, Wisconsin, 1931)

The Rise of the Novel Ian Watt (London, 1957)
Henry Fielding, Mask and Feast Andrew Wright (London, 1965)

Tobias Smollett

Tobias Smollett L. R. M. Brander (London, 1951)
A Study in Smollett H. S. Buck (New Haven, 1925)
Tobias Smollett, Traveller-Novellist G. M. Kahrl (Chicago, 1945)
Tobias Smollett, Doctor of Men and Manners L. M. Knapp
(Princeton, New Jersey, 1949)

Samuel Johnson

Johnsonian and Other Essays R. W. Chapman (Oxford, 1953)
Samuel Johnson Joseph Wood Krutch (New York, 1944)
'*Rasselas* Reconsidered' Mary Lascelles, *Essays and
Studies*, n.s. IV (1951)
Six Essays on Johnson Sir W. Raleigh (Oxford, 1910)
Doctor Johnson S. C. Roberts (London, 1935)
'*Rasselas* and the Persian Tales' Geoffrey Tillotson, *Essays in
Criticism and Research* (Cambridge, 1942)

Laurence Sterne

Laurence Sterne, The Early and Middle Years Arthur H. Cash
(Methuen, 1975)
Laurence Sterne and Yorick Willard Connely (London, 1958)
The Life and Times of Laurence Sterne W. L. Cross (third edition,
New Haven, Connecticut, 1929)
The Unsentimental Journey of Laurence Sterne E. N. Dilworth
(New York, 1948)
Laurence Sterne: The Making of a Humourist M. R. B. Shaw
(London, 1957)
Tristram Shandy's World John Traugott
(Berkeley, California, 1955)

Horace Walpole

The Tale of Terror Edith Birkhead (London, 1921)
The Castle of Otranto edited by O. Doughty (London, 1929)
Horace Walpole: A Biography R. W. Ketton-Cremer
(revised edition, London, 1946)

Horace Walpole and the English Novel K. K. Mehrotra
(Oxford, 1934)
The Haunted Castle Eino Railo (London, 1927)
Horace Walpole D. M. Stuart (London, 1927)
The Gothic Quest Montague Summers (London, 1938)
The Gothic Flame D. P. Varma (London, 1957)

Oliver Goldsmith

The Vicar of Wakefield edited by O. Doughty (London, 1928)
Oliver Goldsmith William Freeman (London, 1951)
The True Genius of Goldsmith R. H. Hopkins (London, 1969)
Oliver Goldsmith R. M. Wardle (Lawrence, Kansas, 1957)

Frances Burney

'Fanny Burney' in *Poets and Story-Tellers* David Cecil
(London, 1949)
A Degree of Prudery Emily Hahn (London, 1951)
Mme D'Arblay's Place in the Development of the English Novel
W. T. Hale (Bloomington, Indiana, 1916)
The History of Fanny Burney Joyce Hemlow (Oxford, 1958)
Life of Frances Burney, Madame D'Arblay C. Lloyd
(London, 1936)
Evelina edited by F. D. Mackinnon (Oxford, 1930)

William Godwin

Shelley, Godwin and their Circle H. N. Brailsford
(London, 1913, new ed. 1951)
William Godwin: A Study in Liberalism David Fleisher
(London, 1951)
William Godwin and his World R. Glynn Grylls (London, 1953)
William Godwin: A Biographical Study George Woodcock
(London, 1946)

Jane Austen

Jane Austen: Her Life and Letters J. E. Austen-Leigh, edited by
R. W. Chapman (Oxford, 1926)
Jane Austen David Cecil (Cambridge, 1935)

Jane Austen, A Biography R. W. Chapman (Oxford, 1953)
Jane Austen: Facts and Problems R. W. Chapman (Oxford, 1948)
Jane Austen: A Biography Elizabeth Jenkins (London, 1938)
Jane Austen: Her Life, her Work, her Family, and her Critics
R. B. Johnson (London, 1930)
Jane Austen Margaret Kennedy (London, 1950)
Jane Austen and her Art Mary Lascelles, (revised edition, Oxford, 1941)
The Novels of Jane Austen: An Interpretation Darrel Mansell (Macmillan, 1973)
A Jane Austen Companion, A Critical Survey and Reference Book
F. B. Pinion (Macmillan, 1973)
Jane Austen: Irony as Defence and Discovery Marvin Mudrick (Princeton, New Jersey, 1952)
Jane Austen's Novels: A Study in Structure A. H. Wright (London, 1953)

Walter Scott

Sir Walter Scott John Buchan (London, 1932)
Epic Suggestions in the Imagery of the Waverley Novels
C. F. Fiske (New Haven, Connecticut, 1940)
Sir Walter Scott, Bart. H. J. C. Grierson (London, 1938)
Sir Walter Scott Lectures, 1940–1948 H. J. C. Grierson *et al.*
(Edinburgh, 1950)
Sir Walter Scott Today edited by H. J. C. Grierson (London, 1932)
The Waverley Novels and their Critics J. T. Hillhouse (Minneapolis, Minnesota, 1936)
Scott and Scotland: the Predicament of the Scottish Writer
Edwin Muir (London, 1936)
Sir Walter Scott: His Life and Personality Hesketh Pearson (London, 1954)
Sir Walter Scott Una Pope-Hennessy (London, 1948)

Thomas Love Peacock

Peacock O. W. Campbell (London, 1953)
Thomas Love Peacock: A Critical Study A. M. Freeman (London, 1911)
Thomas Love Peacock J. B. Priestley (London, 1927)

The Life of Thomas Love Peacock Carl van Doren
(New York, 1911)

Frederick Marryat

Captain Marryat and the Old Navy Christopher Lloyd
(London, 1939)
Captain Marryat: A Rediscovery Oliver Warner (London, 1953)

Charles Dickens

Dickens at Work John Butt and Kathleen Tillotson
(London, 1957)
The Violent Effigy: a study of Dickens's imagination John Carey
(London, 1973)
Charles Dickens G. K. Chesterton and F. G. Kitton (London, 1903)
Charles Dickens: A Critical Introduction K. J. Fielding
(London, 1958)
Dickens and his Readers: Aspects of Novel Criticism since 1836
G. H. Ford (Princeton, New Jersey, 1955)
Life of Charles Dickens John Forster, revised by J. W. T. Ley
(London, 1928)
Charles Dickens: A Critical Study George Gissing (London, 1898)
The Dickens World Humphry House (Oxford, 1950)
Charles Dickens: His Tragedy and Triumph Edgar Johnson,
2 volumes (New York, 1952)
The World of Charles Dickens Angus Wilson (London, 1970)

Benjamin Disraeli

'Disraeli the Novelist' by Eric Forbes-Boyd: *Essays and Studies*,
new series, 111 (1950)
'Disraeli's View of Life in the Novels' by John Holloway: *Essays
in Criticism*, 11 (1952)
Peacocks and Primroses: A Study of Disraeli's Novels Muriel
Masefield (London, 1953)
Novels of the Eighteen-forties Kathleen Tillotson (Oxford, 1954)

Emily Brontë

The Brontës Phyllis Bentley (London, 1947)
The Brontës and Their World Phyllis Bentley (London, 1969)

The Brontë Novels W. A. Craik (London, 1968)
The Sources of Wuthering Heights F. S. Dry (Cambridge, 1937)
Their Proper Sphere: A Study of the Brontë Sisters as Early Victorian Novelists I. S. Ewbank (London, 1966)
Emily Brontë Winifrid Gerin (Oxford, 1971)
The Four Brontës L. and E. M. Hanson (Oxford, 1949; revised edition, Hamden, Connecticut, 1967)
Emily Brontë J. Hewish (London, 1969)
The Symbolism of Wuthering Heights C. Kavanagh (London, 1920)
'A Fresh Approach to Wuthering Heights' Q. D. Leavis, in *Lectures in America* F. R. and Q. D. Leavis (London, 1969)
The Life and Eager Death of Emily Brontë V. Moore (London, 1936)
The Brontës' Web of Childhood F. E. Ratchford (New York, 1941)
The Structure of Wuthering Heights C. P. Sanger (London, 1926)
Charlotte and Emily Brontë N. Sherry (London, 1970)
Emily Brontë C. Simpson (London, 1929)
The Genesis of Wuthering Heights M. Visick (Hong Kong, 1958)
All Alone: The Life and Private History of Emily Jane Brontë R. Wilson (London, 1928)
The Brontës and Their Background: Romance and Reality Tom Winnifrith (Macmillan, 1973)

Charlotte Brontë

The Sources of Jane Eyre F. S. Dry (Cambridge, 1940)
The Life of Charlotte Brontë E. C. Gaskell (two volumes, 1857)
Charlotte Brontë: The Evolution of Genius W. Gerin (Oxford 1967)
The Art of Charlotte Brontë E. Knies (Ohio, 1969)
The Brontë Story: A Reconsideration of Mrs Gaskell's Life of Charlotte Brontë Margaret Lane (London, 1953)
The Accents of Persuasion: Charlotte Brontë's Novels R. Martin (London, 1966)

William Makepeace Thackeray

Thackeray: A Critical Portrait J. W. Dodds (New York, 1941)
Thackeray: A Reconsideration J. Y. T. Greig (Oxford, 1950)
The Buried Life G. N. Ray (London, 1952)
Thackeray: The Uses of Adversity G. N. Ray (New York, 1955)

Thackeray: The Age of Wisdom G. N. Ray (New York, 1958)
A Consideration of Thackeray G. Sainsbury (Oxford, 1931)
The Showman of Vanity Fair Lionel Stevenson (New York, 1947)
Thackeray, the Novelist Geoffrey Tillotson (Cambridge, 1954)
The Art of Thackeray H. N. Wethered (London, 1938)
William Makepeace Thackeray Charles Whibley (London, 1903)

Charles Kingsley

Charles Kingsley and His Ideas Guy Kendall (London, 1947)
Canon Charles Kingsley Una Pope-Hennessy (London, 1948)
The Social Novel of Kingsley M. Marmo (Salerno, 1937)
Charles Kingsley, 1818–1875 M. F. Thorp
(Princeton, New Jersey, 1937)

Elizabeth Cleghorn Gaskell

Mrs Gaskell Yvonne French (London, 1949)
Mrs Gaskell and Her Friends E. S. Haldane (London, 1931)
Elizabeth Gaskell: Her life and Works A. B. Hopkins
(London, 1952)
Elizabeth Gaskell G. D. Sanders (New Haven, Connecticut, 1929)
Mrs Gaskell: Her Life and Work A. S. Whitfield (London, 1929)

Anthony Trollope

Anthony Trollope: Aspects of his Life and Art B. A. Booth
(Bloomington, Indiana, 1958)
Anthony Trollope B. C. Brown (London, 1950)
Anthony Trollope: A Critical Study A. O. J. Cockshutt
(London, 1955)
Anthony Trollope James Pope-Hennessy (London, 1973)
Trollope: A Commentary Michael Sadleir
(London, revised edition 1945)

George Eliot

George Eliot: Her Mind and Her Art Joan Bennett
(Cambridge, 1948)
George Eliot, a Biography G. S. Haight (London, 1968)

Marian Evans and George Eliot L. and E. M. Hanson
(London, 1952)
The Novels of George Eliot Barbara Hardy (London, 1959)

Wilkie Collins

Wilkie Collins R. P. Ashley (London, 1952)
The Life of Wilkie Collins N. P. Davis (Urbana, Illinois, 1956)
"Collins and The Woman in White": by C. K. Hyder, in **P.M.L.A.**
LIV (1939)
Dickens, Reade and Collins: Sensation Novelists W. C. Philips
(New York, 1919)
Wilkie Collins: A Biography Kenneth Robinson (London, 1951)

Lewis Carroll

The Life and Letters of Lewis Carroll Stuart Dodgson
(Collingwood, 1878)
Lewis Carroll Walter de la Mare (London, 1930)
The Annotated Alice: With an Introduction and Notes Martin
Gardner (London, 1974)
Lewis Carroll Derek Hudson (London, 1954)
The Field of Nonsense Elizabeth Sewell (London, 1952)

George Meredith

The Comic Spirit in George Meredith. An Interpretation
J. W. Brach (New York, 1967)
Meredith Now Edited by Iain Fletcher (London, 1971)
George Meredith, His life and Work Jack Lindsay
(London 1956)
*A Troubled Eden, Nature and Society in the Works of George
Meredith* N. Kelvin (Edinburgh, 1961)
Meredith, Hardy and Gissing Patrick Yarker, in *The Victorians*,
Edited by Arthur Pollard (London, 1970)

Henry James

The Complex Fate Marius Bewley (London, 1950)
The Eccentric Design Marius Bewley (London, 1959)
Henry James F. W. Dupe (London, 1951)

The Question of Henry James: A Collection of Critical Essays
edited by F. W. Dupe (London, 1947)
The Ordeal of Consciousness in Henry James Dorothea Krook
(Cambridge, 1962)
The Great Tradition F. R. Leavis (London, 1948)
Henry James: The Major Phase F. O. Matthieson (Oxford, 1946)

H. Rider Haggard

*Le Roman et les idées en Angleterre. (ii) L'Anti-intellectualisme
et l'Estheticisme 1880–1900 (iii) Les Doctrines d'Action et
l'Aventure* M. L. Cazamian (Paris, 1935, and 1955)
*The Cloak that I Left: A Biography of the Author Henry Rider
Haggard* L. R. Haggard (London, 1951)

Robert Louis Stevenson

Robert Louis Stevenson and His World David Daiches
(London, 1973)
The Strange Case of Robert Louis Stevenson Malcolm Elwin
(London, 1950)
Robert Louis Stevenson James Pope-Hennessy (London, 1974)
Robert Louis Stevenson and the Fiction of Adventure Robert Kiely
(Harvard, 1965)
*Henry James and Robert Louis Stevenson: A Record of Friendship
and Criticism* Janet Adam Smith (London, 1948)

Oscar Wilde

Oscar Wilde: A Collection of Critical Essays
edited by Richard Ellman (New York, 1969)
The Last Romantics Graham Hough (London, 1949)
The Life of Oscar Wilde Hesketh Pearson (London, 1954)
Into the Demon Universe: A Literary Exploration of Oscar Wilde
Christopher S. Nassaar (Yale, 1974)
A Study of Oscar Wilde Arthur Symons (London, 1930)

Thomas Hardy

Thomas Hardy Douglas Brown (London, 1954)
Hardy the Novelist David Cecil (London, 1943)

The Great Web: The Form of Hardy's Major Fiction Ian Gregor (London, 1974)
Thomas Hardy: His Career as a Novelist Michael Millgate (New York and London, 1971)
A Hardy Companion F. B. Pinion (London, 1968)
The Novels of Thomas Hardy: Illusion and Reality Penelope Vigar (London, 1974)

George Gissing

Collected Articles on George Gissing edited by Pierre Coustillas (London, 1968)
George Gissing: A Critical Biography Jacob Koig (Washington, 1963; London, 1965)
George Gissing, An Appreciation May Yates (Manchester, 1922)

George Moore

George Moore: A Reconsideration M. J. Brown (Seattle, Washington, 1955)
A Portrait of George Moore in a Study of his Work John Freeman (London, 1922)
The Life of George Moore Joseph Hone (London, 1936)

Joseph Conrad

Joseph Conrad: A Biography Jocelyn Baines (London, 1960)
Joseph Conrad, England's Polish Genius M. C. Bradbrook (London, 1941)
Joseph Conrad: The Modern Imagination C. B. Cox (London, 1974)
Joseph Conrad: the Making of a Novelist A. J. Guerard (London, 1959)
Conrad: A Reassessment Douglas Hewitt (London, 1952)

H. G. Wells

The Early H. G. Wells Bernard Bergonzi (Manchester, 1961)
Wells, a Biography Vincent Brome (London, 1951)

The Time Traveller: The Life of H. G. Wells Norman and Jeanne Mackenzie (London, 1973)
H. G. Wells Norman Nicholson (London, 1950)

Index

Note: fictional characters have been indexed only where reference has been made to them other than in the chapter devoted to the particular novel in which they appear